PRAISE FOR THE FIRST EDITION

"[MacKinnon] keeps to the present moment...blending
crime thriller pace with a barrage of details—half
Agatha Christie and half dutiful crime reporter."
— Martin Wightman, *Telegraph-Journal*

"*Shadow of Doubt* is a fast-paced account of one of the most
sensational murder trials in recent history. Bobbi-Jean MacKinnon
covered the case from start to finish and loads her story with new
details and revealing anecdotes, briskly sketching how a family
soap opera turned to tragedy. For Oland trial junkies, this is the big,
satisfying hit they've been waiting for—by the only journalist
who could have told the story so compellingly."
— Jacques Poitras, author of *Pipe Dreams*

"[MacKinnon's] coverage of the trial was best-in-class.... The book's
relentless accretion of detail is impressive. It shows a laser-like focus."
— Eric Andrew-Gee, *Globe and Mail*

"Bobbi-Jean MacKinnon's *Shadow of Doubt* provides a fly-on-the-wall
viewpoint to one of Canada's most sensational murder cases. The reader
is taken on a roller-coaster ride from the crime scene to the grieving family
to the cops, the Crown, and the jury trial. It's an epic tale that both engages
and teaches—Canada's criminal justice system with all its twists
and turns is in full view right from crime to verdict."
— Kevin Donovan, author of *Secret Life*

BOBBI-JEAN MacKINNON

Revised &
Expanded
Edition

SHADOW OF DOUBT

THE TRIALS OF DENNIS OLAND

GOOSE LANE

Edited by Jill Ainsley.
Cover and page design by Julie Scriver.
Cover image: The Canadian Press/Andrew Vaughan.
Printed in Canada by Marquis.
10 9 8 7 6 5 4 3 2 1

Library and Archives Canada Cataloguing in Publication

Title: Shadow of doubt : the trials of Dennis Oland / Bobbi-Jean MacKinnon.
Names: MacKinnon, Bobbi-Jean, author.
Description: Revised and expanded edition.
Identifiers: Canadiana (print) 20190151730 | Canadiana (ebook) 20190151749 | ISBN 9781773101668 (softcover) | ISBN 9781773101675 (EPUB) | ISBN 9781773101682 (Kindle)
Subjects: LCSH: Oland, Dennis—Trials, litigation, etc. | LCSH: Oland, Richard—Death and burial. | LCSH: Oland family. | LCSH: Trials (Murder)—New Brunswick—Saint John. | LCSH: Murder—New Brunswick—Saint John.
Classification: LCC HV6535.C33 S3532 2019 | DDC 364.152/30971532—dc23

Goose Lane Editions acknowledges the generous support of the Government of Canada, the Canada Council for the Arts, and the Government of New Brunswick.

Goose Lane Editions
500 Beaverbrook Court, Suite 330
Fredericton, New Brunswick
CANADA E3B 5X4
www.gooselane.com

For Jean, Colleen, and Craig,
for your unconditional love and support

PREFACE

This is a book of first-hand research. As a reporter for CBC News, I covered this case from the day Richard Oland's body was discovered. I attended press conferences, jury selection, numerous court proceedings, and the entire trial, which I live-blogged. I've conducted interviews and combed through legal documents, financial records, and scientific reports. On occasion in the pages that follow, I draw from the work of other media or secondary sources, and I cite them when I do. Although I made every effort to speak to a member of the Oland family about the case, to my regret they declined to participate in this book. They have said that they will comment publicly only after the appeal.

Speech is reported substantially verbatim: most stumbles, repetitions, self-corrections, and verbal tics have been edited out. The result, I believe, accurately captures individual speech style without sacrificing readability. When quoting from emails and texts, a similar approach is used. I've quietly corrected obvious typos rather than repeatedly (and pedantically) adding *sic*. Words enclosed in square brackets are additions I've made for clarity.

Trials can be exercises in frustration. Rarely do the proceedings follow a clear narrative path. Lawyers pose questions that can seem random and unconnected, only to revisit the issue again days or weeks later. For this book, I've eschewed a strictly chronological account of the trial in favour of a thematic approach that pulls together testimony from different witnesses at different times to provide coherent accounts of particular evidence and issues.

A GRISLY DISCOVERY

At around a quarter to nine on the morning of Thursday, July 7, 2011, Maureen Adamson's husband dropped her off at work. She carried a tray of Tim Hortons coffee she had picked up en route. Her boss, Richard Oland, loved his coffee, and as his personal secretary for twenty-five years, she tried her best to anticipate his every need. It would be another busy day. The prominent New Brunswick businessman had been travelling most of the previous two months, and they had a lot of catching up to do.

Adamson, a sturdy and serious woman in her late middle age, usually arrived first at Oland's investment firm office, located in a commercial building at 52 Canterbury, a narrow one-way street in the heart of historic uptown Saint John. She dug for her key and inserted it in the street-level door of the three-storey brick building, but it was already unlocked. *Odd*, she thought. The last person to leave at night was supposed to lock the door.

Adamson climbed the narrow, windowless stairwell to the second floor, only to find that door, also normally locked, not completely closed. Now she was irritated. Grumbling, Adamson pushed the door open and turned left into the foyer, which led to Oland's Far End Corporation, marked by a modest brass plaque. As she opened the french door, a "terrifically vile odour" struck her. She couldn't imagine what it could be; she had never encountered anything like it before. She stepped inside the multimillionaire's surprisingly modest, "pack-ratty" office full of stacked bankers boxes and electronic equipment, but nothing immediately seemed amiss; nothing, that is, but the air conditioner on full blast. It was normally turned off overnight. Adamson made her way to a long table in the centre of the room and set down the tray of hot coffee. That's when, as she later recounted, she spotted "two legs" on the floor under Richard Oland's desk. "You couldn't miss it, really," she later said in court, her voice momentarily breaking with emotion.

In shock, Adamson didn't realize who was sprawled on the floor in a large pool of blood, and she didn't stay long enough to find out. She raced downstairs and burst into the print shop on the ground floor, calling out for help.

"Something's wrong," Adamson blurted out. "I see feet upstairs."

"She seemed panicked," Preston Chiasson, who didn't work at the print shop but was a frequent visitor, remembered later. His thoughts automatically turned to Richard Oland. Chiasson had known him for around twenty years and always enjoyed their conversations, which ranged from sailing to politics.

Worried Oland might need some help, Chiasson, who was trained in first aid, rushed upstairs with Adamson. He noted an awful, nauseating smell in the office, and then Adamson pointed. Just five feet away, underneath Oland's desk, two legs were splayed on the floor. Chiasson didn't move any closer. He knew right away there was nothing he could do. Oland was, as he put it, "slaughtered."

Chiasson would later say he couldn't remember much about that day, but he would never forget that macabre scene. He and Adamson hurried out of the office and back into the foyer. He hadn't known what he was getting into on his way in, but he was careful on his way out to avoid stepping in any blood, he said. Chiasson used his cellphone to call 911. "There's a man down," Chiasson reported, describing the condition of the man's head. Adamson, still reeling, pulled out her own cellphone to warn Robert McFadden, Oland's business associate, not to enter the office. Out of habit, she dialled Oland's number first by mistake. Within minutes, police sirens wailed down the street—the sound still haunts her.

Constable Duane Squires of the Saint John Police Force and Trinda Fanjoy, an Atlantic Police Academy cadet, were on patrol just two hundred metres away, in squad car 123, when the dispatch call came in: male, not conscious, not breathing. They arrived at the scene within four minutes, and Constable Don Shannon, who had been working at the police station a couple of blocks away, soon followed.

Chiasson pointed them to the front door and said, "Second floor." They bolted up the wooden staircase. The stench of the office also struck Squires but, in contrast to Adamson and Chiasson, it was familiar to him after nearly five years on the job, that of "a decaying body." Shannon described it as "dried blood."

Squires scanned the chaos. A man was lying face down in a large pool of coagulated blood, and the injuries to his head were "severe." His arms were crumpled beneath him, his neck twisted to the left. A knocked-over garbage can was by his feet. A TV remote control, an iPad, and a set of keys were on the floor, along with some scattered and blood-soaked papers. Shannon searched the office for a suspect or anyone else who might have been hurt, trying to stay close to the walls to avoid disturbing the crime scene, as he had been trained to do when he became a police officer, just a couple of years before. Fanjoy entered behind the two officers. The three spent mere minutes in the office and had retraced their steps to the foyer when the paramedics arrived.

Phil Comeau and Christopher Wall had been having coffee on nearby Germain Street when they received the Code 2 call indicating "gunshot, penetrating and stab trauma." Unsure exactly what they were dealing with, they didn't know what equipment to lug upstairs. "Bring everything, everything you have!" Fanjoy shouted down. But Squires told them they didn't need any gear; they were too late.

Comeau, an EMT with almost twenty years' experience, readily recognized "the odour of death" on his way up the stairs, a piercing smell that assaults the nostrils and clogs the back of the throat. "It kind of lingers in the air, stays with you for a couple of hours," he observed. His first glimpse of the body and the wide swath of blood, almost a full square metre, supported his suspicion. "It appeared he had injuries incompatible with life," he later explained in court. Crime-scene photos would show bits of brain and bone on the man's navy sweater and the hardwood floor. Wall, who was just shy of his one-year anniversary of working part-time as a paramedic, had been to approximately ten other crime scenes, but never one like this. This was an abattoir. He let Comeau take the lead.

Patient care always comes first for paramedics, but they are also trained to avoid contaminating any evidence at a crime scene. Comeau knew the drill. He had attended roughly one hundred other crime scenes during his career, but this time he had a difficult time positioning himself, given the size of the blood pool and the blood spatter radiating from the body. He gingerly put his foot on the victim's right thigh to check for rigor mortis, a stiffening of the limbs caused by chemical changes in the muscles after death. "When the whole body moves, that's rigor." Sure enough, rigor had set in; the man had been dead for "quite some time," at least two or three hours. Comeau declared "time of no resuscitation" at 9:01 a.m.

The two officers and cadet sprang into action. Squires "guarded" the scene, advising those who entered not to go beyond the table with the coffee on it, which he believed marked the point where the blood evidence started. Shannon and Fanjoy went downstairs to take preliminary statements from Adamson and Chiasson while the details of their grisly discovery were still fresh in their minds. By that time, Chiasson was "pretty traumatized." He was dizzy and his chest felt tight, so the paramedics came back to assess him.

Shannon jotted down some notes then went to search the third floor of the building, but he found nothing. Fanjoy returned to the second floor to keep a log of the flurry of comings and goings that shortly ensued.

Stan Miller, an acting sergeant, was called to the scene as the senior officer on duty. After Squires briefed him, a staff sergeant, the forensic identification unit, and the major crime unit (MCU) were also called in. The MCU deals with the city's most "serious, complex, and sensitive property and person crimes," including homicides, assaults, robberies, kidnappings, and missing persons.

At around nine thirty a.m. Sergeant David Brooker, the head of the elite unit, asked Constable Anthony (Tony) Gilbert to respond to the DOA and to take Constable Stephen Davidson with him. Although Davidson had been a police officer for around twelve years, seven years in Saint John and most recently with the RCMP's integrated proceeds of crime unit in Moncton for five years, he had joined the MCU only three days earlier. July 7 was supposed to be an orientation day for him, a chance to observe how his new unit operated. Little did Davidson know that when the lead investigator retired three months later, he would be put in charge of the high-profile case.

Gilbert had only been with the major crime unit for about nine months and had less overall experience than Davidson, having just reached his ten-year mark on the force. But he too detected the "distinct" fetor of death at the scene. After they spent "under a minute" together in the bloody office, observing the significant trauma to the victim's head from about eight feet away, Gilbert knew he'd better call David Brooker with a status report. Up to that point, as far as he knew, no one had conveyed it was a suspicious death.

Gilbert and Davidson didn't touch or move anything and retraced their steps. "It doesn't look very good down here," Brooker would later recall Gilbert telling him.

Brooker headed to the crime scene shortly before eleven with his superior, Glen McCloskey, who oversaw the major crime unit as inspector of the criminal investigations division. The head of the forensic identi-fication unit, Sergeant Mark Smith, was already on-site, assessing the situation and determining what equipment he'd need. Forensic officers, known as "ident," have special training and technology to photograph, collect, and examine evidence, such as fingerprints, footwear impressions, blood, and DNA.

This scene screamed out for every tool in Smith's arsenal. Blood was 360 degrees — on the floor, on the desks and computers, on the filing cabinet and shelving units, on the lamps, and even on an empty pizza box perched in the garbage can. It was "one of the bloodiest" crime scenes in Smith's twenty-year-plus career, with the most blows to a victim he had ever seen. To make matters worse, Smith was working alone that day. None of the other forensic officers were available. One with a broken leg was limited to desk duty, another was away doing an understudy, one was "fairly new" and about to go on an eight-week course, and the fourth was off. Smith was in for some back-to-back, around-the-clock days.

Smith raced back to the station and returned with a panel van packed with equipment. He donned full protective gear before he went back into the bloody office. The white disposable coveralls, latex gloves, mask, and shoe covers, or booties, were intended to prevent the transfer of any hair, skin, or fibres that would contaminate the scene.

He waved in Brooker and McCloskey to observe the body some time before noon. They, like all the officers before them, were not wearing any protective gear, but they were under the watchful eye of Smith, who directed how far they could go and where they could step. Staff Sergeant Mike King, who was in charge of patrol services, went in with them. This was actually his second traipse through the crime scene, and as he later admitted, "There was no purpose for me to be in there." King had no investigative role. As the on-site commander, his job was to coordinate his patrol officers to assist the investigators with whatever they needed: crime-scene security, canvassing, searching for evidence, or obtaining security videos.

Smith carefully moved the body to check for any weapons. He found only the victim's eyeglasses underneath his left arm. Smith also checked the victim's pants pockets, hoping to ID him. He retrieved a brown leather wallet, and the driver's licence confirmed the dead man was sixty-nine-year-old Richard Henry Oland of one of Atlantic Canada's most prominent and wealthiest families. The Olands, founders of Moosehead Breweries, are often mentioned in the same sentence as the Irvings and the McCains.

At one point during those first hours, a slender blonde woman approached the entrance to 52 Canterbury. She told an officer at the door that she had an appointment in the upstairs office, but he refused to let her pass.

Word of Oland's violent death had hit the streets by the time Saint John police confirmed the identity of the body. Saint John is a city of about seventy thousand, but it has a small-town feel. It's the kind of place where if you don't know somebody, chances are you know somebody else who does. People greet one another as they pass on the street, neighbours keep an eye out for one another, and when someone needs help, the community always seems to pull together.

Saint John is located on the south coast of New Brunswick, on the Bay of Fundy. Since its incorporation in 1785, the city has boasted a long line of accomplishments: Canada's first chartered bank, oldest public high school, first public museum, first labour union, first YWCA, and first public playground. For many years, the city prospered on shipbuilding. Today, the various industrial pursuits of the Irving family (forestry, pulp and paper, and oil) remain an important economic force, but the city is increasingly focused on culture, tourism, and IT. What in most cities would be termed "downtown" is known as uptown, because the original urban core was built on a hill that slopes steeply up from the harbour. Uptown is a quaint neighbourhood of narrow streets lined with beautiful Victorian buildings. From his office, Richard Oland could have walked almost anywhere — the shopping mall and office towers at Brunswick Square, the Saint John City Market, the exclusive Union Club — within minutes.

The port city has its share of crime, most of which involves property- or drug-related offences. Murder is rare. And this, only the second that year, was no ordinary murder. It would become one of the most sensational cases to grip the Maritimes in decades, the region's "crime of the century." Who could have killed Oland so viciously? And why?

Staff Sergeant King's cellphone rang. Chief Bill Reid wanted to know what was going on. Although it wasn't unusual to get a call from a higher ranking officer "at a scene like that," King couldn't recall the chief ever calling before in his roughly three decades of service. The "suspicious death" was deemed an all-hands-on-deck situation. Police would deploy as many resources as possible to find out as much as they could, as quickly as they could, during those crucial first hours before any trail went cold. Other cases would have to wait.

Constable Rick Russell, a thirty-one-year veteran, was called in from vacation and appointed the lead investigator, in charge of the "speed, flow, and direction" of the case. Russell was the most experienced officer in the unit, with eight years in MCU under his belt. He had spearheaded about six other homicide investigations and been involved with many more throughout his career, starting with just guarding the scenes in his early years.

Russell stopped by Oland's office for a few minutes to familiarize himself with the layout and get "a contextual grasp," which often proves useful later in an investigation, once the information starts "flowing in," he said. Unlike some of his senior officers, however, Russell resisted the temptation to gawk and did not enter the crime scene. "I didn't want to contaminate," he said. "At that time, there's no value in me going in."

A briefing was scheduled for two thirty, when the officers involved would gather at the police station and share what they had seen and done so far. But first, police had to notify the family. Oland was a husband, a father of three, and a grandfather of seven. Constables Davidson and Gilbert, who had returned to the station to take statements from some of the witnesses, were assigned the grim duty. The force's victim services coordinator, Mary-Ellen Martin, accompanied them.

Richard Oland's family lived in Rothesay, a genteel neighbouring town of manicured lawns nestled along the Kennebecasis River. Rothesay is only about a fifteen-minute drive northeast of the industrial city and yet, some might say, is worlds apart. It's home to billionaire industrialist James Irving and other wealthy elite. The average household net worth is in the $2-million range. In Saint John, the unemployment rate hovers around 10 per cent and nearly one-third of children live in poverty.

The Oland mansion was at 5 Almon Lane, an exclusive tree-lined street. Oland had referred to the property as Far End House, a nod to his investment firm, Far End Corporation; it had been the house where his mother grew up. Oland's wife of forty-six years, Constance (Connie) Oland, was home. She knew what was coming. In the approximately five hours between the discovery of her husband's body and police showing up at her door, a woman phoned her to ask if she knew why police cars were outside her husband's office, prompting Connie to call Robert McFadden, who told her, but not explicitly, that her husband was dead. Connie had gathered her family around her. Connie, a trim brunette with dark eyes and a kind face, was sitting on the couch with her son, Dennis Oland, and daughter-in-law, Lisa Andrik-Oland. Daughter Elizabeth

(Lisa) Bustin and brother Jack Connell were also there. Dennis was still trying to reach Connie's other daughter, Jacqueline Walsh.

Davidson was nervous. It was a trying task. He informed them Richard Oland had been "found deceased" and said police didn't have much information yet in terms of the cause or manner of death. "I didn't provide details of the injuries," he later noted. "It was a gruesome scene and I didn't want to pass that along to the family. I was trying to present it in a way that's respectful to the family."

He couldn't recall later what questions, if any, the family asked, but he did most of the talking during the estimated thirty-minute visit. He requested they all go to the Saint John police station to provide statements. Investigators needed to establish a timeline and were hoping the family could help fill in the blanks: where was Oland last, what was he doing, who was with him? Police also wanted to gather as much information as possible about his family life, business life, and social life — anything that might help them figure out who committed this heinous crime. At that point, they had no suspects.

All of the family members agreed to be interviewed, but Dennis Oland said he needed to speak to his children first, to break the news about their grandfather's death. He promised to come to the police station later.

Back at the crime scene, the forensic officer, coroner, and funeral home employees were coordinating the removal of Oland's body. Smith had already taken numerous photographs. It's important to document the position of the body as it relates to other evidence, he later explained. He charted a course to minimize contamination. "There was going to be some [contamination] for sure," he said. "The scene was too messy to avoid it." They decided to place Oland face down on the stretcher, because the damage to his head was so severe. This was definitely not the norm, according to funeral director Adam Holly, but it was his first crime scene. It was also a first for his colleague Sharlene MacDonald, who was grateful the coroner forewarned them about what they were walking into. She knew it would be bad when he suggested they bring extra towels. "I watched where I was going and kept my hands to myself," said MacDonald.

Smith enlisted Squires to assist him. Fortunately, Squires wasn't squeamish. When he was a rookie cop, he dealt with a victim who had been attacked with a sword and had such a severe gash to his head that Squires could see his brain. Squires did his best to reassure the man as he held his cracked skull together until paramedics arrived, but the victim later died in hospital.

Squires put on latex gloves and cloth booties. Then he straddled Oland's torso, standing smack dab in the sticky, coagulated blood. He lifted the left side of Oland's body, while Smith, who was hunched over Oland's legs, tucked a blanket underneath. Squires lifted the right side, and Smith pulled the blanket through. They tied the ends of the blanket into a makeshift sling and hoisted Oland onto a stretcher and into a waiting "pouch" — funeral home vernacular for body bag. Squires discarded his soiled protective gear somewhere in the crime scene and put on a fresh pair of gloves.

They fastened two straps on the stretcher and shrouded it with a blue blanket, and then Squires, the two funeral home directors, and another officer grabbed a corner each and struggled their way down the steep flight of stairs to the funeral home's Dodge Caravan. Sharlene MacDonald had such a hard time managing the twenty-one steps that another officer offered to take her place, and MacDonald held the doors open.

No one told them about the back door, which would have been much easier to manoeuvre. The building was constructed on a slope with a rear door that exited almost at ground level. The back exit also would have been more discreet than Canterbury Street, where curious onlookers and reporters had gathered. A photograph of the removal of the body appeared on the front page of the *Telegraph-Journal* the next morning under the banner headline, "Dick Oland Dead."

Smith escorted the body to the morgue at the Saint John Regional Hospital, where Oland was officially declared dead at 3:03 p.m. and locked in a police cooler.

At police headquarters at 15 Market Square, Rick Russell, the lead investigator, was prepping for the first team briefing and the "wave of information that was going to start coming in." The officers would tell Russell what they saw, what they heard, whom they spoke to, and what they did, and Russell would write it all down on a big flip chart. This would give him "the lay of the land," and then he would start assigning tasks. The major crime unit was so small that, as Russell said, "everybody's interchangeable." Every officer gained experience over the years doing all kinds of different tasks, big and small. The expectation was whatever was asked of you, you'd step in, he said.

An officer from the fraud unit, Constable John Braam, was named file coordinator, responsible for collecting and categorizing any information that came in. Fraud officers are routinely assigned the task because they are used to dealing with large volumes of documents.

It was also decided "right off the bat" to request the RCMP tech crime lab's assistance with Oland's electronic equipment, because it might "afford information," said Sergeant Brooker. He also planned to contact Rogers Communications about getting Oland's cellphone records after he got the victim's cell number from one of his business cards. Oland's green BMW — parked in its usual spot, number 12, at the corner lot — was towed to the police garage with a police escort, parked in the detention area, and taped off as evidence.

Officers were also going door to door to ask area residents and business owners if they had seen or heard anything unusual, but they faced more questions than answers. The officers were also seeking all available surveillance video. They were particularly interested in the nearby Pizza Hut, given the pizza box in Oland's office garbage can, as well as another restaurant, Thandi, directly across the street from the office.

An article search was also underway. Canine unit Constable Mike Horgan, his sniffer dog, Leo, and several other officers fanned out across the uptown business district, looking for a possible murder weapon or anything else that might be related to the crime, such as blood or clothing. They checked the back alleyway, the parking lot across the street, and an adjacent courtyard, and scoured every other lot, entrance, bush, and grassy area in at least a two-block radius. Horgan, a dog handler for roughly fifteen years, identified only one spot he didn't search, because he couldn't access it with his dog: a small grassy space behind the office building that was at a higher elevation.

Shannon "poked around a bit" at a construction site one block over, where there was a big pile of concrete debris and heavy equipment. Other officers checked out a nearby building under renovation, peering inside the clear plastic wrapped around the building and running their hands underneath the tarps. Two officers also dumped garbage cans collected from surrounding streets into the back of a pickup truck and picked through the trash, wearing white gloves. They searched for about an hour in the hot sun and through a ten-minute torrential downpour but found no clues.

Despite the heavy police presence and very public investigation, the force was tight-lipped about the case that day, as it would continue to be for the next four years. "We're investigating the discovery of a body," Staff Sergeant King initially said. He later confirmed only that Richard Oland was the victim and that he had died under suspicious circumstances.

Meanwhile, the police had started interviewing the family at the station. The lead investigator was most interested in hearing from Oland's widow, Connie, because, as Russell explained, spouses and significant others tend to know the most and thus can be a wealth of information. "We didn't know a lot," he noted. "It's important to start from square one."

Three interview rooms were on the go. Russell made a point of monitoring the interview with Richard Oland's widow, making sure nothing was missed and suggesting follow-up questions. Investigators also interviewed Oland's two daughters. His son, Dennis, and Dennis's wife, Lisa, arrived, but the other statements were "dragging on," each taking about an hour, so Russell suggested they leave to grab a coffee and come back. Finally, at 6:01 p.m., Davidson, who was still getting his MCU feet wet, began to interview Dennis Oland.

two
TEAM OLAND

The news that Richard Oland was dead, and apparently in suspicious circumstances, stunned many Saint Johners because Richard Oland and the Oland name were so prominent in the city's history they seemed like permanent fixtures. The Halifax Explosion had brought the Oland family to New Brunswick. Richard Oland's father, Philip Warburton Oland, known to everyone as P.W., was only seven years old on the morning of December 6, 1917, as he faced a blackboard in Sacred Heart School, learning the catechism in preparation for his first communion. The explosion at the harbour blew out the windows on the opposite wall of the room. P.W., uninjured, picked his way home through the ruined city. The family brewery on the Dartmouth side of the harbour was destroyed and several people inside were killed, including Philip's great-uncle Conrad. P.W.'s grandfather, George Wodehouse Culverwell Oland, purchased the Red Ball Brewery in Saint John and chose as manager his oldest son, P.W.'s father, George Bauld Oland.

The Olands became brewers in 1867, when the family purchased a small Dartmouth brewery a few years after arriving in Halifax from England. Although the new venture bore the name John Oland and Son, everyone who met Susannah knew she was the driving force. Company history credits this formidable woman with developing the first recipes and instructing her sons in the art of brewing, and when John died in 1870, the brewery became S. Oland, Sons and Co. The company experienced its share of setbacks, and at one point Susannah had to give up her controlling interest, but the business flourished, expanded, and diversified, and when Susannah died in 1885, George W.C., the youngest but apparently the most capable of her three sons, became the dominant figure. His death in 1933 triggered a lasting split in the family.

George W.C. had five sons, three of whom — George, Sidney, and Geoffrey — followed him into the family business, and in his will he left each of these three a brewery. Sidney inherited control of S. Oland and Sons and Keith Brewery, plus a 21.8 per cent share in New Brunswick Breweries. George inherited the remaining shares in New Brunswick Breweries, and Geoffrey inherited Red Ball Brewery. George and Geoffrey both felt cheated, as Sidney's breweries were larger and worth far more, and Sidney's financial interest in New Brunswick Breweries placed George and Geoffrey in the unpleasant position of having to pay dividends and share corporate information with a competitor. The commercial rivalry and family bitterness endured for decades. In 1947, George Oland, seeking to expand his market beyond the province, changed the company's name from New Brunswick Breweries to Moosehead.

George's son P.W. grew up in Saint John and joined the family business as head brewmaster at age twenty-two, in 1932. He remained in the business for the rest of his working life, and he became the sole shareholder when his father died. He married Mary Howard, and they had two sons — Derek, born in 1939, and Richard, born in 1941 — and a daughter, Jane.

P.W. and his wife were civic-minded, a value they passed to their children. Mary Oland started the Rothesay Pony Club, while P.W. was a driving force behind the New Brunswick Youth Orchestra in 1965, was one of the founding members of the United Way of Greater Saint John, and was the first chair of the Greater Saint John Community Foundation, which since 1976 has donated millions of dollars to charitable causes in the community. P.W. served on many boards and committees. Philip W. Oland Hall at the Saint John campus of the University of New Brunswick is named in his honour, and he also lent his support to numerous arts organizations.

Richard — Dick, as his friends and wife called him — enjoyed a privileged upbringing. He was privately educated, attending Rothesay

Collegiate School as a boy and boarding at Regiopolis College in Kingston, Ontario, for his high school years. He attended the University of New Brunswick in Fredericton, where, according to a story told at his memorial service, he lobbied the administration to construct a student union building. Oland was persistent in his appeals to Colin Mackay, president of the university. "I understand he bothered Dr. Mackay so much that his father was called," Pat Darrah, one of his closest friends, recalled. P.W. asked if the campus needed a student union building, and Mackay said it did. P.W. advised Mackay "to let Dick work on getting a SUB built." Oland graduated from the University of New Brunswick with a bachelor of arts in 1966. He obtained a certificate of brewing technology at Wallerstein Laboratories in New York before joining the family business.

He was smart and capable. While at Moosehead, he helped design and build a beer packaging line that was one of the world's fastest and most efficient. At his memorial service, Pat Darrah described the innovation as "well-researched and thought out" — classic Oland. "Research and efficiency were two of Dick's key strong principles," Darrah said, also noting that "the manufacturer would have never expected that a corporate executive would be so hands-on during its installation, needing to know the intricate details and indeed, making suggestions on how they could do it better."

Oland became vice-president of Moosehead and served in that capacity until he left the company in 1981. He went on to run several other companies, including Brookville Transport, Brookville Carriers, Brookville Manufacturing, Kingshurst Farms, and, most recently, Kingshurst Estates, a woodlot and property rental company, and Far End Corporation, his personal investment-holding company. Oland served on Rothesay's town council and was a director on the boards of several firms and organizations, including the St. Stephen–based chocolatier Ganong, Eastern Provincial Airways, Newfoundland Capital Corporation, the Huntsman Marine Science Centre in Saint Andrews, and the United Way of Greater Saint John. He was also involved with development agencies — such as Enterprise Saint John, the Saint John Development Corporation, and the Waterfront Development Committee — served as chairman of ParticipACTION, and was a life member of the Miramichi Salmon Association.

Pat Darrah, the executive director of the Saint John Construction Association, felt Oland's true legacy was his tireless efforts to bring the Canada Games to Saint John in 1985. In the early eighties, the city struggled with disinvestment and an unemployment rate of 15.8 per cent. Oland knew hosting the games would mean the construction of new sports facilities, and he believed providing recreational infrastructure for youth would give them better opportunities in life. "I believe that this project was one of his greatest thrills and greatest accomplishment," said Darrah, who worked alongside him for six years as vice-president. The fourteen-day event attracted more than three thousand young athletes and their families to the city, and the extensive media coverage gave Saint John national exposure, showcasing the stunning river views at the cleverly chosen venues. Oland also established a cultural component, Festival by the Sea.

"When Dick was hatching a plan, he had an impish grin. As the plan rolled out, he was all business," said Darrah. "One of Dick's favourite sayings was, 'Get a clean piece of paper and I will just go over a few points we should endeavour to get covered today.'" Darrah remembered some "bumps in the road" and "trying times," but under Oland's leadership, the Saint John event was the most successful edition of the national amateur sports competition — and it ended with a profit of $2 million. Oland used the surplus to create the 1985 Jeux Canada Games Foundation to support young athletes and sports organizations across the country. Twenty-five years later, the Canada Games Stadium and Canada Games Aquatic Centre continue to serve the region. "Only once does a city our size have a chance to show what we can do," Oland said at the closing ceremony. "I believe we have done it."

Oland's community involvement did not end with the Canada Games. He served as president of the board of the New Brunswick Museum in the 1990s, spearheading a significant reorganization, renewal, and expansion that saw the museum's exhibits moved from a deteriorating 1930s building on Douglas Avenue, in the city's north end, to a more inviting and accessible site at Market Square in Saint John's uptown.

Oland hobnobbed with Prince Charles at the 1996 opening of the museum's new exhibition centre. Oland also developed a program of touring exhibits to showcase the province's history.

"He was certainly driven," remembered Jane Fullerton, the chief executive officer of the museum. "He was passionate. He was focused on getting things done. He had an ability to bring people together and to get them to work together."

The day before his death, Oland was working on his next community project. He and Darrah met with Bishop Robert Harris of the Diocese of Saint John to discuss a capital campaign to raise an estimated $10 million to restore the Cathedral of the Immaculate Conception. The historic landmark on Waterloo Street, one of the few structures that survived the Great Fire of 1877, opened in 1853 after thousands of Irish Catholic immigrants flooded into the city, making it New Brunswick's first Catholic cathedral. It needed a new roof and repairs to the exterior sandstone and interior plaster walls.

Oland's community work and contributions to public life earned him many awards over the years, including Sport New Brunswick Executive of the Year, Transportation Person of the Year, an honorary doctorate from the University of New Brunswick, the Rotary Paul Harris Fellowship, and the Saint John YM-YWCA's Red Triangle award. Oland was appointed an officer of the Order of Canada, one of the country's highest civilian orders, in recognition of his "creation of cultural and recreational opportunities for his region," as the governor general of Canada's website notes. "His devotion to the community has borne fruit in many forms and he has distinguished himself as an entrepreneur with a social conscience." Oland credited his appointment to the work and community spirit of the countless volunteers who contributed to his many successful projects (approximately seven thousand contributed to the Canada Games alone), but he took particular pride in the honour, because it was also bestowed on his father in 1970 for his "services to the community in many different fields."

In more recent years, competitive sailing became Oland's passionate pursuit. Skimming the water with the wind snapping his sails was a lifelong love, one that began as a nine-year-old boy on a small boat on the Kennebecasis River and progressed to ocean racing around the world on the 52-foot state-of-the-art carbon fibre yacht he ordered from New Zealand and dubbed *Vela Veloce* — Italian for "sail fast." At the time of his death, he was having a new boat built in Spain and had listed the *Vela Veloce* for sale for $850,000.

"The last three years, he took it to a new, very high level — a level where very few Canadians go," said Darrah. Oland participated in nine of the ten events in the 2010 US-IRC National Championship, a series of races spanning the east coast of the United States from Florida to the Caribbean over a ten-month period. Oland had the highest-standing average of 134 participants, and he earned the Canadian Sailing Association's International Sailor award. Ben Bardwell, a professional sailor and member of the *Vela Veloce* crew for about two years, described Oland as the best boss he ever had. "He certainly had high expectations, but he built such a great team," Bardwell said. "He was the leader and you know, we loved him, and we had just such a great dynamic, such an intense but comfortable dynamic, on the team. It's just sad. It was a great run we had with Dick."

But Oland's family, Darrah said, was his true "pride and joy." He started dating Connie Connell, when she was only sixteen years old. During their courtship, he would take her across the Kennebecasis River to Long Island, where they would picnic and spend the afternoon together on the beach. Connie pursued a teaching degree in the 1960s but dedicated herself to her family. Both her contemporaries and the friends of her children praise her as an unfailingly gracious and kind-hearted woman and mother. The couple's only son, Dennis James, was born on Valentine's Day, February 14, 1968. His childhood was, by all accounts, filled with love. Connie was "a very nurturing individual who was always very attentive," and his father ensured he received the best care money could buy for the 45 per cent hearing loss he was born with. At a young age, Dennis was sent to Toronto to attend speech therapy. He was also fitted with hearing aids, and the interventions proved successful. Dennis was able to play unencumbered with his older sister, Elizabeth (Lisa), and younger sister, Jacqueline, with whom he had close relationships, and the other children in their affluent Rothesay neighbourhood. Dennis's godmother, Margot Doyle, remembers him as a "quiet and polite little boy." Anne and Michael Bruce, who have known him for forty-five years, described him as "kind, mild-mannered, and a truly gentle soul."

"Each time Dick and I got together, we would have a catch-up session, a brief discussion about how things were with Connie, the children, and what they were doing," Pat Darrah said. "He had a wonderful bond with them and an active relationship. Family events were Team Oland events."

It was an idyllic time, when children could chase adventure all day as long as they were home before dark. And in Oland's family, there was always adventure. Richard Oland, whose mantra was "Go for it" was always planning activities for his young family. On winter weekends they headed to Poley Mountain near Sussex, where the three children learned to ski, with their father at their side, helping them hone their skills and taking them down "the steepest hills," as Dennis later recounted. Oland enjoyed downhill skiing with his wife and he, "one for always raising the bar," would challenge her to higher and more difficult hills. "Connie might have rolled her eyes once in a while," Darrah recalled, "but [she] proceeded to enjoy the day."

The Olands were also horse enthusiasts. In the winter they galloped on horseback across the frozen Kennebecasis River and up the trail to Minister's Face to enjoy the snowy view. "So you can imagine how exciting that was," Dennis said. Richard and Connie's daughters particularly shared their father's love of horseback riding. He was "always helping them along to improve their skills in equestrian events. He would encourage them to try the next jump a little higher up. Again, raising the bar," said Darrah. "They would make it over the jump, but even if they knocked it down a few times, he would insist they kept trying and indeed they did."

In the summers, the family could be found on the river, boating and swimming and enjoying bonfires on the beach. Dennis loved the outdoors, especially being on the water. Some of his fondest childhood memories involve time spent on the family's boat, *Aloma II*. "With my father as the captain, you could always count on a big adventure for every trip, and he never let us down," Dennis wrote in an essay presented to the Royal Kennebecasis Yacht Club after an electrical fire destroyed the *Aloma II* in St. Petersburg, Florida, in 2008. The 60-foot motorboat, with a distinctive canoe stern, had been part of the Oland family since Richard's grandfather purchased it in 1947. The vessel, like the family, had a long and proud history. Built in Sydney, Nova Scotia, in 1910, as a 45-foot sailboat, she was lengthened in 1923, converted to a motor vessel, and renamed the *Aloma II*. In 1939, she was called to service in the Second World War and served the Royal Canadian Air Force as a supply and rescue boat. In 2000 she was part of the Tall Ships Festival in Halifax, and before being sold in 2002, economic development organizations, such as Enterprise Saint John, used her to wine and dine potential investors, courtesy of the Oland family. "Dad knew the boat better than anyone, and he was certain to make sure that I learned all I could about the boat and the river," Oland wrote in his tribute, which was posted online. "And what an adventure it was. If there was water, we went there. And if there wasn't, we sometimes tried anyway."

Dennis took sailing lessons and boating turned into a lifelong interest. Under the tutelage of his father and grandfather, according to his cousin and friend Andrew Oland, he became an expert on every tributary, island, and hazard on the Saint John and Kennebecasis Rivers. One windy day, when Dennis was twelve, his father handed him the helm and told him to steer the boat ashore, which he managed to do on his first try. "I was as proud as any twelve-year-old could ever be," he wrote. At around that same age Dennis learned to operate a front-end loader at his father's quarry, Brookville Manufacturing.

Dennis became a self-professed "gearhead" with a fascination for vehicles and all things mechanic. It started when he was very young, playing the game "Name that Car" on road trips. He was also his father's helper with his seemingly endless mechanical tinkering over the years, fixing and maintaining everything from washing machines and stoves, to cars and boat motors. "I was glued to his side as a kid," Dennis remembered. When Dennis was nine and something went wrong with his motorbike, his father suggested he take it apart and fix it himself. "Many hours of work, a few days later, after numerous consultations and suggestions, Dennis had his motorcycle back together and he knew how it worked," recounted Pat Darrah. The motorbike also served as a financial lesson. Richard Oland purchased the bike, but Dennis got a paper route and paid him back in instalments. "He helped with every motorcycle after that," Dennis said, "with me paying over time."

Father and son sometimes toured back roads and fields in a 1970s GMC four-wheel drive pickup truck. One day, they got stuck in a mud hole. "No tow truck would do—and no truck was called," Darrah said. Instead, many hours later, covered in mud, the pair made it home. Darrah quoted Dennis's observation that "It didn't take long for us to understand what Dad would expect us to achieve or push ourselves to achieve: the very best." As the children grew older, the challenges got bigger. "As a team, they would strive to do their best, and Dick would help them along to do a little better," said Darrah. "Team Oland understood what was expected of them."

Despite the many material advantages their father's wealth afforded them, Dennis and his sisters were expected to pull their weight. They were assigned chores around the home. They also helped with stabling horses at the Rothesay Pony Club, operated by their grandparents, P.W. and Mary Oland, at their nearby estate. Dennis even assisted with chores at his friend Val Streeter's house. The boys, who lived just a few hundred yards apart, had been friends since they were five years old. "From day one Dennis and I were inseparable," recalled Streeter, who describes himself as Dennis's "best friend," a term he doesn't use lightly. "We slept and played at each other's houses. We went to the same school. We skied together in the winter. We boated together in the summer. We went to Camp Glenburn together. We took horseback-riding lessons together at his grandparents' farm. Ask anyone who resided in Rothesay in the 1970s, and they would certainly remember our duo."

Susan Streeter, Val's sister, agrees the two were "virtually inseparable." "Perhaps because each was 'saddled' with only sisters, they became fast friends," she said. Whatever the reason, Dennis was also like a brother to her. He was "quite simply, always around. He accompanied our family on ski trips and summer weekends," she remembered, "and my parents generally accepted him as an addition to their own four children." When Val and Susan's sister Sarah died in 1981, Dennis served as a pallbearer.

Dennis attended Rothesay Collegiate, his father's old school, for grades six through ten; in the years since Richard was a student, the school had become closely affiliated with the all-girls school Netherwood and is now known as Rothesay Netherwood. Also like Richard, Dennis went to boarding school, although in his case it was only for the eleventh grade. He attended a boarding and day school, Bishop's College, in Lennoxville, Quebec, where he was a cadet officer and head of a unit. He also participated in sports and leadership training, his mother later wrote. Missing his family and friends, Dennis returned to New Brunswick and attended Saint John High School for twelfth grade, where he was respected and well liked, according to Jill Oland, who attended high school with him and later married his cousin Patrick. The Reverend Canon James W. Golding, chaplain at Rothesay Collegiate in the 1970s, remembered Dennis as a "kind and caring" person who "learned the values of hard work . . . loyalty and great friendships."

Dennis impressed people as likeable and unpretentious. Jill Oland notes that he "makes friends easily and is fun to be around." Dennis "goes out of his way to make people feel important and that they matter," said Gord McNamee, who has known him since kindergarten. "Just like the rest of the Oland family, there is no pretense with Dennis. He is down to earth and approachable." Reverend Michael LeBlanc, a friend and confidant of the Oland family after more than twenty years as their pastor, observed that although Dennis was "brought up in what some would call a life of privilege," he had "a sense of compassion and understanding of others."

LeBlanc attributes Dennis's ability to relate to others to the summers he spent working and residing at the Saint John YMCA's Camp Glenburn during his teens. Located on the shores of Belleisle Bay on the Kingston Peninsula, about forty minutes outside the city, Camp Glenburn is New Brunswick's only non-denominational overnight camp. It boasts thirty wooded acres, a sandy beach, and lots of opportunities for outdoor exploration. Between 1983 and 1987, Dennis, whose camp nickname was "Brewer," served as a counsellor-in-training, counsellor, and canoeing instructor. He eventually became canoeing director and maintenance worker, and even served as camp director for a few weeks when he was eighteen, until they found someone to fill the position, according to his mother. "It's just fantastic. It's a wonderful spot," Dennis remembered. "He really enjoyed his time there, learning new skills, and made lifelong friends and memories," said his sister Jacqueline Walsh.

Scott Wardle said he reaped the benefits of Dennis's friendship in 1986, while attending the University of New Brunswick in Fredericton with him. "Dennis was so careful to make sure I knew everyone and always made me feel at home," said Wardle, who was from Toronto. They shared many common interests — as well as a shared distaste for peas and Brussels sprouts, "a vile food group" — and became "fast friends," he said. "I cannot count — or recount, for that matter — the number of ski trips, sun trips, and road trips that Dennis and I shared during those school years," Wardle later wrote. "Dennis and his family always made me feel welcome in their home. These were the best years of my life."

Dennis remained close to Val Streeter throughout university. They both studied political science, rented a house together, and booted around in a beater Volkswagen Beetle Dennis bought for $500. It was a wreck, Dennis remembered, and his father wouldn't let him drive it until he paid to fix it up. Richard Oland occasionally went to Fredericton to see Dennis and take him out to dinner, and in the summers Dennis worked for his father as a dispatcher at Brookville Transport, his trucking company, "very often on the night shift," as Connie Oland recalled.

Dennis graduated with a bachelor of arts degree in 1990 and worked for Moosehead Brewery in the maintenance department for a few months before moving to Halifax to attend Dalhousie University. After a term, however, he got a job selling household water treatment systems. During these years Dennis met Lesley Phinney, who would become his first wife, and Val Streeter met the woman he, too, would marry. "Both women attended Dalhousie and were great friends themselves," Streeter said. The two couples moved to Toronto in 1991, and both men got jobs in the investment industry. Richard Oland made some phone calls, and Dennis got a job in the mailroom of RBC Dominion Securities. Within four years, Dennis rose to stockbroker's assistant. "We saw each other constantly during our Toronto years," Streeter said. Dennis also became a "fixture" in the family of his UNB friend Scott Wardle, who had moved back to Toronto. "He was welcomed into my mother's home as long as he cheered for the Jays."

Despite living in Toronto, Dennis still joined his family for their annual ski trip. After four years in Toronto, "the Maritimer in both of us called us home," said Streeter. They returned to Rothesay with their girlfriends, bought homes close to each other, and became investment advisers. Oland worked for Richardson Greenshields and married Lesley in 1995, with Streeter serving as his best man. Two years later when Streeter married his wife, Dennis was in the wedding party. Between 1996 and 2000, Dennis and Lesley had three children: Emily, Hannah, and Henry, named for his paternal grandfather's middle name.

Up until July 6, 2011, Richard Oland and his family seemed to live charmed lives, at least to many outside observers. True, Dennis and Lesley divorced in 2009, but he was now happily remarried. Approximately two weeks before his death, Richard Oland had chartered a private plane from Rhode Island to attend the one-hundredth birthday of Connie's cousin, Marg Bourne. After the celebration, the Olands and some of Connie's family gathered at Dennis's home to view photographs from a recent trip to England. It was "a very happy time," Connie recalled. Richard and Dennis planned to get together when Oland returned from a fishing trip to talk about the family genealogy project they were working on. Oland returned from that trip in a "great mood," and he and Connie went out to dinner that night with her visiting family. The next morning, he left for work, and Connie never saw him again.

But all was not quite as it seemed. The relationship between father and son was fraught with tension. Beneath his boyish and affable exterior, and despite his father's wealth, Dennis Oland kept hidden his increasingly dire financial situation. And Richard Oland had another, less exalted side, one that the police investigation would fully expose in the days and weeks to come.

three
THE INVESTIGATION BEGINS

Sergeant Mark Smith, the head of the Saint John Police Force's forensic identification unit, donned a fresh set of protective gear when he returned from the morgue at around 3:40 on the afternoon of July 7 to photograph the crime scene. He took pictures of the outside of the building, the front door, up the stairs, the foyer and washroom outside Oland's office, and the office itself, being careful not to move anything. He was methodical, as he was trained to be, and at one point returned to headquarters to upload photographs from Oland's cameras before returning to take additional pictures and process for fingerprints and DNA. Smith, a PEI native who graduated from the police academy in 1988 and was hired three days later, had worked his way up the ranks from patrol constable to head of the forensic unit in 2006. He had extensive forensic training, including courses in fingerprints, processing of exhibits, digital imaging techniques, and blood spatter. In 2000 he was qualified by the national DNA data bank.

As he worked, he inspected all the doors and windows for any sign of forced entry, such as damage or paint chips or other debris on the floor. He saw none. It did not appear to be a break-and-enter gone awry. Besides, Oland's wallet, Rolex watch, electronic equipment, and the keys to his BMW, which was parked out front when his body was discovered, were left untouched.

Smith took hundreds of photographs, trying to capture everything from every angle. "You can never take too many," he said. "You have no idea what may be important down the road." Then he returned to the office to test for fingerprints, using a magnetic powder and magna brush. Smith dusted any items the perpetrator may have touched, including computers, cameras, and phones, but everything in the office had been handled too frequently for him to find usable prints.

Shortly before seven p.m. two RCMP tech crime experts the Saint John police called in to assist in processing Oland's electronic equipment arrived, but Smith still needed to collect and catalogue blood samples for DNA testing, and he asked them to wait in the foyer while he finished processing the scene. It was a painstaking procedure.

Smith used a drop of sterile water on a swab, rubbed the swab in the coagulated or dried blood, and placed the swab in a plastic tube with a screw-top lid, known as a SWUBE tube. He labelled the sample with an identification number, the date, the time, and his initials, and placed it in a plastic exhibit bag, which was also labelled. He also placed an adhesive ID marker and scale next to the area tested and took a photograph before swabbing the next area.

He finally let the RCMP tech crime experts in at around eight thirty. He gave them gloves and protective shoe covers to wear and asked them to "be as careful as possible" and to stay away from the main blood pool. Smith supervised while the RCMP officers seized twelve items they hoped might provide some clues, including computers and digital cameras. They placed numbered miniature orange pylons beside the items of interest and photographed and documented them. Then they loaded the items into their vehicle and drove them to their lab in Fredericton for detailed analysis. Smith packed up for the night a short time later, around ten thirty, and headed to police headquarters to take care of some administrative duties. An officer remained on guard in the foyer outside the office when Smith left.

At the forensics office on the fifth floor of the station, Smith secured and documented all the evidence he had collected, following procedure to ensure continuity. He logged each exhibit on a flow chart in the computer system, and locked the DNA samples in a special drying cabinet. Once DNA is dry, it's quite stable, he explained. He placed the other exhibits in one of the forensics lockers at the back of the office; despite their name, these cabinets had no locks. Used for short-term storage, each of the lockers had a file on the outside that indicated what was inside, who placed it there, and when, said Smith. The forensics office itself was on a security card system, to which only a few officers had access. Other officers who wanted to access the exhibits were supposed to consult Smith. Items moved to the sixth-floor property control office for long-term storage would be logged to track and protect them. Access to property control was limited to the employees of that section and was armed with an alarm system.

On July 8, Oland family members remained behind closed doors at their Rothesay homestead but issued a statement through the family lawyer, William (Bill) Teed. "This is a very difficult time for our family and we hope everyone understands our need for privacy," they wrote. "We are very proud of Richard's many personal and business achievements and contributions to Saint John and the region. We will remember him fondly and truly appreciate the outpouring of support and heartfelt remembrances we have already received."

Oland's prominence was not lost on Chief Reid, a thirty-three-year veteran. Although any mysterious sudden death was treated seriously, he realized his force would face more intense scrutiny during this investigation. "This is obviously a person who is well-known in the community," Reid told the *Telegraph-Journal*. "He's known in the province, and nationally. So those types of things are important." His officers were working around the clock to solve the case, he assured the public. Nearly twenty men and women continued to comb the crime scene, canvass the neighbourhood, and seek out surveillance video from local businesses. The police would leave no stone unturned, he said.

But Reid revealed little else. Investigators were waiting for the results of the autopsy, scheduled for that day, to determine whether Oland's death, which he continued to refer to as "suspicious," was an accidental death or a homicide, he said. "It's not a natural cause, I can absolutely tell you," he said, and police did not suspect it was a suicide. Still, Reid felt confident enough to say Oland was not killed in a random act of violence.

"This is an isolated situation," he said. "There's not someone out there trying to cause havoc." Clearly the chief knew more — or thought he knew more — than he disclosed.

Smith attended a debriefing in the major crime unit's boardroom that morning before heading to the morgue at Saint John Regional Hospital. A pathologist would conduct an autopsy to determine the exact cause of Oland's death, but first Smith would examine the body for evidence, treating it as part of the crime scene. He asked forensic Constable David MacDonald to assist. "I effectively cancelled his holidays," he later admitted.

They each donned a hospital surgical gown, cap, mask, gloves, and shoe covers. Smith retrieved Oland's body from the locked cooler at 9:47 and rolled the gurney into the autopsy room. The body was as it had been transported, face down to maintain the integrity of the skull. Smith unzipped the white body bag, carefully pulled down the sides, and took photographs of the body. When he died, Richard Oland was wearing a white shirt with vertical red and blue stripes, a dark blue sweater, dark blue pants, dark blue socks, and black leather loafers. He also wore a navy belt with red trim and "Block Island Race Week" in white lettering, the sailing competition he had recently attended.

Constable MacDonald inspected Oland's prone body from head to toe, using a bright light and magnifying glass to look for any traces of evidence on his clothing. He repeated the process using a special forensic light with multiple bandwidth settings called a CrimeScope, which is designed to make various compounds fluoresce and provide contrast between evidence and the surface on which it is found. During the examination, a minor incident occurred when the CrimeScope touched Oland's body. MacDonald had to scrub the light down and note the event.

Smith took more photographs and used tape, resembling packing tape, to remove some hair and fibre samples. He also found some metal shards, something never explained in court. He placed each item on clear plastic and documented and bagged it.

Next, they rolled Oland's body over. Rigor mortis was fully developed in his extremities. Both his arms, which had been crumpled beneath his torso, were flexed. His face was covered in clotted and liquid blood. Smith removed the body bag that was labelled with Oland's name, seized it as evidence, too, and went through the same steps all over again: photographs, inspection, evidence collection, and cataloguing.

Smith found some strands of hair in between Oland's fingers. He used tweezers to remove them. He plucked a dozen strands of hair from Oland's head, trying to get the roots for DNA testing. He swabbed Oland's knuckles, the inside of his palms, and underneath his fingernails. He took fingernail clippings. Oland's bloodstained clothing was removed, and his body was searched again using a UV light, which can show any bruising or bite marks not visible in fluorescent light. Nothing was found. The body was washed down to remove all the blood, and a penile swab was taken "to cover all the bases," said Smith.

The pathologist had to wait until around four thirty that afternoon for Smith and MacDonald to finish their work so he could begin his. Dr. Ather Naseemuddin had reviewed Smith's crime-scene photos of the body in preparation for the autopsy. The coroner, Andrew Cavanagh, and a morgue attendant, Kirk Sweeney, were also present. Sweeney took samples of blood, urine, and eye fluid for toxicology tests. MacDonald also took some blood as a DNA sample. The only thing of note the toxicology tests revealed was the presence of a small amount of alcohol in the urine.

"The body appears to be that of a well-developed, well-nourished, late middle-aged Caucasian male," Naseemuddin noted in his postmortem report, PM-11-166. Body length, 182 centimetres; weight, 88.6 kilograms. Oland wore a hearing aid in his right ear. Blood partially covered the Rolex watch on his left wrist.

Oland's injuries were "readily apparent," but Naseemuddin ordered X-rays of his head, neck, chest, and hands to "bolster those findings." He then began to inventory the injuries, starting with Oland's hands, which had "sharp-force wounds." He measured the lengths, widths, and depths of each one, marked them with a numbered piece of medical tape, and photographed them. "There were so many injuries I risked being confused and missing one, or counting one twice," Naseemuddin would later explain of his decision to number as he went.

No. 1 was a deep gash on Oland's left index finger. "It was deep enough to reach the bone," said Naseemuddin. The back of Oland's right hand had a cut about five or six centimetres long and one and a half centimetres deep. The bones beneath the cut were broken. The underside of his right wrist bore another laceration. Naseemuddin counted six "defensive-type" wounds to Oland's hands that sliced through his flesh and shattered his bones, but none, he noted, were life threatening.

He moved up to the neck and head area.

One injury wasn't assigned a number because it would have been too complicated. Oland's left orbital plate was cracked like an eggshell, indicating "some degree of frontal impact," said Naseemuddin. He also noted bruising on Oland's eyelids and concluded the damage may have been caused by Oland falling forward. Other unnumbered injuries included a 0.8-centimetre scratch on the bridge of his nose, two small bruises on his right cheek that measured about 4 centimetres in diameter, and a faint "historical" bruise, about 5 centimetres in diameter, on his upper left chest.

The damage to Oland's head was obvious, but Naseemuddin wanted to investigate the injuries in more detail. He shaved Oland's head and documented five blunt-force injuries, and thirty-four sharp-force injuries, "consistent with chop wounds." Then he peeled back the scalp to document the skull fractures. He counted fourteen. Some were superficial; others exposed brain tissue. Naseemuddin took more photos and sketched three diagrams. "The skull bones are removed by removing the upper portion of the scalp with a bone saw," he wrote in his report. He removed Oland's brain and sliced it into sections.

Oland's body was also sliced open, using the standard Y-shaped, vertical midline, thoracoabdominal incision. Naseemuddin removed the chest plate and exposed the organs, which he removed for examination and dissection.

It took until shortly after nine o'clock that night for Naseemuddin to complete the autopsy. "Death, in my opinion, resulted from multiple sharp and blunt force injuries to the head," he concluded.

—

The investigation continued through the weekend. At eight a.m. on Saturday officers gathered in the major crime unit's boardroom for yet another debriefing. Afterward, Sergeant Smith headed to the police garage to examine Oland's seized BMW 750 Li, licence plate number NBW 713, for any sign of damage, struggle, or blood. Smith spent about an hour processing the car and seized an iPod but "noted nothing unusual." The vehicle was "very neat and in order," he said. Years later, Smith was still able to recite the licence plate number from memory.

Smith hustled back to Oland's office, where a number of officers were conducting a search. It was two days since the discovery of Oland's body, likely three days since the murder, but the crime scene "had not been thoroughly searched yet," according to David Brooker, the head of the MCU. They were looking for a "weapon or any other type of evidence," he said. Smith's job, as a forensic officer, was to document any items seized.

Brooker, who had been with the force for about twenty-three years at that point, doesn't recall wearing any protective gear, such as gloves or booties, when he re-entered the crime scene that day. Constable Stephen Davidson, who accompanied him, also could not say with certainty whether he was wearing protective gear but "most times" police do for "that type of scene," he later said. Constable Shawn Coughlan remembers putting on latex gloves, a construction-style dust mask, and booties, but isn't sure what, if any, protective gear anyone else wore. There "weren't any real precautions" to avoid disturbing the scene, as far as Davidson recalls, other than to go straight to the areas of interest. He doesn't remember touching or moving anything on Oland's desk "because of the blood and whatnot," he said. None of the officers could say where exactly they stepped. "I certainly didn't step in any blood, if that's what you're asking," Coughlan would later say.

They searched for about ninety minutes. Coughlan focused his efforts on the wall-length bank of filing cabinets, where he found two USB sticks that Smith labelled and packaged. He also pointed out three pieces of paper on the desk of Robert McFadden, which were also seized, although, curiously, the police did not seize any of the papers on Richard Oland's desk. Brooker located "an electronics device" in a plastic case on a shelf behind the curtain. He wasn't sure what it was exactly, just that it was "electronics," and it was seized. Davidson also identified numerous electronic items for seizure. Laptops, camera memory cards, and CDs were catalogued. Inspector Glen McCloskey, who was off that Saturday, spent part of the early afternoon at the crime scene "for support." He wanted his officers to know "somebody at a higher level is there and cares about what they're doing," he later explained. One of the officers found a small toy-like wooden hammer, "something a child might use," according to McCloskey. He didn't know if it was seized, though. Like the metal shards, the small wooden hammer is an unexplained mystery.

Near the end of the search, Brooker contacted Oland's secretary, Maureen Adamson, and asked her to come in and see if she noticed "anything out of the ordinary." Adamson identified a logbook, a genealogy book, Oland's will, and his iPhone as missing. Police would subsequently find everything except the iPhone. It appeared to be the only thing that went missing from the crime scene. Adamson told the officers Oland always kept his cellphone on him, and it would be unusual for him not to have it. When police left at around three p.m., an officer was still on guard.

The police contracted All-Sea Atlantic to provide five divers to search the Renforth wharf in Rothesay. Coughlan was present while the divers searched underwater for any evidence related to the case, including the murder weapon and Richard Oland's missing iPhone, although at the time police wouldn't say what they were searching for, or even confirm if the search was related to the Oland investigation. The divers searched in front of the wharf, down its sides, and around the nearby rowing club. The divers filmed the search with video cameras, and Coughlan watched the search on a monitor on the wharf. The divers searched for more than four hours, according to the underwater video the defence lawyers later got in disclosure from the Crown. They found plenty of debris at the bottom of the Kennebecasis River, including a piece of metal pipe, but no clues in the case.

Brooker, meanwhile, contacted Rogers Communications again about Oland's missing iPhone. Police needed a production order for Oland's cell records, which Justice William Grant of the Court of Queen's Bench authorized. Brooker sent the order that day.

Back at the crime scene, Smith gathered the pieces of the puzzle: photographing, collecting samples, and running tests. He took more DNA swabs from the main blood pool and measured the hundreds of spattered bloodstains for analysis. Smith was not a certified blood-spatter analyst. The closest expert was at the RCMP forensic lab in Halifax. Inspector McCloskey asked that day — two days after the body was dis-covered — if Smith "would like to have the assistance of an analyst," Smith recalled. "And I agreed."

Smith continued, however, to take measurements of the stains that radiated from where Oland's bludgeoned body was found, essential data for the analyst. He also drew a sketch that mapped the distances of various items in the office from the body. From Oland's severely battered head to the curtained area leading to McFadden's office was about six feet, Smith noted, and the curtain had staining more than five feet high. From Oland's head to the blood-spattered tabletop was nine feet and about thirty-six inches off the floor. At least one stain was approximately nine feet from the centre of the blood pool.

In the washroom, located off the foyer outside the office, Smith found a paper towel in the garbage can and subjected it to a presumptive test for blood. It came back positive. Smith seized the paper towel and the garbage bag and its contents for further testing.

On the afternoon of July 11, the chief of police held a news conference at police headquarters to confirm what many people in Saint John already suspected. "Preliminary results of the autopsy, coupled with evidence at the scene, clearly indicate that Richard Oland was a victim of foul play — homicide," Bill Reid said into a bank of microphones as video cameras rolled. Oland met his "untimely death" sometime between six p.m. on July 6 and the morning of July 7, when his body was found, the chief said. But Reid remained circumspect about other details. He would not say how Oland died or whether a weapon was involved. That information, he said, "will remain with the investigational team at this time."

Reid did say that Richard Oland likely knew his killer, but he would not divulge why police believed that or whether they had identified any suspects. He said no evidence suggested the crime was a robbery gone wrong or a random act, nor did police have any reason to believe that other members of the Oland family — or anyone else — was in danger.

Police were still in the fact-finding stage, collecting and analyzing forensic evidence from the crime scene and reviewing more than thirty-six hours of security video collected from several local businesses to "marry" to information obtained from interviews with Oland's family, friends, and business associates, he said. "These are crucial times for us. Our members are working long hours to come up with some idea of what took place." He had assigned a core group of ten to fifteen officers to the investigation, but he stressed it would be a slow and detailed process.

Asked how far police were from identifying a suspect or arresting someone, Reid reiterated that they were still in the fact-finding phase. "It can always be said that you've got tunnel vision in an investigation if you're focusing on one person or a specific thing. I would rather say that the analogy here is that we're using a funnel. We're grabbing all this information, and hopefully we can come to a suspect or suspects in this investigation. That is a very long process. Our folks are being very methodical, analyzing the information. We do not want to make a mistake," Reid said. "We want to be able to prove this case without a shadow of a doubt."

As Chief Reid declared Richard Oland's death a homicide, visitation for the prominent businessman was ongoing at Brenan's Funeral Home on Saint John's Paradise Row. Oland's sudden death was, of course, the talk of the town, dominating newscasts and coffee-shop chatter. But the fact police were now looking for a suspect in the tight-knit community made it all the more unsettling, and gossip worthy. The announcement he had been killed, and likely at the hands of someone he knew, left the entire region reeling, Rothesay's mayor Bill Bishop said. "After the shock wears off, people will be more responsive then," Bishop observed. "But at the present time, people are just shocked that it happened, and in the fashion it happened." Neighbour and friend Kelly Patterson expressed disbelief. "If anyone in Saint John could be murdered, he'd be the last person, I would think."

In the days following Oland's death, the flags of municipal buildings in Saint John and at the Rothesay Yacht Club were lowered to half-mast. John Ainsworth, the owner of 52 Canterbury Street and operator of the print shop that occupied the ground floor, had set up a memorial outside his building. "We're really, really hurting over this. Really hurting," Ainsworth said at the time. He struggled with "the ghost of it," he said. His poster-board display, flanked by fresh-cut flowers, included a smiling photograph of Oland and the message: "Richard, you will be sorely missed. Thank you for all that you've done! God speed, friend." Ainsworth encouraged people to sign the poster.

Richard Oland's siblings, Derek Oland and Jane Toward, had released a joint statement through Moosehead Breweries spokesperson Joel Levesque. Derek Oland, the executive chairman, was fishing in a remote part of Labrador when his brother's body was discovered. The family had difficulty reaching him, and he wasn't able to arrange transportation back to Saint John until July 8, arriving home late in the afternoon on July 9. Their statement expressed their condolences to Connie Oland and her children and grandchildren.

"Richard is being remembered kindly by many in the community and elsewhere and we truly appreciate these words of comfort. Like our father and mother, Richard gave a great deal of himself and his resources for the betterment of Saint John and the larger New Brunswick community. We are grateful for these and his many other contributions," they observed. "Our thoughts now are with Richard's family and our focus is to help them through the difficult days ahead."

The next day, on Tuesday afternoon, about four hundred and fifty grief-stricken family and friends filled Our Lady of Perpetual Help Roman Catholic Church in Rothesay beyond capacity to honour the late pillar of the community. It was a who's who of politicians and business leaders alike. Senator John Wallace, several cabinet ministers, MLAs, and area mayors joined the congregation of the bereaved. Ben Bardwell, whom Oland employed as a member of his sailing crew, drove overnight from Connecticut with three friends to attend his former boss's funeral. "It was pretty important to us to get here," Bardwell explained. "Just, I guess, to say goodbye." The mourners filled the pews and extra chairs and lined the back of the modern, airy sanctuary, located mere steps from Oland's home. It was an apt locale for his obsequies. Just a few years earlier, Oland devoted his fundraising skills, engineering experience, and endless energy to help build the new, bigger church to accommodate the growing community.

Premier David Alward numbered among the attendees. "Mr. Oland's contributions to his community of Greater Saint John and to New Brunswick were as generous as they were significant," Alward said in a statement. "He was a great businessman with an equally great regard for his fellow New Brunswickers. He will always be remembered with deep respect by the people of Greater Saint John and of our entire province." Lieutenant Governor Graydon Nicholas said he felt "fortunate" to attend the service. "I think it's always difficult in the best of circumstances for a life to be lost. And when you stop and think of all the good that this man has done for this community and all of New Brunswick, I think this is a beautiful celebration of life for him."

"God loves us all and receives us all in His own way," Reverend Michael LeBlanc said at the beginning of the mass, as the sun beamed through the skylight and the stained glass windows, bathing the casket, draped in a white and gold pall, in a glow. "Let's always be thankful for all of the good things Dick did for us."

Family members, including his son, Dennis, read from scripture during the hour-long service. The Saint John String Quartet accompanied a number of vocalists. Pat Darrah delivered the eulogy, fighting back tears as he paid homage to his "dear friend" of nearly thirty-five years, describing Oland's myriad achievements and contributions to the community. Darrah remembered that he'd sometimes choose a subject for fun and challenge Oland, saying, "You wouldn't know about [such and such]." Invariably, Darrah recalled, "I would get a lecture of how that situation or institution worked. And be brought up to speed to the very fine points," he said. "And if he didn't know the details, I could guarantee that within twenty-four hours my telephone would ring, and I would have a full, detailed description." Darrah also paid tribute to Oland's widow, who sat in the front row with one of her grandchildren on her lap. "Connie," he said, "Dick may have been the skipper, but you controlled the rudder. We all knew that he could be impatient, but one of your hands on his shoulder and things turned — calm, kind, and considerate of others."

At the end of the service, family and guests exited the church to the strains of the Frank Sinatra classic "My Way" — a fitting tribute, according to Darrah. Video cameras rolled and camera shutters clicked as the casket was lifted into the hearse; Oland would be cremated. The mourners exchanged handshakes and shared hugs of condolences with few outward signs of sorrow. The Saint John police were also there, watching.

One photographer captured a curious moment: the kind of photo that makes people look twice and seems to invite speculation. The image would grace the front page of the *Telegraph-Journal* and be picked up by newspapers right across the country, but not for nearly two and a half years: Dennis Oland, eyes downcast — and with what many viewed as a slight smile on his face.

four

FATHER AND SON

In the days following Richard Oland's murder, many lauded him as a successful entrepreneur and community leader known for his business savvy and philanthropy. Friends and associates used words like "passionate," "intense," "driven," "tough," and "exacting" to describe him. He was "larger than life" and "dominated a room," they said. No one likes to speak ill of the dead, especially someone who personally, and whose family, had contributed so much to the region. But as time passed, it became clear those putative positive attributes were a double-edged sword. The man with the wide, dimpled smile had another, lesser known, less talked about side. He was well known, yes, but not necessarily well liked. Could this have played a role in his violent death?

Oland's uncompromising, unreserved nature led to rancorous relations with his older brother, Derek, and his eventual departure from the family business, Moosehead Breweries, the oldest independent brewery in Canada. "Dick would argue with anybody. It didn't matter who it was," Derek once said in an interview for Harvey Sawler's book *Last Canadian Beer: The Moosehead Story*. The brothers both aspired to succeed their father, P.W., as president — succession disputes an all-too-familiar theme in the Oland family dynasty. In 1980, fearing P.W. would put Dick in charge, Derek tendered his resignation and planned to move his family to New Zealand. "I couldn't work for Dick because of the nature of the guy," he told Sawler. P.W. promptly appointed Derek executive vice-president, sending a clear — and public — message about his succession plans. "The younger one wanted to be president, and he hadn't the experience," P.W. later told *Financial Post Magazine*. Richard Oland gave a different account in a 1992 interview with the *Financial Post*, one that downplayed the personal significance of the family business. "I was just looking for opportunities, and if they weren't present in the existing system, I had to leave," he said. "Moosehead was just a career option like any other."

Oland left Moosehead in 1981 and went on to run Brookville Transport, a trucking company that initially owed the bulk of its business to the brewery, hauling beer to the United States. Derek became president and CEO of Moosehead Breweries the following year and was instrumental in launching the brand in the United States and, later, globally. P.W.'s death in 1996 brought Richard back into the fold, with a 33 per cent share willed to him; Derek got 53 per cent, and their sister, Jane, 14 per cent, according to Sawler. Rising costs and the loss of its largest customer, Repap, led to the sale of Brookville Transport in 1997, and Richard twice sued over Derek's management of Moosehead before Derek bought out his siblings in 2007 and took full control of the company, which now has estimated annual revenues of $200 million. Richard Oland, a multimillionaire, settled into semi-retirement, running his investment management company, "basically for his investments," as his secretary put it. He travelled the world, drove a BMW, and ordered high-end suits (and suspenders) from Italy and Harry Rosen in Toronto. He frequented the Rothesay Yacht Club, located near his recently renovated mansion, and lunched at the Union Club, a private, old-fashioned gentlemen's club housed in an 1890 Victorian building just steps from his uptown office; a room in the club bears his father's name, and the club asks its members to restrict the "conspicuous use of business papers" to the P.W. Oland room or one of the private function rooms. He skied and sailed, and he threw himself into community service.

Yet despite his considerable personal success, Richard Oland's personality remained difficult. He may well have found losing the presidency of Moosehead to Derek more publicly humiliating than he admitted. In fact, his wife, Connie, felt that his disposition became "more severe," after his father passed him over. After Oland left the brewery, she said, he distanced himself from his family and was never the same toward their children. Connie said she had quickly "realized his personality was different" when they started dating. She learned during their marriage that he could be, as she put it, "verbally and emotionally abusive." He "did not always seem to understand how his words might offend someone." She would sit him down at the kitchen table and explain it to him. He would then make amends and peace would be restored, she said.

Connie attributed Oland's shortcomings, in part, to the way she says his father, P.W., raised him — through "yelling and put-downs." Dennis Oland also described his father's relationship with the steely P.W. as difficult. "I think his upbringing was, you know, tougher than mine," he told investigators. "His father was a military guy and grew up with that generation...living through the Depression and everything. His father wasn't easy on him." Dennis blamed his grandfather for Oland's "life-long battle with his brother," Derek. "It's his father's fault because his father basically said, 'You two are against each other. Fight for it.' Which is dumb, right?"

All three of Richard and Connie Oland's children "had issues" with their father (or he with them), Connie noted. Behind the stories Pat Darrah shared at the funeral of the proud father riding with his daughters, back-roading with his son, and skiing with his wife was a man with high and exacting expectations, urging "Team Oland" to attain perfection. "'Push to achieve' is a quality that Dick lived every day," Darrah had said, and he expected the same of those around him. Just as Oland couldn't seem to please his own father, he seemed to be "hardest" on his only son. Dennis was barely a teen when his father's ambition to control the family business was thwarted, and he later said he felt he bore the brunt of the acrimonious fallout. Dennis told investigators that his relationship with his father had been "probably perfect," until that point, but his teenage years were "very difficult" because of his father's "really high expectations." As the only son, he "took most of the pressure," he said. "Things got complicated." As a teen, Dennis looked forward to the summer months, when he could escape to Camp Glenburn. "I'd be gone," he said. "It was great."

Dennis said his father was "never violent" and didn't use corporal punishment as a means of discipline, but he would "say and do things that...could be hurtful." He was "quite meticulous" and would verbally correct Dennis in front of others, which Dennis found embarrassing. It was like Oland was just waiting for his son to mess up. And yet Dennis doesn't seem to have been a problem child. Like many teens, he experimented with marijuana and alcohol, mostly on weekends. His parents shipped him off to boarding school in Quebec for eleventh grade, but he returned home to Saint John for grade twelve. "We concluded...he was responsible enough to choose wisely," his mother said. Dennis never caused her any major concerns during his formative years, she said, and she wasn't worried about his alcohol use.

Richard Oland was much harder to please. If Dennis borrowed something without permission or didn't return it on time, he would "get in trouble." His father kept him on his toes. They used to enjoy sailing together, but his father was "a real hard guy to be on a boat with." He "had no fear" and wanted to do everything his way. The people Richard Oland paid to sail with him may have enjoyed the experience, but not his son. "He just barks and barks and barks," Dennis remarked. Dealing with somebody with "such a quest for perfection" became too frustrating, Dennis said, so he stopped boating with him. "It was just... It wasn't good for our relationship."

Dennis's friend Dale Knox, a Saint John businessman, acknowledged the father-son relationship deteriorated over the years. "And I understand that. I think back to my own father who's been gone for a lot of years now. Sometimes those relationships are tough." Knox thinks Oland may have thought he was helping Dennis: his version of tough love.

Connie's sister, Jane Mackay, didn't see it that way. She felt Oland sometimes tried to provoke his son. She remembered the wedding of one of the Oland daughters, when Dennis served as the master of ceremonies. "His father was annoyed that rain had delayed the ceremony schedule, and began yelling behind the scenes at Dennis as the cause of the problem," she said. "Dennis was called a number of names. Dennis refused to rise to the bait and calmly continued with a modified schedule." Through the years, Dennis exhibited patience, respect, and an unwillingness to engage in confrontation, said Mackay. Dennis himself told investigators that family occasions were "not always pleasant." Everything was "intense" and "regimented" and "had to be perfect," Dennis said, recalling a recent Christmas dinner when his father "blew a gasket" because Dennis let the flame of a rum cake extinguish before he got it to the table. "It was ugly," Dennis said. "Dick's personality was the norm for our family, and we all knew how to work around that norm," Connie observed.

Despite Oland's expensive personal tastes, home life was a different story. Oland allotted Connie $2,000 a month for household expenses and would only reimburse her if she submitted receipts for her expenditures; Maureen Adamson would prepare a report for him to review, and he'd sign a cheque. He "could be very difficult and controlling at times," Connie said. "In our family, you know, you don't get given stuff," Dennis observed. "I mean, you know, we've had a very fortunate upbringing, OK, but...he doesn't go out and buy you things, he doesn't take you on trips and spend the money." Oland's daughter Jacqueline Walsh was running the Rothesay Pony Club, started by P.W. and Mary Oland. Richard Oland owned the property and demanded, Dennis alleged, an "exorbitant" amount of rent. "And you know, the farm itself is in some ways almost derelict," Dennis said.

Nor was it only his family members who found him difficult. Long-time friend and lawyer Gerald McMackin knew Oland for more than sixty years. One of his first summer jobs was working for Oland at the Rothesay Horse Show and later at Moosehead Breweries. He rented a house from Oland when he got married and often socialized and travelled with him and Connie over the years. McMackin didn't mince words. "Dick was at times a difficult person to get along with and was disliked, or even despised, by many people." Family friend Valerie Teed found him "overbearing" and "narcissistic."

Even Pat Darrah, who spoke of him as being like a brother, acknowledged his disagreeable side. "The legacy of what he's done for the community shows in every corner of it," and "his heart and soul" was always in the cause, he said. But Oland was not always diplomatic when he was determined to get something done. He often ruffled feathers along the way and Darrah, who worked with him on many projects, would follow behind, trying to smooth them out as best he could.

Dale Knox, who knew Richard Oland for years, initially as a classmate and friend of Dennis and later as a member of the Canada Games Foundation board, admired him for his business acumen. "I think from a business perspective Dick was brilliant. You could tell it from a financial aspect, you know. Numbers really spoke to him." But he recalled being exposed to Oland's forceful personality when he attended his first board meeting. "I had a question. It was a question around some of the financial stuff, and Dick didn't like my question. And it was basically: 'You talk when I tell you that you can talk,' and of course I didn't take that very kind," said Knox. "And after the meeting, he comes over and he says, 'You're going to be a great addition to this board.' [He] puts his arm around my shoulder and says, 'We're going to do great things.' And I walked out, and I thought, 'OK, what just happened?'"

Former mayors of both Saint John and Rothesay said Oland would often stop by their offices to offer his unsolicited advice on municipal matters. He was not afraid to share his opinions, they said. He was not one to ingratiate himself. "He seemed to go through friends," Dennis noted. "He just seemed to exhaust them, I think. You know, his intensity would just exhaust them, and they would just throw their hands up." His father didn't seem to have any filters and would say inappropriate things. "It was unfortunate for him because he did, you know, push the wrong buttons sometimes."

Even making small talk could pose a challenge. Dennis found himself reaching for topics to ask his father about: his boat, or his last fishing trip, "because it's not a two-way conversation. If he asks you how you're doing, he doesn't want a long answer," he explained. Dennis concluded, "it was a lot easier to keep your distance.... It just kept the peace." A friend who was a clinical psychologist later told Connie that she felt Oland showed many of the signs of Asperger's syndrome, an autism-spectrum disorder characterized by difficulties in social interaction and non-verbal communication.

———

Dennis wasn't like his father, everyone agreed. Connie, having observed the results of P.W.'s parenting, made a conscious choice to raise her children "in a loving manner, with the tools of structure, reason, and a sense of others," she noted. "I was not going to use yelling and put-downs." Family friends thought that Dennis took after Connie more than his short-tempered and brusque father. He "is like his mother, not his father," remarked Gerald McMackin. "Dennis has always been an easy-going person. I have never seen him angry; I have never heard of him threatening anybody or hurting anybody. In fact, I can't really recall having heard him say anything negative about anybody." Valerie Teed also felt Dennis, whom she described as pleasant, sociable, and "non-confrontational," took after his mother.

Connie herself felt that Dennis had a "gentle" way about him. "Dennis has always had a caring personality and 'stood up' for the underdog," she said. It was a trait Connie said her husband had admired in her late uncle, Gordon Fairweather, the head of the first Human Rights Commission and later founding chairman of the Immigration and Refugee Board of Canada. Richard Oland was "fond" of Fairweather. When Richard's mother died in 1995, Richard turned to Dennis to help plan her funeral, Connie noted. In the aftermath of her husband's murder, Connie leaned on Dennis for emotional support and advice. Derek Oland described his nephew as "one of the most decent and kindest of men." Friends noted his devotion to his three children. "Dennis has done everything possible to ensure his children feel as secure and happy as they can possibly be," his long-time friend Stephen Turnbull observed, particularly after their grandfather's brutal death. Both Turnbull and Susan Streeter, the sister of Dennis's closest friend, Val, praised him for always putting the well-being of his children first.

Dennis Oland's struggles to meet his father's expectations continued into adulthood. After trying his hand at some other jobs in his teens and early twenties, Dennis pursued a career as a financial adviser at CIBC Wood Gundy. From the beginning, his father was one of his "sizeable" clients (Oland invested a few million dollars, a small percentage of his considerable fortune, with CIBC Wood Gundy), but his business relationship with him was, as he put it, "a bit different" than with his other clients. Dennis was one of several stockbrokers who managed parts of Richard Oland's diverse investment portfolio, but as Dennis acknowledged, "With him I'm more of an order-taker." Oland, not surprisingly, was "a demanding client," according to branch manager John Travis. The firm installed a dedicated phone line, one programmed on the speed dial at Oland's 52 Canterbury Street office. The line rang at Dennis's desk and the desk of Dennis's assistant. Oland expected someone to answer within the first three rings. If they didn't, Travis was the backup. "Was it a perfect relationship? No," Dennis frankly admitted. "If something went wrong, you know, he would fly off."

Wallace Turnbull, a retired judge who had a long family friendship with the Olands and described himself as a "sometime confidant of Dick's" said: "As parents, we shared with each other the normal concerns and challenges faced by parents with maturing children. I heard from him about the occasions when he was proud of Dennis's successes and also when he felt Dennis required his support." Larry Cain became close friends with the adult Dennis. They boated together and took trips with their children. Cain believes having to cope with a mercurial father helped build Dennis's character. He was expected to work hard, and he did. "I think Dennis was not one of those kids that had everything handed to him," he said. "Dennis worked for everything that he earned, and I think he learned that from his dad."

But Dennis struggled financially. His protracted and bitter split from his first wife, Lesley, which began as a separation in 2006-07 and ended in divorce in 2008-09, threatened to cost him his home, the Gondola Point Road property that his paternal grandparents had owned and where Richard Oland and his siblings grew up. To his credit, Oland refused to see that happen. He asked his business associate, Robert McFadden, to help Dennis negotiate the terms of the divorce. "He certainly wanted to have some input in how things were settled," McFadden said.

Oland advanced his son approximately $538,000 to provide a cash settlement to Lesley Oland and settle the existing mortgage and line of credit. The terms of the loan required Dennis to make interest-only payments each month (the principal would be deducted from his inheritance when Connie Oland died); Oland also took ownership of the property that encompassed the barn, stables, and riding ring used for the Rothesay Pony Club, which Dennis estimated was worth around $125,000, and he then rented that part to his daughter Jacqueline.

Dennis was grateful for his father's help and credited him for never throwing the loan in his face. But even here one senses that Oland judged his son and found him wanting. He wanted Dennis to enter into a "domestic contract" with Lisa Andrik, the significant other who became his second wife in August 2009, to protect the family interests against another failed relationship. "I was cognizant of Dennis's struggle through his divorce and achieving career success that would please his father," Wallace Turnbull noted, "but I never saw Dennis wear those struggles on his sleeve. Rather, his head was up, and he always greeted you warmly and with respect."

Dennis didn't see much of his father. None of the family did. He was often away sailing, skiing, or fishing. "This is probably an exaggeration, but he's gone six months out of the year. I mean he's back and forth, but he could be gone for a month, and then back for a couple of weeks, and then gone," he told the police. "I mean, look, this guy had a whole other life outside his family." Richard Oland, it turned out, was having an extramarital affair.

Richard Oland and Diana Sedlacek, a local realtor, met around 2003 at a public event. At the time, Sedlacek had been married since 1987 to Jiri Sedlacek, who was approximately two decades her senior. Originally from Saint John, Diana met her husband in Toronto in 1981, where Jiri Sedlacek was a senior executive of Bata, a prominent shoe manufacturer. They moved to the Saint John region because they liked the area and wanted their son (approximately twenty-three when Oland was killed) to attend Rothesay Netherwood. They lived on an acreage on Darlings Island, a small community of mostly older people outside Saint John, tucked between Hampton and Quispamsis, with only one route in, through Nauwigewauk. Sedlacek, a slim blonde, was probably in her fifties when she met Oland. They embarked on an affair soon after.

They saw each other frequently, their marriages notwithstanding, and they took numerous trips together, although they were careful to book separate flights.

Jiri Sedlacek later said he had no idea about his wife's infidelity. Connie Oland apparently did not know, either, although she knew Sedlacek as "Dick's friend." The Olands and Sedlaceks occasionally saw one another at group social occasions at each other's homes. Oland involved his mistress when he and Connie renovated their Almon Lane home in 2008. Maureen Adamson, Oland's long-time secretary, remembered meeting Sedlacek when she was brought in to assist with the decorating. She oversaw the painting and helped to choose draperies and furniture. On occasion in the years that followed, Oland would get Adamson to make Sedlacek's travel arrangements.

Not surprisingly given the size of Saint John and the small social circle in which they moved, Richard Oland's adult children became aware of his adultery, daughter Lisa Bustin in particular. She became suspicious in 2008 or 2009. "I think at first, she just sort of... You turn a blind eye to it," Dennis told investigators. According to Dennis, his sister became convinced that "this was a legit thing" after she found a bottle of Viagra, presumably in Oland's name, and she eventually confronted him. They argued, and Dennis's impression was that the two hadn't talked much after that. Dennis told investigators that he'd heard a story about Sedlacek being on his father's sailboat after a race. After she left, according to Dennis "all the crew said, if [she's] ever on the boat again, we're not coming back, 'cause she's just a bitch!" Dennis felt guilty about not telling his mother, but because he didn't know for certain if Lisa's suspicions were valid, he tried to stay out of it. When Robert McFadden was helping him with his divorce, Dennis asked McFadden to have a word with his father. Dennis was concerned that other people would find out about the relationship—including his mother. "This is the story out there, and if it's true, you don't need to tell me," Dennis said he told McFadden. "But if you know about it, you need to tell Dick that, you know, people know—and that it should stop." McFadden reportedly replied: "Duly noted."

And yet, despite all the resentments and tensions, some outside observers did not doubt that father and son shared a meaningful bond. Valerie Teed felt that "like his mother, [Dennis] has always been able to assimilate the stark differences between himself and his father. The result, I surmise, was a guarded but genuine affection for him." Dennis and his father spoke on the phone or emailed and texted frequently about the investments Dennis managed, and the two shared an interest in genealogy. They both got "real enjoyment" out of doing "family history stuff," he said. It was one subject they could discuss "without it getting heated." It was also one realm Dennis excelled in. "I think just being a bit more Internet savvy or that sort of thing, I was able to really progress [our research] along," Dennis said.

Dennis told investigators that his father undoubtedly "pissed a lot of people off, but not to that point where someone would, you know, want to kill somebody," although he allowed for the possibility that Oland finally drove someone to say, "I'm not going to put up with this anymore." He named his father's mistress as a potential suspect. Investigators, however, thought that if Diana Sedlacek played a role in Richard Oland's death, it was only as a motive.

Was the relationship between father and son so acrimonious as to lead to murder? Investigators thought so, especially when they learned that Dennis Oland's debts went beyond the more than half-million dollars he owed his father—and that he kept those debts a secret from Richard Oland.

five
FAMILY SECRETS

Saint John police began interviewing members of Richard Oland's immediate family on the day his body was discovered. It didn't take investigators long to uncover the long history of strained, even stormy, relationships and secrets.

Oland's wife, Connie, had not reported him missing on July 6. When he didn't show up for dinner, she figured he must have gone to a meeting at Ganong, the candy manufacturer, in St. Stephen, roughly an hour's drive from Saint John. "Earlier in the day I had been talking to a friend of mine whose husband was attending such a meeting," she would later explain. "Ganong was in a dire financial position, and Dick had put money into the company." Later that evening, when he still didn't come home, she figured he had spent the night in St. Stephen. It was not uncommon for her husband not to come home at night, she said.

Connie told police her husband had high expectations of their three children, expecting them to perform at "150 per cent" all the time. Oland did not have much to do with the children, but Dennis had "always tried to connect with his father," she said, and the father-son relationship had improved recently because of Dennis's work on family genealogy. Dennis and her husband "developed a connection" over this shared interest. She did not believe Dennis would hurt his father.

Oland's daughter Lisa Bustin told police her parents essentially lived separate lives and described their relationship as "out of convenience for the kids." Although she had an unresolved argument with him about his affair, she said she had a good relationship with him. He was "pure business, and if you worked hard, you would get his respect." Her father was a "hard-nosed businessman" who "could have anyone as an enemy." Oland had "high expectations" of Dennis, which he was unable to live up to, she noted. Oland's other daughter, Jacqueline Walsh, told police her father was "the type of guy some people got along with and some people did not." She said he could be "very difficult to deal with at times," but "could be very loving and caring, too." Still, she learned to keep him at a distance.

Dennis's wife, Lisa Andrik-Oland, told police her husband had always tried to earn his father's respect but felt he could never live up to his standards. She said the relationship had been strained for years, but Dennis thought his involvement in the Oland family tree was of interest to his father and was allowing them to build on their relationship. On the night of July 6, Dennis told her that he met with his father at his office, and they had a "really nice" meeting, talking about family history. She did not see Dennis when he first got home, she said. He came in, went straight upstairs, and got changed.

Police also interviewed Diana Sedlacek, who told them she had been in a "romantic relationship" with Richard Oland for eight years. She believed that most of his family was aware of their affair. Recently, they had started talking about getting married, she said, although they were both still married to and living with other people. Oland arranged for her to see a lawyer to go over the details, she said. She told police Oland was distant from his family and had complained to her about his son's work ethic. He thought Dennis was lazy, and he didn't have a lot of respect for him, she said.

Police knew from Maureen Adamson's statement that Dennis Oland visited his father at his office the night before, making him the last known person to see his father alive. He was therefore a particularly important witness. Constable Stephen Davidson took him to Room 2, a small, mirrored interrogation room equipped with two video cameras.

"Long day, huh?" Davidson started out.

"Oh yeah," replied Oland, sitting with his feet flat on the floor, his hands in his lap. Davidson asked Oland to write down "all the important details" about the previous day, from the time he got up in the morning until he went to bed that night. Davidson left him alone, and after about twenty minutes, Oland called out, "I'm done." Davidson returned and Oland handed him a two-page printed statement.

Davidson opened the routine questioning by asking if he had anything on his mind he wanted to talk about. "The biggest thing that's on my mind is, what happened?" Oland said. "It's pretty clear in my head that he didn't have a heart attack and die. Something's happened to him." But instead of asking Davidson for more information about how his father died, Oland, unsolicited, offered his own theory. "So the first thing that runs through your head is, you know, is this one of those, uh, crackhead type things or whatever, where someone goes in and, you know, does that kind of thing or, you know, like sort of being in the wrong place at the wrong time." (Only later would Dennis ask, "What happened to him? What did they do?" Davidson replied that he didn't know any details.)

Oland said his mind was "racing" and it was all "troubling," but he showed no flicker of distress during the videotaped interview. Rather, he appeared relaxed and chatty. He chuckled as he talked about how his father — to whom he referred as "this guy" — was "living his dream," sailing "like crazy," winning races, and skiing about forty days a year. And yet, within three minutes, he described him as not being "the easiest guy in the world to get along with." Some people might say he was a "ruthless bastard," Oland noted. His father was "intensely, intensely, intensely intelligent," but lacking "certain social skills," Oland said, suggesting he "had some sort of spectrum thing" that would "rear its ugly head at times," alienating both family and friends.

They did not have a close father-son relationship; his father "had this thing that you can't be friends with your son," he said, launching into a laundry list of his father's past offences, including the episode involving the Christmas rum cake. But that was about two years ago, he said, and while there was "a ton" of smaller arguments, it was "amazing how quickly water would be under the bridge" between them. Being an adult had given him some perspective, he said. "You know there's that overall blanket, that this guy is a really difficult person to get along with. And I think when you're a teenager, you wear it differently, like, 'This guy's coming down on me. He's a jerk all the time; he's so hard on me.' When you're my age, you actually... I can actually look at him and say, 'You know, it's not all his fault,' because he had such a hard upbringing." His father was "a product of his generation," he said. Oland also spoke fondly of how his father had "stepped up" and "bankrolled" his divorce. "That's very powerful stuff," he said.

His father's suspected extramarital affair was a more recent "family concern," and Oland told Davidson "the only person that comes to mind" as someone who might have caused his father's death was "this supposed girlfriend." Oland noted that he didn't know Sedlacek himself, but "this woman's reputation is a real kind of hot-blooded type of person." According to Oland, his sister Lisa had on more than one occasion answered the phone at their parents' home only for the caller, a woman, to laugh or hang up. He also said that his sister had told him she'd seen someone she believed to be Sedlacek around the Oland house, "sort of stalking, for lack of a better term." He told the police about the time his sister found a bottle of Viagra and, he said, she felt he was a "dirty pig, I guess, because of it."

The conversation shifted when Davidson asked Oland to focus on the events of the previous twenty-four hours. "Until I went over to his office, it was a very typical day," Oland said. If this cryptic comment registered with Davidson in the moment, he did not let on. He did not ask Oland to explain himself. Instead, he let the near-monologue continue, offering the occasional, "Mmm hmm," "Yeah," or "OK," in response. Davidson wanted to keep his subject talking.

Oland said he had spoken to his father on the phone and emailed him earlier that day about a stock trade he did for him. The transaction went "a bit hooky," he said. "There was a stock split, so what he wanted sold and what actually got sold were different things." Later, after work, he went to visit his father at his office to talk about genealogy, but he ended up making two trips because he forgot some of the documents he wanted to show him. "I went to the top of the stairs, and I might've used the bathroom [located in the second-floor foyer], and then I left." He was just steps away from the Far End Corporation door, but he didn't tell his father he was there. Instead, he started back toward his own office to get the documents he had forgotten, driving even though his office was at most a three-minute walk away. He realized he didn't have a pass card to access the work elevators after hours. "So I went back and just said, 'Oh well, I have enough information; I have what he wanted.'" They had their visit and "that was it, then I left," Oland said. He drove home to Rothesay, stopping along the way at Renforth wharf to see if his children were swimming, he said.

Davidson let him finish, then circled back to the beginning, asking questions in a calm, non-accusing manner. So you got there around what time? Was that the first time or the second time? And what time did you leave, approximately? Which way did you go? Where did you park? He was probing for Oland's inconsistencies.

Eventually, approximately halfway through the interview, Davidson said, "Dennis, I have to ask you this: did you have any involvement in your father's death?"

"No," he replied, impassive.

"I ask you that because you were the last person there."

"Yeah."

"And, you know, it's something that I have to cover."

"Yeah.... I have no reason to want my father dead, to kill him, to... I mean, no. I mean, we've had our things, but no, I wouldn't rob someone of the fun that they're having and... You know I... He's just... No."

Davidson excused himself for a few minutes and left Oland alone in the room. When he returned, he apologized for the interruption, saying new information was coming in all the time. In truth, Davidson had gone to consult with the officers secretly monitoring the interview from the next room. Normally, only one officer monitors a police interview. Oland had three.

Davidson said he wanted to "clarify a few things" with Oland. He stressed the importance of the timing of different events and explained that he needed to make sure everything lined up with the videos from the security cameras that were "all over the place." Having alerted Oland to the probability that some of his movements were documented on video, Davidson led Oland through the chronology of events again. This time, new details emerged.

Oland didn't make it all the way back to his office. He only started to go back, "then gave up," he said. Why did he take his car back to the office instead of walking, Davidson wanted to know. Another new detail: "Because I wasn't sure I was going to be going back. I was just probably going to leave." What happened after the visit? More new information: Oland remembered crossing the street, away from his parked car, back toward his father's office. His account was becoming increasingly convoluted.

Davidson asked Oland what he wore so he could be identified on security video. "Um, these pants, these shoes, a dress shirt, and a navy blazer," Oland replied.

"You were wearing those pants, those shoes..."

"Those shoes, a dress shirt — not this, you know, a collared dress shirt."

"Yeah."

"And a navy blazer."

"And a navy blazer."

"Yeah."

Oland's assertion he wore a navy blazer when, in fact, he wore a brown sports jacket would become a central part of the investigation, but Davidson would later testify he only became aware of the discrepancy after the interview. Davidson asked him to again go over the time between his first and second trip to his father's office. "That's just a little bit confusing to me and I just want to clarify it," he said. This time, Oland said he thought he might have sat in his car "for a bit and did some texting or business." Davidson let the incongruity pass and moved on, trying to nail down the exact sequence of Oland's whereabouts. He asked Oland to describe the route he travelled. "It's really important that you remember," Davidson said. "I mean it was yesterday, right?" It was at this point that Oland said he might have gone the wrong way on a familiar one-way street.

"I might've got confused when I was going along, and I might've turned up Princess Street, into the gravel parking lot." Canterbury Street crosses Princess, a one-way street running down the steep hill to the harbour. At the corner is a gravel parking lot with an entrance off Princess. Accessing this lot from Canterbury would normally mean circling the block, but Oland described making a left at Princess and driving briefly in the wrong direction before turning right into the gravel lot.

"You went the wrong way?" Davidson asked, surprised by the revelation but unsure of its relevance.

"Yeah, I might've done that because it's such a short little zip up there, right?"

"Why wouldn't you have mentioned that to me the first time?" Davidson asked. "I mean, that's a significant thing."

"I'm sorry, it's not a hundred-per-cent clear to me," Oland said. "I mean, I don't know how I get to work sometimes. I don't. I can be, you know, totally zoned out on what's going on."

"Is there something else that happened that you're not telling me?" asked Davidson, still treading lightly but intimating that he did not believe Oland. "Tell me what happened," he insisted.

"You've got me all confused," said Oland. "You have me intimidated now, so now I'm getting a mental block."

"Just give me one sec, OK?" Davidson stepped out again.

Once he left, Oland mumbled to himself, using his finger to retrace his route on the table in front of him, pausing frequently as he mapped out his thoughts. "So I went up the driveway . . . and sat there . . . and then I parked . . . there, there . . . no . . . I went in . . . and sat there. . . . I drove in and I parked . . . then I left . . . went around and then I stopped there . . . and then I went in. . . . So I . . . I came in and I parked there . . . then . . . I left there, and I went around, and I stopped there. . . . Then where did I go after that?" Before Oland left the station that evening, Davidson advised him that the police suspected him of involvement in his father's death and would execute search warrants against him. For the time being, at least, Oland was free to go.

From the moment Oland left the police station, "at or around 11:01 p.m." on July 7, 2011, members of the street crime unit of the Saint John Police Force had him under surveillance. It was "pretty much" twenty-four hours a day for a full week, his lawyer Gary Miller would later say. No wiretaps were used, however, as the Crown would later disclose during a pre-trial conference. The lead investigator at that point, Constable Rick Russell, said the surveillance was not his decision. Criminal investigations division Inspector Glen McCloskey and Sergeant David Brooker of the major crime unit set it up without consulting him, he said. (McCloskey would later testify that then Deputy Chief Bruce Connell and David Brooker were the ones who organized the surveillance.) But Oland was "a suspect-slash-person of interest, in my mind," Russell said.

Even while Oland was still being interviewed, at around eight thirty that evening, Brooker dispatched an officer to search the Renforth wharf area, where Oland mentioned he had stopped on his way home after visiting his father the night before. The next day police conducted a two-hour "secondary search" of the wharf area, from a quarter to four to a quarter to six. Dog handler Mike Horgan and his dog, Leo, along with Constable Shawn Coughlan scoured the wharf, around the Bill McGuire Centre on Renforth Drive and its baseball field and playground, and along Regatta Row to the water, two small docks, the shoreline, and the beach.

Constable Anthony Gilbert, meanwhile, went to Rothesay to try to retrieve security videos from the places Oland said he went on the evening of July 6, including Cochran's Country Market; Kennebecasis Drugs, a Guardian pharmacy outlet; and the Irving gas station on Marr Road. A member of the Rothesay police accompanied Gilbert, since it was their jurisdiction. The two also went to the Bill McGuire Centre and the Rothesay Rowing Club, seeking security videos. On July 9, Constable Davidson was assigned to interview people Dennis Oland came into contact with on July 6, including some of his co-workers at CIBC Wood Gundy. On July 13, watchful police seized fast-food wrappers Oland had discarded at a Rothesay gas station, hoping to get a cast-off DNA sample.

On July 14, 2011, one week after the discovery of Richard Oland's battered body, police prepared to execute search warrants at Dennis's home. Oland lived at 58 Gondola Point Road in Rothesay with his wife,

Lisa, his three children from his first marriage (he shared custody with his ex-wife, Lesley), and his stepson. The large yellow and brown, vine-covered house, largely hidden behind trees, had been in the family for about seventy years. Oland moved into the home in 1998, following the death of his grandfather, Moosehead patriarch P.W. Oland.

Lead investigator Rick Russell briefed the search team. They needed to search approximately twenty rooms plus the basement and attic and the sprawling property. Russell divided the officers into teams of two, assigned them areas, and told them what they were looking for. The list included a brown sports jacket, a navy blazer, a blue-and-white-check dress shirt with a button-down collar, khaki pants and dress shoes, as well as genealogy documents, a red bag, computers, cellphones and other electronics, and "any other items relating to this offence," according to the search warrant.

Russell instructed the officers to search each area completely before moving on to the next. If they found anything of interest, they were directed to stop and promptly notify him. "The entire process was carefully mapped out and then controlled in that environment on that day," he later said.

Russell acted as the "search leader" inside the home, while MCU Constable Keith Copeland took charge of the exterior search of the nearly three-hectare property, which included horse stables, a large detached garage with a loft apartment, several small outbuildings, and a large, fenced pasture, horse-riding ring, and woods. Some of the property was, of course, owned by Richard Oland, who purchased it from Dennis as part of the terms of the loan that allowed Dennis to keep the house when he and his first wife divorced.

Forensic Constable David MacDonald served as the seizing officer. When any of the other officers located an item to seize, MacDonald would photograph it, bag it and catalogue it, then document it on a handwritten flow chart that described each item and where it was found. He would enter the flow chart into a computer later, back at the station.

Russell and two other colleagues went ahead of the other officers to serve the warrant. They walked up the gravel driveway to the front porch, adorned with potted geraniums and a welcoming wicker rocker.

Oland's wife, Lisa Andrik-Oland, was home when they arrived. She phoned her husband and told him to come home. Oland was, in fact, at the police station, having been called in for further questioning. He went in at ten with his newly retained lawyer, Gary Miller, and spoke briefly with Constables Sean Rocca and Greg Oram of the MCU before returning home for the search. Russell sat down with the couple at the dining-room table to explain the "rules of engagement," as he put it. He read the "whole document to them, start to finish." They were welcome to remain in the home, he said, but they would have to be accompanied by an officer. They decided to leave, but not before police showed the warrant to Gary Miller.

Miller, one of the most prominent and experienced criminal defence lawyers in New Brunswick, is also one of only a few in the province who practise criminal law exclusively. He once headed the New Brunswick Criminal Defence Lawyers' Association and has earned a reputation for fiercely protecting his clients and disdaining the media. Miller gained notice in 1984 as part of former premier Richard Hatfield's defence team, which won an acquittal on a marijuana possession charge; Hatfield denied any knowledge of the marijuana found in his luggage. At the time he took on Dennis Oland's case, Miller was perhaps best known for representing the late aboriginal rights activist Noah Augustine, who in 1999 was found not guilty of second-degree murder in the shooting death of Bruce Barnaby of Eel Ground First Nation.

A Saint John transit bus loaded with about thirty officers descended upon Dennis Oland's property shortly before noon. At least two forensic vans and six unmarked police cars parked outside the house. Just down the road, other family members grieved at the Almon Lane home of the late Richard Oland and the newly widowed Connie.

Media soon found out about the search, tipped off either by sources, chatter on newsroom police scanners, or calls from area residents about the heavy police presence. Reporters started arriving on the scene. But in keeping with the silence surrounding the high-profile case, Saint John Police Force spokesman Sergeant Glenn Hayward would not confirm the activity was related to the homicide investigation, saying only that the major crime unit was "executing a criminal search warrant." He would not comment on what police were seeking or even say who lived in the house, which had a handmade wooden sign that read "Private, Friends Welcome." Reporters searched city property records to confirm the home belonged to Dennis Oland. CBC News tried to get copies of the information police filed in support of the warrant, but the documents were sealed by order of a provincial court judge. Every search warrant in the case, and all the police's findings, would be sealed until media successfully fought to have them made public.

Although police wouldn't comment, the identity of their suspect was now an open secret; an unthinkable tragedy for the Oland family, said neighbour and friend Kelly Patterson. "It was such a brutal vicious crime to somehow get your head around while you're grieving the loss. I think that's a pretty tall order. And then, right on the heels of that, you realize that one of our own is in the police's sights. I think that's, to me, one of the real tragedies of this is that family, I don't think, ever had an opportunity to properly grieve the loss of their father or husband [or] grandfather."

Officers covered some of the windows with cardboard, preventing reporters and other onlookers from seeing what they were doing inside. Approximately ten officers searched the interior while the others worked outside. Russell sketched the layout of each of the three storeys of the house, numbering each room. He also made diagrams of the grounds and outbuildings. As the search progressed, Russell wrote in red what, if any, items were seized from which rooms. When "nothing of evidentiary value was recovered," he wrote "neg" for negative.

Constable Stephen Davidson was paired with Sergeant Jay Henderson. They searched the sunroom — and found nothing. The dining room: nothing. The butler's pantry: nothing. The kitchen: nothing. They moved on to the staircase and upper foyer, still nothing. A child's bedroom: nothing. In another child's bedroom they seized a laptop. And in the upstairs bathroom, a USB stick found on the windowsill was seized.

Years later, Henderson couldn't remember wearing latex gloves for the search, but it was part of his training to do so. It's like putting on shoes and tying the laces — "automatic," he'd later explain. Besides, he said, he remembers rummaging through the contents of a white garbage can that had a reddish stain on it. He wouldn't even search his own garbage without gloves on, he said.

At about 3:20 p.m., Davidson and Henderson reached the master bedroom, where a brown duvet cover and brown throw pillow, which both had stains on them, were seized. Then Henderson turned his attention to a closet full of men's clothes. "I noted several items that were contained in the warrant," he said, including a brown sports jacket, which had a dry-cleaning tag attached to the collar, and a navy blazer. The jackets were hanging side by side. Henderson didn't touch either of them. He used coat hangers to move through each piece of clothing. "I stayed quite a bit of time at the closet," he said.

Henderson then searched a chest of drawers, where he found an iPhone, passports, ID, and "lots" of receipts, including one of particular interest from VIP Dry Cleaners. It was under Oland's wife's name and dated July 8, at 9:08 a.m., roughly ten hours after police questioned Dennis Oland and told him he was a suspect. The receipt listed one pair of pants, two sports jackets, and sixteen shirts. The items were due to be ready by July 11 at three p.m., but that was crossed out and "SAT" for Saturday, July 9, had been handwritten instead as the pickup time.

The forensic officer, David MacDonald, was systematically working his way through the house, covering the ground floor first, starting with the front entry closet, and then the basement and upper floor. He was asked to seize and catalogue the items of interest that Henderson found in the bedroom closet, including the two jackets, seven dress shirts, a golf shirt, and six pairs of shoes.

MacDonald was methodical about the seizures, donning a fresh pair of latex gloves to handle each item. He put clothing in paper bags in case they were wet or soiled, so they could breathe, while other items, such as electronics, went into plastic bags. Each bag was labelled and catalogued.

Outside, a canine unit circled the grounds, where horses grazed and brown hens clucked. Constable Mike Horgan and his dog, Leo, searched in front of the house, the pasture area, and the driveway. They searched around the barn but not inside because, as Horgan later explained, other officers had already "contaminated" it in a "hand search." They also searched around piles of compost and manure—but not in them. "I did not find any evidence at all," said Horgan, who wrapped up at around three p.m. Other officers wearing latex gloves used shovels and rakes to roll back large strips of sod approximately four car-lengths from the end of the tree-lined driveway. They dug through the soil beneath the grass before rolling the sod back into place.

By the time the search ended, police had seized a total of fifty-seven items, ranging from financial and legal documents to a note found in a purse, a pair of brown work boots, and the lint trap from the clothes dryer. Police also seized Dennis Oland's Blackberry. Police hauled four orange garbage bags, some brown paper bags, several large cardboard boxes, a desktop computer, and two metallic suitcases from the house and loaded them into a forensics van parked out front.

After about seven hours, the officers gathered for a debriefing. Although the warrant was valid for another three days, between seven a.m. and nine p.m. each day, police "determined it was a thorough search," said Russell. The property was turned back over to the family lawyer by 7:50 p.m., he said.

The head of forensic identification did not participate in the house search. Mark Smith's only involvement was to seize Dennis Oland's silver 2009 Volkswagen Golf from the driveway, which was towed to the police garage shortly before one. Oland actually had three vehicles registered in his name at the time, according to the motor vehicle branch. The other two were a 1998 black Mazda and a 1996 Toyota Land Cruiser, but the Golf was the vehicle Oland drove on July 6.

Smith cordoned off the car in a secure area of the police garage with limited access and turned his attention to some of the other case files that were "backing up." By a quarter to six, Smith was back on the Oland case. He photographed and examined the impounded car. He didn't note anything unusual about the exterior of the vehicle, he said. It appeared to have been washed recently and didn't test positive for bloodstains.

The interior, on the other hand, "was untidy and did not appear to have been cleaned for some time." There was "dirt and debris" on the floor and mats, and stains on the backseats. Documents, business cards, and receipts were strewn across the dashboard, tucked into the centre console, and stashed in the glove compartment. Some of the papers were seized, including a receipt found in the front passenger door from the Irving gas station in Saint John's north end, dated July 7 at 9:24 a.m., shortly after the victim's body was discovered in his uptown office.

In the trunk, Smith found a socket wrench tool kit, a sail cover, a receipt for repair to a sail cover, lawn mower blades, plastic cups, dog toys, a dog bed, and "other miscellaneous items." Although no one ever made much of it later, Oland purchased five "No Trespassing" signs and three "Private Property" signs, each measuring 8" x 12", at Canadian Tire at 11:10 on the morning of July 7. Smith also found a red reusable Sobeys grocery bag, which contained a cellphone charger, a large orange garbage bag, a Canadian Lifesaving manual, a CPR worksheet with handwritten notes, a 2011 herb and vegetable catalogue, and publications related to Oland's genealogical research.

Smith used a magnifying glass and a forensic light to go over "the entire inside" of the car, looking for any "anomalies," or stains that might be blood. He continued working on the car until after ten.

The next morning, a security car blocked the driveway at the Oland homestead and the newspaper remained uncollected. Just a few minutes' drive down the road, about fourteen officers had started another search. They spent the morning combing a wooded area near the Bill McGuire Centre.

The officers, clad in dark T-shirts, dark pants or jeans, and in a few cases, baseball hats, stood shoulder to shoulder, examining the area one foot at a time. They did not appear to be carrying anything when they emerged from the woods at around twelve thirty, after roughly four hours of trudging through the thick brush. To some witnesses, it looked like nothing more than a training exercise.

But it was at least the third time people had spotted police scouring the area since the prominent businessman was found dead. Two days earlier, kayak instructor Emily Benson saw officers combing through garbage bins at the nearby Renforth beach, and other area residents had seen the canine unit a few times. Saint John police still weren't talking, but

Rothesay police (now Kennebecasis Regional Police Force) confirmed the searches were not related to any of their investigations.

Back at police headquarters in Saint John, Smith resumed his examination of Oland's car for a second day. He swabbed for DNA and tested for trace or latent bloodstains. If Oland had killed his father and fled the bloody scene in his car, there might be transfer stains. Smith swabbed eleven areas, including the door handles, inside and out; the trunk release button; the steering wheel; the headlight and turn-signal switches; the emergency brake; and the passenger seat — anywhere Oland might have touched after leaving his father's office.

Smith got "weak positive" results from the front passenger-door handle, seat, and headrest, the front and back of the steering wheel, and the emergency brake handle. But it "took a while" for the swabs to turn green/blue when he applied the testing chemical, and there "wasn't a lot of colour," he said. "Other areas had very weak positive results, and some, not at all."

Next he sprayed the interior with two different chemical reactants, Bluestar and Leucomalachite Green, which would fluoresce in the possible presence of blood. He sprayed the fabric seats, the floor, pedals, dashboard, and steering wheel. All produced negative results for blood. Smith spent all day inspecting the car, a full eight hours, on top of the approximately four hours' of inspection the day before. It was a long and arduous task, he admitted. But he still wasn't done.

On Sunday, July 17, Smith formally seized the red grocery bag from the trunk, along with some of the documents it contained. And on July 18, twelve days after the murder, he devoted two hours or so to giving the car a final once-over. He checked under the seats and the trunk lining, delving into every nook and cranny he could think of to locate items that might be related to the offence. He seized some more receipts and documents before finally turning the car back over to Dennis Oland.

On July 20, police were granted another search warrant and a general warrant for a 25-foot sailboat co-owned by Oland's wife, Lisa Andrik-Oland, and her friend Mary Beth Watt. Police made the request after speaking to Oland's new assistant at CIBC Wood Gundy, Ethel Harrison

Wood. She told police Oland had emailed her between ten thirty and eleven on the morning of July 7, the day his father's body was discovered, saying, "'It is too nice of a day to work' and he was going to work on his boat." Oland's former assistant, Karla Yurco, corroborated that in an interview. She said she saw Oland in the office that morning, and at eleven he told her he was going to work on the boat, called *Loki*.

Doug Orford, who used to work at CIBC, told police he saw Oland that afternoon at the Royal Kennebecasis Yacht Club, where the boat was docked. Orford, who also had a sailboat at the north-end club, arrived at around twelve thirty to drop something off, he said. When he arrived, Oland was talking with three men whom Orford named as Sean Keyes, Dave Richards, and Chris Gilmore.

Mary Beth Watt, who had purchased *Loki* with Lisa Andrik-Oland years before she married Dennis, told police she had been out on the boat with friends on July 6 when she experienced a problem with the boat. She called Dennis Oland for help, he told her how to deal with it, and he went the following day to fix it, she said. The next time she went to the boat, the tools were left out, said Watt.

The search at the private yacht club at 1044 Millidge Avenue was conducted on the morning of July 21, but once again police refused to confirm if the search was connected with the Oland homicide investigation, or what they were looking for. The warrant listed many of the same items as the other search. Police also wanted to "forensically examine [the *Loki*], swab, record, log, or duplicate, photograph, measure and seize items, and any other forensic investigative procedures necessary," according to the sworn documents filed with the provincial court.

Police blocked off access to the club to everyone but members for approximately six hours; a uniformed officer stood guard at the gate. One member at the club that day, Ken Ward, noticed that the divers searched under most of the roughly two hundred boats at the club but paid special attention to the avocado-coloured *Loki*. Ward didn't know what the divers were looking for, but he knew they'd be hard-pressed to find anything in the murky water surrounding the marina. "Be almost impossible to find anything," he observed to the media, "especially if they don't know what they're looking for."

In the hours, days, and weeks following the murder, police obtained search warrants for Dennis Oland's office computer at CIBC Wood Gundy, a camp logbook, and the cellphone records of Oland, Richard Oland, and Diana Sedlacek. Police also interviewed more than sixty people. For the next four years, the investigation wound on, even after Dennis Oland was arrested and charged with second-degree murder, ending just a few months before his trial started.

six

ARREST

On November 9, 2013, Dennis Oland switched his Facebook profile photo to one of actor Harrison Ford in the 1993 movie *The Fugitive*, in which Ford plays a man wrongfully convicted of murder who escapes and tries to find the real killer, a team of US marshals in hot pursuit. Just three days later, members of the Saint John Police Force arrested the forty-five-year-old Oland in connection with his father's death. And although defence lawyer Gary Miller had earlier told prosecutors that if the Crown approved charges against his client, Oland would surrender himself at the station, the police opted for a public takedown in Rothesay, a town outside the jurisdiction of the Saint John force. Police cornered Oland in the middle of the afternoon at a self-serve car wash on a busy thoroughfare not far from his home.

Security video from King's II Car Wash on Hampton Road showed Oland drive his green SUV into the fifth bay. Seven minutes later, a police cruiser and two unmarked police vehicles pulled in behind him. The video, obtained by Brunswick News, showed that Oland offered no resistance. He dropped the water hose and stepped toward the two plainclothes officers, his arms at his side, palms open. Police placed his hands behind his back, handcuffed him, and took him into custody.

The arrest that was nearly two and a half years in the making took less than ninety seconds.

—

Prior to his arrest, Oland lived in the community under a cloud of suspicion. Police had not identified him as their suspect, but in a city the size of Saint John, they didn't need to. Oland was, as he put it, "unceremoniously dismissed" after more than a decade as a financial adviser at CIBC Wood Gundy. Oland was initially told to take a leave of absence after police searched his home and interviewed some of his colleagues, said branch manager John Travis. But as word spread that Oland was a suspect in the slaying, he began losing clients. Bosses higher up the chain made it clear he wouldn't be able to return to his advisory role, said Travis, and Oland was forced to take a retirement buyout.

Oland already had a new job. After his father's death, he became president of his father's main numbered company, and secretary of the two subsidiaries: Far End Corporation and Kingshurst Estates, which together were worth an estimated $36 million. Before his murder, Richard Oland was on the verge of leasing a new space at the nearby Brunswick Square office tower, but Dennis Oland, his now co-director Robert McFadden, and secretary Maureen Adamson decided to stay at 52 Canterbury Street. Oland set up shop in his father's office. But not right away. It took about six months to clean and renovate the space.

They moved into the vacant adjacent office while a professional disaster cleanup company that specializes in biohazardous removal and restoration work hosed, mopped, and scoured to eradicate all traces of Richard Oland's barbaric murder and the lingering stench of death. The floor had to be stripped down to the boards. Blood had seeped through "three, maybe four" layers of flooring into the ceiling below, explained McFadden. The walls were patched and painted; office furniture and equipment replaced. It cost nearly $30,000, according to court records filed in a dispute with the insurance company.

Dennis Oland came to the office "on an irregular basis," said Adamson, but he had his own space. "When he was there I often assisted with such things as correspondence and filing," until she retired in June 2014, she said. "I always found Dennis to be very easygoing and easy to get along with. He was friendly and outgoing as much as could be expected during a very difficult time." They never discussed "the incident," she said. "I just didn't discuss that with anybody, even my husband."

Oland, who signed cheques "from time to time," earned about $50,000 a year for his work as director of Far End and Kingshurst. He also received about $30,000 as co-trustee of his father's estate, although that amount was "subject to adjustment," according to court records.

He upgraded his boat from a Boston Whaler 13 to a Grand Banks 42 Motoryacht called *Heritage* worth an estimated $175,000. He kept his new boat at the Rothesay Yacht Club, the same club his father's *Vela Veloce* once graced. Pam Vincent remembers meeting Oland around that time. "I was just learning everything about being on a boat. He was wonderfully patient, teaching me things and respectful of the fact that I knew nothing about boats and everyone around me had years of experience," she said. "I have wonderful memories of laughter, stories, silliness and adventures, fun times socializing and boating with Dennis and [his wife] Lisa. My favourite memory is the look of gentle peace and true contentment on his face one of many summer nights when he was at the wheel."

Oland's childhood friend, Val Streeter, believed he saw beyond his countenance. "The years between Dick's death and the trial were very difficult for Dennis. First he was a suspect, then the only suspect. It became a waiting game for him, a sort of slow water torture if you will," he said. "'How can they have a case? Are they going to charge me? When are they going to charge me?'"

Streeter felt that Oland's "main concern remained his children and trying to shield them as best he could from the storm that was brewing." Family dinners, boat trips, and school events were proof of "life as usual," Streeter said. "He tried so hard to make their adolescence a fun, carefree time, despite the ever-present cloud over their lives."

In fact, Oland seemed to begin living more publicly than he had before, often spotted at auctions, restaurants, and bars with his wife. He was, said his friend Larry Cain, living his life. "He didn't hide." Money was apparently no concern. Oland took several trips, travelling to Bermuda, New York City, Texas, Florida, and Turks and Caicos, among other places. In the winter of 2012, the self-described gearhead flew to

Ontario to purchase a 1967 Volvo 123GT to restore and a 1968 122 for parts. He was inspired, he said, by the stories he'd heard of the twin 544s his father and his uncle had owned in the early sixties; Richard's was red, and Derek's was light green. Later, in the midst of the preliminary inquiry that would determine whether or not he'd stand trial, Oland wrote a "customer spotlight" post for the Volvo-aficionado website iPd. He boasted that he "went all out on parts." He raced a Volkswagen GTI "on a ten-mile stretch of twisty roads," he said, and "while [the GTI] pulled away on the straights, I caught up on the turns." He concluded: "This car is a real head turner, and I am enjoying it a lot."

In November 2012 Lisa Andrik-Oland opened Exchange on Germain, a high-end consignment boutique carrying items from exclusive labels such as Chanel and Prada, just one block up from the Far End Corporation office. Andrik-Oland formerly worked for Saint John Conservative MP Rodney Weston, and in 2010 she ran the campaign for Dorothy Shephard, who was elected MLA for Saint John Lancaster, with Dennis helping in the background. He also helped with the new shop. On June 26, 2013, he appeared with her before a Saint John Heritage Development Board seeking permission to install a projecting black fascia sign with gold leaf lettering. Earlier that month, the shop's Facebook page featured a photograph of the smiling couple, decked out to attend the Live Life Awards, which celebrate the best retail shops in uptown Saint John. He sported a dashing black suit and bow tie, with a red handkerchief, his arm around the waist of her red-and-white polka-dot halter-top dress. In October of 2014 Andrik-Oland also became co-owner of Handworks Gallery with Leslie Oland, the wife of Dennis's cousin (and Derek's son) Andrew, when the previous owner ran into financial difficulties. The shop, which carries local artwork, jewellery, pottery, woodwork, stained glass, and ironwork, is prominently located on King Street.

Saint John police were facing their own share of scrutiny. They were still hard at it, investigating the murder and building their case against Oland. Details of the investigation, however, remained shrouded in secrecy.

"I've been getting several [media] inquiries regarding the Oland case, which is understandable, but I still have no update," spokesman Sergeant Glenn Hayward had said.

Gossip and rumours filled the void. Theories on the killer ranged from angry investors to the Russian mafia. The case featured prominently on online discussion boards devoted to unsolved murders. The family's high profile fuelled the insatiable curiosity. It was a whodunit among the rich and famous and became as popular a topic of conversation as the weather, but far more titillating.

Few were fearful about a killer being on the loose. The chief had assured the public that Oland's death was an isolated incident and the victim likely knew his killer. But as days passed, then weeks and months, people grew restless. They wanted some answers. What was taking police so long? When were they going to make an arrest? Why the cone of silence?

Michael Boudreau, a criminology professor at St. Thomas University in Fredericton, defended the force in the early days of the investigation. It's often difficult to strike the right balance, Boudreau noted. Secrecy could fuel innuendo about who may have killed Richard Oland and how he was killed. But revealing too much information could also backfire. "People may start to have the wrong idea and start publicly blaming people or naming people. Then you have the issue of vigilantism, and that can be very, very dangerous as well." Seasoned Saint John lawyer Allen Doyle felt the way police were handling the case was "par for the course" for a homicide investigation. "Generally speaking, you're going to be more thorough—you're going to make sure all your i's are dotted and t's are crossed." Doyle defended Carmen Tessier, who was charged in 2000 with second-degree murder in the death of his girlfriend, Brenda Cosgrove, after a decade-long investigation. Police had a videotaped confession, but the trial judge threw it out and the Supreme Court of Canada ultimately dismissed the charge. Doyle said he could understand police taking their time.

By the fall, Oland's family offered to post a reward for information leading to the arrest of Richard Oland's killer, according to a sworn affidavit filed with the courts by Dennis Oland years later. "I am advised by [family lawyer] William Teed, and do verily believe, that on September 27, 2011, acting on behalf of my mother and sisters, he met with Police Chief Bill Reid to offer a reward on behalf of my family for anyone providing information leading to the arrest of my father's killer," the affidavit states. (No dollar amount was indicated.) "Reid declined the offer, telling [Teed] that it would be unethical for the Saint John Police to accept it from my family because they believed that I was the person responsible for the death of my father." Someone quietly hired more than one private investigator. The family has declined through their lawyers to confirm their involvement, but their lawyers fought to keep the information suppressed through a court order.

However it may have appeared to the public, the investigation remained active. Stephen Davidson started to review with a civilian crime analyst the hours of video surveillance gathered from some of the places Oland told him he went to on July 6 and 7. They obtained a court-ordered production order for Oland's cellphone records and the records of his father and his father's mistress. Officers visited the dry cleaners whose receipt they found when they searched Oland's home. On July 17, they scoured around Renforth wharf yet again with, yet again, no results. On July 19, Davidson and Constable Greg Oram interviewed Derek Oland. (In February 2015, three and a half years after the murder, police would put Derek Oland under surveillance in an attempt to obtain a cast-off DNA sample from him. After a nine-day stakeout of his New River Beach home and the brewery proved futile — Derek Oland was out of the country at the time — they later seized a fork and a glass he used at a Saint John restaurant, the Bourbon Quarter. When the DNA sample was admitted into evidence at the trial, Derek Oland promptly emailed a statement to CBC News, noting that police had never asked him to provide a sample and that he was willing to help the investigation into his brother's death in any way he could.) Forensic Constable David MacDonald examined Oland's Blackberry, testing the keypad and buttons for blood. And in August, the force recruited a forensic accountant to help sift through the reams of financial information for Oland and his father — a possible financial motive already flagged.

Sergeant David Brooker said that the major crime unit had only eight officers, including himself, and handled up to five hundred files a year. But they continued to "front load" the Oland investigation with help from other units.

In October, the case lost its lead investigator when Constable Rick Russell retired. Inspector Glen McCloskey of the criminal investigations division said he learned only in September that Russell was planning to retire. Constable Stephen Davidson, still new to the major crime unit, the fourth most senior of the seven officers in MCU, was named as his replacement. The decision was based on a discussion between Russell, McCloskey, and Brooker, the court would later hear. No details were provided. Forensic Sergeant Mark Smith said he was "maybe somewhat" surprised Davidson was chosen. He couldn't remember working on any other homicide investigations where someone so "junior" was in charge. He later clarified he meant "junior," in terms of rank, not years of service.

Russell was one of about eight officers set to retire by the end of the year. The Oland file coordinator also retired and Constable Sean Rocca took his place. Not only was the force losing some of its most experienced officers, but it also looked like they might not be replaced. Chief Bill Reid was holding off on hiring any new recruits at the request of city council until the 2012 budget was finalized. The city was facing a huge pension deficit, the worst in the region at $123 million. By December, it reached $161 million. The city and its four unions reached a deal to switch to a shared-risk pension plan, which would see the city and its workers share the risk of future deficits and give the city the option to temporarily reduce benefits if the fund fell behind. But council still cut $9 million from the overall 2012 budget.

Reid's budget of $22.7 million was $134,600 less than the previous year and $1.05 million less than what he was counting on when the budget was being drafted in the fall—the equivalent of about ten officers when payroll expenses, such as pension contributions, and other costs, were considered, officials had said. The Saint John police union called on the local police commission to fight city council over the cuts, even if it meant suing the city. Commission chairman Christopher Waldschutz was unwilling to "butt heads."

Reid committed to work within his new budget restraints and remained confident his officers would solve the "complex" Oland murder. But he requested the public's patience as they continued to investigate what had quickly become the most highly publicized case in the city in years. It catapulted the Saint John Police Force into the national spotlight, with Reid front and centre. The son of a Cape Breton coal miner, Reid had dreamed of becoming a policeman since he was a boy. In 1978, an imposing broad-shouldered man, he started his career in Saint John on patrol and worked his way through the ranks to the major crime unit and polygraph section. He went on to become staff sergeant, inspector, and deputy chief before his promotion to chief in 2008.

He prided himself on crime reduction through "intelligence-led" policing: data-driven operations with support programs in place, such as methadone treatment. He boasted double-digit drops in some categories since he took the helm. Arson, for example, was down 65 per cent, break-and-enters, 52 per cent, and robberies, 50 per cent. The Saint John force also fared well among the thirty largest police forces across the country in solving crimes, according to Statistics Canada. In 2010 it ranked fifth highest for the total weighted clearance rates, where crimes are assigned values, based on their seriousness. Saint John stood at 45.4 per cent, about 6 per cent higher than the national average.

Still, the sentiment Saint John police were in over their heads was growing. The force, formed in 1849, is believed to be one of the world's oldest, but it had more experience dealing with crimes like prostitution, break-and-enters, and drugs. Homicides were rare, although there was one in the city earlier that year: Jason Dow, twenty-nine, was stabbed to death in the north end on March 11, but the perpetrator turned himself in within two hours. In the previous five years, the city had seen only six homicides. All were solved, but statistics show the longer a murder goes unsolved, the more difficult it is for an arrest to be made. The Oland investigation was already six months old, and no new information had been released—no word on a suspect or even the cause of death.

The case was progressing, the chief insisted. Several search warrants had been executed, but they all remained sealed by a judge's order. In December 2011 CBC News and Brunswick News launched a joint legal challenge, seeking to gain access to information related to the court-issued search warrants. The Supreme Court of Canada ruled in 1982 that once a search has been executed and evidence has been seized, the documents should then generally become public. The court declared that openness is the rule and is essential as a means of protecting the integrity of Canada's justice system. "One of the greatest intrusions of the justice system into private lives is the search warrant," said journalist and author Linden MacIntyre. MacIntyre initiated the legal action that led to the precedent-setting Supreme Court case — *MacIntyre v. the Attorney General of Canada* — affirming the principle of transparency in the courts. "It's a suspension of your right to privacy, it's an invasion of your home, or your workspace, or your property in some form or another, so it has to be taken very seriously... and according to the law, people have to justify these search warrants [being sealed]," he said in a 2012 interview. With regard to the Oland case, MacIntyre observed: "There is something about this murder that is being treated differently than an ordinary murder, and I think it's the public's right to know why. Why is this being treated with such deference to everybody?"

At a hearing on December 15, 2011, Halifax-based lawyer David Coles, who represented the media outlets, argued the search warrants, the information used to obtain them, and information about the items seized should be made public. The courts have ruled that search warrants should only be sealed in a handful of situations where "the ends of justice would be subverted by the disclosure," he said. Based on case law, search warrants may only be sealed when the information they contain would compromise the identity of a confidential informant, compromise an ongoing investigation, endanger a person engaged in intelligence-gathering techniques and thereby prejudice future investigations, or prejudice the interests of an innocent person. Coles argued that the media should have access to the search warrant information to be able to reassure the citizens of the community that the investigation was proper, that it was proceeding, and that the rights of the people who were searched were protected. "Right now, we're operating in a vacuum," he argued, adding he found it "hard to accept" that all the information must remain sealed.

Crown prosecutor Patrick Wilbur told the court police had key forensic evidence related to the Oland murder, and releasing any information about it would compromise the ongoing investigation. Wilbur argued it's "too simplistic to suggest it's a kernel" of evidence. "It encompasses all of the evidence," and one search warrant "builds upon the other," he said. Police have "very, very significant concerns" about releasing the information, said fellow prosecutor John Henheffer, referring to it as "hallmark evidence." Freedom of the press and the public is not an absolute right, he said.

Gary Miller made submissions on behalf of Oland, as well as for William Teed, who was representing Lisa Andrik-Oland, her friend Mary Beth Watt, and Connie Oland's brother, Jack Connell. Miller argued the court should lift the sealing order to allow him to assess the grounds of the searches and challenge their legality and constitutionality. He questioned how disclosure of information to "an interested party," such as whether forensic testing of seized items was done and if anything was found, could compromise the police investigation. Miller also argued his client should have "special status" and get access to the search warrant information before the media and the public. He could argue it's necessary to prevent prejudicing the interests of an innocent person, he said, but not without knowing what the information contains. "There's no great shame in delaying access to the media in such situations," Miller said, urging the court not to rush such "important, even potentially ground-breaking issues," pointing out: "The sky's not going to fall."

Provincial court Chief Judge R. Leslie Jackson decided to hold an *ex parte* hearing to allow the Crown the opportunity to present detailed evidence as to why "justice would be subverted by disclosure." The following day, he said he was satisfied releasing the documents would compromise the police investigation. They contained information only the killer or killers would know, he said, including details about the condition of the victim's body. He also said he was satisfied it was still an active, ongoing investigation, noting some of the objects seized had been sent elsewhere for forensic testing. "Police are proceeding diligently with the investigation," he said. "This is not a cold case." Jackson ruled the documents should remain sealed, but he took the unusual step of putting a six-month time limit on the continuance of the sealing order. It would expire on June 15, 2012.

Coles said the case illustrated the need for New Brunswick to follow the lead of other provinces, such as Alberta, and adopt new rules requiring interested parties be notified when an application to seal a search warrant is filed. "If the Crown wants to seal, people have a right, according to law, to stand up and oppose," but without notice, they likely don't even know the applications exist.

On June 15, 2012, on the same day the sealing order was set to expire, Crown prosecutors sought a temporary extension until a court date could be set to argue the merits of a six-month extension. Coles opposed, arguing the Crown did not provide the minimum fifteen days' notice required and did not present any evidence to justify the extension. "You are operating in a total, absolute, evidentiary vacuum," Coles told the judge. "They're asking today that you extend something you already decided was dead after six months."

Jackson said he would not dismiss the matter on the "technicality" of "lack of timely notice," but he felt having a "full and complete" hearing on the merits of keeping the documents sealed for another six months was "necessary." At that June 27 hearing, Jackson said he would not agree to keep the warrants sealed for another six months without hearing new evidence. He adjourned the matter until July 31 when the lead investigator, Constable Davidson, testified behind closed doors as to why the documents should remain sealed. Then, in a surprise move, the Crown abandoned its application to keep all the documents sealed. Instead, the Crown argued during a closed hearing as to what specific information should continue to be withheld.

"The material that we're looking for is material that there is no justification to keep confidential," Coles told reporters outside the court. CBC News and Brunswick News were not trying to impede or jeopardize the investigation, he stressed. "It is so that the process works as it's supposed to, as opposed to shielding from public scrutiny that what ought to be known." The media were acting as surrogates for the public, he said.

On August 1, a nine-page affidavit by Davidson in support of keeping the search warrants sealed was made public, with the exception of two words at the request of Miller and Teed. The redacted words appeared in a section describing why some witnesses had become reluctant to help police. "I have spoken to three persons who have been approached by [redacted] on a number of occasions," Davidson said. "After speaking with these [redacted], they are now questioning whether they are prepared to continue to offer their assistance in this investigation as a result of the actions of these [redacted]." The affidavit also outlined delays investigators faced in getting exhibits analyzed by the RCMP forensic labs. Davidson said 378 exhibits had been seized. Of those, 243 required forensic analysis.

Lab staff decided which exhibits to accept, and no additional exhibits could be submitted until the results from the previously submitted exhibits were reported, said Davidson. At that point, only forty-three exhibits had been sent, with the most recent results received on June 26. "It is difficult to determine how much longer this investigation will continue, due to the potential results that will be received from evidence already gathered that has been analyzed or is currently being analyzed," he wrote. A month earlier, during an interview marking the one-year anniversary of the murder, Chief Reid told CBC News he believed investigators were "very, very close" to laying charges. Davidson stopped short of saying he disagreed with the chief's assessment, but he said it was difficult to say, since evidence was still coming in.

Reid's comments came on the heels of criminology professor Michael Boudreau's suggestion that an outside force help with the investigation. "Another police force, notably the RCMP, would bring a fresh perspective," argued Boudreau, who had previously defended police against unrealistic public expectations for how quickly crimes can be solved based on TV crime shows — the so-called *CSI* effect. The *Telegraph-Journal* also had the force under fire, publishing a series of editorials and cartoons that questioned the force's ability to solve high-profile cases and suggesting the RCMP take over. Dean Secord, president of the New Brunswick Police Association, complained that the Irving-owned daily was producing "some of the worst cases of yellow journalism we have witnessed from any media outlet in North America," and the president of the Saint John Police Association, Jamie Hachey, called the editorials inappropriate. Even Vic Toews, the federal Public Safety minister, weighed in, denying allegations that bottlenecks at RCMP crime labs were slowing down important investigations. In June, the RCMP had announced plans to close its forensic labs in Halifax, Winnipeg, and Regina, consolidating services at its existing labs in Ottawa, Vancouver, and Edmonton. The RCMP estimated the change would save $3.5 million annually while reducing duplication and improving services.

Chief Reid rejected calls for the RCMP to take over. Three officers remained actively assigned to the file, he said. "There's no question in my mind we have very competent investigators. They've done excellent work."

On August 16, seven of nine search warrants and several other related documents in the year-old case were made public, but they were heavily redacted by order of Judge Jackson. The documents revealed, however, that police believed Richard Oland was murdered. Police had publicly only referred to Oland's death as a homicide — an umbrella term that includes the lesser offence of manslaughter, which is not premeditated.

Among the information that was withheld by the court at the request of the Crown and the lawyers representing members of the Oland family were lists of items police were looking for and lists of items seized, names of people Oland was seen with on the day he died, and descriptions of Oland by some of the people police had interviewed. The court gave four reasons for redacting the information: it was considered hallmark evidence, it could compromise the investigation if disclosed, redaction protected an innocent party, and redaction protected the privacy of a third party.

The documents were so heavily redacted that many paragraphs contained only a word or two.

Sgt. Brooker was advised by [redacted]. [Redacted] told Sgt. David Brooker that they are [redacted]. [Redacted] told Sgt. David Brooker that they did [redacted]. He asked about the [redacted]. He was advised [redacted]. In conclusion, [redacted].

On August 17, Coles argued for the release of more information. "People like their privacy and everybody understands that, but unless you have a process that opens these things to the light of day, you run the risk of abuse... because there's no public supervision," he said.

On September 28, Judge Jackson ruled in favour of releasing additional details. "I have concluded that police have not demonstrated a serious and specific risk to the investigative integrity of the Oland homicide investigation; indeed their position is based on vague and general assertions of risk," he said. But Jackson imposed a publication ban on the names of individuals searched and on information that would identify them. The additional details, released on October 5, described Richard Oland's final hours and suggested a financial motive. CBC News and Brunswick News applied to the Court of Queen's Bench to have the publication bans lifted on the names of people subject to police searches, on the in-camera testimony of the lead investigator, and to have four more search warrants and related documents unsealed. Parts of the search warrant documents were released in April 2013. They showed police had obtained the cellphone records of a "viable suspect." On April 23 David Coles argued it was unreasonable to keep the identities of those who were subject to the search warrants under wraps when the searches had been observed and reported. "It brings the court into disrespect with the public when we try to stuff genies back into bottles," he said. Coles described the case as an attempt to rewrite history and likened it to George Orwell's *1984*. He pointed out that Jackson hadn't ordered the names of the people searched be blacked out when the search warrants were made public. Anyone willing to pay ninety dollars could get copies of the search warrants from the court and share that information. But many people rely on the media, he said, and the media were prohibited from printing or broadcasting the names.

Gary Miller argued the publication ban protected the rights of innocent people. There had not been "one shred of evidence" that anything seized from anyone had "any forensic significance" to the investigation, he argued. He called for an end to the media's "never-ending barrage" of coverage. "Enough is enough," he said. Coles countered that "enough will be when the public in Saint John is satisfied that the police and the judiciary have done their jobs." Justice William Grant ruled Jackson "made an error of law" in imposing a publication ban. Dennis Oland was publicly identified on May 17 as the prime suspect in his father's murder. Chief Reid said the revelation wouldn't affect the investigation and continued to pledge that police would make an arrest before the end of the year.

On September 6, the media outlets went back to court to seek the release of the remaining documents and Davidson's in-camera testimony. Gary Miller argued a "poison climate" against Oland already existed. The coverage, he suggested, was becoming "tabloid journalism." Family lawyer William Teed agreed. The privacy of his clients, he said "has not only been invaded, it has been run over by a truck." Teed called it a "lynching."

Information about the blood on Dennis Oland's jacket was released on October 4. The DNA findings were released on October 25. The following month, he was arrested.

A week before Dennis Oland's arrest in November 2013, Chief Reid told the *Telegraph-Journal* that investigators were keeping close tabs on the suspect in the case. He explained that was routine procedure. "We make sure that we're monitoring those individuals and we know where they're at, at all times," he said. "That would be consistent with what we're doing here." The scene at the car wash was the force's "first opportunity to arrest Dennis Oland," Reid said at the time. "We made a determination we wanted to talk to him, so that was an opportunity for us to find him. We did find him, and we brought him in to have a conversation." It would later be confirmed through sworn testimony that police had in fact kept Oland under surveillance for five days in late October to establish his daily routine.

Word of the arrest spread like wildfire. Police issued a rare evening news release. Oland was scheduled to appear in provincial court the following afternoon, the release advised, but it did not indicate what charge he would face. Oland would remain in custody, in a holding cell, until his court appearance, and police would hold a news conference at ten a.m. the next morning. Reporters raced to file the breaking news. Gary Miller, who had to drive more than an hour from his Fredericton office, was seen entering the police headquarters shortly before seven p.m. He declined to comment. William Teed, the Oland family lawyer, also declined to comment.

Derek Oland, the victim's brother and the accused's uncle, was used to dealing with the media in his capacity as executive chairman of Moosehead Breweries. He promptly issued a statement, saying his family believed police had the wrong man. It would be the first statement of many with a recurring theme in the years to come, as the legal proceedings dragged on.

> This situation truly is a tragedy for all of us who are part
> of the Oland family, and we are striving to understand and
> deal with the many implications. We will rely on the court
> of law, believing in the judicial process. We believe our
> nephew and cousin, Dennis is, in fact, innocent and we will
> support him and his family members through the course of
> whatever legal actions unfold. Right now, it is of no help or
> value to engage in dialogue or speculation about what did
> or didn't happen in the murder of Richard Oland. Rather,
> we must allow the evidence to be examined and the rule of
> law to unfold as it will.

But much speculation did ensue. Why now? Oland had been publicly identified as the prime suspect for at least six months, when the court released the search warrant documents. Had investigators finally secured a missing piece of the puzzle? Or did mounting public pressure trigger the arrest? Just the week before, Reid commented on the unprecedented attention the case had garnered. "You don't see the amount of information that's entailed in the investigation [as] news in the media every day as we have seen for this particular file," Reid had said. "Having said that, that hasn't deterred the Saint John Police Force and our investigators to pursue this file to its ultimate conclusion, which is to take this file to court."

Some observers surmised police and prosecutors felt they had gathered all the evidence they could; it was time to put the case before a jury and see what would happen. The chief, of course, painted a much different picture when he strolled into the news conference the next morning, decked out in his formal uniform. He never doubted they would make an arrest and see the case go to court, he told the roomful of reporters. "I've always believed that, and that's been fulfilled today." The media seemed to be "under a time constraint," Reid said, but police were not. "We were in no hurry to make a mistake." Reid compared the complex investigation to assembling a mosaic. In the absence of witnesses, police had to rely largely on forensics. "We got a little piece of evidence. That would direct us [to] an area. We had to get another piece of evidence and keep going. So we built a case from nothing, essentially."

Investigators took the file to Crown prosecutors a year earlier, he noted, but prosecutors asked for "a multitude of things," including additional interviews and forensics, to strengthen the case before they would approve charges. (New Brunswick is one of three provinces in which only Crown prosecutors have the authority to lay criminal charges.) About three weeks before the arrest, after some "massaging of the file," prosecutors approved a second-degree murder charge against Dennis Oland. In Canadian law, murder is either first- or second-degree. First-degree murder is planned and deliberate (premeditated) or is committed in the course of another offence, such as sexual assault or forcible confinement. All homicides involving identified police officers are automatically categorized as first-degree, regardless of the circumstances. Second-degree is essentially a catchall category for all intentional killings that don't fall under the specifics of first-degree. It is the customary charge in so-called heat-of-the-moment killings. The second-degree murder charge indicated that the Crown believed it could prove Dennis Oland intended to kill his father but not that he planned the murder in advance.

First-degree murder and second-degree murder both carry automatic life sentences. The main difference is the minimum term. Those convicted of second-degree murder can become eligible for parole after ten years, while those convicted of first-degree murder must serve at least twenty-five years before being considered for parole. The lesser charge was not a strategy to get a guilty plea, said Reid. "There was no plea bargaining." He stated unequivocally that second-degree was the "appropriate" charge in this case.

Police did not expect to lay additional charges against Dennis Oland, or to charge anyone else. He allowed for the possibility that police could receive information "that would make us look at someone else or others, but as it stands today, our investigation is pointing clearly to one individual: Dennis Oland."

Oland appeared tired and dishevelled, wearing a baggy grey sweatshirt, sitting in the prisoner's box after spending the night in lock-up. He looked straight ahead during the brief proceedings, but he did glance over at his visibly shaken relatives who filled the first two rows, including his mother and wife, and offered them a weak smile. They did their best to return the expression. About seven police officers, including Stephen Davidson, the lead investigator, were also present to witness the pivotal event.

Judge Marco Cloutier asked Oland if he understood the charge against him. He nodded and quietly replied, "Yes, sir." Oland did not enter a plea. That would come much later. Oland was remanded into custody and ordered to appear on November 19, when the court would set a date for the preliminary inquiry. Gary Miller did not request a bail hearing, so Oland was expected to remain in custody for another six nights. As sheriff's deputies escorted Oland from the courtroom, Derek Oland waved at him.

None of the family members spoke to reporters after court, but his mother, his wife, and his two sisters issued a statement, asserting their confidence in his innocence. "We wish that the police would turn their attention to finding out who is really responsible for Dick's death," the statement said. The previous two years had been the most difficult in all their lives, they noted, and they were "devastated" that "this nightmare" would continue. "We know that he will be found innocent in an objective and fair process in a court of law." The arrest was "preposterous," friend Larry Cain said. "The Dennis Oland that I know is just simply not capable of such a horrific act."

On November 18, the day before Oland was scheduled to return to court, media caught wind that a bail hearing for him was underway in the Court of Queen's Bench. Oland wore a dark suit, crisp white shirt, and a tie for the court appearance. Approximately fifty supporters attended the proceedings, including family members and his father's long-time friend, Pat Darrah. Oland also had a second defence lawyer acting on his behalf. The high-profile (and high-priced) Toronto lawyer Alan Gold joined Gary Miller. At the time, Gold was representing Toronto police officers facing Police Service Act charges stemming from the 2010 G20 protests. He's also represented members of the Hells Angels in his distinguished career, which dates from the early seventies. In a single year, 1990, Gold won three cases in the Supreme Court. Most relevant to the Oland case was Gold's reputation for debunking scientific evidence. He's written extensively about science and the law. "The last two decades have witnessed an ascendancy of two phenomena: junk science and miscarriages of justices," Gold has stated.

Under the Criminal Code, a judge must consider whether it's necessary to keep an accused in custody to ensure he or she will attend court, to protect the public safety, or to maintain public confidence in the administration of justice. For three and a half hours, Justice Hugh McLellan listened to testimony from witnesses and arguments from the Crown and defence.

The Crown opposed Oland's bail application. Alan Gold countered with an argument that used Chief Bill Reid's own words. Gold pointed out that for the past two and a half years, Reid had repeatedly said "there was no danger to the public, the police knew who they thought it was, and they were continuing in their investigation, and there was nothing to be worried about." Dennis Oland was "the only suspect virtually from the day the body was found," and yet police had not considered him a threat to public safety or a flight risk. On the stand, lead investigator Stephen Davidson denied that Oland was the police's only suspect from the beginning; he acknowledged that police had told Oland that when they interviewed him, but that was simply a "tactic" called "reposited confrontation," he explained. "These sort of things, even though we have not determined 100 per cent on that day, are sometimes said in police interviews."

Gold, like reporters and pretty much everyone following the case, expressed curiosity as to why, exactly, police had suddenly arrested Dennis Oland. Davidson attributed it to a gradual accumulation of evidence. About a month earlier, newly released court documents revealed key forensic information in the Crown's case against Oland: blood on a brown sports jacket seized from his bedroom closet matched the victim's DNA. But, as Gold pointed out and Davidson confirmed, Saint John police had known about that DNA result since the beginning of March 2012.

Alan Gold prevailed. Justice Hugh McLellan granted bail. Dennis Oland and his supporters smiled and sighed with relief. The judge imposed a number of conditions on Oland's release, including a $50,000 surety that Derek Oland posted. Oland was also ordered to surrender his passport, to maintain his residence at 58 Gondola Point Road, and to advise Saint John police of any change in his address or any travel outside the province.

When the hearing ended, Oland exited the prisoner's box and fought back tears as he shared a long embrace with his wife and his mother. His sister Jacqueline Walsh handed him tissues. He then walked around the courtroom, hugging or shaking hands with each of his supporters, who offered their congratulations. One man encouraged him to "take a deep breath." By the time he left the courthouse at around two p.m., Oland was smiling as he walked arm-in-arm with his wife to a waiting SUV.

When Oland and his team returned to court the next morning to set a date for the preliminary inquiry, Gary Miller requested an adjournment until January 21, and the Crown agreed. Outside the courthouse, Miller told reporters he requested the adjournment because the defence had just received the disclosure file from the Crown the day before. "It's voluminous," he said. "They've had almost two and a half years with it, with all kinds of Crowns and all kinds of cops. It's only fair that we have the time to review it and read this material before we decide how much time we're going to need for a preliminary and all of that." The adjournment was not unusual, he noted. "It wouldn't make sense to set a date now when you don't even know what you're talking about."

Oland returned to court on January 21, 2014, to set a date for his preliminary inquiry. The inquiry would test the strength of the prosecution's case and determine if the Crown had enough evidence to proceed to a trial. It was scheduled for May 12 and was expected to take twenty non-consecutive days, stretching into mid-July. Judge Ronald LeBlanc from Bathurst, in northern New Brunswick, was brought in to hear the matter. Chief Judge Pierre Arsenault selected him based on several factors, including availability and absence of any conflict of interest. LeBlanc, who was named to the bench in 2002, previously served as a Crown prosecutor in the Moncton area for several years.

On the first day of the hearing, Oland arrived at the Saint John Law Courts with several family members. He chatted and laughed with Gary Miller and greeted supporters with a handshake or a hug. Then he took a seat in the front row of the courtroom. Right away, LeBlanc imposed a publication ban on the evidence, at the request of the defence. Publication bans are common during preliminary inquiries to avoid prejudicing potential jurors. LeBlanc also ordered all witnesses to leave the courtroom when they weren't testifying and instructed them not to discuss their testimony with any pending witnesses.

The Crown called Sergeant Mark Smith as its first witness and several photographs were entered into evidence, including graphic ones from the crime scene and autopsy. Miller suggested the judge turn off the monitor facing the public gallery for those images, but the judge refused, saying the exhibits were displayed in an open courtroom to everyone who wanted to see them. He did advise the gallery that some of the photos would be graphic, and they were welcome to leave if they didn't want to see them. Oland's mother and sister Jacqueline stepped out during part of the proceedings. Oland averted his eyes, sitting with his elbows resting on his knees and his chin in his hand, but he appeared to be listening intently.

By the end of day two, the preliminary inquiry was already falling behind schedule. Crown prosecutor John Henheffer could not estimate how far behind they were, but said he hoped they would be able to make up the lost time along the way. The hearing was extended several times. It lasted a total of thirty-seven days, spread out over six months, until November. The court heard testimony from forty-two witnesses, including police officers and medical experts.

During closing arguments on November 26, Henheffer took an hour to review the evidence and timeline of events. He also discussed the Crown's theory of a financial motive. He said the prosecution's case was based on a "series of circumstantial facts" and forensic analysis which, when viewed in totality, made the "reasonable and logical inference" that Dennis Oland was the assailant.

Defence lawyer Alan Gold joked that the only thing Henheffer was right about was how long his closing arguments would take. He challenged the Crown's evidence and motive and suggested the entire investigation was flawed by the "tunnel vision" of the Saint John Police Force. Officers focused on his client and failed to follow other "trails," he said. Gold argued no reasonable inference of guilt existed in the case and stressed that preliminary inquiries are aimed at filtering out "weak cases that do not warrant a trial."

On December 12, Oland sat in the front row of the courtroom with his wife and mother, surrounded by other relatives and friends, to await Judge LeBlanc's decision. It could mark the end of the lengthy criminal proceedings against him. He might walk out a free man. But it could also launch a whole other phase. LeBlanc spent more than two hours going over the evidence. The details of his decision could not be reported at the time, because of the publication ban that would remain in place until the jury was sequestered to begin its deliberations.

LeBlanc stressed his role was not to determine whether Oland was guilty, or whether a jury would likely convict him. The test was whether a properly instructed jury acting reasonably could return a guilty verdict on the evidence presented. LeBlanc also noted that at the preliminary inquiry phase, when faced with evidence where more than one inference can be drawn and with competing theories, he must consider the prosecution's case in the "best light" and decide in its favour. As a result, he ordered Oland to stand trial for second-degree murder in the death of his father.

Oland showed no reaction to the decision. He stood, nodded solemnly, shook the hand of at least one supporter, and then quietly left the crowded courtroom. He would continue to live in the community under the same conditions and would return to appear in the Court of Queen's Bench on February 2 to be indicted.

Several of Oland's family members were teary-eyed after the decision. They did not offer any comment outside the courthouse, but his mother, wife, and other relatives issued a written statement shortly after the ruling, maintaining his innocence.

> Throughout this ordeal, our faith in him continues to be absolutely unwavering. We are devastated that we will have to endure a trial but we know Dennis will be found innocent in an objective and fair process in a court of law. The question of who is really responsible for Dick's death haunts us. We despair at the time that has been lost and worry the perpetrator of this terrible crime may now never be found and brought to justice.

The statement expressed gratitude for the support the family had received throughout "this most difficult time."

Derek Oland issued a statement as well, saying the extended family also stood behind him. "As we have previously stated, we believe our nephew and cousin is innocent and we will continue to support him and his family members throughout the upcoming legal proceedings. The evidence and testimony presented during the preliminary inquiry will now be examined at trial where we will wait for the judicial process to run its course."

Miller told reporters he and Gold were disappointed with the judge's decision, but the threshold the Crown has to meet at the preliminary inquiry stage is "incredibly low," he noted. "I mean, I've been doing this thirty-seven years, and this is the first time I've ever contested a murder committal at a preliminary inquiry," he said. "But plain and simply, we remain very confident that Dennis will be vindicated at trial."

seven

THE TRIAL BEGINS

Approximately twenty reporters, photographers, and videographers from local and national news organizations jostled for a position on the front steps of the Saint John Law Courts on September 16, 2015. More than four years after the violent death of multimillionaire Richard Oland, his only son, Dennis Oland, was about to stand trial for second-degree murder. It was a day many people thought would never come, and the media hoped to document the moment with the perfect image.

Oland, who was not in custody, sauntered toward the front doors, the bright morning sun shining on his face, with his mother, Connie, at his side. He did not shy from the cameras; rather, he looked straight at photographers and videographers, the corners of his mouth upturned in a hint of a smile, which infuriated some people, but others believed it was his resting facial expression. He wore a dark blazer, grey pants, a powder blue shirt, and a navy tie with red-and-white diagonal pinstripes. Connie toted a blue seat cushion for the hard wooden bench at the front of the courtroom where she would faithfully sit for the duration of the trial, expected to take three months. Several other family members, friends, and supporters also filed into the courthouse.

The trial attracted its share of curious spectators and self-proclaimed Oland murder aficionados, who had been following the case from the beginning. Such high-profile cases were few and far between in Saint John, and this one had the essential elements of a sensational event: money, betrayal, and a certain celebrity status. There had been nothing like it in Saint John since the 1982 kidnapping of industrialist Jack Irving. Here, in their own backyard, was a case worthy of true-crime TV. Some dubbed it the Maritime version of the O.J. Simpson trial. Those who wanted to be guaranteed a seat in the small fifth-floor courtroom had to arrive well ahead of the scheduled nine thirty start.

The sheriff's deputies, hoping to move people through more quickly, added a second queue for security screening. Everyone had to take off their coats, empty their pockets, remove their belts (and sometimes their shoes), and put any other personal belongings, such as purses or bags, into bins to be run through an X-ray machine while they walked through a metal detector.

In the courtroom, Oland didn't sit in the prisoner's box. Instead, he had a special table and chair set up at the front of the courtroom, near his defence team's two tables. His lawyers requested this unusual arrangement in March, during a pre-trial conference with Court of Queen's Bench Justice John J. Walsh, the details of which were under a publication ban until the end of the trial. Gary Miller argued there was no need for Oland to sit in the prisoner's box, noting he had been free on bail "basically from the beginning." Miller initially requested Oland be allowed to sit at one of the counsel tables, next to his third lawyer, James McConnell. "It just shortens the time frame when we have to talk to him," if he's closer, Miller explained. Walsh eventually ruled against Oland sitting at the counsel table, but he agreed he didn't have to sit in the prisoner's box. "We've come a long way from the day where we wheeled the box into the middle of the courtroom. I know that," Walsh said. "But at the same time, he is the accused." The table beside his lawyers was the compromise. "For the record, I'm doing this because no one has given me a good reason why the accused needs to sit in the prisoner's box — what's euphemistically referred to as the prisoner's box — during the course of this trial," Walsh said. Because no one had raised any security concerns about Oland, who was on bail, "this is what I have to do," Walsh said, even if it would "play havoc" with the sheriff's protocol.

Directly behind Oland and his three defence lawyers, on the right-hand side of the courtroom, his supporters, including his mother, wife, and uncle Derek filled the pew-style benches of the public gallery. Most of the members of the public sat in the centre section, while the media were on the left side, behind the Crown prosecutors.

No cameras were allowed, but many reporters had their smartphones or laptops ready to live-tweet the proceedings, a practice that had only been permitted in New Brunswick courtrooms since 2012, when Court of Queen's Bench Justice William Grant allowed it during the jury trial of former Saint John city councillor John Ferguson, who was unsuccessfully sued for defamation by the city's pension board over allegations of wrongdoing in its handling of the city's deficit-plagued pension fund. Although the provincial Department of Justice had recommended Grant ban live tweeting, other judges subsequently followed his ruling.

The $50 million Saint John Law Courts building was only two years old in 2015, and Oland's trial was being held in the best-equipped court-room. It had around ten monitors, three the size of the flat-screen TVs popular in sports bars, and the public gallery came equipped with head-sets for observers to wear if they needed the proceedings amplified. An interactive screen at the witness box would allow whoever was testifying to mark any photos or documents displayed on the monitors, and the markings could be printed right in the courtroom and entered into evidence as an exhibit. Richard Oland, a "techie" with a lot of leading-edge "gadgetry," according to his secretary, would no doubt have approved of the set-up.

The large monitors would soon display the graphic crime-scene and autopsy photographs of the prominent businessman's bludgeoned body, making the disturbing images almost impossible for anyone in the court-room to avoid.

Dozens of bankers boxes filled with four years' worth of evidence were stacked around the Crown's two tables. There were so many exhibits, the Saint John Police Force's file coordinator for the Oland investigation, Constable Sean Rocca, sat with the prosecutors to help them quickly access whatever they needed and to assist with some of the technology.

The Crown and defence lawyers busily shuffled papers and adjusted their formal trial attire: white shirts with winged collars and tabs, grey pants, black waistcoats, and knee-length black robes. The long-awaited trial would begin in moments.

"All rise," a sheriff's deputy called out, announcing the arrival of Justice Walsh, who wore similar garb, the red lining on the front of his robe indicating the level of court. After some preliminary "housekeeping" matters between the judge and lawyers, a sheriff's deputy escorted in the members of the jury panel.

The jury summonses had started popping up in mailboxes across the Saint John region in June 2015. The court orders sent by the New Brunswick Department of Justice did not state they were for Dennis Oland's second-degree murder trial, but they were for September 8, 2015, which the media had reported as the day of Oland's jury selection. The location, though, was the real giveaway. Prospective jurors were directed not to the Saint John Law Courts building but to Harbour Station, the city's largest arena.

About five thousand people from Saint John and Kings Counties were summonsed for the Oland case — nearly ten times the usual number for a trial in New Brunswick. It may have been the largest jury pool in a criminal case in the province's history, possibly the largest ever in Canada, although no one seemed able to say for sure.

Unquestionably, the pool was larger than in some of Canada's most notorious criminal cases. The 1991 trial of New Brunswick serial killer Allan Legere saw five hundred people summonsed. Legere was facing four counts of first-degree murder for a killing spree that occurred after the previously convicted killer escaped from prison guards in May 1989, creating widespread terror along the banks of the Miramichi River. For the first-degree murder trial of serial killer (and serial rapist) Paul Bernardo in 1995, Ontario sent out ten times the normal number of summonses in that province, calling 1,500 people to report for jury duty. The first-degree murder trial of Luka Magnotta for the killing and dismemberment of Chinese engineering student Jun Lin in Montreal in 2014 started with 1,600 people being summonsed. In that case, jurors had to be fluent in both English and French. And in 2006, approximately 3,500 British Columbians were summonsed for the trial of pig farmer

Robert Pickton, charged with killing twenty-six women and eventually convicted of six of those charges.

Normally in New Brunswick, only about three hundred people are summonsed. The last time more than five hundred summonses had been sent out in the Saint John area, according to veteran defence lawyer David Lutz, was for the trial of the "Grand Manan Five" in 2006. The five men were among a group of forty people—some reportedly armed with guns, knives, and baseball bats—who stormed the house of an alleged crack cocaine dealer, fought with the occupants, fired gunshots, and finally set the house ablaze. The mob then blocked firefighters and the RCMP from dousing the flames, chanting, "Let it burn." Two thousand people received jury summons in that case; of those, three hundred and fifty showed up and, in the end, only ten of the required twelve jurors were selected. The rest were excused for a variety of reasons, such as a conflict of interest or financial hardship, or were rejected by the Crown or defence. The judge filled the remaining two spots by ordering sheriff's deputies to hit the streets and conscript twenty-five more prospective jurors. That was only the second time in Lutz's career of more than thirty years that a judge had to resort to the unusual measure to fill out the jury.

Given the extensive pre-trial publicity in the Oland case, authorities were worried they wouldn't be able to find enough impartial jurors. The relative smallness of the community also raised concerns that many summonsed would be related to or know someone involved in the case, whether members of the Oland family, witnesses, investigators, or lawyers. Some observers were surprised the defence didn't request a change of venue.

The anticipated length of the trial, sixty-five days, was another concern. Employers in New Brunswick, unlike in some jurisdictions, are not required to pay employees' wages while they serve on a jury, only to guarantee the employees' jobs. The government pays jurors $40 a day for the first nine days and $80 for each full day thereafter, but these fees are low compared to some provinces (jurors in Quebec earn $103 a day for the first fifty-six days and $160 a day thereafter) and haven't kept pace with current wages. Officials knew some people simply couldn't afford to be off work for a long trial.

The court thought summonsing three thousand people would be adequate. The number jumped to five thousand, however, once the initial mail-out saw the courthouse inundated with people trying to get out of jury duty. Under the Jury Act, anyone who receives a summons has up to five days to apply to the head sheriff to be excused in advance. Otherwise, they must attend jury selection at the place and time indicated on their summons or risk being held in contempt of court. Anyone caught misleading the court with a bogus excuse in an attempt to shirk their civic duty could be fined between $500 and $50,000.

So many people showed up at the courthouse seeking to be discharged that the sheriff's deputies set up a designated table at the entrance. Here they took the potential jurors aside to answer questions and explain the procedure. By September 8, the first day of jury selection, the head sheriff had exempted nearly four thousand. The reasons cited, said Dave MacLean of the Department of Justice, "pretty much ran the gamut," with health problems and financial hardship among the more common ones. The remaining 1,131 prospective jurors would have to plead their case to Justice Walsh, who was brought in from Miramichi, a city with a population of about twenty thousand in northern New Brunswick, to hear the high-profile case.

It was no coincidence that Walsh was chosen to preside at the Oland trial. He has practical experience in the legal application of forensic DNA typing—and DNA would play a large role in the Crown's case. As part of the Allan Legere prosecution team, Walsh was one of the first lawyers in Canada to introduce DNA evidence against an accused (securing convictions on all four counts of first-degree murder). In 1994 Walsh authored a public consultation paper that formed the basis for the federal DNA warrant legislation and the DNA data bank legislation. Four years later, he addressed the federal Standing Committee on Justice and Human Rights on the subject of DNA-related legislation. And in 2003 he received the Canadian Bar Association's prestigious John Tait Award of Excellence for his public and professional contributions.

The horde of people heading to Harbour Station for nine a.m. caused traffic snarls and parking headaches in the city's uptown area during the morning commute. The prospective jurors also faced long lines to get into the makeshift courtroom. It took hours for everyone to register at one of the six desks set up and go through the security check, which resembled that of an airport. One end of the floor of the arena was set up as the temporary courtroom, with desks for the Crown prosecutors and defence lawyers and a horseshoe of seats behind them for the prospective jurors. The concession stands along the concourse were open, selling popcorn and pretzels, giving the proceedings an oddly festive feel.

Once everyone was settled and court was in session, Oland was officially arraigned for second-degree murder and asked by Walsh to enter a plea. More than four years after his father's bludgeoned body was discovered, Oland stood, leaned forward into the microphone and said in a clear, slow voice, "Not guilty."

Walsh thanked the prospective jurors for their patience. "I'm not one to blow smoke: this will be a long, slow process," he said, offering the first glimpse of his unvarnished approach. He pledged to do his best to minimize the disruption to their lives and explained how the process would unfold. The rest of the day was spent dividing the jury pool into eight groups of 142 people. Prospective jurors had each been assigned a number when they registered, which was put into a box. Justice staff drew the numbers at random, announced them over the public address system, and displayed them on the large scoreboard above centre ice. Each group was then assigned a day and time later in the week to appear at the Saint John Law Courts for the actual selection process. It was a tedious process that, some people joked, should be recorded and used to help insomniacs.

Later in the evening, Walsh asked a handful of the prospective jurors to stay behind for possible selection as so-called triers, a rare procedure in New Brunswick. Triers are citizens appointed from the jury pool to assist the judge and lawyers with jury selection. The proceedings moved downstairs to a small room on the lower level of the hockey rink, near the dressing rooms. Only the judge, prosecutors, defence lawyers, Oland, and a few observers, mostly Oland's relatives and members of the media, attended. The potential triers were brought in one at a time. Walsh interviewed them about their profession, explained the role of a trier, and asked if they were up to the task. He then sought input from counsel on whether the individuals were suitable. The first two men brought in, both retirees, were chosen.

The following morning at the courthouse, Group A, the first group of 142 people, faced a multi-step process that started with Walsh calling them up individually and asking if they had any reason why they might be unable or ineligible to serve. People who were self-employed, suffered from anxiety issues, had vacation plans, or who knew any of the witnesses were excused. Next, Walsh posed three questions. First, had they seen, heard, read, or written anything about this case in any form of media, or in discussion with others? If they answered in the affirmative (and most did), they were asked if anything they had seen, heard, read, or written had caused them to form an opinion about Dennis Oland's guilt or innocence. Finally, prospective jurors were asked if, despite any opinion they may have formed, would they be able to set that opinion aside and decide the case based only on the evidence at trial and the instructions of the judge. The two triers would confer and deem the prospective juror either "acceptable" or "not acceptable." Those deemed acceptable moved to the third step, which involved the Crown and defence. The two sides could each accept or reject sixteen prospects without having to give any reason for their decision. They could also challenge potential jurors for cause if, for example, they had reason to believe the person was not impartial.

Jury selection was scheduled to take a week, but the panel of sixteen was complete by noon the following day.* Nine men and seven women were chosen from among the first 217 people who presented for consideration. Walsh was pleasantly surprised. "The jury selection has gone much more quickly than any of us, quite frankly, thought possible," he told the remaining members of the jury pool, offering his "sincere thanks" for their willingness to serve. "Without you, our system of justice would

---

*Normally, juries consist of twelve members, but fourteen jurors and two alternates were selected because the anticipated length of the trial increased the chances someone might get sick or be unable to serve for some other reason. A minimum of ten jurors is required to deliver a verdict, and their decision must be unanimous.

suffer greatly," he said. "You did your duty as citizens of this great democracy."

Five months later, Walsh would have harsh words for the thirty-three people who failed to show up for jury selection. They were ordered to appear before him at the Saint John Law Courts on February 12, 2016, to explain why they ignored their summonses. Walsh said paying taxes and appearing on a jury summons are the only two things the state can force citizens to do. "If everybody decided they didn't have to come, the system would collapse," he said.

Under the Jury Act, the no-shows could have each been fined up to $1,000, and faced "any other penalty that a judge of the court may impose in contempt proceedings," which includes jail time. Walsh excused fifteen, accepting their reasons as valid. The remaining eighteen were each fined $300.

The trial began with Walsh introducing himself to the jury as Jack and advising that juror No. 4 was no longer able to serve. An alternate selected only the week before as a precaution was elevated to juror, and Walsh discharged the other alternate, who was no longer needed now that the trial was starting. Walsh said the remaining fourteen jurors would sit through the entire trial, hearing all the evidence and arguments, but only twelve would deliberate and deliver a verdict. Any extra jurors remaining at that time would be eliminated by a random draw, he said. "Nobody knows who will be the final twelve, so all of you must pay close attention," he cautioned.

Walsh told the jurors to focus only on what they would see and hear in court and instructed them to avoid any media reports or discussions about the case. He warned them against becoming amateur investigators, trying to dig up their own information or develop their own theories. He also said that only the witnesses' answers mattered, not the lawyers' questions. Walsh urged them to keep open minds and reminded them that Dennis Oland was presumed innocent.

The only agreed facts, submitted to the court at the beginning of the proceedings, were that Richard Oland was the victim, and his death occurred on or about July 6, 2011. The key issue, said Walsh, was the identity of the person who caused his death.

Prosecutor Paul (P.J.) Veniot would lead the Crown's case. Veniot took over on August 11, just weeks before the trial began, when former lead prosecutor John Henheffer had to step aside for health reasons.

Veniot, the former senior regional Crown prosecutor for northeastern New Brunswick, was plucked out of retirement for the high-profile case. He had dealt with many other notable cases over the years, including the murder trial of Justin Bourque, who went on a shooting rampage in Moncton in June 2014, killing three Mounties and wounding two others. The veteran prosecutor was also respected for recommending provincial fisheries officers lay charges in 2011 against the brother of then deputy premier Paul Robichaud in defiance of a directive to drop the case and subsequent pressure to find a way to withdraw the charges against Donat Robichaud. Veniot said he was so worried about interference in the case that he made copies of all documents and emails and took them home for safekeeping. Most recently, Veniot served as counsel to the coroner during the May 2015 inquest into the still-unexplained 2012 death of twenty-two-year-old Serena Perry, an involuntary psychiatric patient at Saint John Regional Hospital.

As experienced as Veniot was, he wouldn't handle the Oland trial alone. He had two other capable prosecutors with him, Patrick Wilbur and Derek Weaver, who both had some history with the file.

Many details of the case were already publicly known, after the CBC and *Telegraph-Journal*'s joint successful fight for the release of the search warrants. So-called "hallmark evidence" that only the killer would know, such as how Richard Oland died and the nature of the weapon used to kill him, had yet to be revealed.

When Veniot rose to speak, he had everyone's undivided attention. The relationship between the victim and accused was at the heart of the modern tragedy, Veniot argued, and money played a key role. "Richard Oland held his children to a high standard," he said. "While public-ly Richard Oland may have been known as generous, at home it was a different story. . . . In Richard Oland's household, you were not given things."

Richard Oland's investments at the time of his death were worth an estimated $36 million. But Dennis Oland, a financial adviser, was in dire financial straits, Veniot said. "As time went by, we submit, the relationship between Richard Oland and the accused evolved into one more like a client and banker, rather than father and son." Richard Oland loaned Dennis more than $500,000 to ensure he didn't lose his home during his divorce. But the assistance "did not come without a cost," said Veniot. The loan was supposed to be secured against the property, and Dennis had to make monthly interest payments. He also had child and spousal support obligations and his own living expenses. And his debts were considerable. In addition to the money he owed his father, his $163,000 line of credit, secured against his house, was maxed out by July 2011. His $27,000-limit credit card was also tapped out, and he had requested an advance on his pay from CIBC Wood Gundy. In May and June 2011 Dennis Oland failed to make the interest payment to his father.

"The accused, we submit, was a man living beyond his financial means," Veniot declared. Dennis Oland was "on the edge financially" and "difficult financial circumstances might point one towards a path one might never expect," Veniot ominously noted. Oland was also upset about his father's extramarital affair with local realtor Diana Sedlacek, argued Veniot. Oland "did not approve," once describing the affair as a "family concern." Word about the relationship was getting out, Veniot said. Richard Oland was planning a trip with his mistress when, early on the evening of July 6, 2011, his son, Dennis, visited his investment office. The next morning, the victim's secretary discovered Richard Oland's bludgeoned body lying face down in a pool of blood on the floor near his desk.

Oland had suffered forty-six sharp- and blunt-force blows to his head, neck, and hands, said Veniot. (Veniot used the original figure in the pathologist's report, but the pathologist made a mistake and later corrected the number of wounds to forty-five.) "The manner and cause of death point to an act committed by a perpetrator who, in a rage, intended to kill Richard Oland, but not in a simple senseless act of a strike — or two, or three — to the head," Veniot told the jury. "The perpetrator for whatever reason or reasons continued way beyond what was required to cause Richard Oland's death."

No weapon was ever found and there was no sign of forced entry. The only thing missing from the crime scene, he said, was the victim's iPhone, which suggested the murder was not part of a robbery. The crime stemmed from a much more personal motive. Richard Oland's tight-fistedness and infidelity provoked his killer, Veniot posited. "Whatever faults and shortcoming he had, he did not deserve to die in such a gruesome manner," he said.

Veniot turned to the evidence that pointed to Dennis Oland as the guilty party. Oland told police he wore a navy blazer when he visited his father that night, but the victim's secretary remembered him wearing a brown jacket, which video surveillance confirmed. A week after the murder, Saint John police seized a brown Hugo Boss sports jacket from Oland's bedroom closet. The jacket had recently been taken to a local dry cleaner and still bore the dry-cleaning tag on its collar. Tests on the jacket revealed four areas of blood, and the DNA profile matched that of Richard Oland, said Veniot.

"Anyone is capable of doing bad things," said Veniot, as Dennis Oland and his friends and family looked on.

The defence chose not to make an opening statement.

July 6, 2011, started out as "just an ordinary day," according to the Crown's first witness, Maureen Adamson, Richard Oland's long-time secretary. In an eerie irony, Oland's first meeting that morning concerned his life insurance policy. "Little did Richard Oland know," Veniot dramatically declared, "that the life insurance policy's proceeds were about to be paid out. Richard Oland would never again see the sun rise."

Oland had been away most of the previous two months participating in sailing races. He returned home for one day to attend his wife's cousin's hundredth birthday on June 25, but the next day, the multimillionaire was off again on a fishing trip at the Miramichi Fish and Game Club. He returned and popped into the office briefly to pick up some paperwork related to a meeting he had on July 5 regarding the cathedral project, but July 6 would be his first full day back at work, said Adamson. The insurance meeting was scheduled for ten, so when Oland hadn't arrived by nine thirty, the ever-diligent Adamson called him to make sure he hadn't forgotten. Adamson called his cellphone first but got no answer, so she sent him a text message. When she didn't hear back from him, she called his home in Rothesay, she said, reciting the numbers four years after the fact with ease. It was what she described as her "reminder procedure" with Oland—one she was used to after twenty-five years of working for him.

Adamson first met Oland in the early eighties, when she worked as a receptionist on the Canada Games project. She later went to work for him at Brookville Transport and in 1999 became his secretary at Far End Corporation. Her primary role was as secretary—taking dictation, writing letters, filing reports, and reconciling accounts—but she did "a little bit of everything" and also assisted with outside projects, such as his competitive sailing and volunteer work, she said. "Work was never dull or boring. I really miss those busy days," she later wrote, wistfully.

She reached Richard Oland at home, and he told her he was on his way. Oland said goodbye to his wife and some of her relatives who were staying with the couple, then he climbed into his BMW. The next thing Adamson knew, at around 10:05, he was at the office. "I used to say he was a lead foot," she said. Oland met with the two life insurance agents and then sat at his desk to take care of some investment business. As always, he tuned his overhead TV to financial news, Adamson remembered. He also looked into some yacht races he was considering entering in 2012. It was a full day, with lots of catching up to do from his time away. "The inbox was quite filled," said Adamson. She didn't think he left the second-floor office all day, but she couldn't say for sure, because she went out during the lunch hour to bring him back some pizza from Pizza Hut, which was located within walking distance.

She was getting ready to leave for the day when Dennis Oland showed up at around five thirty. Richard Oland seemed pleased by the unexpected visit. He swivelled in his chair and greeted him warmly. "He said, 'Hi, Dennis,' in a very happy way," she said, and asked how he was making out with the family tree project they were working on.

Adamson had already closed the lateral blinds and turned off the Keurig coffee maker as part of her daily office "wind down" routine, but she left the air conditioner "blasting" at her boss's request. He was reviewing some reports and said, "I'll be here for a while," Adamson recalled. She noted that Dennis Oland was wearing a brown jacket. It was a hot day, she explained, and she wondered how he could stand it in the stifling heat. "That is how it stuck in my head," she said, as the jurors listened attentively, some taking notes.

Adamson spoke briefly to the younger Oland, whom she had known since the mid-to-late eighties, when he spent his summers as a teen and young adult working at Brookville Transport. She knew him well, she said, but didn't see him very often. She asked him to take a book home to his mother so it could be returned to his uncle Jack Connell. It was an old logbook for a family camp, which Richard had borrowed to scan. Adamson said the last time she saw the book it was on a table near her boss's desk as the two men chatted away. Richard Oland was seated at his desk, and his son was standing beside him. They were "so engrossed" in their conversation, Adamson said, she didn't think they even heard her when she left them alone together at around five forty-five, saying, "Goodbye fellas."

On her way out, Adamson checked that the door in the second-floor foyer that led to a back alleyway below was locked, but she did not check the vacant adjacent office. She said it was undergoing some work (although the landlord would later dispute this) and it was kept locked most of the time, she said, noting they would sometimes have to call the landlord for access if the power went out, because the fuse box was in there.

Adamson didn't lock the exterior street-level door, because the office rule was the last one to leave for the day locked that door, she said. Only four people had keys: her; Richard Oland; his business associate, Robert McFadden; and the building's owner, John Ainsworth.

Adamson's husband of thirty-seven years, William Adamson, was waiting for her, parked in his usual spot in the loading zone at the front of the building. He had arrived at around 5:20 and given "a couple of taps on the horn" to let her know he was waiting, which was their routine, he said. It was a beautiful, sunny day without much pedestrian traffic, William Adamson recalled. He saw McFadden leave the building with his son Galen, who was helping out that summer, scanning old photos for the Oland genealogy project.

Then, out of the corner of his eye, he noticed a man walk in the front door. He said he only took note of the man because it was around five thirty, and he was worried it might mean last-minute work for his wife. The man was between five foot eight and five foot ten, average build, clean-shaven, wearing tan slacks and a "medium to dark brown" sports jacket. He was also carrying a red "grocery store tote bag," which appeared to have something in it but not something heavy enough for the man to be exerting himself, Adamson said during cross-examination by the junior defence lawyer, James McConnell, who was called to the bar only in 2012. Adamson could not identify the man he saw as Dennis Oland, but his description matched.

Veniot asked Maureen Adamson about her arrival at work on the morning of July 7. He began by leading her through some photographs of the outside of the three-storey commercial building. Adamson testified that she was surprised but not shocked to find the street-level door unlocked. John Ainsworth sometimes allowed bands to practise on the third floor at night. She was more surprised to find the door at the top of the stairs ajar, she said, but she still wasn't alarmed. In damp weather, the door would sometimes stick, she noted, and so she was annoyed, if anything, that someone failed to pull it tight and turn the lock the night before. Once she opened that door, however, she smelled the "terrifically vile odour."

The door to Far End Corporation was closed, although she could no longer remember if it was locked because she had put her key in the lock out of habit. Only when she reached the centre of the office and looked toward Richard Oland's desk did she see a body on the floor and flee. "I panicked, I guess," she testified. Adamson went downstairs to Printing Plus for help, and Preston Chiasson agreed to go up with her. Adamson couldn't remember which one of them went up the stairs first or into the office first. "I was just so upset," she explained.

When Preston Chiasson took the stand, he was clearly as uncomfortable about testifying as he was with the harrowing memories of what he saw on July 7. He spoke in barely more than a whisper, and he frequently drank deeply from a court-supplied bottle of water. He apologized to those struggling to hear him. Chiasson told the court that he had known "Dick" for years and occasionally went up to the Far End office for a chat. He always found him "very approachable." He initially thought Oland might have suffered a heart attack.

When shown photographs of Oland's bloody and badly beaten body, Chiasson closed his eyes and looked away. "All I seen was Richard," he said, his voice full of emotion. He hadn't noticed anything else on the floor. "As soon as he came into view, I stopped moving." Chiasson snapped shut the binder of photographs and handed it to a sheriff's deputy, as though he couldn't get rid of it fast enough.

Chiasson couldn't be certain how long he stayed in the office. "When I saw what I saw, I kind of had a weird experience," he said, speculating that he was in shock. Adamson, he remembered, was in a "bad, bad way," and Chiasson worried about her navigating the steep stairs on her own, so he escorted her out to the street. He couldn't remember exactly where they went or what they did next. "By then," he testified, "I was kind of freaking out." Police arrived quickly, he remembered, and an officer, "a big, tall guy," sat him down and asked him questions. Defence lawyer Gary Miller posed a single question to Chiasson: did he remember whether any renovations were underway in the building at the time? Chiasson couldn't recall.

Robert McFadden, Richard Oland's business associate, testified that he was parking his car a few minutes before nine on July 7 when Maureen Adamson called him. She told him not to go up to the office, to meet her at Printing Plus instead. McFadden recalled walking past Oland's BMW and thinking, *Gee, how come he's in so early?* Then he saw the first responders. "I had a sense there was foul play," he said. McFadden phoned his wife and asked her to pick up their son, who had accompanied him to work that day.

At around ten thirty, the police on the scene asked McFadden and Adamson to go to the station for formal interviews. When they finished, the two went to a Tim Hortons around the corner from 52 Canterbury Street, and "tried to make sense of what had happened in the day." At twelve thirty, McFadden's cellphone rang. It was "sort of spooky," he said, because the call display showed Richard Oland as the caller. McFadden answered. It was Connie Oland, who had received a call from someone about the emergency vehicles outside her husband's office. "I, in not so many words, indicated that Richard Oland was dead, without saying that Richard is dead," McFadden remembered.

Police had cautioned McFadden and Adamson not to talk to anyone about the case. He was registered for a golf tournament that afternoon, and he thought he could avoid talking to anyone for at least four hours if he played, so he decided to go. When he arrived at the course, however, it seemed to him that everyone was aware that "something had happened," so he didn't play for long.

On cross-examination, defence lawyer Gary Miller argued that Dennis Oland knew the Far End office routine. If William Adamson was sitting in his usual spot in the loading zone, in the blue 2008 Saturn Astra he always drove when he picked up his wife, Dennis Oland would have known when he arrived that Maureen Adamson was still at work. If he didn't want to be witnessed as the last person to see his father alive, he could have waited until after six o'clock, when everyone was gone. He could have even parked down the street and watched as they left, said Miller.

Miller painted a picture of the father-son relationship that differed dramatically from the Crown's depiction. Maureen Adamson testified to being surprised by media reports about Richard Oland and Dennis Oland's strained relationship.

"I had never observed that myself," she said. "I had never seen them arguing in all the time I had worked with Richard Oland." They seemed to have a relatively good relationship, Adamson said, "as far as I observed," but she had only ever really observed them in an office setting and didn't see Dennis Oland very often, she added. Her boss would occasionally "grumble" about his son if he couldn't reach him on the phone or if he loaned him something and it wasn't returned in pristine condition, she said. But the complaints were minor, and he complained about other people too.

Their shared interest in family genealogy, Miller stressed, was the reason for Dennis Oland's visit. The two really seemed to bond over their effort to construct the family tree, he said. In fact, in May 2011 Dennis and his wife, Lisa, had returned from a trip to England, during which he traced the prominent beer-brewing family back to an illegitimate child of Worthington Brice, a Bristol merchant who died in 1826. Richard Oland was delighted to hear the family may have originated from a "bastard" birth, Miller said, because the Nova Scotia Olands had long claimed they came "practically from royalty." The documents Dennis Oland unearthed in England were among the many blood-spattered papers found at the crime scene, Oland would later tell the court, papers not seized by police.

To illustrate the bond, Miller introduced email exchanges between father and son with the subject line "Family Tree."

"Dennis, I am very interested in our conversation and the document you gave me the other day," Richard Oland had written on May 16, 2011. He asked his son some questions and signed off, "Dad." Within thirty-six minutes, Dennis Oland sent a lengthy reply, explaining that records prior to 1700 "start to become a problem."

"This job is sort of like trying to find a special one-of-a-kind quarter in a big pile of quarters. You want them all, but without that one prized quarter your pile is worth a whole lot less to you."

Miller also submitted some emails exchanged in June about Dennis Oland's daughter Hannah. Richard Oland had sponsored his grand-daughter's U13 basketball team, which had won the provincial title and was heading to the eastern Canada championship in St. John's, Newfoundland and Labrador, from July 1 to 3.

"Dad, a very big thank you for the anonymous donation to Hannah's basketball fundraiser. This will be very helpful in sending them off to

Newfoundland. Thanks," Dennis Oland had written on June 7. Hannah Oland's team won, and Richard Oland congratulated her in a formal letter dated July 5, the day before his murder. "Congratulations on your team's win," he wrote. "I understand, as well, that you were voted Tournament All Star! We are so very proud of you for all your hard work and accomplishment. This sort of thing is important in life. Well done!... Love, Granddad."

LEFT: Richard Oland, ca. 1996.
(detailed from Court of Queen's Bench of
New Brunswick exhibit)

BELOW: July 7, 2011. Police investigate
at 52 Canterbury Street.
(Bobbi-Jean MacKinnon/CBC News)

TOP TO BOTTOM: An aerial view of uptown Saint John. (Court of Queen's Bench of New Brunswick exhibit)

The back door and alleyway behind 52 Canterbury Street. Note the small garage upon which, the defence argued, the killer could have climbed to escape. (Court of Queen's Bench of New Brunswick exhibit)

The two different alleyways the defence argued the killer could have taken if they had escaped through the back door. (Court of Queen's Bench of New Brunswick exhibit)

ABOVE AND BELOW: A diagram of Richard Oland's office indicating where his body was found, between his desk and the table. The diagram above, marked by Greg Oram, shows the routes he said he and Glen McCloskey took during their unauthorized visit. McCloskey marked their routes on the diagram below. (Court of Queen's Bench of New Brunswick exhibits)

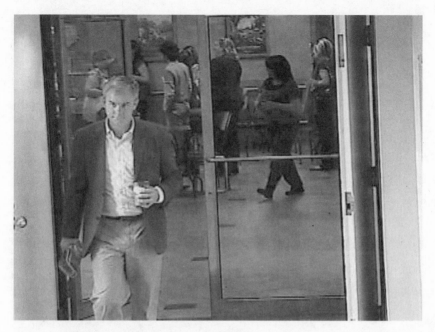

ABOVE: Video still of Dennis Oland on July 6, 2011, wearing a brown sports jacket.
(Court of Queen's Bench of New Brunswick exhibit)

BELOW: Video still of Constable Keith Copeland interviewing Dennis Oland, hours after his father's body was discovered. (Court of Queen's Bench of New Brunswick exhibit)

TOP TO BOTTOM: Forensic tests revealed bloodstains and Richard Oland's DNA on the brown sports jacket seized from Dennis Oland's closet. (Court of Queen's Bench of New Brunswick exhibit)

Evidence photo of the bloodstain on the back of the jacket that was originally missed during inspection by Saint John Police Force forensic constable David MacDonald and two inspections by RCMP bloodstain pattern analyst Sergeant Brian Wentzell.
(Court of Queen's Bench of New Brunswick exhibit)

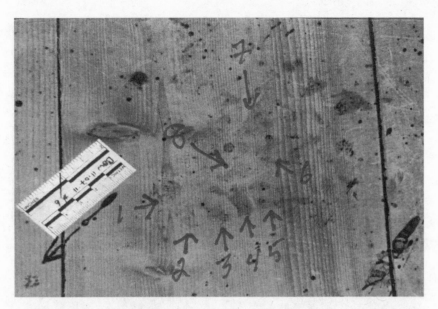

ABOVE: The possible footprint at the crime scene with markings by footwear impression expert, retired RCMP Corporal Brian Babin (Court of Queen's Bench of New Brunswick exhibit)

BELOW: Evidence photo of the sole of one of the shoes Dennis Oland said he was wearing when he visited his father on July 6, 2011. (Court of Queen's Bench of New Brunswick exhibit)

TOP TO BOTTOM: Connie Oland, Dennis Oland's mother and Richard's widow.

Dennis Oland and his wife, Lisa Andrik-Oland.

Diana Sedlacek, Richard Oland's mistress.
(CBC News)

ABOVE: Dennis Oland and his lawyer Gary Miller in court during his first trial in 2015.
(Andrew Robson for CBC News)

BELOW: Video still of Dennis Oland in custody, February 2016. (CBC News)

ABOVE: Dennis Oland and defence lawyer Michael Lacy following the court's crime scene visit, March 12, 2019. (CBC News)

BELOW: Dennis Oland and his wife, Lisa Andrik-Oland, emerge from the courthouse after the announcement of a "not guilty" verdict, July 19, 2019. (Roger Cosman/CBC News)

THE KILLING

It was a few weeks into the trial, not long before Thanksgiving weekend. The start of proceedings was delayed, and defence lawyer Gary Miller, remembering when someone's cellphone rang in court a few days earlier, broke the bored silence with a story about a similar experience in Truro, Nova Scotia. A cellphone rang, and Miller turned to the other lawyer. "What idiot left their phone on in court?" he demanded. "I don't know," the other lawyer replied, "but it's coming from your briefcase." Everyone laughed. Then the testimony of the pathologist who conducted the autopsy on Richard Oland's body starkly reminded those present that a horrific, violent loss of a human life was at its crux.

Dr. Ather Naseemuddin presented graphic post-mortem photographs to illustrate his findings. The jurors had some previous exposure to images of Richard Oland's violent death on September 16, the first day of the trial, when 119 photographs of the crime scene were entered into evidence. The images showed a wide halo of blood, bone, and tissue around Oland's head, his lifeless legs sticking out from under his office desk, pants askew, pale flesh exposed, three Werther's Original candy wrappers by his feet. "There was a piece of skull in that area" and "what appears to be tissue and blood and hair on the back of his sweater," Sergeant Mark Smith noted when he led jurors through some of the images in early October.

Jurors had also glimpsed the thirty autopsy photos when they were entered into evidence but not reviewed on October 2. Walsh examined the photographs before binders of hard copies were distributed to the jurors. He questioned whether all were necessary. The Crown replied they were.

Walsh warned jurors that the crime-scene images were "going to be a bit of a shock." He urged them to "steel" themselves. When the autopsy photos were entered into evidence, Walsh told the jury, "If at any time you feel uncomfortable and you feel you need to take a break, don't be embarrassed about that. Everybody's different. You'll get through this. It's just going to be a little tough for a while." He also imposed publication bans on the photographs of both the crime scene and the autopsy; the media successfully challenged the ban on most of the crime-scene photos deemed "blood" images but did not challenge the ban on the head wound images or the post-mortem photos. Walsh offered another caution when Naseemuddin took the stand. He advised people in the public gallery they might wish to leave or at least avoid looking at the monitors. They could leave anytime, he said. But nothing could have prepared the jurors or spectators for the gruesomeness.

A wide-angle shot of Richard Oland face down on a cold metal gurney at the morgue came first. Next were close-ups of the deep gashes to his hands. Then came images of the massive head wounds — his scalp slashed open, his skull shattered, and bits of his bone and brain, a testament to the ferocity of the attack. As disturbing as the photographs undoubtedly were, the jury had been spared some of the worst ones used at the preliminary inquiry, which depicted a probe in the wounds to measure their depths, Oland's skull hacked open, and the removal and dissection of his brain.

Naseemuddin testified he had done about 150 autopsies, but that was as of the time of his testimony; he was not asked how many autopsies he had conducted prior to Oland's. He started working at Saint John Regional Hospital a year before Richard Oland's death and had previously completed his residency in 2008 and fellowships in 2009 and 2010.

Richard Oland's autopsy was gruelling and took about five hours to complete, the court heard. Naseemuddin's final report numbered twelve pages in addition to three sketches he made of Richard Oland's head injuries. Naseemuddin counted forty-six wounds: six to Oland's hands and forty to his head. Although Crown prosecutor P.J. Veniot mentioned neck injuries in his opening statement, Naseemuddin's testimony did not.

The doctor took pains to number each wound with a piece of medical tape in a bid to keep them straight, but Walsh pointed out a discrepancy between his report and his testimony. Naseemuddin inadvertently counted one wound twice. He initially thought the wound was a laceration and assigned it twenty-six but later realized, when examining the skull, that it was a fracture and assigned it forty-five, he explained. "I regret the error," he told the court. No need to apologize; we're only human, Walsh reassured him.

Naseemuddin systematically inventoried Oland's wounds for the jurors — left side of the head, right side, top and back; length, width, and depth; horizontal or vertical; and whether they were bevelled left to right or right to left. Five of the head injuries were blunt-force and round, he said. They measured between two and two and a half centimetres in diameter and had a "faint cross hatching pattern in them." The other thirty-four were sharp-force injuries, "consistent with chop wounds." Seven of the lacerations on the right side of Oland's head were parallel and closely spaced together. "It would appear these injuries were made in quick rapid succession," said Naseemuddin as the jurors followed along with the photos, either on the overhead monitors or in the binders open on their laps. They appeared increasingly uneasy with the images of Oland's scalp peeled back to expose his skull and brain as Naseemuddin noted that several of the incised wounds cut through or crushed bone.

The accused did not look at the photos on display. He leaned forward with his elbows on his knees, eyes cast down. His mother averted her gaze. His wife did, too, at first, until she left the courtroom.

Underneath the scalp, Naseemuddin counted fourteen fractures as the "skin and soft tissues broke apart," he said. The spindly doctor turned in his seat to face the jurors and motioned to his own head as he tried to explain his specialized report in layman's terms. His testimony was enthusiastic and animated, his speech rapid. During Naseemuddin's two days on the stand, Crown prosecutor Patrick Wilbur reminded the doctor to slow down. "Haste makes waste," he said.

Four of the six fractures on the left side of Oland's head created a concave in his skull measuring ten centimetres in length, seven centimetres in width, and two centimetres in depth, said Naseemuddin. Some of the wounds "breached the outer table of the skull," and "entered the cranial cavity," exposing the brain. The injuries were "not survivable," he said. Even if Oland received prompt medical attention? asked Wilbur. "I do not believe so," Naseemuddin replied.

When asked, Naseemuddin said he could not estimate the time Oland's injuries were inflicted. He found no overt signs of decomposition. The decomposition process starts immediately after death but doesn't "manifest" itself for a few hours, and it can be affected by a number of factors, he noted, including temperature, humidity, and air circulation. As Maureen Adamson had already testified, the office air conditioner was running when she discovered the body. Sergeant Smith noted the office temperature was 19°C. Decomposition starts inside the body and works outward, said Naseemuddin. It may manifest as discolouration of the skin or an offensive odour, he said. Oland's secretary and several other witnesses had testified to the vile odour at the crime scene.

Although Naseemuddin could not comment on when the injuries were inflicted, he did say the six wounds to Oland's hands likely came first, when he was still conscious and able to fight for his life. "In the early part of the assault, the victim made defensive motions with his hands." But Oland was no match for his attacker and whatever weapon was wielded against him. Naseemuddin said Oland likely survived only minutes into his vicious bludgeoning. "In my opinion these injuries would be rapidly fatal," said Naseemuddin. "Maybe ten minutes. Maybe five." That meant the attack likely continued after Oland was lying on the floor, unconscious and defenceless. "There are so many injuries... which are terribly incapacitating," Naseemuddin observed. "I would think those would have come after the victim was able to make any defensive motion."

During cross-examination, defence lawyer Alan Gold raised the notion of two perpetrators. He suggested Oland was "physically quite capable of defending himself," because he was a "healthy, robust man," nearly six feet tall and 192 pounds in weight. "There must have been some initial involvement...with the attacker or attackers?" he asked, referring to the defensive wounds to Oland's hands. Naseemuddin agreed that Oland tried to defend himself, but he could not say how many assailants were involved or whether they were left- or right-handed.

Gold described Oland's death as a "vicious beating." He asked if Naseemuddin had ever seen such a "massive amount of head injuries before" in terms of the number of blows. "It's a very high number," Naseemuddin replied.

"This poor man's skull was completely broken, correct?" asked Gold.

"Yes, that's fair to say," Naseemuddin said.

Gold suggested breaking the skull would have taken "considerable force" and created noise. "I presume you haven't heard skulls being broken by weaponry," he said, "but it's obvious to say some noise would be created?"

"That's correct."

Gold also asked about a bruise on Oland's chest that Naseemuddin determined predated the attack, although he could not say when it occurred. Gold suggested the bruise was in an odd place. "People get bruises all the time in different places," Naseemuddin replied. Bumping into a table or a wall could cause such a bruise, he suggested.

Blood evidence at the crime scene supported the theory that many of Oland's injuries were inflicted after he fell to the floor, according to the blood experts for both the Crown and defence. RCMP Sergeant Brian Wentzell, a bloodstain pattern analyst who examined the bloody office on July 11, 2011 at the request of Saint John police, gave a lengthy, detailed PowerPoint presentation to the jury on the laws of physics that govern the distribution of blood spatter and the mathematics used to interpret the patterns.

Wentzell, who bore a physical resemblance to the comically clumsy Peter Sellers character Inspector Clouseau, was anything but. He held a bachelor of science degree and had been with the RCMP since 1987. Wentzell completed a four-year forensic identification specialist apprenticeship, later earned certification as a bloodstain pattern analyst, and is now the acting non-commissioned officer of the forensic identification services division based in New Minas, Nova Scotia. Walsh declared him an expert qualified to give opinion evidence on the size, shape, location, and distribution of bloodstains and in the interpretation of the physical events that gave rise to their origin.

The soft-spoken Wentzell appeared relaxed on the stand, looking directly at the jurors as he explained the technical information. He seemed to command their full attention. Wentzell told the jury blood patterns are "predictable and reproducible." Whether the victim is old, young, male, female, drunk or sober, their blood behaves the same. It's often possible, based on how the blood has travelled, to determine the position of the victim and assailant or assailants during the attack, any movements during and after the bloodletting, the minimum number of blows delivered and the force involved, the mechanism used, and whether the spatter is from impact or weapon cast-off. The three main categories of bloodstains are passive, spatter, and transfer, said Wentzell. Passive stains are primarily caused by the pull of gravity. Blood from an injury drips straight down and pools or splashes if it is flowing quickly and trails if the injured person is moving. Spatter stains result when some form of force is applied to the blood. Some of the different types of spatter stains are impact, cast-off (the blood shed by a bloody object in motion), and blood expirated from the victim's nose, mouth, or an injury to the airway or lungs, said Wentzell. Transfer stains result from an object touching blood and then contacting another surface, leaving wipes, swipes or patterns behind, such as a shoe that tracks blood on a floor.

The volume of blood, the texture of the surface, and the distance it falls affect the shape of bloodstains, he said. If blood drips straight down, it creates a circular shape. If it strikes a surface at an angle, the shape is elliptical. The direction of movement at the time the blood was deposited, known as directionality, can also be determined by "scalloping," which will be prominent on the side the blood was moving.

Wentzell found that some of the stains on Richard Oland's main computer monitor were "associated with an event in front of the desk." They were circular, indicating the source of blood was directly in front, where Oland would have been sitting, he said. Oland's body was found on the floor. Wentzell directed the jury's attention to bloodstains on the chair mat beneath the desk. He determined the area of origin of some of that spatter was 27 centimetres from the floor, 187 centimetres from the north wall, and 333 centimetres from the west wall. Those measurements would be consistent with where Oland's head was located when his body was discovered, he said. Wentzell wasn't explicit, but he implied the blood showed that Oland was attacked while seated, and the attack continued after he was on the floor.

Wentzell showed the jury a photograph of the victim's left loafer-style black leather shoe, which he examined at the RCMP forensic lab on December 7, 2011. It had two spatter stains on the outstep side, near the heel, and a minimum of three stains on top, in the toe area of the instep side, he said. The location and shape of those stains suggested they were deposited while the shoe was sole-down on the floor.

The defence had its own blood-spatter expert, Patrick Laturnus, a retired RCMP forensic specialist and former forensic instructor at both the Canadian Police College and Ontario Police College. In fact, as Laturnus pointed out, he taught Wentzell; "I'm not going to ask you what his marks were," defence lawyer Alan Gold joked. Laturnus now works as a consultant and serves as the president of the International Association of Bloodstain Pattern Analysts. He's been doing forensic work since 1975 and has been a bloodstain analyst since 1990, working primarily on homicide investigations across Canada but also internationally. As with Wentzell, Walsh deemed Laturnus an expert in his field. Laturnus said the blood spatter was consistent with Oland being struck while seated at his desk and while on the floor. He could not comment on the sequence, but he did say the patterns indicated the assailant, or assailants, were moving around.

What killed Richard Oland? No weapon was found at or near the scene of the murder. Earlier in the trial, forensic Sergeant Smith, who had been present during the autopsy, testified the blunt-force wounds were round, measured about three centimetres in diameter with a "whirl" pattern in them, and appeared to have been caused by a hammer-type instrument.

He believed a sharp instrument about six or seven centimetres in length made the "long and slender" incised wounds. Naseemuddin could not comment on the type of weapon or weapons used to kill Oland, but he did say the injuries were inflicted by two separate surfaces: one blunt and round that left a "faint cross hatching pattern" imprinted in the wounds, and one with a sharp edge, strong enough to deliver the force to cut through bone without breaking apart and leaving pieces in the wounds. Whether it was two weapons or two different surfaces on the same weapon, he could not say. At the time of the autopsy, Saint John police "did not ask me to speculate about any specific weapon, and I did not do so," Naseemuddin said. It was "entirely possible" that police asked him about the weapon at a follow-up meeting "at least a few months later," but he could not recall.

Alan Gold asked if Naseemuddin had ever seen round wounds like the ones Oland sustained. Never, he said.

"So you, like everybody else, have no idea what that could have been, is that correct?" asked Gold.

"Correct."

"The implement remains a puzzle," said Gold.

When Sergeant Wentzell examined the victim's clothing, he found two unusual patterns he thought might provide a clue. One was a linear indentation mark on the blood-saturated navy sweater. Whatever contacted that area had that shape and had blood on it, he testified. A similar linear transfer stain was also located on the front right side of the victim's blood-soaked white-striped shirt. Below the back of the shirt collar, which had "hundreds" of blood-spatter stains on it, Wentzell found a transfer stain "indicating some kind of pattern detail" with small wavy lines. "I'm not able to say what that was," he said.

(When retired Staff Sergeant Mike King was questioned by prosecutor Patrick Wilbur about a possible weapon, he said, "I made my own assumption." He said he believed he had mentioned it to two senior officers, but before he could continue, Justice Walsh cut off the line of questioning, saying he wasn't interested in King's conjecture. At the preliminary inquiry, however, Judge Ronald LeBlanc noted that King, a former roofer with seventeen years' experience, speculated that the weapon was a roofer's hatchet, a tool with a blade on one end and a cross-hatched pattern on the surface of the hammer end.)

The suspected weapon wouldn't be revealed until several weeks later, when the lead investigator, Stephen Davidson, told the court that Saint John police surmised that a drywall hammer or "hammer-type" instrument was the murder weapon as early as the day after the discovery of Oland's bludgeoned body. Drywall hammers, also known as drywall hatchets, are hand tools that typically have a bevelled hammerhead with a waffle design on one side to nail gypsum board in place and a sharp axe on the other side to score the drywall. Davidson testified that "speculation" about a drywall hammer arose after the autopsy revealed the cross-hatch pattern. "That was the idea that was passed around" among officers, he said.

Davidson said he searched online to see what drywall hammers look like. Asked whether he ever looked into the availability of drywall hammers at local hardware stores, he said he did. Defence lawyer Gary Miller asked when. "Through the course of the investigation," Davidson replied. "Nothing formal; just to get an idea of what they looked like and what different styles there were," he said. "There are many different kinds." He never bought one, and he never showed one to Naseemuddin for his opinion on whether it could have been a possible weapon, he said.

But Miller noted Davidson had testified at the preliminary inquiry in September 2014 that he didn't take any steps to investigate the type of weapon, other than some Internet searches. There was no mention in any police reports about officers going to local hardware stores either, said Miller. Davidson said he went on his own time.

"Is there any evidence that Dennis Oland ever owned or was in possession of a drywall hammer?" asked Miller.

"No."

"Was that something police were looking for when they searched Dennis Oland's home?"

"Yes."

The police searches at Renforth wharf and the community centre near Dennis Oland's home also failed to produce a weapon. Nor did it seem that the crime scene furnished whatever object the killer used to murder

Richard Oland. When Robert McFadden, Oland's business associate, testified, he told the court that the only tool he kept in his office was a small screwdriver he used for minor repairs.

Could the killer have found a weapon in the vacant adjacent office? This may never be known. The question of whether that office was under renovation that July also remains, frustratingly and bafflingly, unresolved, with two equally credible witnesses — the building's owner, John Ainsworth, and Oland's secretary, Maureen Adamson — making conflicting assertions.

nine

POLICE IMPERFECT

The Crown called its first police witness on the fourth day of the trial. Over the next several weeks, many more police witnesses would appear in the witness box. By the time their testimony concluded, the defence had revealed so many problems with the conduct of the investigation that the judge provided the jurors with mid-trial instructions: "At the end of the trial, it will be for you to determine whether evidence about the inadequacy of the police investigation alone, or along with other evidence, causes you to have a reasonable doubt about whether Dennis Oland committed the offence charged."

Constable Duane Squires was the first officer to respond to the 911 call on July 7, 2011, and the first officer subjected to the defence's grilling. Squires described what he saw that morning when he entered with Constable Don Shannon and Cadet Trinda Fanjoy: "a deceased male," approximately three-quarters of the way into the room, lying in a pool of blood that was "coagulating, hardening on the floor." The man had "severe injuries to his head," and there was significant blood spatter. "It was obvious to me the death was suspicious and violent," Squires testified.

They exited swiftly to minimize contamination of the crime scene, Squires said under questioning by Crown prosecutor Patrick Wilbur, and Squires stood guard in the foyer to prevent unauthorized entry, recording the arrival and entry of senior officers and investigators: acting Sergeant Stan Miller at 9:22; Constables Anthony Gilbert and Stephen Davidson from the major crime unit at 9:35; Staff Sergeant Mike King at 9:39; forensic identification Sergeant Mark Smith at 10:18; criminal investigations division Inspector Glen McCloskey at 10:52; MCU Sergeant David Brooker at 11:07; and Constable Greg Oram from the MCU at 12:23. Staff Sergeant Mike King, as previously noted and he himself admitted, had no reason to enter the crime scene, but he went in not once but twice that day. Mark Smith, the forensic sergeant, was the only officer who wore protective clothing, Squires said, although Smith would later testify that while he put on a body suit, shoe covers, and latex gloves the second time he entered the office, he wasn't wearing any protective gear the first time.

Squires went back into the office around 2:22 to help remove the body, and he put on a pair of latex gloves he had with him and shoe covers that Smith gave him. By the time they got the body onto the stretcher, his gloves and booties were "pretty covered in blood," he said, so he took off the booties and put on a new pair of gloves before they carried the stretcher out. Wilbur asked where he disposed of the blood-covered items. Squires cleared his throat. "I don't remember exactly where I put them," he said, as some of the jurors jotted down notes. "I know I didn't take them with me when I left the office. I know I left them somewhere, discarded them, but I don't remember exactly where that was."

Constable Trinda McAlduff (formerly Fanjoy, and formerly a cadet), who had been with Squires and Shannon that morning, also testified. She, too, said they withdrew soon after entering. She estimated she was in the office for only seconds and while she went "pretty far" in, she said she did not get close to the body. "I didn't want to further contaminate the crime scene," she explained. While Squires stood guard in the foyer, she went downstairs with Constable Don Shannon to talk to the witnesses. McAlduff said she later returned to the foyer and, like Squires, took notes of who was there, when they arrived, and when they left. She remembered seeing a set of double doors to the Far End office, another set of double doors, a single door that led to a bathroom, windows, and a door to the outside.

The testimony of Constable Don Shannon was postponed for a few days, because he was in Nova Scotia attending the funeral of Catherine Campbell, his former squad mate. Campbell, a Truro officer, had been killed off-duty, her body dumped over an embankment in a wooded area under the Macdonald Bridge in Halifax. Shannon had lost another officer friend just the year before, when Codiac Regional RCMP Constable Douglas Larche was one of three Mounties gunned down in the line of duty by Justin Bourque.

Shannon testified that he entered the crime scene in haste. He explained that he arrived on the crime scene believing, based on the information he'd been given, that someone was injured. "I wanted to locate the person who was hurt — from the information I was given at that time," and assess their injuries, he said. But he soon found Oland's body. "He had been there for quite some time," based on the dried blood, said Shannon. "There was quite a bit of blood." He estimated he came within about three feet of the body and the only blood he noticed was around the body, although others would testify to the hundreds of blood-spatter stains radiating 360 degrees.

Wilbur presented Shannon with a diagram of the office and asked him to show the path he travelled in and out. "Once I realized this was not a normal call for service," Shannon said, "I immediately stuck to the side walls." He was in for only about two minutes before going downstairs to talk to witnesses. He then went back inside to check the third floor. "No one had done that yet," he noted.

Alan Gold, known for his deft handling of forensic evidence, took the lead for the cross-examination of Duane Squires. Surprisingly, Gold didn't harangue him over the misplaced bloody shoe coverings and gloves. Instead, Gold wanted to know about the door in the foyer outside Oland's second-storey office. The door locked with a deadbolt from the inside and exited to a rear alleyway out back, almost at ground level because the building was on a slope.

Gold asked Squires if the exit to the alley was in his field of view the entire time he was guarding the scene. Squires said it was. Had he seen anyone approach that door? Squires didn't remember seeing anyone, no. Gold wanted to know if an exit sign appeared above the door. Squires replied that he didn't remember seeing an exit sign, but he knew it was a door to the outside because he could see through the window next to the door.

"If someone has killed a gentleman in this office and presumably wants to escape as quickly as possible, wouldn't the nearest door to the outside — especially if it leads to an alley — at least be of interest to police?" asked Gold, his voice rising to a boom that eliminated the need for anyone to use an amplifying headset. Some jurors recoiled at his forcefulness. Rather than go down the stairway and out the front door to a main street, with a restaurant directly opposite the building, Gold argued, "would it not occur to the police that this might be the killer's preferred exit route?" The back door was the "nearest, more surreptitious, most hidden exit route." Squires said he didn't check the back door; he was protecting the crime scene, but he didn't recall anyone else going in or out the door, and he didn't make any notes about it, either.

Gold noted that Squires seemed like the kind of bright, conscientious officer who wanted to rise up in the ranks, who kept his eyes and ears fully alert to what he could learn for when he sought promotion. Didn't he think that if an officer had opened that door, jumped down, and climbed back inside, it would be something he'd notice? Squires reiterated that it wasn't something he had taken notes on, and it was a long time ago.

Don Shannon didn't check the door leading to the rear alley on July 7, but when he returned on July 11 to guard the scene, he noted the back door was open. He did not know who opened it. The two funeral directors who transported Richard Oland's body to the morgue testified under cross-examination that police had not mentioned the back exit to them as they struggled down the steep staircase to the front door.

Staff Sergeant Mike King, now retired, told the court he noticed the back door when he arrived at the scene at approximately 9:39 that morning. The door was closed, and he looked out the adjacent window to see where it went and what was out there. "I didn't do anything to the back door," he said under direct examination by Wilbur. He did not make note of the door when he left at around 2:43, he said, but it was open when he returned over the lunch hour the next day to relieve the officer guarding the scene. He could not say who had opened it or when.

Wilbur asked King, the senior officer in charge of patrol officers, what instructions he gave, if any, about securing the scene on July 7. He replied that he didn't give any instructions until he left. Constable Shanda Weir was in charge of security at that point, and she had a cadet, Robin Govindsamy, with her, he said. On cross-examination, King admitted that he made no notes about the back door when he first observed it on July 7. He didn't draw the attention of any other officers to the door, and he had no recollection of any conversation about the door needing to be checked or whether or not the door was locked.

Constable Weir began guarding the scene at around two forty-five, following removal of the body. She testified the back door was open at that time. Alan Gold asked her if she went outside. No, it was elevated, she said, explaining she could see the canine officer outside, but only his upper body. She didn't know who had opened the door or whether it had been locked; it was open when she got there, she said.

Constable Ben MacLeod, who relieved Weir at around 6:13 p.m., said the door remained open the entire time he was there, about eleven and a half hours. He said he either sat on a chair near the doorway or stood in the doorway, hoping to catch a breeze on the hot night. "Did it ever dawn on you the perpetrator of this dastardly deed may have left that way?" Gary Miller asked during cross-examination. "[The killer] could have left through that door and any other door in that building," MacLeod replied.

When forensic Sergeant Mark Smith took the stand, he plunked a large binder, at least four inches thick, down in front of him. Smith said that on July 7 he was fingerprinting prisoners for court when he was advised of the "sudden death." He finished what he was doing at ten a.m. and was on-site within minutes. He assessed the situation before leaving to get equipment. He didn't leave any instructions about protecting the scene when he left, he said, but he expected it "would be maintained" to minimize contamination and the destruction of possible evidence "and nobody would go in." When he returned at 11:20, three officers were standing guard outside the office, he said. Smith "suited up" in full protective gear, including a coverall, gloves, shoe covers, and a mask, but he allowed other officers without protective gear to enter the office under his supervision. Smith said he didn't move anything before taking photographs, and he didn't see anyone else move anything either.

Smith led the jury on a virtual tour of the crime scene, using 119 of the photographs that were submitted into evidence and precise descriptions of its layout and contents from his remarkable memory. Along the north wall was a curtain hiding storage shelving; to the left, McFadden's office, which overlooked Canterbury Street; farther down the north wall, a bookcase full of books. A drafting-style table with electronic equipment on its surface was in the northwest corner, a water cooler was in the southeast corner, and left of the entrance stood a coat rack. On and on it went. Smith had dealt with a huge amount of detailed information in the case — he personally processed 564 pieces of evidence — and his comprehensive testimony took six days to plow through.

The forensic sergeant said he normally checks all doors and windows at a crime scene for "anything unusual," such as signs of forced entry or other evidence. He noticed the back door when he first arrived and planned to test the deadbolt. "I wanted to fingerprint it," he said, but he was the only forensic officer available that day and other tasks — such as photographing the crime scene, helping to remove the body, and escorting the body to the morgue — consumed his time. When he returned from the morgue at around 3:20 p.m., the door was open "a good amount," he testified, and he could see the dog handler searching the area outside. Smith had "no idea" who had opened it, but it was already contaminated, "negating" his plans to check for fingerprints, he said.

Not only were the door and its deadbolt contaminated and never tested, but Smith, who had asserted earlier in the trial that "you can never take too many" photographs at a crime scene because "you have no idea what may be important down the road," also admitted that he didn't take any photos of the door until July 23, 2015 — four years after the murder. "It was overlooked during my examination," he told the court. "It was always in the plan to do that at some point, but it wasn't completed."

Wasn't it pretty basic policing that officers not touch anything at a crime scene, Gary Miller asked Smith. "That would be implied," Smith agreed. Miller asked if an investigator should have checked to see if the door was locked or unlocked before touching it with an ungloved hand; Smith agreed.

Miller introduced a close-up photograph of the back-door handle and deadbolt. The deadbolt was engraved with the word "locked," indicating when it is in a locked position. He proposed that if someone wanted to check whether the door was locked or unlocked, they could simply look at the deadbolt. "Correct," said Smith. Miller asked Smith if he would expect this hypothetical investigator to make a note, a record, of their observation that the deadbolt indicated the door was locked from the inside. "I suppose so," Smith said, although he added that he would personally be more likely to make a note if it were open. He might not if it were locked, he said.

Miller continued to press the issue. He asked whether or not an officer who noticed the door was locked should have advised the officers guarding the scene not to let anyone touch it and contaminate it. Smith agreed. He acknowledged that if that had been done, he could have tested and photographed the door. He also admitted, when asked, that he did not document his intention to test the door in any of his voluminous notes. Miller chided him, prompting him to agree that the omission showed the value of keeping complete notes in the event of questions years down the road. "You can never take enough, apparently," replied Smith.

Miller wanted to know why he "all of a sudden" took photographs of the door. Smith said the Crown had instructed him to. He was also told to go back and take measurements of the height and width of the steps, which he did a month later, on August 24, 2015, and took more photographs, he said. Miller asked if Smith was aware the back door had become "an issue" at Oland's preliminary inquiry. He said he was not.

Miller asked if Smith used the steps when he measured them, or did he have to jump down and then boost himself back up? Smith said he used the steps. The photos showed the distance between the base of the door and the alley as fifty-nine inches, nearly five feet. Miller commended Smith for the overall "incredibly meticulous work" he did on the case but suggested that, darn it, he simply forgot about the back door. "No, sir," Smith replied.

On redirect, prosecutor P.J. Veniot asked Smith how close he would have gotten to the deadbolt on July 7. Smith said he would have examined between the door and the jamb for any pry marks or any other signs of a break-in. Did he "take note of" the engraved word "locked?" asked Veniot. No, Smith said.

—

When he cross-examined Ben MacLeod, Gary Miller suggested the killer, once out the back door, could have ducked down a northbound alleyway, wide enough for a car, that exits onto Grannan Street, a side street that's quieter than Canterbury, or climbed onto the roof of a small garage behind the building, pulled themselves up over a low retaining wall to a grassy area, and then escaped down a narrow passageway, wide enough for a person, that exits onto Germain Street. A pile of dirt and debris behind the garage would have made the roof easily accessible, Miller suggested. There are "many possibilities," said MacLeod. "That may be one, depending on the person." MacLeod said he did not "thoroughly examine [the alleyway] for every nook and cranny." His assigned duty was security detail, he said.

Constable Mike Horgan from the canine unit did search the alleyway and surrounding area at around three thirty with his dog but found no evidence of the killer's escape route. Prosecutor Patrick Wilbur asked Horgan to mark on an aerial photograph of the area the route he took with Leo. Horgan used a red marker for the search route, which included Canterbury, Grannan, Princess, and Germain Streets, and blue arrows to indicate the direction of travel. There was one area he said he couldn't access with his dog, which he marked in green: the elevated grassy area Gary Miller suggested as a possible escape route. Horgan estimated he spent twenty-five minutes of the approximately hour-long search in the alleyway, which he described as a dead-end loading zone. "No evidence was found as a result of the search," Horgan said.

Alan Gold moved to submit into evidence twenty-two photos of the alley area, taken by a professional photographer on June 17, 2014. Veniot objected, saying the Crown hadn't seen the photos and wanted an opportunity to review them. Justice Walsh suggested an early lunch.

When court resumed, the defence agreed to remove one of the photographs. Gold showed Horgan the other twenty-one, which illustrated the warren of old buildings, narrow passages, stairwells, and fences typical of the historic city core. He peppered Horgan with questions about where he searched and what he remembered. Horgan had difficulty recognizing several of the scenes in the recent photographs of an area he had searched more than four years earlier, including a photo of the alleyway leading to Grannan Street, which Miller had previously suggested was a possible escape route. "I can say I went down an alleyway," said Horgan, but he could not confirm if it was the one depicted in the photo. He didn't remember steps at the back door of 52 Canterbury, either. "It looks a little different," he said. Gold showed him photos taken from the top of the garage and the grassy area, the other proposed escape route. Gold pressed him. Did he check here? What about here? "Not that I recall," Horgan replied.

Gold argued that unless a helicopter picked up the killer "like in a James Bond movie," only three possible exit routes existed: out the front door, or out the back door and down one of the two alleyways. "Whatever way the killer or killers left, you didn't find any evidence of their departure, did you?" he asked. Horgan agreed. Without any evidence, Gold submitted, none of the escape routes could be ruled out. Again Horgan agreed.

The door the defence argued would have been the killer's preferred exit was never forensically tested, nor was it photographed during the early investigation. Nor did it appear that police had thoroughly searched the network of lanes and passageways that connected the area at the rear of 52 Canterbury with the surrounding streets. Gold and Miller would go on to question whether the officer who later became the lead investigator on the case, Stephen Davidson, ever really checked the back door, casting doubt on his credibility — and on the integrity of the entire investigation he led.

The first hint that the defence had painted a target on Constable Davidson's back occurred during cross-examination of Trinda McAlduff, which focused less on the contested back door and more on her observations of Davidson during the estimated hour he was at the scene. Did she see him go in to view the body? Did she see him go upstairs? McAlduff said she didn't remember anything about Davidson's movements that day. Constable Stan Miller, a twenty-one-year veteran of the force who was an acting sergeant that day and the senior officer on-site until others arrived, was also asked during cross-examination about Davidson's whereabouts. Did he observe Davidson go into the office? Did he see him go downstairs to interview people? Miller couldn't recall. "I wasn't concerned with what they were doing at that point," he said.

The jury first heard, briefly, from Constable Davidson on October 1. His testimony would take seven days, stretched out over nearly a month. On July 7, Davidson recalled, the major crime sergeant, David Brooker, asked him and Constable Anthony Gilbert to respond to a report of a male, "not conscious, not breathing," at 52 Canterbury Street. That was the only information they had, he said. "It could mean a number of things."

Once they arrived on scene, Don Shannon told them a "deceased male" was on the second floor. Davidson entered the office "far enough to see this male," he said and concluded, based on "the condition of his body," that he was deceased. Davidson estimated he got within eight feet of the body and stayed in the office less than a minute. He didn't touch anything, he said.

In the foyer outside the office, he testified, he unlocked the back door, looked outside, and locked it again. He said he also stepped out the door to look around the alleyway, but he could not recall if that was on July 7 or when he returned to the crime scene on July 9. Whichever day he went out, he only took a "general look around... nothing in depth" for just a few minutes to get an idea of what was out there, he said. Davidson was adamant the door was locked when he arrived. He also checked the third floor, he said, before going downstairs to get some preliminary information from some of the witnesses.

He interviewed the victim's business associate, Robert McFadden, back at the station from eleven fifteen until about noon, headed to Rothesay to notify the family, and then returned to the station for a group briefing at two thirty with the lead investigator, Constable Rick Russell. The lead investigator acts like a "nerve centre," assessing what needs to be done next and who's going to do it, said Davidson. He was assigned to take a videotaped statement from Richard Oland's daughter Jacqueline Walsh, which he did from 3:47 p.m. to 5:07 p.m., with Constable Keith Copeland monitoring from the next room. He interviewed Oland's son,

Dennis, next, and Copeland assisted. P.J. Veniot asked Davidson if the accused was in the courtroom. Dennis Oland popped up from his seat, smiling, and faced Davidson.

Gary Miller pointed out Davidson made notes that day about talking to the witnesses, but his notes didn't mention anything about the back door. There was nothing about the door in the more detailed report Davidson typed up a few days later, either, Miller said. "Or the third floor," Davidson tersely pointed out. The court heard Davidson was a sparse note-taker with a "sum total" of twenty-six pages of notes on the case between July 7, 2011 and March 4, 2015. He testified it would be "impractical to mark everything down," but his practice was to jot down "significant points" and type up more thorough reports later. He had seventy-five additional pages of reports, known as police narratives, the court heard.

None of the other officers who testified remembered Davidson checking the back door or had any notes or reports about him doing so, continued Miller. The first mention he could find of Davidson checking the back door, he said accusingly, was during his testimony at Oland's preliminary inquiry on June 9, 2014. At that time, Davidson said he was with Constable Anthony Gilbert, said Miller. He quoted from the transcript: "We checked to see if it was locked" and went outside "to see what we could find," Davidson had testified.

When Gilbert had testified at the trial, Gold asked him if he had touched the back door that day. Gilbert said no, he didn't touch it; he hadn't noticed it. Gold asked if, had he noticed it, he would have touched it. "Probably not, no," Gilbert replied. "I would think not," said Gold. Wouldn't Gilbert "make every effort to disturb absolutely nothing" until forensics had a chance to test for evidence, the lawyer asked. "That's what I would do," Gilbert confirmed. He said he did not see Davidson touch the back door or open it and look outside.

But Gilbert had also testified under direct examination that he wasn't always aware of Davidson's whereabouts. After they went into the office together and observed Oland's body, Gilbert called David Brooker, the sergeant of the major crime unit, to let him know that the DOA report actually "appeared to be something suspicious." Asked what Davidson was doing at that time, Gilbert said he wasn't sure. He said they went downstairs at the same time to talk to witnesses, and when they decided to leave, Davidson was downstairs, but he didn't know if Davidson ever went back up to the second floor. "I wasn't focused on what he was doing," he said.

Miller said it was only later, at the preliminary inquiry, that Davidson testified that he couldn't remember whether he checked the door on July 7 or July 9. In response to a question from the Crown about what he did once the door was open, Davidson said he remembered "jumping down" to the alleyway below and "kind of boosting up" to get back in. The drop was about three feet, he had said. The Crown also asked if anything was engraved on the back-door deadbolt. "Not that I recall," Davidson had replied. But photos showed the deadbolt was engraved with the word "locked," and three wooden steps led from the back door to the ground below. The photos were recently taken, but according to the testimony of the building's owner, John Ainsworth, the steps were in place when he bought the building in 1999, Miller noted. Robert McFadden confirmed the steps' existence prior to 2011.

Miller implied that Davidson lacked experience with homicides; he'd joined the major crime unit only two days before the murder, but he had been a police officer since 1999. Davidson admitted that he did not check another doorway in the foyer: a set of double doors adjacent to Oland's office. The doors led to a vacant office, the court had heard, but Miller argued they could have also been an exit, and Davidson wouldn't have known. If Davidson had made notes on July 7 or July 9 about checking the exit and jumping out to check the alleyway, Miller suggested, "there would be much less controversy than there is today about that." Davidson agreed, but he maintained he had checked the door and didn't remember any steps. Miller showed him the photos. Davidson pointed out a sill, likely either granite or limestone, approximately two feet below the base of the door with only a small step between it and two wooden steps to the ground. Miller countered that Davidson never mentioned anything about the sill at the preliminary inquiry. "You were under oath and telling the truth?" Miller thundered.

"I was telling the truth," Davidson replied uncowed, his voice steady.

What the jury thought of Davidson's testimony was unknown, but people who followed media coverage of the trial were forming their own opinions. Saint John police had already faced harsh criticism for how long it took to lay charges and how tight-lipped investigators had been. Then the trial revealed that more than one officer paraded through the crime scene and touched potentially crucial evidence without any protective gear. Gobsmacked citizens started to bandy about the term "Keystone Kops." Now Stephen Davidson's cross-examination suggested something worse. To Cathy Urquhart, the details of the potential back-door escape route for the killer should have been crucial for the prosecution. "The fact that the officer didn't know that there were steps to the back door, that he [said he] had to jump down and climb back up? Come on. Something's wrong," she said. She added that the case would have been "done a long time ago" if investigators "had done the job properly." Barbershop owner Blaine Harris suggested the testimony was making it easy for the defence. "You've got an incident that happened four years ago, you've got what appears to be a very bungled investigation, and you've got evidence that's coming out that, if I were sitting on a jury watching it, I would say, 'Not guilty.'"

Danny Hennessey, on the other hand, sympathized with the investigators. Richard Oland's murder was such a huge event, he observed, that it was no surprise the Saint John police struggled. "I don't know how many constables in southern New Brunswick would have experienced a violent, brutal homicide," he pointed out. He felt the police deserved credit for their investigation. Paul Cherry also pointed to the scope of the high-profile murder. "It was such a shocking event, and I think that has sort of come through," he said. "Perhaps the police weren't as well-equipped as they might be to handle this type of investigation."

Davidson wasn't the only officer who didn't remember any steps at the back door. The dog handler, Horgan, who had spent about twenty-five minutes searching the alleyway, said he didn't remember the steps, and Constable Weir, who described the door as elevated, did not mention steps. Later in the trial, Glen McCloskey, an inspector in 2011 who had since become the deputy chief, also testified to the steps being different than he remembered on July 7. McCloskey said he noticed the back door was open sometime after twelve thirty that afternoon, when he was in the foyer. He said he thought it had been closed earlier, so he decided to walk through and look outside.

"When you first arrived, what, if anything, can you say about the status of that door?" asked Wilbur.

"I don't know for sure," McCloskey answered. "I thought it was closed, but I don't know." He described the back step as being "peculiar," farther down than a normal step. McCloskey estimated he was outside for three or four minutes before returning to the foyer, where he remained until around 2:35 p.m., when the body was removed. He didn't remember what, if any, instructions were given about the back door and couldn't say with any certainty if he touched it at that point.

McCloskey returned to the scene in August 2014, following a conversation with Wilbur about what he remembered about the back door. He had thought there was no step and was surprised to find otherwise, he said, so he took a photo of the back door with his Blackberry and emailed it to Wilbur on August 15. "Now I know it's time to retire. Quite a drop there," McCloskey wrote. McCloskey said he also remembered a metal fence about his height, six foot one or "maybe higher," blocking the end of the alleyway.

McCloskey's direct testimony triggered a barrage of derision from Alan Gold. What a coincidence, he said, his words heavy with sarcasm, the lead investigator didn't remember the steps either. He insinuated Davidson and McCloskey concocted a story about the "overlooked" steps. McCloskey denied even discussing the steps with Davidson. Gold noted McCloskey's email to the prosecutor expressed surprise over there being "quite a drop" at the back door, not surprise that there were steps. McCloskey agreed that was true, but maintained he took the photograph and sent the email because his recollection was there were no steps. McCloskey also agreed with Gold: the back door was a possible escape route for the killer or killers.

"Do you know who opened that back door?"

"I don't," McCloskey replied.

"I take it the door was open enough for you to go out and come back without you touching the door?"

"I couldn't say that. I probably touched the door."

Gold continued to press until McCloskey admitted that he could have opened the door. "It's been so long ago, I could have opened the door," he said.

"OK, so let me get this straight," Gold responded, his tone incredulous. "You're at a crime scene, you're concerned about criminals getting in and getting out of a crime scene. You just walked up to a door and opened it? A door, an exit door that's proximate to a crime scene, a homicide scene? You just walked up to it and opened it? Is that your evidence?"

"I could have."

At the end of Gold's tirade, Walsh addressed the lawyers without McCloskey or the jury present. He noted McCloskey had testified the door was open before Oland's body was removed, but the funeral directors testified they never saw any door. Smith said the door was closed when he left the scene but open when he returned from the morgue. Walsh said he was curious to know if McCloskey remembered closing it when he went back in, "for what it's worth." The lawyers agreed, court resumed, and the judge asked McCloskey: did he close it, touch it, or do "anything of that sort" to the back door? McCloskey said he couldn't recall.

The washroom in the foyer outside Richard Oland's office proved an equally embarrassing subject for the Saint John Police Force. Mark Smith, the forensic sergeant, had testified that a paper towel he found in the garbage can tested positive for the possible presence of blood, as did a swab he took from the sink. The preliminary findings stirred up anticipation. Surely these results would be critical evidence for the Crown's case. If, as the defence argued, blood would have covered the killer, a post-murder wash-up might explain the lack of blood evidence found elsewhere. Smith's findings did come with a big reveal, but not what anyone expected. He said the police officers who were supposed to be guarding the crime scene, had used the washroom for two days before he found the time to examine it for evidence.

Lead prosecutor P.J. Veniot responded to the jaw-dropping news with the understatement of the trial. "Did that concern you at all?" he asked.

"Yes, it did," Smith replied sedately. But he persevered and processed the washroom anyway, he said. The jury heard details about a battery of subsequent tests, which included obtaining DNA samples from several officers who had been at the scene and citizens who had used the washroom to eliminate them from the investigation. But the results — which were only disclosed later in the trial, after everyone spent weeks wondering how much evidence the blunder might have washed away — ultimately showed the blood had no relationship to the murder. It predated the killing and belonged to Galen McFadden, the son of Robert, who was working at the office that summer, assisting with the genealogy project, the court heard.

Another black eye came through the testimony of Brian Wentzell, the RCMP blood-spatter expert who assisted Smith with the analysis of the crime scene. Wentzell wasn't called in until July 10, three days after the discovery of Oland's body. He left Nova Scotia early the next morning, arriving in Saint John shortly before noon, and began examining the crime scene at around 1:40 p.m. By that time, the body had been removed, several people had been in and out of the crime scene, and items had been moved, including Oland's desk, a chair, a backpack, and some papers. That put him at a disadvantage, he said. Bloodstain pattern analysis is best "when the body is still present and things are not disturbed." Evidence might have been on the body and lost, and removing the body while the blood was still wet could have altered the blood evidence, he explained, "so you are limited in your interpretation." There was also "a lot of alteration to the blood," because of the amount of time that had passed, said Wentzell. It was dry and "flaking upward," he noted, "different than if I had been there initially."

Despite his delayed arrival and the absence of the body, he noted he had photographs Smith took before the body was removed and autopsy photos to work with and consider in his analysis. Wentzell also agreed, when questioned by Veniot, that it wasn't the first homicide scene he had examined without the body present, although he did not say how many other cases there had been. But he did say that he had, on occasion, offered blood-spatter analysis based on photographs alone, without ever attending the crime scene.

Still, the defence preyed on the information. It stressed how important blood evidence was in the case, pointing out police had sought the input of Dr. Henry Lee, one of the foremost forensic experts in the United States. Lee gained notoriety as a defence witness at the trial of O.J. Simpson for the murders of his former wife Nicole Brown and her friend Ronald Goldman. Lee testified the crime scene indicated the murders involved a protracted struggle, which became an important part of the defence strategy, and that critical evidence was improperly handled, including blood samples. Lee was also involved in the JonBenét Ramsey case and a reinvestigation of the John F. Kennedy assassination.

On September 13, 2011, Inspector McCloskey wrote to Lee. "On behalf of the Saint John Police Force, I am requesting your assistance in reviewing the forensic evidence of a current homicide investigation. This is a high-profile murder that is receiving national attention in Canada," the letter, submitted into evidence, states. "While we are confident in the abilities and quality of the work of our investigators and forensic specialists, we would greatly value the objectivity, nuance and vision of an experienced authority with your credentials in criminalistics in the analysis of physical evidence and interpretation of crime-scene patterns relating to this case," wrote McCloskey. "If you are interested and available to consult on this matter, I would be pleased to discuss it further with you at your convenience."

On January 26, 2012, McCloskey sent an email to Mark Smith, Stephen Davidson, file coordinator Sean Rocca, and David Brooker. "We need to put a package together to send Dr. Lee. This is directed from the Chief so it needs to be done. Please set aside some time Monday afternoon so this can get accomplished. I would suggest crime scene photos and ?" When asked at the trial, neither McCloskey nor Smith seemed to know whether the package was ever prepared and sent to Lee. If Lee received the package, he apparently did not reply.

Other blood evidence proved problematic. When Smith and Wentzell sprayed Leucomalachite Green on the office floor to detect latent blood, they found a geometric pattern near the main blood pool, which appeared to be a partial footwear impression. Smith initially believed it was a boot-print transfer created by Constable Duane Squires when he helped remove Oland's body. But when Smith reviewed photographs he had taken of the scene, he realized the marks were there before the body was removed. Smith also found two other transfer-type stains between the filing cabinets and folding table, each measuring about four centimetres by one and a half centimetres. He sent photographs to the Shoeprint Image Capture and Retrieval database in Ottawa, hoping to determine the make and model of the footwear, but the prints lacked detail and unique identifiers, he said. He compared the staining to Squires's footwear, but the results were inconclusive. He also reviewed video surveillance of Dennis Oland taken on July 6, 2011, to see what shoes he was wearing that day, and created impressions of six pairs of footwear seized from his home to compare the tread marks to the patterns at the crime scene. "My results were the same: insufficient detail to be able to come up with any kind of meaningful comparison," he said.

Defence lawyer Miller agued it was a "reasonable possibility" the killer caused the transfers. "It's possible, yes," said Smith. When asked, Smith acknowledged that blood would have been on the killer's footwear. Shoes, he agreed, are a "fruitful source" for blood evidence.

Miller introduced a security video of Oland at Kent Building Supplies in Saint John on July 7, 2011, around eight a.m., shortly before his father's body was discovered. Smith agreed the shoes Dennis Oland was wearing in the video appeared to be the same ones he wore when the police interviewed him later that day. During that statement, Oland told police he was wearing the same shoes the night before, when he visited his father at his office. No blood was found on the six pairs of footwear seized from Oland.

Other deviations from procedure involved a bloodstained brown sports jacket seized from Dennis Oland's bedroom closet, the Crown's key piece of physical evidence. Rick Russell, the original lead investigator in the case, handled the jacket without protective gloves, forensic Constable David MacDonald testified. Russell "grabbed [the jacket] by the sleeve with his bare hands," MacDonald alleged. "Before I could say, 'Don't touch that,' he'd already touched it."

MacDonald, who had carefully donned a new pair of latex gloves for each of the fifty-seven items seized, to avoid contaminating any evidence, told the court he was upset about Russell's actions, but he couldn't recall if he voiced his displeasure. Russell, who retired about three months after the search, was not asked about touching the jacket when he testified just four days earlier. MacDonald said he did not circle the area Russell had touched. He said he placed the jacket into a paper evidence bag that measured about thirty centimetres by thirty centimetres. "It barely fit in there, so I just folded it up as best as I could and put it into it," he said under direct examination by Patrick Wilbur.

The jacket remained in the bag for nearly four months. MacDonald said he didn't get a chance to examine it until November 9, 2011, even though the jacket had been at the top of the list of items police were searching for. MacDonald blamed a staffing shortage. He had to juggle testing seized items with some of his other duties, he said. The jacket was noticeably wrinkled when MacDonald removed it from the bag; a photo of the crumpled jacket was submitted into evidence. Alan Gold asked MacDonald whether it occurred to him that folding the jacket would cause different areas of the jacket to touch and might cause evidence to migrate from one area to another. MacDonald, who now works in patrol, said it did not occur to him at the time. But, he noted, it was a "dry exhibit." MacDonald did acknowledge the collection and storage of the jacket "could have been done better." If he had to do it again, he said, he would probably put the garment in a larger bag.

The cross-examination of Brenan's Funeral Home employee Sharlene MacDonald, who helped remove Oland's body and embalmed him before his funeral, revealed another issue. She confirmed under questioning by Gold that police didn't interview her until sometime in 2014, more than two years after the murder. "As a result, it was more difficult for you to remember things?" Gold asked. Yes, she said. The two paramedics who responded to the crime scene also testified to long delays before the police asked them to make formal statements. Christopher Wall couldn't remember the exact date, but he said it was "quite some time after." Phil Comeau told Miller police didn't contact him until November 1, 2012. Comeau said he is normally contacted sooner, while his memory is still fresh. The man who dry cleaned Oland's bloodstained brown sports jacket wasn't asked to give a full police interview until February 2015, more than three and a half years after the fact.

"There were a lot of things we could have done better at the scene," Deputy Chief Glen McCloskey acknowledged. "We certainly learned some valuable lessons from what we did."

ten
THE McCLOSKEY ALLEGATIONS

The most explosive testimony about the police investigation came on October 13, in the fifth week of the trial, when the alleged conduct of a senior officer at the crime scene raised new questions about the force's abilities, already under the critical scrutiny of Oland's defence team.

The morning was uneventful. An officer testified about his role at the crime scene on July 7, 2011 — when he was called, when he arrived, where he walked, whether he wore protective gear, whether he touched anything, what he did, and who was with him. By that stage of the trial, the questions had become routine, even predictable. The day took a dramatic turn after lunch, when retired Staff Sergeant Mike King took the stand. Crown prosecutor Patrick Wilbur opened with the standard questions he posed to every police witness. Then, about forty-five minutes into his direct examination, Wilbur reminded King he was under oath and had sworn to tell the truth.

"At any time previous to this, did anyone suggest to do otherwise?" asked Wilbur.

"Yes," replied King. A faint collective gasp arose as stunned observers looked at one another quizzically, wondering what they were about to hear.

King alleged his former supervisor, Glen McCloskey, encouraged him to not reveal that McCloskey entered the crime scene to view the bludgeoned body. McCloskey was the top-ranking officer involved with the case at the time. He was the inspector in charge of the criminal investigations division, overseeing both the major crime unit and forensic identification unit. King said the conversation occurred sometime in 2014, either before or during Dennis Oland's preliminary inquiry, when they were alone together in McCloskey's office. McCloskey referred to another officer as an "idiot" for telling people that he, McCloskey, was in Richard Oland's office, he said.

As noted, King had entered the crime scene purely out of curiosity not once but twice that day, including one trip with McCloskey, and he said he responded by saying, "You were in the room." He alleged that McCloskey replied, "Well, you don't have to tell them that."

King did not appear to enjoy his time on the stand, but he did not shrink from it, either. His testimony was soft-spoken and straightforward, without embellishment or prevarication. King said he didn't see McCloskey go "near the body." In fact, he said, McCloskey was behind him when they entered the office. King also said McCloskey never used the word "lie," but he believed McCloskey was asking him to suppress information about McCloskey's presence at the crime scene. "There was no misunderstanding for me," King testified. He told McCloskey he had "never lied on the stand in thirty-two years," and he "wasn't about to start," he said. "I didn't care if it was a murder or a traffic ticket, I was telling the truth." According to King, McCloskey didn't say, "You misunderstood me." His only reaction was to stand, walk over to a window, and look outside, King testified.

King's testimony also described another visit to McCloskey's office. He alleged McCloskey had a box of exhibits related to the Oland investigation in his office and asked King to arrange for another officer to deliver the box to the RCMP in Fredericton. King did not say what was in the box or why McCloskey wanted it delivered to the RCMP, but he did say under cross-examination by Alan Gold that the request was highly unusual.

"Normal procedure was that exhibits seized would stay in the possession of the forensic identification officer," King said, and any movement should be documented.

"And that is because every person who handles exhibits has to be a witness to the continuity of those exhibits?" Gold asked.

"Basically, yes," King replied.

King said he never told any superior officers that McCloskey wanted him to alter his testimony. McCloskey was subsequently promoted to deputy chief in January 2015 and served as the acting chief for about six months after Bill Reid retired in April 2015. King confided only in his wife, mother, and two lower-ranked officers, Sergeant Charles Elgee and Constable Grant Lyons, he said, "a long time ago, probably last winter." More recently, on September 8, shortly before the trial began, he also told the lead investigator, Constable Stephen Davidson.

As King described it, Davidson was talking about wanting to get out of the major crime unit; the Oland case was wearing him down, said King. "He was pretty worked up," King testified. "He felt like things were making him look bad, and he didn't want to look bad." King said Davidson told him "the testimony was taking a toll on him and he wanted out.... There has been a lot of attention on the case, and he was feeling he would take a hit if something goes wrong." King encouraged Davidson to hang in. "I said, 'Just tell the truth, just report the facts; that is all you can do.'" That's when King disclosed to Davidson that McCloskey wanted him to alter his testimony, he said. Davidson responded, according to King, "That could be career-ending." King retired in April 2015, around the same time that McCloskey became acting chief.

Stephen Davidson corroborated King's testimony about their conversation on September 8. He told the court he was aware of King's allegation that McCloskey suggested he mislead the court, but he couldn't remember if he described King's allegation as "career-ending," and he hadn't made any notes of their discussion. "It was a serious thing he said to me, so it's likely I would have said something like that," he said when cross-examined. Davidson also didn't report what King told him to senior officers.

The allegation was that McCloskey was essentially "counselling perjury," an incredulous Gary Miller noted, and yet the lead investigator on the case didn't see fit to report this to his superior officers. Davidson said he didn't tell anyone because he only knew what King had told him. "I didn't know the truth of it," he said. King had told him he planned to tell the Crown himself, Davidson testified, "So I had every belief it was going to be known."

King said he told the prosecutors on September 29, just before he was originally scheduled to testify. On that day, the trial ended early and abruptly, with little by way of explanation, but Dennis Oland and his defence team appeared jubilant, smiling, sharing whispered exchanges, and strutting confidently around the courtroom. "An unexpected issue has arisen," the judge told the jury. Court would not sit the following day, he said. "Don't speculate about anything. You have enough on your plate," he instructed.

Gold showed self-restraint when he cross-examined Mike King, his questions stretching over two days.

"I take it it was not a pleasant decision for you to blow the whistle on what took place at this time?" he asked.

"Very difficult," replied King.

"Didn't look forward to it?"

"No."

Gold then read from King's statement to the prosecutors. "It's been bothering me for some time. I just wanted to get it off my chest," he quoted King as saying, which King confirmed was correct. Gold asked about the fact King applied for an inspector's position before he decided to retire. King said he applied while on sick leave with what he described as a "bad case of vertigo," but after a conversation with his physician, he decided not to follow through.

"What would you say to the allegation you're just saying these things about McCloskey because you got turned down for inspector and you're bitter?" Gold asked.

"False," said King. He wasn't turned down, he said; the process hadn't started when he decided to withdraw his application. He was not a disgruntled former employee; that was not the reason for his testimony, he stressed.

The courtroom buzzed as everyone waited for Glen McCloskey to take the stand. But the judge was informed McCloskey hadn't yet left the police station, so he suggested it was a good time to take the mid-morning recess. Within twenty minutes, the courtroom was packed with more people than had been there on day one, a few of them standing along the back wall.

McCloskey arrived via an underground pedestrian walkway between the police station and the courthouse, managing to avoid any news cameras. Unlike other officers, who testified in their dress uniforms, McCloskey wore a suit and tie.

Crown prosecutor Patrick Wilbur led the deputy chief through his work history, as King listened from the back row of the crowded courtroom. McCloskey had been with the force since November 1998, when he started as a constable. He was promoted to sergeant in May 2005 and promoted again to staff sergeant the following January. In April 2010 he became inspector of patrol services, overseeing about 110 officers, as well as the community policing, canine, and traffic units. Two months later, he became inspector of the criminal investigations division. The CID investigates crimes that either require extensive follow-up by trained investigators or would be too time-consuming for a member of the patrol division to handle. The various units within the CID have specialized expertise in investigating different types of crime, including major crime, forensic identification, street crime, stolen auto, fraud, family protection, and polygraph. McCloskey described his job as a "macro role." He was not an investigator. Rather, he was responsible for overseeing human and financial resources and reviewing files — "how we made out; where we're going," as he put it. The CID handles about a thousand files a year, he said.

On the morning of July 7, McCloskey testified, he received a call from Mike King about a "dead body" on Canterbury Street. "He wanted me to come to the scene," he said. King told him the victim was believed to be a "prominent businessman."

McCloskey said it was not unusual for other officers to call him to a crime scene. He attended all five homicide scenes in Saint John between 2008 and 2011. McCloskey walked to 52 Canterbury Street with David Brooker, the head of the major crime unit, arriving at 10:59. At first Brooker stayed outside and McCloskey went in. His role was only as an "observer, resource person," he said. Brooker eventually went inside the building, and he and McCloskey, along with King, entered the blood-spattered office under the direction of forensic Sergeant Mark Smith sometime between 11:20 and 11:50 for, he said, "observation of the person that's deceased." Smith led the way into the "inner crime scene," along the table in the middle of the office, and they followed the same route, stopping where he instructed. "I could see most of the body," said McCloskey. None of them wore protective gear to avoid contaminating the scene, as far as he could recall. "I don't remember touching anything," he said. They were in and out quickly, "somewhere around forty-five seconds to a minute," said McCloskey. He believed he was at the back of the group, because he was the tallest, and suspected they backed their way out because it was such "close quarters."

"Were you assisting the investigation in any way?" asked Patrick Wilbur.

"No," said McCloskey. His voice periodically dropped during his testimony, prompting Justice Walsh to remind him to speak up.

If those in the courtroom thought the only shocking thing they'd hear about McCloskey was Mike King's allegation, they were in for another surprise. Approximately thirty minutes into his testimony, McCloskey revealed that he entered the crime scene a second time — without Mark Smith. At around twelve thirty p.m., he went back into Richard Oland's office with Constable Greg Oram, a polygraphist with the major crime unit; it was Oram whom McCloskey allegedly called an idiot for mentioning that he and McCloskey had been in the office.

"Had he been assigned to the file to your knowledge?" Wilbur inquired.

"I didn't ask him that question, but David Brooker may have. I don't know."

"Is that something you would ask someone — why is someone here or not — as an inspector?"

"Well, I probably should have."

"And why do you say that?"

"Well, it's important. Why are all these people here, right? What are we doing?" He said he and Oram were "chit-chattin' for a bit" outside the office doors in the foyer, and then they went in. At first they walked "roughly where Sergeant Smith had taken us to," McCloskey explained, but then they took another step, closer to the filing cabinets, and headed deep into the office, to a room at the back (Robert McFadden's office). McCloskey testified that he noticed some small drops of blood on the floor as they passed through the office. "[I] just tried to step over and into the room," he said. Neither officer wore protective gear. Wilbur asked McCloskey the purpose of this second visit to the crime scene.

"Curiosity, I guess," the deputy chief replied, as reporters scribbled furiously in their notebooks and pounded away on their keyboards, already knowing this would be their lede for the day's proceedings. "It was just to look around in general and very quickly come back out." Mark Smith walked by and saw McCloskey, his superior officer, and Oram in the crime scene. "Hey, guys, get out," he said, or "words to that effect," McCloskey recalled, and they obeyed. He estimated they were inside for "probably a minute."

McCloskey said he asked Smith if he wanted him to "stay for support, and he did," because McCloskey could assist him with getting extra resources. It was at this point that McCloskey said he noticed the door to the rear alleyway and went out to look around. He couldn't remember whether or not he touched the door, and he did not remember any steps leading from the door to the ground below. Wilbur asked McCloskey to mark on a diagram of the office floor plan the routes he took on his two trips. McCloskey marked one in green, the other in orange. The diagram was shown to the jury and submitted into evidence.

It wasn't until after the court lunch break that Wilbur addressed King's accusations. He started with King's testimony that McCloskey had kept a box of Oland-related exhibits in his office, contrary to proper procedure. "Did you handle any exhibits?" he asked. "Not to my knowledge," said McCloskey.

Wilbur turned to King's other serious allegation. "What, if any, suggestion did you make to anyone to change their testimony in relation to your attendance at the scene?"

"None," McCloskey testified under oath.

Asked whether King's retirement was "amicable," McCloskey said, "Not in my view." He said they had shared a professional and personal friendship for years, but problems between them started in March 2014, when King failed a Canadian Police College course in critical incidence command, which is required to lead the emergency tactical services (ETS) unit he was already in charge of. McCloskey asserted that King was interested in becoming an inspector, but budget cuts in January 2015 began to limit his chances. He seemed concerned the department was considering promoting a woman who was an acting staff sergeant at the time and had seven years less service than him, according to McCloskey. "That's when the relationship really started to break down," he said. Other restructuring stripped King of some of his duties, including responsibility for the ETS unit. "It didn't go over well," McCloskey said. He claimed that King came to his office, and they had what he called a "heated conversation."

King went on sick leave for three months and then retired. He declined, McCloskey said, to come in to accept a retirement ring from him, the acting chief at the time. According to McCloskey, King told him to leave the ring at the front desk, and his wife would pick it up. "I didn't allow that to happen," said McCloskey. He claimed that King appeared at the station in June and said, "Just give me the ring" and "Shame on you" to McCloskey; McCloskey believed the latter remark referred to the appointment of a female inspector, the first woman in the force to hold that rank. McCloskey said he had no doubt in his mind that King was bitter that he was passed over for promotion.

Alan Gold handled the cross-examination for the defence and was aggressive with McCloskey from the start. First, he pointed out that some forty other officers—essentially everyone who had anything to do with the case—were called as witnesses at Dennis Oland's preliminary inquiry.

"Why were you not called? Do you know?"

"Yes."

"Why? You weren't feeling well that day? You had a tummy ache?" he asked with unmistakable sarcasm.

McCloskey responded that he had a conversation with prosecutors about, he said, "some things going on with my personal life." Later, on redirect by Patrick Wilbur, McCloskey elaborated on the personal issues that kept him from testifying at the preliminary inquiry. In 2013 his older sister, a Toronto police officer who inspired him to follow her into policing, died of cancer, and his younger sister was diagnosed with cancer. The next year, his younger brother succumbed to a heart ailment and McCloskey was diagnosed with the same condition. He was off work for about seven weeks.

"And who was the other officer that just happened not to be called? I'll give you a hint: Oram," Gold said, naming the officer with whom McCloskey entered the crime scene the second time. "Just a coincidence that you and Oram were the only two officers not called at the preliminary inquiry?" (Oram did not testify at the trial, either.)

Gold theorized that McCloskey, who had testified in approximately one hundred other court cases during his career, would have known the easiest way to get away with not telling the truth in court is to say something for the first time at the trial so no one can check it out beforehand. Had McCloskey testified at the preliminary inquiry, the defence would have had the opportunity to properly prepare its cross-examination of him and to verify McCloskey's claims with other witnesses, Gold said.

McCloskey said he told Wilbur on April 30, 2014, that he was at the scene. "Yes, but before that, you had asked Officer King to lie about it, hadn't you?" asked Gold.

"No," replied McCloskey.

"And you told the Crown you were at the scene. You didn't tell the Crown you'd gone too far into the scene and that Sergeant Smith had yelled to get out of there. You didn't tell the Crown that then, did you? Did you?"

"I'm not sure what I told the Crown, now."

"Is it any wonder [Smith] yelled at you to get out of there?"

"No, I was wrong, I shouldn't have been in there," the veteran with twenty-seven years of experience conceded.

"You knew you were wrong?"

"Absolutely."

Gold also quizzed McCloskey about using the pejorative term "idiot" to refer to Oram. Oram, he noted, was saying that he and McCloskey had gone into the murder scene. In what way was he wrong?

"He wasn't wrong," McCloskey replied. "I was embarrassed that we went in there so I just didn't want to talk about it."

The lawyer, however, offered a different theory. He posited McCloskey created the suspected partial footwear impression in blood that Mark Smith found at the crime scene. As noted, Smith originally thought the geometric pattern may have been created when the body was removed, but he later realized, upon reviewing photographs of the crime scene, that the pattern had been there before the removal, the court had heard. Gold suggested Smith contacted McCloskey in April 2014, before the preliminary inquiry, to tell him about the discovery, saying the perpetrator could have made it.

"When Sergeant Smith came to you about this footprint, didn't you become worried that maybe you and Oram had perhaps made the print and that you didn't want any evidence about this second time into the crime scene [to get out]? Is that what was troubling you?"

McCloskey said he didn't recall Smith coming to him about a partial footprint.

"But you understand how it sort of fits with what Sergeant King is telling us, because he says that you told him that Oram was saying you went into the crime scene — that would certainly fit with the second trip — and you called Oram an idiot, and you wanted King to deny that you'd gone in on the second trip. Is that what happened? Is that what this is all about?"

"No," McCloskey said, reiterating that he didn't recall any such conversation with Smith.

"This was such an important case. The whole police department is under pressure. You don't remember a discussion about a partial footprint in the blood, officer?"

McCloskey's response was inaudible. "He's indicating no," said Justice Walsh.

"For a senior officer in your position, it was quite a professional disgrace to have to hear publicly in evidence what you had done at this murder scene, and you wanted to cover it up. That's the long and the short of it, isn't it? Isn't it? I'm not hearing an answer, 'No,'" Gold sneered.

"Well, I was embarrassed that it happened, that's for sure," said McCloskey, but he denied trying to get King to lie. As noted, Smith's attempts to match the suspected footprint to the footwear of those who attended the crime scene or to Dennis Oland proved unsuccessful.

Gold also raised a series of emails McCloskey sent to King after their alleged conversation. McCloskey emailed King several times, asking if he had testified at Oland's preliminary inquiry yet, the court heard, and Gold asked him to account for the messages. McCloskey said he was "concerned" about King. They had both just returned from assisting RCMP in Moncton with the two-day manhunt for Justin Bourque. Several Saint John officers were involved — around 350 officers from across the country joined in the search for Bourque — but King and McCloskey had roomed together. They were "very close," he said. McCloskey wasn't sure if King was the only officer whom he repeatedly emailed about testifying at the preliminary hearing.

Gold submitted the email exchanges into evidence. The first began on the morning of Friday, June 13, 2014, when McCloskey asked King: "Did u testify yet?"

"No, adjourned to June 23rd...." King replied.

"Heard [Constable Stephen] Davidson got a scolding?" McCloskey asked.

"I talked to him after and he said it was over frivolous things that u wouldn't be expected to remember and the defence preys on it," King replied. "He didn't seem concerned."

"OK," McCloskey responded. "[Davidson] got the next day off from [Sergeant David] Brooker as Brooker advised he was worked up. It probably was frivolous things but that's what they do."

"That's what we talked about," King wrote. "They go after what they think you won't know to make u look bad."

On Wednesday, June 25, 2014, McCloskey again emailed King about his appearance at the preliminary inquiry. "Did u make it court?" he asked in an email that also discussed other, unrelated issues. King responded: "Still haven't testified." A few minutes later, King answered another email from McCloskey, writing: "Not going today. They'll let me know. Supposed to switch back to DNA stuff again."

On August 22, 2014, King declined an email invitation from McCloskey to attend a mock incident-planning session slated for September 3. "Scheduled for Oland," he wrote, to which McCloskey replied, "Oh I think that will be moved a few more times."

On Monday, September 1, 2014, at eight-fifteen p.m., McCloskey emailed the force's crime analyst, Angela Totten, and copied King. "Can u review PDF file Oland and advise SSGT Mike King when his name appears?" he asked. A few minutes later, McCloskey emailed King directly. "Mine appeared 29 times," he wrote. "I had no idea until I had her look."

"What is the PDF file?" King asked.

"It is the whole Oland file and she can submit your name and determine what page your name appears," McCloskey wrote.

"Nice to know," King typed back. "I've gone through all the supplements by guys I gave direction to. All looks good. We'll see . . . ."

On the morning of September 3, 2014, the day King expected to be "scheduled for Oland," King emailed McCloskey, letting him know his prediction had been right. "Not required today. Now it's tomorrow morning."

Gold revisited McCloskey's suggestion that King had lied about him in court because he was bitter about being "passed over" for inspector.

"Are you blaming that as the reason why someone would come to court and testify under oath that they got tired of carrying a burden for so long and they wanted to tell the truth that you essentially had asked them to lie under oath?"

"I never said anybody lied under oath," said McCloskey.

"Because certainly the Mike King you knew would never lie under oath, correct?"

"I would hope not."

"And of course, he told you that in your office. He said he hadn't lied under oath in all his years as a police officer, and it doesn't matter whether it's a traffic case or a murder case, he's not gonna lie under oath. Do you remember him saying that to you?"

"Maybe words to that effect. I don't know. I go around and say that to all kinds of officers, the same thing: 'Don't lie, never lie under oath for a traffic ticket or anything.'"

Gold asked McCloskey if he ever had a box of exhibits related to the Oland case in his office. McCloskey said he couldn't recall. He shouldn't have, unless someone else signed them out and brought the box to him for him to take somewhere, he said, "but I don't remember anybody giving me exhibits."

The lawyers had no more questions for McCloskey. After nearly four-and-a-half hours in the witness box, he was free to go. He raised his husky frame, straightened his suit jacket, and held his head up as he exited the courtroom into the turmoil that awaited him.

That same day, the Saint John Police Force's new chief, who had only taken the helm a few weeks earlier and, having come from Ontario, was the first chief appointed from outside the force in more than fifteen years, ordered an investigation into "the recent allegation" against his second-in-command "pertaining to the Oland murder trial."

Chief John Bates directed the force's professional standards unit to open an investigative file, and both the Saint John Board of Police Commissioners, the governance authority for the police force, and the New Brunswick Police Commission (NBPC), the independent oversight body that investigates and resolves complaints relating to any aspect of policing, had been advised, "as per procedure," Bates said in an emailed statement to CBC News. Bates said he would be in contact with the NBPC "with regard to conducting a thorough investigation into the allegation." In the meantime, McCloskey would remain on active duty. Bates declined to comment on any of the testimony, noting that would be improper. "The men and women of the Saint John Police Force have and will continue to deliver exceptional and first-rate service to this community each and every day," he said. "Our members go about their duties with my full confidence; they have already earned and continue to hold the confidence and respect of the greater Saint John community."

City councillors Susan Fullerton and John MacKenzie exchanged emails (obtained through a right-to-information request) on the subject. Fullerton, who "nearly fell over" when she read a media report about the

McCloskey allegations, wrote, "I surely hope it is not true." MacKenzie agreed, noting, "We have enough problems." Rick Caswell, a sergeant, sent an email to Chief Bates, describing the allegations as "the most embarrassing and humiliating event ever in the history of the force, and in my twenty-eight years. Even people I know are bashing us on social media with conviction." He urged the chief not to "give up on us in the trenches." Bates responded, in part, "We will, as a force, get through this."

On October 15, Bates contacted the commissioner of the Ontario Provincial Police, to ask him to undertake an external investigation. "Needless to say," Bates wrote, "the whole city/province is in an uproar." In the end, the NBPC announced the appointment of former Fredericton Police Chief Barry MacKnight to look into the matter. The investigation under the provincial Police Act would not begin until after the trial concluded, the commission noted. As it turned out, the commission's probe wouldn't be the only investigation McCloskey would face. And the commission would end up investigating more than just the allegations against McCloskey.

eleven

A TIMELINE FOR MURDER

Dennis Oland was the last known person to see his father alive on July 6, 2011, when he visited him at his office on Canterbury Street at around five-thirty p.m. That much was clear. And it was agreed he was alone with him for roughly forty-five minutes, from a quarter to six, when Maureen Adamson left, until approximately six thirty p.m., when he said he left. The Crown's position was that he had the opportunity to kill him, but prosecutors needed to establish a timeline. What happened after Dennis came to visit? The Crown called a number of witnesses to use the activity, or lack of activity, of Richard Oland's iPhone and computers to establish his time of death and to match the probable movement of the iPhone with Dennis Oland's whereabouts.

The junior prosecutor, Derek Weaver, handled the examinations of many of the technology-related witnesses. Weaver, a Moncton native who was only called to the bar in 2009, had acquired experience in the technology field in 2013 as part of the team that successfully prosecuted former Saint John city councillor and youth pastor Donnie Snook on forty-six charges, in one of the biggest child sex-abuse cases in New Brunswick history. Snook's collection of pornography included 14,457 unique images and 620 videos.

Weaver called to the stand Payman Hakimian, a senior technological crime forensic analyst at the RCMP headquarters in Fredericton. Hakimian was one of the computer forensic experts who attended the crime scene on July 7, 2011, at the request of the Saint John Police Force. He has been with the RCMP's tech crime unit since 2007. It started as an informatics unit, dealing mostly with the RCMP's server security, but the investigative arm developed with the growth of tech crime, he explained. Hakimian uses specialized tools and training to extract and restore deleted digital data from electronic devices, such as computers and cellphones. "People think that it's wiped, but it's really not completely gone," he told the modest crowd of approximately twenty-five people in the courtroom that day. The data remains preserved in hidden corners of the device's memory, even after it's purged, and it's accessible to someone who knows how to recover it, like Hakimian. He told the court he works on a variety of cybercrime cases, such as child pornography investigations, and has assisted various policing agencies, including the US Secret Service and FBI, Homeland Security, and border security. Justice Walsh deemed Hakimian an expert qualified to give "opinion evidence" in the forensic analysis of computers and related electronic devices and in the recovery and interpretation of electronic data. Walsh instructed the jury that expert opinion is just like the testimony of any other witness. "Give it as much or as little weight as you think it deserves," he said.

Hakimian said he arrived at Richard Oland's office at 6:55 p.m., about ten hours after Oland's body was discovered, but had to wait until about 9:00 to begin his work because forensic Sergeant Mark Smith was still processing the crime scene. Hakimian donned gloves and booties and slowly, methodically, worked his way through the office, checking each computer, documenting where it was located, whether it was on, and what systems were running. He then photographed and unplugged each one. Pulling the plugs, he explained, preserves the data and prevents the operating system from making any changes during the shutdown. Before he shut them down, he used write-blocker software on the hard drives to ensure no new information could be added.

Oland's main computer, a Dell Precision, was on but in power-save mode. When Hakimian nudged the mouse, the monitor lit up, displaying Oland's email program, Microsoft Outlook. The user log-in and password box was on the screen, prompting the user to click "OK." At some point, it had lost its connectivity to the mail server due to inactivity, he said, so any emails that were sent during that time weren't received. Whoever used the email program last was working in a folder labelled

"2aaaa 2011 race program," said Hakimian, noting Oland's emails were extremely organized. Some of the other email folders had titles like 5 Can Games, 6 family and friends & PIC, 9 jokes, and 7 FISHING. The email that was open was from Sue Costa at New England Boatworks in Portsmouth, Rhode Island, sent on June 15 at 3:41 p.m. The subject line was "Vela Volce invoice attached," referring to Oland's yacht. A USB cord, used to charge or backup Apple products, such as iPads and iPhones, was attached to the computer, he said. An envelope containing $110 in cash for Oland's gardener and a can of Coca-Cola were also visible in the photographs of his desk.

To the left of the desk, on a white two-tiered shelving unit, was another Dell computer, a Precision 490, said Hakimian, marking the location of each computer he processed on a diagram of the office for the jury. That computer had three monitors, which is uncommon, particularly in 2011, he said. People use multiple monitors when they have several applications open that they want to monitor simultaneously, he said. Oland had open eSignal, a stock charting software. The screens looked like electrocardiogram readouts: a rainbow of spikes and dips. Oland's third computer, a Dell Precision T5500, was located on the shelf above the 490. It had two monitors attached, but no programs were open. Hakimian also located an external hard drive. It was 1 terabyte (TB), which was one of the largest, if not the largest, available in 2011, he said. It "could probably fit multiple libraries."

Hakimian processed and seized a total of twelve items to drive back to his Fredericton lab for further analysis, including computers, an iPad, the external hard drive, and digital cameras. The jury viewed photos of the guts of the computers as Hakimian explained how he checked to ensure the accuracy of the time clocks on each machine before he opened them up to access their hard drives. He created a duplicate of each one using a forensic imaging program. The duplicates ensure the originals are "safe and intact," and multiple copies can be created, enabling more than one analyst to work simultaneously on different elements. "Divide and conquer," he said.

Hakimian performed a time analysis on each computer to determine when each was used. He looked at three time stamps: create, modify, and access, starting with Oland's main computer. "All activities stopped at 5:39 p.m. on July 6," he noted. That was around the time his son stopped by to visit and Maureen Adamson and Robert McFadden left for the day. No clicks or keystrokes were documented after that time, the court heard. Activity on the other office computers ended a bit earlier but at around the same time. "To me it's very clear: all systems, basically shortly after five thirty, they hadn't been used," Hakimian testified. The last activity on Oland's iPad was a draft email on July 6 at 2:31 p.m., but no information about its content or to whom it was addressed was revealed in court.

Defence lawyer Alan Gold set out to dismiss the significance of documented human activity on Richard Oland's computer ending minutes after his son came to visit. Gold was immediately aggressive and confrontational with Hakimian. He argued some human activity, such as accessing certain websites and closing certain browsers, doesn't leave a forensic "footprint," meaning Oland could have been on his computer after his son left, with no way for police to know. Hakimian stood his ground. He said he wouldn't be "cornered" into a "simple yes or no" answer, which could mislead the court. Closing some browsers doesn't leave a trace, but others do; it depends on the page the user is visiting, he said.

Gold pushed. Is it possible to close a website and leave no trace? "Everything is possible," Hakimian replied. Reading documents without changing them can leave no trace? That's possible, Hakimian agreed. Gold suggested someone might stop using their computer if they become engrossed in something else. "I'm not here to speculate," said Hakimian. Even if 5:39 p.m. was the last human activity, Gold argued there was no way to know if it was unusual or significant, because Hakimian did not analyze Oland's computer activity for any other days. Hakimian said he was not asked to look at any other day and could not comment.

The defence called their own computer expert to counter Hakimian's testimony. Geoffrey Fellows, who specializes in digital analysis, travelled from the United Kingdom to testify at the trial. Fellows started out as a police officer, doing forensic work for a small force near Oxford. He has dealt with hacking, forgery, and murder cases, as well as some recent counter-terrorism work. The "celebrated" cases he has worked on in Britain include the 2010 murder of Joanna Yeates in Bristol, where the suspect had used Google Street View to look up the site where her body was eventually found. Justice Walsh also deemed Fellows an expert qualified to give opinion evidence in the forensic analysis of computers and the recovery and interpretation of digital data.

Fellows said he analyzed Richard Oland's three office computers and found police followed the proper procedure to preserve the data on them by pulling the plugs. He agreed the last evident human usage of Oland's main computer was at 5:39 p.m. when Oland was visiting a yachting website for the Southern Ocean Racing Conference. But Oland could have been using the computer "for hours" after his son left, according to Fellows. Reading a static website does not leave any traces, provided the user doesn't change the page, he said. It could have been open for "ten to twelve hours," with no way to know. Other activities, such as closing a browser or a document, are also generally undetectable, said Fellows.

The police may have focused narrowly on the day of Oland's death, but the defence asked Fellows to analyze his computer usage history to determine how unusual it was for human activity to stop at around 5:39 p.m. Fellows looked at June 13 to June 17, 2011, the last full week Oland was in the office prior to July 6, and found human activity on all three of Oland's office computers on those days ended between 3:05 p.m. and 6:30 p.m.

Under cross-examination by Weaver, however, Fellows agreed that while the yachting website could have been open "for hours," it could have also been open for only "one second." He also agreed that it wasn't a very "content heavy" page and to "read it once wouldn't take very long." The browser was closed by the time Oland's body was discovered. Fellows could not say when it was closed, only that it was "at some point" prior to police taking a screen shot of the computer. Weaver asked whether it was true that all three computers had been used frequently throughout the day, up to that point. Yes, replied Fellows. Weaver also challenged Fellows's statement about the number of human activities on computers that don't leave traces, arguing they are limited. Some of the more common types of human activities — such as opening a browser, a web page, or an email, or updating, saving, or deleting a document, for example—can be detected, submitted Weaver. Fellows agreed. As to Richard Oland's prior computer history, Weaver asked Fellows whether the data he used in his analysis is frequently unreliable. Fellows said it is, because it is constantly being altered and overwritten. He drew the analogy of an airplane's contrails: the farther back, the more detail is lost. You can't say for certain what occurred on those days, Weaver suggested. Correct, said Fellows.

Hakimian, during his analysis, had discovered an iPhone was connected to Oland's computer during a reboot at 1:46 p.m., when someone logged on using Oland's username. The content of the iPhone was backed up at that time. "I'm very comfortable saying that up to 16:41, an iPhone was attached to that computer," said Hakimian. That's when the backup process was completed, he said. Oland's iPhone was, allegedly, the only item that vanished from the office, and it was never recovered, while the multimillionaire's wallet, Rolex watch, electronic equipment, and the keys to the BMW parked outside were all left untouched.

Robert McFadden testified Oland was "generally attached" to his iPhone. He had "migrated through a whole series" of cellphones over the years—and broken many of them, said McFadden, who was the one who helped set them up and sync them with his computer. Oland usually carried his iPhone in his pants pocket or jacket pocket or put it on the table beside him, McFadden said. Maureen Adamson testified that whenever she needed to reach her boss, she would always try his cellphone first. It was how they stayed in contact, she said. As far as she knew, he had it with him all the time.

Saint John police believed the killer took the iPhone. They followed up on Hakimian's findings with a request to the RCMP in Halifax. Neil Walker, also a senior technological crime forensic analyst, provided a more detailed analysis of Oland's computer in March of 2012. He agreed with Hakimian: the iPhone backup process was completed at 4:41 p.m. Walker determined the iPhone was disconnected from the computer at 4:44 p.m., less than an hour before Dennis Oland visited. Weaver asked if Walker compiled a report on the iPhone backup. He said he tried twice, using two software programs, but both were "unusable" because all the email formatting and computer data was also printed. The first report was twenty-six thousand pages, he noted. He ended up using another software, BlackLight, to extract some of the information, including text messages between Oland and his mistress, Diana Sedlacek. Those text messages were entered into evidence and would be discussed in detail later in the trial, when Sedlacek was examined.

No other information about the content of the iPhone was revealed during the trial. And why anyone would have taken the phone after it had been backed up on the computer—with apparently no incriminating information uncovered—remains a mystery. But it was clear Oland's iPhone was in his office up until 4:44 p.m., less than an hour before his son came to visit.

Rogers Communications officials attempted to help Saint John police in locating Oland's missing iPhone on July 9, 2011, but received a "roaming error" message. That could mean one of three things, according to an agreed statement submitted into evidence: the phone is registered on a foreign network with which Rogers doesn't have a roaming agreement; Rogers can't locate the device because records of its location were purged after a period of inactivity; or the location can't be obtained for "some unspecified reason."

Sylvie Gill, a Montreal-based investigator with Rogers, told the court the company has a law enforcement support unit that routinely assists police to locate cellphones in emergencies, such as missing person cases, or under judicial authorization. A service provider can manually initiate a registration signal, a forced registration, to locate a particular cellphone. When a cellphone is on, it emits periodic signals to communicate with the network, so when calls are made and received, the network will have a general idea of the phone's location for service delivery. During a forced registration, a signal is sent from the closest communications cell tower, and the phone responds, providing its geographic location in real time. On July 9, one of her colleagues received such a request regarding Oland's cellphone from Sergeant David Brooker of the major crime unit. But the attempt failed, coming back with a "roaming error" message, said Gill. Two other possible fail codes exist: absent subscriber, and unrecognized subscriber. The Crown and defence submitted into evidence an agreed definition of "absent subscriber." It could mean the cellphone is off, out of the coverage area, or unregistered, the agreement states. If a cellphone can't be located, Rogers can also look at the subscriber's "call detail records" to determine the last usage and the cell tower used, said Gill. Police obtained warrants for Oland's records and those of Diana Sedlacek.

Spreadsheets entered into evidence by the Crown showed the date and time of calls and text messages, the calling number and called number, as well as which cell towers picked up the signals. On the morning of July 6, while Oland was still at his Rothesay home on Almon Lane, his cell pinged off a tower in Rothesay, said Gill. During the day, while he was at his Saint John office, a tower just steps away, at 1 Germain Street, transmitted all calls and messages, including several with Sedlacek about a trip they were planning together to Maine.

At 6:44 p.m., Sedlacek texted, "U there??" But Oland did not respond. The records showed Sedlacek continued to try to reach him several times throughout the evening. She called six times, starting at 6:46 p.m., sent a text message at 7:19 p.m., followed by another six calls, and then a final text message at 11:12 p.m. Her cell pinged off a tower in Quispamsis, near her Darlings Island home, where she and her then husband Jiri Sedlacek would both testify they were that night.

The 6:44 p.m. text was transmitted to Oland's iPhone by a cell tower in Rothesay, said Gill. Rogers has three towers closer to his office than the Rothesay one, she noted. Two are on the roof of the Brunswick Square business tower at 1 Germain Street, and the third is on the city's east side, at 292 Westmorland Road. That text was the final communication ever received by Oland's cell. After that, it went silent.

Gold noted the records showed Oland let all calls to his cellphone go to voicemail that day. Gill confirmed that was correct. He asked about the other messages that never got through, and Gill confirmed it was true the network continues to try to deliver messages for up to three days. It's possible the messages sent to Oland on July 6 and July 7 that weren't delivered could have been delivered on July 9 or 10. But Gill was only asked to provide records for July 6 and July 7, Gold pointed out, taking another shot at Saint John police, so there was no way to know if the messages might have gone through on the following days. Gold also questioned if police could have done more to find Oland's cell after the ping on July 9 came back with a "roaming error" message. Could AT&T in the United States have been asked to look? Gill was unsure. Gold noted Oland's Rogers bill for June 24 to July 24 showed "roaming" charges during periods he was travelling outside of Canada.

The timing of that final text and the fact a tower in Rothesay transmitted it suggested Oland's missing iPhone had been transported to Rothesay by whoever killed him. Weaver called on Joseph Sadoun as the Crown's next cellphone witness to bolster that premise, but he was three floors down in the courthouse. Weaver apologized to Justice Walsh for the delay. "Big building," he said. "No big whoop," Walsh replied, suggesting it was a good time for the morning recess.

Sadoun is a radio frequency engineer and the director of engineering for the wireless division of Yves R. Hamel & Associés in Montreal. He manages, designs, and participates in the deployment of wireless communications systems for a number of cellular operators from in-building and DAS systems to full-sized macro sites. He is also the president of the Canadian Association of Broadcast Consultants. He deals with coverage and capacity issues of cell towers. Weaver sought to have him deemed an expert, but defence lawyer Alan Gold wanted to ask him a couple of questions first. He said he had no doubt Sadoun is an expert in the design and operation of cell communication systems, but he wanted to know what experience he had with towers in the Saint.John area. None, other than through this case, Sadoun admitted, but he joked that he could see a couple of them through the window from the witness box. Gold continued the banter. You're an expert in cell towers, he said. "You're not going to tell us why Rogers charges us so much?" Walsh agreed to declare Sadoun an expert qualified to give opinion evidence in analysis and interpretation of cell communications and data and cell records in terms of the location and movement of cell devices in conjunction with towers.

Sadoun conducted a mini-seminar for the jury on how cellular networks work. He said a group of towers provides a blanket of services in an area to run phones, computers, and other devices. More towers are provided in highly populated urban areas and fewer in suburban and rural areas. Each tower has a coverage area, and those areas overlap. Cellphones are designed to seek out the best (strongest) signal and will switch from tower to tower as they move through a coverage area. The so-called switch is the "core of the network," the "big database of information" that knows where cellphones are located and routes them to the best signal. As a signal degrades, a cellphone looks for a better signal and will request a "hand off" to the next cell tower, he said. Networks are also designed to send a call to a second-best tower if there is a problem with the best one.

It's all based on "wave propagation," explained Sadoun. There are three types: direct wave, refraction, and reflection. Terrain is one of the biggest design problems, he said. Cell signals can be blocked by buildings, bounced by flat surfaces, or split by sharp edges. Trees, for example, can cause "arc absorption" and "attennuation" — a reduction in the signal strength. Different types of antennas are used, depending on the requirements. Some operate 360 degrees, while others are directional, just "a 33-degree sliver." Different towers also have different levels of capacity. A cell tower's range can diminish during high call volumes, also known as "call loading," but that mostly affects older 2G networks, like Bell and Telus, he said. Rogers is generally not affected, and Oland was a Rogers customer.

Sadoun studied the Rogers network towers in the Saint John and Rothesay areas, considering factors such as their height and power, the tilt of their antennas, and their frequency band. He showed the jurors a map of the overall area and the location of each tower. He also produced a colour-coded map to illustrate the best coverage area for each tower. He referred to the Saint John sites as being yellow, purple, and grey. Justice Walsh commented the grey looked more brown to him but joked it might just be his age. Defence lawyer Gary Miller said he also thought it looked brown, which didn't comfort Walsh. He noted Miller was even older than him. The occasional jokes were no doubt a welcome reprieve for the jurors.

Sadoun concluded the tower that would have provided the best service to Oland's office at 52 Canterbury Street would have been the one on the Brunswick Square business tower at 1 Germain Street, which had been transmitting his messages all day. The Rothesay tower that transmitted the final 6:44 p.m. text message to Oland's missing iPhone, known as the Fairvale tower, is located at 2524 Rothesay Road, near the Renforth wharf. That tower would provide the best service to the wharf area and to Dennis Oland's home at 58 Gondola Point Road, Sadoun said. He reiterated that cellphones usually connect with whichever tower will provide the best quality signal and typically, that is the closest one, he said. "The closer to the tower, the stronger the signal." It's highly unlikely Richard Oland's missing iPhone was still in his Saint John office when it received its last message from the Rothesay tower, the jury heard. Weaver asked Sadoun what the chances were that a phone located in the city's uptown would communicate with a tower in Rothesay. "Minimal," he replied.

Weaver also asked Sadoun about test calls performed by police. In March 2012 lead investigator Stephen Davidson was issued an iPhone 4 and used Rogers to make a series of calls at various locations in the Saint John and Rothesay areas to see which cellphone towers picked up the signals. He started on Canterbury Street, near Oland's office, went to Princess Street, toward Water Street, up to King's Square, back to Canterbury Street, and then down to Harbour Station, making fifty-nine test calls from nine locations in the uptown area. About one hundred and forty-five additional calls were made from fourteen other locations, including Highway 1 eastbound, near Strescon Ltd., and the old Rothesay Road exit, the court heard. Of the fifty-nine calls made in the uptown, forty-one went through. Sadoun predicted those calls would transmit through the Brunswick Square tower on Germain Street. That proved to be correct in thirty-eight of the forty-one calls. The other three calls used the tower on the city's east side. No calls made from the uptown area connected with the Fairvale tower in Rothesay.

During cross-examination, Alan Gold pointed out that some of the other software-generated predictions Sadoun made in his twenty-one-page report regarding which towers would respond to Davidson's test calls were wrong. For example, according to Sadoun's analysis, the fifteen calls made from Renforth wharf should have connected with the Fairvale tower in Rothesay. All used a tower on Mount Champlain, near Welsford, instead. Sadoun acknowledged that was true, but he noted none of the incorrect predictions involved a signal bypassing one or two other towers as would be the case for a phone in uptown Saint John to connect with a tower in Rothesay.

Gold also criticized the test calls themselves, suggesting Davidson should have conducted them during the summer, rather than in March, to best replicate the conditions of the final calls and texts to Oland's cell. Sadoun agreed that would have been a good idea. He also agreed it would have been prudent to place the phone receiving the officer's test calls in Oland's office instead of at the police station. He did not agree, however, that Davidson should have sent texts from Sedlacek's home on Darlings Island. He said it doesn't really matter where the sender of a text is located in relation to what tower is accessed by the receiver. As to whether a cell connects differently with calls than it does with texts, Sadoun said, "Not particularly, no."

Demonstrating his prowess, Gold also pointed out that cell-tower prediction models are based on a cellphone being at a height of 1.5 metres, the equivalent of a person standing at street level holding a phone. If Oland's cellphone was in his office, which was located on the second storey of 52 Canterbury Street, the basic assumption of 1.5 metres wouldn't apply, suggested Gold. True, said Sadoun. Gold questioned whether the Fairvale tower in Rothesay would be strong enough to send a signal twenty-five kilometres to reach Oland's office. Sadoun acknowledged it was possible, if the terrain was flat. Gold also argued a phone that connected with the Rothesay tower might not be located within the primary coverage area of the tower, illustrated in pink on Sadoun's coloured map. The strength of a signal "waxes and wanes" every second, and so-called neighbour towers may take over during technical problems or in peak periods when there is a heavy volume of calls, Gold said. Sadoun agreed the coverage of towers overlap, and he didn't know what the "digital electronic neighbour list" of the Rothesay tower would have been on July 6, 2011. But he reiterated that the best tower to transmit Richard Oland's final message would have been the closest one. In his professional opinion, it was "more likely" Oland's missing iPhone was near the Rothesay tower, located near the Renforth wharf.

Two people saw Dennis Oland at the wharf that night. Barbara Murray and her husband, Douglas LeBlanc, did not testify, but details of what they witnessed were submitted in writing, admitted to by Oland, and read into evidence. Such submissions are called evidentiary admissions. When one side submits evidence that the other side does not dispute, evidentiary admissions can save witnesses from having to testify, which can shorten the duration of the trial. Oland's formal agreement to the evidence — "The accused, Dennis James Oland, admits the following as evidence..." — meant the defence would not challenge Murray and LeBlanc's account. Murray and LeBlanc said they frequent the wharf to watch the boats and activities. On July 6, 2011, "after supper," sometime between 5:40 and 7:00 p.m., they were sitting in their parked Dodge Caravan in the third or fourth parking spot over from the wheelchair space. Murray was in the driver's seat, and LeBlanc was in the passenger's seat. Not many people were around at the time, just "the odd person here and there," said LeBlanc.

As they sat, a man came up from behind their vehicle, "walking very briskly," said Murray. She described the man as Caucasian, about five foot eight to five foot nine, 160 to 165 pounds, with an average build. He had a dark complexion, dark hair — a "regular man's haircut" — no facial hair and no glasses, she said. He was "dressed very nice," wearing a dark green sports jacket and tan or olive slacks, and he was carrying a green and "yellowish" reusable Sobeys bag with a kiwi on it, she said.

LeBlanc described the man as Caucasian, probably a little taller than his own height of five foot seven, with light hair in a "normal" haircut. He did not appear to have glasses. He was wearing a "lighter sport coat, and it looked like he had beige pants on," and black shoes. He was carrying a "typical multi-coloured Sobeys shopping bag with a reddish tint" in his right hand, he said.

The man walked past the passenger's side of their vehicle and down the stairs toward the wharf, near where they were parked. As he approached where "there's some rocks," he bent down and picked something up. Murray had "no idea what it was." The man looked to his left, over toward the lighthouse and playground area, and then walked "briskly straight ahead to the very end of the wharf," where he sat down "sort of sideways, facing toward Rothesay," Murray said. "He opened the bag and took something red out, possibly a bag. He wrapped whatever he had picked up in the red thing and put it right back in the bag." Then he walked "very briskly" past them. Murray saw a "little silver car" in her rear-view mirror drive away. She did not see him leave anything behind, she said. (In her statement to police on July 15, 2011, which the jury never heard, Murray said the way the man was dressed and the way he was walking made her nervous. "I knew it wasn't right," she said. "There was a purpose to what he was doing, a real purpose.")

LeBlanc also described seeing the man head toward the wharf and stop to pick something up. He "thought it looked as if it was a small parcel of some kind, round," according to the court document. He "thought it looked wrapped in red or was red," it states. The man walked to the end of the wharf, carrying what he had picked up in his right hand and the bag, LeBlanc believed, now in his left hand. He sat sideways on the bumper at the end of the wharf, facing toward Rothesay, looked at the object, and put it in the bag. Then he got up and walked "quite swiftly" back to where he had come from, said LeBlanc, adding he lost sight of him after that. LeBlanc did not see him throw anything away. Neither Murray nor LeBlanc knew the man was Dennis Oland.

Oland had told police he stopped on his way home to see if his children were swimming at the wharf. He estimated he arrived at around 6:45 p.m. His phone records showed he received a call from his wife at 6:36 p.m., just as, he said, he was leaving his father's office. The defence argued he wouldn't have answered that call if he had just killed his father. And if he had just killed his father, the phone should have had blood on it, his lawyers pointed out, but no blood was confirmed. His wife had also tried to reach him at 6:24 p.m., but that call went to voicemail, his records showed.

As part of the investigation, Stephen Davidson conducted a series of test drives to determine how long it would take to get from Richard Oland's office to the wharf and from the wharf to Dennis Oland's home. He made fourteen trips, taking different routes each time. All the test drives were conducted during the winter months, between January 23,

2013, and February 14, 2013, the court heard. But Davidson varied the times of day, and the weather conditions weren't consistent. The Crown submitted a three-page chart into evidence. It listed the dates and times, routes and distances, weather and traffic conditions, and the time elapsed. Davidson drove the posted speed limit each time, he said. The total driving times ranged between roughly sixteen and twenty minutes. His fastest trip to the wharf took ten minutes and fifty-four seconds.

The court also heard from two men who were working downstairs from Richard Oland's second-storey office that night. They both testified to hearing "thumping" noises coming from upstairs; noises they believed, in hindsight, were the sound of Oland's murder. John Ainsworth, who has owned the building since 1999 and operates the print shop on the ground level, was one of the two witnesses. Oland had been his tenant since approximately 2005.

Oland's Far End Corporation was in "Suite 1," Ainsworth told the court. The adjacent second-storey office was vacant in July 2011, and no renovations were underway at that time, he said, contradicting Maureen Adamson's earlier testimony. He also let various local bands practise on the third floor at night. Prosecutor P.J. Veniot showed him photographs of the building, but Ainsworth didn't have his reading glasses with him. Several of the lawyers offered to loan him theirs. Ainsworth wondered aloud to a few chuckles if he should take the ones that worked best or the ones that made him look best.

Veniot asked whether the street-level door up to the second floor was normally kept open or closed. "I'd try to encourage them to keep that door shut, but it was up to them," said Ainsworth. He also tried to encourage them to keep the door locked, "especially at the end of the day," he said. The door locked with a deadbolt on the inside and a key lock on the outside. He gave one key to Far End. "However many keys they had made, I wouldn't have known," he said. Ainsworth didn't know how many copies of the key the various bands that used the third floor had for that door, either, but they did not have keys to the door at the top of the stairs, which led to the foyer with the two offices and a washroom. Ainsworth believed the former "Suite 2" tenant, Net Difference, had returned its key when it moved out in March 2011.

Ainsworth said he went to work at his print shop, Printing Plus, on July 6, 2011, at around eleven a.m. His employee left around five p.m., and he was working on a challenging project when his friend, Anthony Shaw, stopped by at around six. "I recruited him to help save my sanity," said Ainsworth. His computer was "glitching left, right, and centre," he explained, and Shaw was computer savvy. While they were working, they heard the noises upstairs. "I could tell it was coming from Far End's space," Ainsworth said. He described an initial thump, a slight lag, and then eight or ten thumps, like "rapid fire." "It was quick." The sounds were "stationary," and seemed to be coming from Richard Oland's desk area, he said. "It didn't sound like someone was thumping directly on the floor." He said it sounded as though something was "in between the floor and what was being thumped on."

Ainsworth said he had soundproofed his shop so the equipment wouldn't bother his tenants, and he rarely heard noises coming from upstairs. But the former tenant, Net Difference, had an employee whose children would run around, "thundering back and forth, full tilt" for ten to fifteen minutes, he said. The noises on July 6 lasted only about ten seconds. "It may seem like it should have been a concerning noise," he acknowledged, but it wasn't "outstanding in the sense that it wasn't prolonged." He did not hear any yelling or screaming, he noted. "Comparatively, it's not disconcerting," he said. He and Shaw "just kind of looked at each other," and when the noises stopped, they continued working.

Veniot asked Ainsworth what time he heard the noises. He said it was sometime before what he described as a Persian-looking, "olive-skinned" man came in to have a document faxed. The document was scanned and emailed at 8:11 p.m., his computer records showed. Ainsworth said he initially told police he thought the noises occurred about thirty to forty-five minutes before the customer came in, but he testified there was "nothing definitive about it." He "wasn't paying a lot of attention to anything," he stressed. He was preoccupied with the project he was working on; he described it as "tunnel vision to the issue at hand." All he could say for sure, he told the court, was that it was sometime between six and eight. He and Shaw left together at around nine.

Anthony Shaw told the court he often stops by to visit Ainsworth at Printing Plus after work. On July 6, he arrived at around six. He described hearing "a loud crash and then many thumping sounds," "maybe eight or ten repeated sounds," coming from Oland's office. The sounds were "loud and unusual." But "it was swift, quick," he said, estimating the noise only lasted about ten to fifteen seconds. Shaw said he and Ainsworth stopped working and looked at each other, "kind of thinking 'What's going on?'" But then the noises stopped, and they kept working.

Shaw said he had been to Printing Plus many times and never heard any unusual noises before. Veniot asked why he didn't do anything when he heard the noises that night, quickly adding, "I'm not blaming you, sir." Shaw said he owns a similar brick building, and when he investigated a noise complaint from a tenant one day, he found another tenant putting together furniture. He figured it was something similar — someone "maybe arranging furniture, hanging a picture," he said. It sounded like someone hammering a nail or banging a wall, he said. Shaw said he did not hear any voices arguing, and he did not hear any other noises before they left at around nine. He didn't notice anything unusual going on outside in front of the building during several cigarette breaks he took that evening, either, he said. "I've since quit," he added, prompting laughter. The noises occurred sometime before eight, he said, when a man in his mid-twenties, whom he described as Saudi or Iranian, came in to have a document faxed. Shaw estimated it was between seven thirty and seven forty-five.

The defence also wanted the jury to believe the sounds Ainsworth and Shaw heard were Oland being murdered, but that the noises occurred between seven thirty and eight, after Dennis Oland was already gone. Gold and Miller reminded the witnesses during cross-examination that when they spoke to police at the scene on the morning of July 7, they both estimated the timing of the noises at around eight.

Gold asked Ainsworth if he connected the noises he heard to the murder when he learned of Oland's death. Ainsworth said he had. "I tried to figure out the time realizing how critical it probably was." Gold said Constable Davidson's notes from the scene indicate Ainsworth told him he heard "stomping five to six times on floor" at eight p.m.

Justice Walsh gave the jury a refresher crash course on hearsay evidence. What Davidson wrote in his notes about what other people told him was hearsay, he stressed. The jurors must consider only the courtroom testimony of Ainsworth and Shaw as evidence, not Davidson's notes. Ainsworth testified he didn't remember what he told the officer, but he believed he probably said, "I think it was eight p.m."

"Were you not trying to be as truthful and accurate as possible?" asked Gold.

"I put a time out there, but the certainty was pretty negligible," Ainsworth replied.

On July 7, during his official statement to police, Ainsworth put the time as being approximately thirty to forty-five minutes before the fax customer came in. So "it could well have been between seven thirty and eight, you're just not 100 per cent sure?" Gold persisted. Ainsworth refused to endorse the later time frame as being accurate. He repeated it was sometime between six and eight. "After that, I'm not sure."

According to the defence, the first time Ainsworth suggested the noises occurred between six and eight was at the preliminary inquiry on August 20, 2014; "I initially was trying to frame or trying to pinpoint the time. But in actuality it was just a wild guess because I really wasn't paying that much attention," he had testified. "Time frame was it happened somewhere between, say, six and eight. That's the real time frame."

Gary Miller had challenged his preliminary-inquiry testimony during cross-examination. "So that very next morning, after the police come and ask you about that, you tell Constable Davidson that it was around eight o'clock, correct? That's what you told him at that time, yes or no?"

"Yeah, that was a guesstimate at the time, that's right," Ainsworth replied.

"And then you went to the police station later that same morning — I think it was some time around eleven o'clock or so. You accompanied the police, or you went down to the station. And Constable Shannon took a statement from you at that time?"

"Yeah."

"And at that time you told him: 'Sometime about an hour before we left, which I think was around nine o'clock. That's like when we left. I heard some shuffling.' So again that same morning you told Constable Don Shannon that you thought it was an hour before you left, which was at nine o'clock."

"Yeah. Emphasize 'thought.'"

Miller noted Shaw was questioned at the scene in the presence of Ainsworth and also estimated the time of the noises to be around eight p.m. He asked if Ainsworth had corrected Shaw when he heard him tell Stephen Davidson that "it was around eight-ish." "Did I? No. I don't know. You got a record of me interrupting or not?" Ainsworth asked.

A private investigator working for the defence questioned Ainsworth on July 27, 2011, and Miller asked Ainsworth about his responses. "And would you agree with me, sir, at that time, when you gave him that statement, he asked you what time you heard the noise, and you told him 'Around seven forty-five; about an hour before we left someone came into the office to get things done?'"

"Yeah. Again, I thought it was that time, yeah."

"You thought it was that time?"

"Mmm hmm."

"So back in July [2011] you say it was around seven forty-five —"

"I'm trying to make you understand it was never definitive relative to how I expressed it," Ainsworth said.

"Right, but it was an approximation, and the approximation —"

"Not definitive."

"— was around —"

"Not definitive."

"— eight o'clock."

"Not definitive."

"And was it made apparent to you that based on your and Mr. Shaw's statement that the noises were around eight o'clock, that it was not helpful to the police case against our client?" Miller asked.

"Not at all. What was that? Rephrase that."

"Did anybody —"

"No."

"— tell you —"

"No."

"— that the fact that you and Mr. Shaw had heard this—"

"Not that I'm aware of."

"— that the noise was around eight—"

"No."

"— or seven forty-five—"

"No."

"— that that did not help the police case?"

"No, no, wasn't aware of that."

"Were you aware of that?"

"Not aware of it."

"You weren't aware of that?"

"No."

Ainsworth said he was less helpful when police came back to talk to him in September 2011 "'cause I realized the fact that I really didn't know what time that was...and I felt guilty about it."

"When you were feeling guilty about saying that you heard the noises around eight-ish, you did not call the police to correct that, did you, sir? Yes or no?"

"Well, no."

Ainsworth was subsequently questioned again by the private investigator.

"And at that time, back in the fall in October of 2011, again under oath, when you were asked when you heard the noises, you said it was around seven forty-five, didn't you, sir? Seven thirty, seven forty-five-ish is what you said at that time, wasn't that correct sir?"

"I didn't say it was definitive."

Miller questioned Stephen Davidson at the trial about the notes he took regarding his conversation with Ainsworth on July 7. Ainsworth "didn't describe it as a 'guesstimate'?" Miller asked. "Not to my recollection," Davidson replied. Miller suggested police considered the noises "serious." He noted Davidson had checked the clock on the Printing Plus equipment to ensure the time-stamp was accurate, and he made several unsuccessful attempts to identify and locate the fax customer off and on for about ten months, including contacting the school in British Columbia where the fax was sent. Davidson also followed up in 2013 on information that the business located next to Richard Oland's might have been moving on July 6, 2011. But it turned out Net Difference had already moved out by then.

"The long and short of it, Constable Davidson, is that you followed up on these noises... quite thoroughly?"

"Yes, that's correct," Davidson replied.

The defence felt the time estimates of the noises posed a problem for the Crown's case. They had time-stamped security video of Oland with his wife at Cochran's Country Market in Rothesay at 7:38 p.m. — before the Printing Plus customer's document was faxed, and about an hour after Oland told police he left his father's office. Cochran's, located on Hampton Road, is at least a fifteen-minute drive away from 52 Canterbury Street, according to Google Maps. Witnesses had seen Oland make the stop at the wharf, and he also stopped at home and went upstairs to change, his wife told police.

In the video, Oland is wearing a change of clothes — shorts and a short-sleeved shirt — instead of the pants and jacket he wore during his meeting with his father. He appears relaxed as he shops for samosas, bananas, and other groceries, and chats with his aunt Jane Toward (Richard Oland's sister), who is also in the store. Another, earlier video (also time-stamped 7:38 p.m.), shows Oland and his wife shopping at Kennebecasis Drugs for cold medicine. Justice Walsh gave the jurors a mid-trial instruction on the security videos. He said it was up to them to decide what person, place, or thing was, or was not, portrayed in the videos and how much weight to give the images in their deliberations.

Could Oland have gone from being the enraged killer described by the Crown — who savagely delivered forty-five blows to his father's body, shattering his skull — to nonchalant shopper in such a short period of time? the defence asked. Miller went one step further and suggested during his cross-examination of Davidson that the videos served as his client's alibi. "If John Ainsworth and Anthony Shaw heard noises [coming from Richard Oland's Saint John office] between seven thirty p.m. and eight p.m., and the noises were the killing of Richard Oland, then Dennis Oland could not have done it?" Miller put to Davidson. Prosecutor Veniot promptly objected. "Sustained," said Justice Walsh.

He admonished Miller, describing his comments as improper. It will be up to the jury to decide, within the context of all of the other evidence, Walsh stressed. (If the cellphone pinging off the·Rothesay tower at 6:44 meant it had already been taken out of uptown Saint John, it was, of course, questionable whether any noises after that would have been the sound of murder.)

The defence also presented evidence suggesting Dennis Oland was not the last person to see his father alive. They noted Richard Oland had asked his secretary to leave the air conditioner on when she was getting ready to leave for the day. He told her he was going to be there a while. Oland had a lot of catching up to do after being away for much of the previous two months and may have been planning to work late, they said. The inbox was quite full, Maureen Adamson had agreed.

Robert McFadden confirmed under cross-examination by Alan Gold that it was not unusual for Oland to stay at the office later than five thirty p.m., when they usually left. If there was something Oland wanted to get done, either Oland stayed, or he asked McFadden to stay. If McFadden hadn't had his son with him that day, he might have had to stay later, Gold suggested. "I more likely would have stayed later, yes," McFadden replied.

Ainsworth had testified he rarely saw Oland work nights or weekends. Oland "didn't make a habit of sticking around" past six thirty because it was, as he put it, "so bloomin' loud" when bands practised on the third floor that "it was like being in a rock concert." "If it was something super critical, he might brave it," Ainsworth said. But Gold argued no bands were practising on July 6. "For all you know, he could have been working late that night?" he asked. He could have been, Ainsworth agreed.

The defence also highlighted the forensic toxicology results from the autopsy. Oland had a "low" amount of alcohol in his urine — 23 mg/dl. "The low concentration of ethyl alcohol in post-mortem urine along with negative ethyl alcohol findings in post-mortem blood and vitreous humour [the clear gel that fills the space between the lens and the retina of the eyeball] indicates alcohol consumption several hours prior to death," the two-page report by Dr. Albert Fraser states.

Gold converted that amount to the more common measurement of milligrams of alcohol per millilitres of blood, which is used in impaired driving cases. It would be the equivalent of 25.8 mg/100 mL, he suggested, noting that a reading over eighty milligrams would result in an impaired driving offence. "I'm not saying [the amount of alcohol in his urine is] large enough to represent a weekend in Vegas," said Gold, but he suggested the initial amount would have been higher, given the normal elimination process and whatever Oland might have urinated away prior to his death. The pathologist who conducted the autopsy, Dr. Ather Naseemuddin, however, pointed out Gold's calculation was for a blood alcohol reading. Oland's was in his urine, he said, stressing the distinction. At the preliminary inquiry, the Crown had presented evidence to suggest the decomposition process can endogenously produce alcohol, but this was not raised at trial.

Oland's secretary previously testified under cross-examination by Gary Miller that Oland didn't keep any alcohol in the office, other than an old can of Alpine in the office fridge, and she didn't think he'd left the office at all that day. Oland's associate, Robert McFadden, didn't think Oland had left the office all day either, but he also couldn't be certain, because he had stepped out for approximately fifteen minutes to go to the bank. He, too, testified no alcohol was kept in office, and he never saw Oland drink alcohol in the office. He said he did, however, on occasion arrive at work to find wine glasses in the office.

twelve

MOTIVE

I was aware of her."

Robert McFadden was speaking of Richard Oland's mistress, Diana Sedlacek. Crown prosecutor P.J. Veniot, having suggested in his opening statement that the pair's adulterous relationship played a role in the murder, had just asked McFadden what he knew about her. The jury had seen Dennis's videotaped statement to police, in which he told Stephen Davidson he was worried "people might be finding out" about the affair and asked McFadden, his father's "right-hand man" and "the guy who's closest to him," to talk to him.

McFadden confirmed the private conversation. He said it took place about a year and a half before the murder, when he was helping Dennis with his divorce. "He sort of said that he had a matter to talk to me about." According to McFadden, Dennis said he had "become aware of Diana, and should I have the occasion to suggest to his father it was getting out and to cool it, to take that opportunity." McFadden said he nodded in response but never passed along Dennis's concerns. "The opportunity never came up," he testified. "Richard was careful" and "never made me aware of [the affair] directly. There was never an opportunity I could say, 'Your family knows about this,' so I didn't."

But it was no secret Oland was having an affair, McFadden added. Airline tickets and texts on Oland's iPhone proved Sedlacek was more than just "Dick's friend." It wasn't difficult, he said, to "follow the money" and "figure out what was going on." McFadden's choice of words was particularly apt. The Crown was arguing that two factors comprised Dennis Oland's motive for murder: one was his anger over his father's adulterous relationship and his determination to see that relationship end before it became common knowledge, and the other was his mounting financial problems. As early as his police statement, Dennis Oland had suggested Sedlacek as a viable suspect in his father's killing. His lawyers at one point floated this idea but later seemed to abandon it, implying instead that Sedlacek's husband might have played a role. For the second, more substantial motive, the defence used the testimony of the Crown's own witnesses to counter every assertion the prosecution made about Oland's debts and his father's responses to his financial difficulties, arguing that Oland's precarious financial situation long preceded his father's murder, and denying that Richard Oland had ever expressed concern or anger about Dennis's difficulties.

The courtroom was full on November 10. Although prosecutors refused to divulge their list of witnesses or the order in which they would be called, word had gotten out: the mistress was set to testify. Sedlacek swept through the front doors of the courthouse looking like Jackie Onassis, a black, white, and grey shawl draped loosely around her head, large dark sunglasses hiding her eyes. In a tailored black pantsuit she sashayed past the extra chairs sheriff's deputies had set at the back of the courtroom to accommodate the large crowd, and she perched herself in the witness box. Veniot asked if she had moved outside New Brunswick. "That is correct," the former real estate agent replied coolly. He didn't ask where, but her Facebook page identifies her current city as Victoria, British Columbia.

Sedlacek said she had been in a "romantic relationship" with Oland for "very close to" eight years. Veniot asked if she was married at the time. "Legally married, at the time, correct," she said; contrary to what Sedlacek might have meant to imply, she was living with her husband throughout the affair, and the couple did not separate until after the murder. She said she saw Oland about three times a week, "fairly frequently" at his Far End Corporation office. "Often after church on Sunday, we would pop in there for a bit," she told the riveted crowd. "He was very interested in wanting to share his week with me, show me what he had done, ask me questions about what he should do." At Veniot's request she described the office layout, adding extra details—the french doors with curtains, old-fashioned water heater, the number of computer monitors—that made clear her familiarity with the space.

They also travelled together "many times," and were planning a trip to Portland, Maine, just before his death, she said. The jury had already heard that investigators discovered entries on Oland's electronic calendar for the weeks following his death: Oland had identified them as trips A, B, and C. Maureen Adamson, who knew about other entries—such as a five-day service appointment for his BMW in Moncton, an hors d'oeuvre luncheon at the Union Club, and when a particular senator would be in town—in a schedule so full his "free" time slots were marked, said she had "no idea what they were." Oland must have entered them himself, she said, either typing them on his computer or downloading them from his iPhone, although Adamson would on occasion make travel arrangements that included Sedlacek. The entries were made at 4:42 p.m. on July 6, 2011, Adamson had said, less than an hour before Dennis showed up at the office, and she left the two of them alone together.

Sedlacek, sounding increasingly confident as she grew accustomed to having all eyes locked on her, said she and Oland had been texting on July 6, 2011, about possible travel dates, discussing whether to leave on July 11, 15, or 20. The jury had already heard about the texts, too. Oland's iPhone was never recovered, but it had been connected to his office computer on July 6, and the data on it had been backed up. The Crown had entered into evidence two pages of the chat log from July 5 and July 6, 2011, extracted by RCMP tech crime forensic analyst Neil Walker. Veniot asked Walker to read the messages between Oland and Sedlacek aloud for the courtroom, as Connie Oland looked on. "Kisses Snuggle me up I need your body," Sedlacek wrote on July 5 at 9:02 p.m. "Snuggle up kkk in bed," Oland replied seventeen minutes later. (K was their code for kisses, the court would later hear.)

Sedlacek had since upgraded her cellphone, she said, but had downloaded the information from her old one. She still had text messages and phone call history between her and Oland, the courtroom heard. Veniot led her through the events of July 6. She said she got up, showered, ate breakfast, and texted Oland. Veniot moved to submit five pages of text messages downloaded from Sedlacek's cellphone into evidence, and the judge ordered a mid-morning recess. A female sheriff's deputy escorted Sedlacek during the break. When court resumed, each juror had copies of the messages from July 6 and July 7, 2011.

At 9:08 a.m. on the last day of Oland's life, Sedlacek messaged, "Morning Lixxxx on Goldn Gun. Drvn 2gym — Did Zu find note? — re Our Trip." Asked by Veniot to explain the first part of her message, she replied briskly, "It's a term of endearment," provoking a few muffled snickers from the public gallery. Less than a minute later, Oland, who was at home with his wife and her visiting family, responded, "Have in [office] just up kkk." She replied, "Kissssss wen U get ther text it — mmm kisss." Sedlacek drove to the gym and missed a call from Oland. "Sorry love in spin class," she texted, "phones not allowed 2 noisy w music Kissss." She showered and went to a Shoppers Drug Mart and a Sobeys grocery store. He texted back at 12:01 p.m.

"3 options all ex St. Stephen nb. Option 1 lv am jul 11 return jul 15 11.00 am Option 2 lv 15 pm return pm 3.00 jul 19 Option 3 lv jul 20. At 4.00 pm return 24th All should be 4 nites would prefer option 2 or 3." Sedlacek said she was driving at the time and pulled over to the side of the road to reply. "I agree 2 or 3 let me think," she replied. At 1:57 p.m., she wrote, "Let's leave at Noon on Fri 15th [so] we can arrive early enough in Portland — So leave 15th come back on 19th. Kisses." It's unclear whether Oland ever read that final text message, the courtroom heard. Neil Walker testified that as of 4:44 p.m., he had not. That's when his iPhone was disconnected from his computer, and there's no log of what happened after that, Walker said.

At 6:44 p.m. on July 6, Sedlacek texted Oland, "U there??" She tried calling before sending another text at 7:19 p.m. "You've turned your phone off!! Why!!!!!!??????? Your not at office & don't tell me U hav a 'Bus' mtg cause U don't — So tell the fucking truth!!! Cause I'm sitting here not doing suspicious things & I hav a lot of men who would love 2 b with me !!!!!! Do stop this fucking around! And answer the damn phone! I wil call at your house." Sedlacek attempted to explain this message. "We were always teasing each other," she said, but defence lawyer Alan Gold objected, and Veniot instructed her to stick to the texts.

Sedlacek said she believed Oland's phone had been turned off, because when she tried to call, it went immediately to voicemail. She tried calling repeatedly that night from her home on Darlings Island, she said, which is about a thirty-minute drive from Oland's office. She could not remember how many times she tried calling; she lost count. Veniot asked if she was expecting a call back. She "absolutely" was, she said. He asked if they had a pattern or routine. Yes, when called or texted, "I had to respond within a period of time," she said, without elaborating. (Sedlacek had told police she contacted Oland every day at 6:30 p.m., "and he always answered," but the jury didn't hear about that statement because Veniot didn't ask Sedlacek about it.)

At 11:12 p.m. she wrote: "Pathetic!"

The timeline of Sedlacek's efforts to reach Oland was important to the prosecutors. Oland's not responding to any texts or calls after 6:44 p.m. supported the Crown's theory he was already dead.

When Sedlacek still hadn't heard from Oland by the next morning, she was even more annoyed. She drove by his office on her way to a hair appointment at a nearby salon and saw his BMW parked in its usual spot. "What the hell is going on with you?????????" she texted at 9:37 a.m. During her appointment, with still no response, she told the court, her impatience started to turn to panic. When she called his cellphone, it was "just dead...nothing." Calls to his office: just "ringing, no answer." She was "texting, calling, praying," she said.

After her appointment, she walked up the hill toward Oland's office and saw police outside. She said she told one of the uniformed officers she had an appointment to see Oland and was told no one was allowed inside. At some point, either before or after she spoke to the police (or both), she sent emails to Maureen Adamson and Robert McFadden but got no reply. By 12:52, she was frantic. "Richard why [are] the police at your office and car in lot — trying to reach everyone — What has happened PLEASE I [love] you God be with My Love — Praying praying." Then she saw Oland's car towed away. "I knew something horrible had happened," she said. "I didn't know what." Sedlacek, thinking he'd had a heart attack, called Oland's home to see if Connie knew what was going on; Dennis would later describe her as "yelling" at his mother over the phone. Sedlacek's call prompted Connie to call McFadden, and she learned that her husband was dead. Sedlacek said it was later that day when she found out Oland was dead. "Somebody had said something to me," she said.

Sedlacek said she never told her husband, Jiri Sedlacek, about the affair. According to her, he only found out after Oland's death, when police questioned him. They were both at their Darlings Island home on the evening of July 6, she said. The Crown called Jiri Sedlacek, eighty-seven years old. He shuffled unhurried up the courtroom aisle. He testified he met Richard and Connie Oland around 2003. The couples socialized together at each other's homes about eight to ten times over the years, along with other friends and acquaintances, he said. The former Bata Shoes senior executive enjoyed talking to Oland; he said he found Oland interesting and well travelled. He believed the last time he saw Oland was at Christmas mass in 2010. They shook hands, he said.

Prosecutor Patrick Wilbur asked Sedlacek about his whereabouts on July 6, 2011. He said he was at home, as he was most days. He had a six-acre property and large garden to tend. (He has since moved from Darlings Island to Hampton.) His wife was "absent" most of the day, he testified, but he believed she was home on the night of the murder. "What, if anything, did you have to do with the death of Richard Oland?" Wilbur asked. "Nothing," Sedlacek replied in a firm voice. He said he found out about the affair in October 2012, when his lawyer showed him a newspaper article that identified his wife as Oland's mistress (not when Saint John police interviewed him, as his former wife had testified). He had been out of the country at the time the affair became public through media reports, he said.

In his police interview, Dennis Oland had suggested that Diana Sedlacek might have reason to harm his father. "The only person that comes to mind is this supposed girlfriend, because she really seemed to be a whack job. Like, they call her the Dragon Lady. You know she's... this hostile... somebody who you think could be that *Fatal Attraction*–type person," he told police. The defence also tried to direct suspicion at

Sedlacek as a plausible alternate suspect early in the trial, suggesting that her relationship with Richard Oland had started to sour in the weeks leading up to the murder. On September 29 Alan Gold had introduced correspondence and phone calls between the pair, including a text she sent on July 4 at 11:20 a.m. "Richard Richard!!!!! It's 2 long now — Hate this waste of time!!!! You're always wasting OUR time OUR life." Two seconds later: "Where are U???? Are u not coming back 2day????" Then at 3:03 p.m.: "What's happening now? Are U here? Want 2C you." They had two brief chats, each lasting less than two minutes. Then Sedlacek started texting again at 5:56 p.m., sending two more texts before Oland responded with a call at 10:10 p.m. "So two days before the date we're all focused on [July 6], it took him over four hours from her first message to respond," Gold noted.

The next day, it was "essentially eight or nine hours before Richard Oland gets back to her after she starts messaging him," he said. The RCMP computer expert, Neil Walker, agreed Oland was "not prompt" in responding during that forty-eight-hour period, based on the extracted data, but suggested Oland might have deleted some of his messages so they wouldn't be seen "at home." Gold countered that Oland retained other intimate messages that would have been good candidates to delete, and Walker agreed.

Sedlacek might have maintained that most of Richard Oland's family knew about the relationship, but Oland attempted to conceal the affair, argued Gold. He noted Oland listed Sedlacek's number under three different names in his iPhone contacts list: Office Jones, Office One Dr. Jones, and Diana Sedlacek. Her photo was not associated with any of them, Gold pointed out; Oland used a photo of three male friends. If you're a married man having an affair, you don't want your mistress's picture popping up, he said.

Gold asked Robert McFadden if Oland's phone habits started to change just prior to his death and whether he had started ignoring calls and letting them go to voicemail. McFadden confirmed he had noticed that. Gold also asked McFadden if Sedlacek's messages in this period included words to the effect of *stop wasting our time, leave your wife, let's start our new life*. Veniot objected, arguing it was hearsay, and Walsh asked the jurors to leave for a few minutes while he discussed the issue with the lawyers. When the jurors were called back fifteen minutes later, Walsh told them to "ignore" what they had just heard about Sedlacek wanting Oland to leave his wife. He said Sedlacek would be called as a witness later, and Gold should put the question to her directly.

But in a surprise move, the defence chose not to cross-examine Diana Sedlacek. Although the jury never heard about it, a polygraph test indicated that she told the truth when she said she was at home with her husband at the time of Oland's death, which may have prompted the defence to abandon the idea of her as a suspect. Instead, Gold grilled her former husband. Gold argued it was difficult to believe Jiri Sedlacek didn't know about an eight-year affair, particularly when his wife went away on trips with Oland, and suggested it was a good motive for murder. He asked Sedlacek if he would have been furious if he'd learned, in 2011, that his wife of twenty-four years was cheating on him. "Probably I would have been very upset," replied Sedlacek. "I was married to that lady." But he insisted he never even suspected the affair.

"If you had something to do with Richard Oland's death, would you come to court and tell the jury you did? Of course not!" Gold retorted. He demanded to know if police asked Sedlacek for his bank records to see if there was any large cash withdrawal, implying that Sedlacek may have hired someone to get rid of his wife's lover. No, said Sedlacek. Nor had they asked him for his phone records or the GPS on his vehicle. The "sum extent of the police investigation" of Jiri Sedlacek, Gold argued, was to speak to him twice and ask him his whereabouts on July 6. Sedlacek said he believed that was true. He had nothing to do with Oland's death, he maintained.

The Crown contended that Dennis Oland simmered with resentment over his father's extramarital affair, but that it was not the real source of his stress. Oland's increasingly dire financial situation was a central part of the Crown's circumstantial case against him. Although it isn't essential to prove motive, prosecutors were confident the money trail would lead to a conviction.

Throughout the trial, the prosecutors called several witnesses who could lend credence to their theory. Maureen Adamson testified on the first day of the trial that Richard Oland was very much in control of his money. He used various firms, including CIBC Wood Gundy, to handle his estimated $36 million in investments, but he made his own decisions about buying and selling stocks, she said. He kept the TV in the office tuned to financial news all day and real-time global market activity running on at least three of the six computer monitors at his desk. He also used e-trade to do some of his own transactions. Oland, as she put it at the preliminary inquiry, "wanted to know where every penny was." He tracked his spending at home and at work. Coded spreadsheets for expenses such as groceries, travel, and car repairs showed him exactly how much he spent in each category.

Adamson testified that she was aware of Dennis Oland's debt to his father. Dennis paid the monthly interest by post-dated cheque, which she deposited. (Although Veniot had told the jury in his opening statement the interest amount was $1,667, Adamson, in her exacting manner, specified it was actually $1,666.67—which totalled exactly $20,000 a year.) Dennis Oland usually sent the cheques in batches of eight to twelve at a time, and she typically deposited them on the fifteenth of each month. In April 2011 his last batch ran out. On May 24, Adamson sent Dennis a reminder email.

"Dennis: Your monthly cheques have run out (I didn't have one for this month). Could you pls send some again for deposit." Within about an hour, he responded. "Ok, and when u say u don't have one for this month u mean May correct?" "Right," Adamson replied. "I did not have one for May—just a reminder." On June 20 she emailed again to ask if he'd sent over an envelope of cheques. Oland replied promptly that he had, either two weeks earlier or at the beginning of the preceding week. Adamson didn't remember seeing the cheques, but Canada Post was on strike at the time, and she assumed they were in the mail. Oland said he would deliver new ones if nothing turned up in the next couple of days. "Not me rushing you, Dennis," Adamson replied. "We'll see how the mail goes and then go from there."

On June 28, she emailed again to let him know the cheques had arrived. He asked if she could wait until the following Monday, July 4, to deposit the first one, even though by this time he had already missed his May and June payments. Adamson agreed. "Okay — I'll wait until Monday." Adamson testified she didn't deposit the cheque until Tuesday, July 5. Not until sometime "after Mr. Oland's passing" the cheque came back marked NSF, for not sufficient funds, she said. Adamson's testimony suggested that Richard Oland was likely unaware that his son's cheque had bounced, but Dennis Oland's financial records showed the rejected payment appeared in his chequing account on July 5, so Dennis could have known about the returned cheque when he went to his father's office on July 6.

The Crown also called Robert McFadden. Richard Oland and McFadden met in 1980-81 when McFadden, a chartered accountant, was seconded from the firm Coopers & Lybrand to be the financial officer for Oland's Canada Games project. McFadden later worked for McCain Foods and Baxter Foods and left a promising position at the latter company when Oland recruited him to work at Brookville Transport. McFadden remained at Brookville after Oland sold the company in 1997, and after the new owners terminated him, he successfully sued for breach of contract.

He began working for himself, handling mergers and acquisitions for various clients while continuing to do some per diem work for Oland. By 2006, "for all intents and purposes, [Oland] consumed all of my available time," said McFadden, and he moved into the Far End office. McFadden said he sat at the end of the folding laminate-top table in the middle of the office for "a long time" — years. But Oland eventually shifted around some of his stacks of boxes, each one filled with records, and McFadden got his own room at the back of the office.

McFadden helped Oland with everything from preparing his taxes and setting up his computer systems and a syncing program for his iPhone to dealing with suppliers and contractors around the world for Oland's new custom-designed, Spanish-built sailboat. There was no typical day, said McFadden. Every day was different, and "they were often very interesting days."

McFadden had given a statement to police on the morning Oland's body was discovered, when he "had a sense there was foul play," as he put it. Veniot asked whether he was approached by police about providing a DNA sample.

"Yes, I was," he said.

"Did you do so?"

"No, I didn't."

"I'm not going to ask you why, sir," said Veniot. Police covertly obtained a DNA sample from him on December 29, 2012, by following him and seizing a straw he used at an East Side Mario's restaurant.

Two money managers at CIBC Mellon in Toronto handled the lion's share of Oland's investment portfolio, McFadden said. He also had some money with Wellington West and a small percentage — a few million — through his son at CIBC Wood Gundy. McFadden also had some RRSPs through Dennis, whom he had known since 1995, the court heard. Like Adamson, McFadden knew about the money Dennis owed his father. He had helped broker the arrangement in 2008-09, he said. Dick, McFadden said, provided a total of $538,000 to his son: $120,000 for the cash settlement of marital property, $303,000 to settle the mortgage on the family homestead, and $115,000 to cover a line of credit. His other company, Kingshurst Estates, also subsequently purchased the adjacent "farm," where the stables are located, he said. Oland had wanted to "formalize" the loan with a mortgage and the first right to buy the home in the event his son no longer lived there, said McFadden. Oland also wanted his son to enter into a "domestic contract" with his then significant other, Lisa Andrik, who went on to become his second wife. None of that happened, said McFadden. Instead, Dennis Oland provided "notes" to document the loan and in September 2009 started making monthly interest-only payments of $1,666.67 on the $500,000 identified as a "mortgage," said McFadden.

Veniot asked McFadden about the life insurance meeting Richard Oland had on the morning of July 6. McFadden said the two men were "peddling" life insurance, hoping to sell Oland a new policy. His existing policy was up for renewal in the "foreseeable future," McFadden explained, and Oland was willing to go through the medical tests to see if he could get a better rate. No evidence was presented about what might have changed under a new policy, but his investment firm, Far End Corporation, was the beneficiary of the existing policy. Oland was the sole owner and lone director of Far End, as well as a real estate company, Kingshurst Estates Limited, both subsidiaries of a numbered company he also fully owned. After his death, his estate held the shares of the companies.

"The executors of the estate appointed new directors of each of the companies," McFadden testified. He and Dennis Oland were the co-executors of the estate, and they appointed themselves as the new directors. Within days of his father's violent death, Dennis Oland became president of his main holding company and secretary of the two subsidiaries. McFadden became the secretary and treasurer of the numbered company and president and treasurer of the two subsidiaries.

A handwritten to-do list found on McFadden's desk at the Far End office had "will" as the sixth and final item. The list was dated July 4, two days before the multimillionaire's slaying. "It was a recurring event," McFadden testified, although the existing will dated back to 1996. "Once in a while he'd say, 'Let's revisit the will.'" Oland had just come back from a fishing trip and was pretty "mellow," he added. The other items on the to-do list included filing the corporation's tax return, negotiating a lease for a new office, dealing with Oland's life insurance policy, and matters related to Oland's sailboats. The terms of the existing will were "relatively simple," said McFadden. Oland's house in Rothesay, along with all of the furniture and fixtures, were to go to his widow, Connie. After his funeral was paid for and his debts settled, any assets realized and the corporations were to be transferred to a spousal trust. Connie would receive income from the residual. And if that was "insufficient," she could receive more money from the capital, at the discretion of the trustees — McFadden and Dennis. Upon Connie's death, the trust would dissolve and the three Oland children would share the residual estate equally. McFadden said Richard Oland wanted to set up an auction process for "his stuff," where survivors could pick items they wanted. He was also interested in setting up a family trust, as some of his wealthy friends had done, which would offer some tax advantages, McFadden said.

The Crown began pushing the money motive in earnest in the eighth week of the trial. The junior prosecutor, Derek Weaver, who had taken the lead with the technology experts, called banking and accounting experts to provide sensational details of Oland's financial problems. Weaver submitted a binder containing hundreds of pages of financial documents obtained from CIBC. The jurors were each given a copy, adding to the numerous exhibits and personal notes they were already balancing on their laps and tucking under their seats. "I don't know how you're doing, ladies and gentlemen, with no desk, because I'm full up here," said Justice Walsh. The court eventually provided a large shelving unit where jurors could store their documents.

Michelle Lefrancois worked at CIBC in personal banking and handled some of Dennis Oland's loan applications. When someone wanted to borrow money, she would ask for proof of income, run a credit history check, prepare a statement of assets and liabilities, and send it all off to the underwriters, she said. If the loan was approved, she would then meet with the client to complete the paperwork.

On August 9, 2010, less than a year after receiving the $538,000 bailout from his father, Oland borrowed $75,000 from CIBC, at an interest rate of prime plus 0.5 per cent, said Lefrancois. It was what the bank called a "home power" line of credit, secured against his Rothesay home, the same property he had already refinanced with his father. Seven months later, on March 8, 2011, Oland applied to increase his line of credit to $163,000. "Because he had the equity, we could make that change," she said. Any amount up to 80 per cent of a home's value is allowed; Oland's home was valued at approximately $650,000.

Weaver asked Lefrancois what Oland had portrayed as his assets and liabilities to get approval. She was trying to remember when Alan Gold objected. The jurors left the courtroom so Justice Walsh and the legal teams could hash out the issue. The Crown was clearly questioning whether Oland had disclosed to CIBC his true financial situation, including his substantial debt to his father, when applying for money from the bank. McFadden had previously testified no contract between father and son was ever signed, presumably meaning there was no public record of that debt for CIBC to check when approving Dennis Oland's line of credit, and thus his home appeared to be mortgage-free. Gold told the judge the defence had looked through the disclosure material from the Crown very carefully and did not find any lists of assets and liabilities provided to the bank to obtain the line of credit—an "obviously important" issue, he noted.

Walsh concluded that, in the absence of supporting documents, he could not allow Weaver to question Lefrancois about what Oland told her about his assets and liabilities. When the proceedings resumed, Weaver dropped the question and moved on to ask Lefrancois about the NSF, or bounced, cheques. She said some clients have discretionary overdraft limit privileges, as long as their account has enough money to cover the cheque within fifteen days. Oland had lost his overdraft privileges, she said. He exceeded his $163,000 limit by $481.02 on June 9, 2011. On June 30, his payment was rejected for not sufficient funds.

June was also when Oland requested an advance on his pay, the court heard from his former supervisor, John Travis, CIBC Wood Gundy branch manager and one of roughly twenty-five financial advisers. Travis had known the Olands most of his life. He'd worked for Richard Oland at Brookville, considered him a mentor, and was a witness to his will. Financial advisers are paid through commissions on trades and fees for portfolio management, said Travis. He estimated Dennis Oland's "book of business" was worth $200,000 to $300,000 in commissions and fees in 2011, "maybe more." But on June 1, Oland had emailed Travis, requesting an advance to carry him through a cash crunch. Travis read their email exchange aloud for the courtroom.

"Hi, I had a good chat with Dick [his father] yesterday and the timeline to see some funds flowing this way looks to have firmed up to the August/September time period. I also met with [redacted] last week and it looks like we'll begin the process of consolidating his assets here starting in September. We are looking at total new assets in the $10-$20m range. So things are progressing very well," Oland wrote. "In the meantime, it does look like I am going to struggle with cash for the next few months and as a result I wanted to revisit your offer to assist me to get through this crunch period." (Travis explained to the court during cross-examination he had asked Oland around May if he might need some help "in the current market environment," which he portrayed as lean.) "Summer is usually slower for me so I am a bit concerned," Oland's email continued. "From what I can see at this point in time, two months of financial help (June and July) would be very helpful and most likely all that is required. So, can we look at this to see what can be done to help me for two months? thanks."

"Dennis, I will look into this immediately," Travis replied. "This is great news re assets which we all know will lead to Revenue. Can you give me a brief outline of what you might require as assistance for the next couple of months. I have also copied Wilma, so she is in the loop." (Wilma Ditchfield was the regional director of eastern Canada and first vice-president.) Soon Travis emailed Oland: "Fyi, Wilma is on side we just need to be clear in the ask." The money was just an advance, Travis testified. Oland would have to pay it back over time, he said. When Weaver asked how, Travis replied that CIBC Wood Gundy would "review" it "going forward," but he did not elaborate.

"Well to cover costs I am looking at a minimum requirement of $7500 per month," Oland wrote. "The monthly expense breakdown is like this; I have $4300 spousal/child support payments, $1650 loan payments, plus cash needs for basic living expenses. The ideal amount would be $8500 as this would insure I keep all expenses paid up (general monthly expenses phone bill, power bill etc.) As I said I am grateful for any amount that can be provided. I do not require funds beyond this two months as August income will be fine based on July being a fee month. September is always a good month and then everything comes into place at that time with the new assets."

Later that same morning, as Oland awaited approval on a salary advance, he and his wife were scrambling to work around their maxed-out $27,000-limit Visas, as a string of emails submitted into evidence showed. The messages, discussing strategies for getting enough money deposited onto one of the credit cards to be able to use it, suggest mounting tension. Just weeks before the trial started, the defence fought to have the emails declared inadmissible by claiming spousal privilege. The Criminal Code protects spousal communications intercepted via a wiretap. Oland's lawyers argued that the Canada Evidence Act, "properly interpreted," extends spousal privilege to other forms of information, including emails and texts, which did not exist when either the Criminal Code or the Canada Evidence Act were created. Walsh ruled that he was bound by the Supreme Court's interpretation that "once a spousal communication is overheard or read by a third party or otherwise lawfully obtained by the police... there is no bar to its admission because of spousal privilege." Walsh also pointed out that "the legal trend" in Canada and England is away from recognizing spousal privilege at all, "or at least not giving it the prominence the defence would place upon it." He suggested Parliament would be the better body to determine if texts and emails should be protected.

The first message came from Lisa Andrik-Oland. "I should not have answered my phone earlier when u called, I cannot come across as pleasant cause I am not in a good place. Hannah [Oland's daughter] prob has flu, and I am very off today! Deadline for Concordia registration is today. I have no money on my visa and I had to wait til today to make a payment. If u add something to your card today will it work?"

"Well, I'd like to at least try something to make you feel a bit better," Oland replied. "As for visa card. Mine is overdrawn by $650, so I'd need to put more than that on the card just to get it to work. How much is your card over drawn?"

"I am $200 over limit and it won't reach them within 48 hrs. Internet does not work."

"Ok, well I'll go to the bank and deposit what I have and move funds to my Visa. I looked to see why my Visa was so bad and I had not realized the extent of the money that was spent for Montreal, it was $1350.00," he wrote.

"Wait now, I can't afford to put the rent check on your card, that's got mortgage etc. I plan on getting some money back from his father," she replied.

"Well [how] else [do] we get the Visa to work today?"

CIBC Wood Gundy agreed to give Oland a $16,000 advance; $8,000 per month for June and July, said Travis. But on June 14, Oland emailed Travis, saying he had received only "a bit more than $4000. Can you inquire why it is not $8000. Thanks. Dennis." "Leave it with [me] I will check to see what the calculations look like," Travis replied. "The calculation should work out to a net pay of $8000," wrote Dennis. "Thanks for taking the time to look into this for me." The next morning, Oland sent another email. "Hi John, I have attached a pay stub for your review, as you will see the pre-tax payment is $7682.27 with net after tax and other deductions coming out to a 'net net' of $4429.02. The 'net net' needs to be $8000. Thanks." At 2:32 p.m., Oland emailed again. "Hi John, I am becoming a bit nervous that this issue will not be resolved today. It is essential that the correct funds be placed into my bank account today so that I can honor my commitments that are due today. For example, my support payment is due today in the amount of $4230.00. Also due is a $1650.00 loan payment. Both items are deducted automatically from my bank account and I do not wish to have these bounce. Can you let me know the present status and provide assurances that this will be remedied today. thanks." Another email from the following morning, June 16, suggested that, despite Travis's assurances, it wasn't resolved that day. Travis told Oland the company would "process a top up asap... I will let you know when this is done."

Oland was less than honest with his wife about that money and his deteriorating financial situation, as the court learned through another email Weaver entered into evidence while she glowered from the front row. On June 16 Oland sent her an email, subject line "$$$," in which he represented the advance as earned income. He wrote: "Money is a bit tight this month. I had a good pay of $8000 but I need a bit more to cover expenses so that they do not bounce." He asked Andrik-Oland, who'd had shoulder surgery and wasn't working at the time, if she could get $1,000 from her line of credit for him to use.

By the following day, Oland's CIBC chequing account was $776.43 overdrawn, the Crown's next witness testified. Eric Johnson, a forensic accountant with Public Works and Government Services Canada since

1998, said the Saint John Police Force's then Inspector Glen McCloskey contacted his office in August 2011, seeking help with the investigation. Johnson, who previously worked for the New Brunswick Securities Commission and two accounting firms in Saint John, was asked by his manager to assist. He often works with RCMP on proceeds-of-crime cases, he said. Johnson looked at Dennis Oland's finances, including his main chequing account, CIBC Visa, line of credit, a collateral mortgage, investment account, and RRSP account, focusing primarily on the period between January 1, 2011, and July 7, 2011, the day Richard Oland's body was discovered, although he had records dating back several years. He prepared an Excel spreadsheet and PowerPoint presentation to help lead the court through the voluminous financial records he reviewed.

Dennis Oland's main CIBC chequing account had reached a negative balance of $1,622.38 by July 7. The account had overdraft protection of $2,000, but "rarely had a positive balance that lasted more than a month," Johnson wrote. "The balance spiked upward when his pay was deposited, but declined as funds were used to pay bills and other living costs." Between January and July 2011, a total of $102,835.93 was deposited into the account and $102,171.58 was withdrawn.

In 2009 Oland increased his Visa limit from $5,000 in January to $10,000 in February and $20,000 in May. In February 2011 he increased it again to $27,000. The card reached that limit on May 31, said Johnson. The RCMP extracted a deleted text message Oland had sent to his wife from his cellphone that day. "Hi, there is no money on my Visa Card anymore so don't bother trying to use it," he wrote. But Johnson's review showed Oland leaned heavily on cash advances from the maxed-out credit card in the days before his father was killed. He withdrew one hundred dollars per day on July 1, 2, and 3, and on July 6 he withdrew $401.50 twice. His balance reached $32,582.89 — $5,582.89 over his credit limit.

Oland also had a personal line of credit, which was separate from the home-backed line of credit, said Johnson. Oland had increased its limit from $15,000 in 2009 to $35,000 in February 2010. Then, in March 2011, when Oland was just shy of his limit, he used his newly increased secured line of credit to pay it off and to retire a $23,080.55 balance on his Visa, which quickly ballooned back up. Three months later, the $163,000 secured line of credit was also over its limit, said Johnson. On July 7, with the over-limit fee and interest charge applied, the balance stood at $163,939.68.

Oland's investments were essentially non-existent. On December 31, 2010, he had $13,676.15 in his CIBC Wood Gundy investment account, but on January 31, 2011, he withdrew almost all of it, leaving just $137.47 behind. His RRSP account had only one cent in it on January 31, 2011. On February 14, during tax season, Oland deposited $4,648.37 into the account, but three days later, he withdrew all but $20.13.

Meanwhile, Oland's income with CIBC was steadily dropping, Johnson found. In 2008 Oland earned about $180,000; in 2009, $110,000; and in 2010, $100,000. Between January 1, 2011, and July 7, 2011, Oland was paid $34,124, with his monthly income ranging between $2,026.68 and $9,450.61. He also appeared to have some rental income, but Johnson couldn't determine the source. (It was never mentioned in court, but Andrik-Oland owned an apartment building, according to her July 7, 2011, statement to police.) Based on the data he had, Johnson said Oland, who estimated his minimum monthly expenditures totalled $7,500, exceeded his income by $86,848 during that six-month period — about $14,000 per month. Despite his considerable debt, however, Oland continued to live well beyond his ability to pay. He spent more than $20,000 on three trips between November 2010 and April 2011, including twenty-three days in Hungary and Italy, eighteen days in England, and twelve days in Florida, the records showed.

In summary, on July 6, 2011, Dennis Oland owed $32,582.89 on his major credit card, $163,481.02 on his secured line of credit, and $16,000 for the advance on his pay. His chequing account, which was overdrawn on July 5, had a balance of $294.18 after he deposited a $650 rent cheque and $780 in cash. His investment account balance was zero, and his RRSP account had $20.13. He was also two months behind on the $1,666.67 payments to his father.

Oland's home had been mortgaged and remortgaged several times since the deed was transferred to him and his first wife on February 5, 1998, the land registry documents showed. The first mortgage was for $280,440. That increased to $307,500 in 2003, and $338,500 in 2006, before being discharged on June 3, 2009, with the loan from his father during his divorce settlement.

Even some of Oland's closest friends didn't know about this aspect of his life. When asked if he was aware of Oland's heavy debt load, friend and local businessman Larry Cain replied, "No, not particularly." Cain noted that in Oland's line of work, "your earnings fluctuate depending on the state of the market and all kinds of other economic conditions. And, you know, I think at the end of the day that Dennis had some debt, but he was managing." The defence took the same attitude and attempted to downplay the significance of Oland's financial squeeze, using the Crown's own witnesses.

The Crown characterized the $500,000 Richard Oland had given his son as a loan, but Robert McFadden testified that Oland viewed it as an advance on Dennis's eventual inheritance, and Adamson also believed this to be the case. The principal would be paid off from the inheritance Connie would eventually leave Dennis in her will, McFadden said. Lawyer Gary Miller argued that the $1,666.67 interest payment each month was only to be fair to the other heirs, Dennis Oland's two sisters. McFadden concurred. The amount, about 4 per cent, was similar to what Dennis Oland would have paid at a bank and similar to what Richard Oland would have made at a bank, he said. Oland did this voluntarily and was "perfectly willing to help his son," Gold suggested. Yes, McFadden replied.

Nor did Oland seem concerned when Dennis missed payments, Miller suggested. He pointed out that Adamson used the joint office email account to contact Dennis Oland about his post-dated cheques. Richard Oland would have had access to those emails and could have read them, said Miller. He asked Adamson if Oland was upset to learn that his son had missed payments for two consecutive months and apparently delayed providing a new batch of cheques. Had he told Adamson to get cheques from Dennis? No, Adamson said. Richard Oland did not micromanage those payments and wasn't complaining, she said. She had previously testified her boss rarely even inquired about the status of the interest payments — maybe once or twice over a couple of years. McFadden, too, confirmed that Oland did not express concern about his son falling behind in his payments. He pointed out that the monthly interest was the equivalent of the cost of a dinner on Oland's sailboat— "Not that big a deal." McFadden testified that he never saw any animosity, any anger, about the debt.

Gold also noted that it wasn't the first time Oland assisted his son financially. He helped him in 1998 when he bought his home and in 1999-2000 when he purchased the adjacent farm property, confirmed McFadden. That was the property later sold back to Richard Oland's real estate firm, Kingshurst Estates, as part of the $500,000 advanced to settle Dennis's divorce. Nor was this the first time Dennis fell behind in payments to his father. One of the $1,666.67 cheques bounced in July 2010, and in 2002 he had difficulty making an annual payment of around $10,000 on the mortgage for the farm property he'd purchased. Adamson confirmed that her boss hadn't stepped in when the interest payment bounced or seemed concerned about the mortgage. In that case, McFadden told the court, Oland simply added a year to the term of the 1999-2000 agreement. He wasn't upset? "It was refinanced," said McFadden. "He was open to modifying terms to accommodate Dennis Oland's financial situation?" Gold asked. "Yes," McFadden confirmed. Similarly, when Dennis Oland missed payments in 2007, 2008, and 2009, his father, Gold suggested, "cut him some slack." "He did," agreed McFadden.

"So Dennis Oland's financial situation in 2011 was another year in the life of a man who, since the turn of the century, had been getting help from his dad, right?" asked Gold.

"Correct," replied McFadden.

"Nice to have a Bank of Daddy, isn't it?" Gold commented glibly. But he overstepped when he suggested that "it cannot be said these were matters that bothered Mr. Oland," prompting Veniot to object. Gold rephrased to ask McFadden if he'd ever heard Oland express dissatisfaction. No, said McFadden.

Miller pointed out that Oland himself had experienced financial troubles during the "long, protracted" legal battle with his brother, Derek, over Moosehead shares. Brookville Transport was teetering on the verge of bankruptcy when he sold it (and subsequently went under).

In 2006, when the Moosehead split was settled, Richard Oland received a "substantial amount of money," said Miller. Exactly how much money is unclear because the court records are sealed, but Miller suggested that's where most of Oland's $36 million came from. After that, he became "a little looser with the purse strings," Miller argued, citing his custom-built, state-of-the-art yachts as an example. Maureen Adamson insisted that her boss was always "very careful," "very detailed" with his money, almost obsessive-compulsive "in some areas," but she conceded he did spend more after the settlement.

Alan Gold asked McFadden about Oland's wish to "formalize" the latest financial arrangement with his son with a mortgage contract, a right of first refusal to buy the family homestead, and a domestic agreement between Dennis Oland and his future second wife to protect against any future breakup. McFadden testified that Lisa and Dennis were together during his divorce and the "possibility of a second marriage" was on the horizon. Legal documents were drawn up but never signed, the court heard, but Richard Oland knew that for almost two years, stressed Gold. McFadden agreed this was true.

Gold asked McFadden when Oland last mentioned his son's debt. McFadden said it was at least six months to a year prior to his death. Gold also asked if he was aware of any occasion when Dennis asked his father for financial help and his father refused him. McFadden said he was not. Gold asked McFadden about the compensation he received for brokering the deal between father and son. "I billed him fees," said McFadden. He didn't divulge the amount, but in his statement to police on July 7, 2011, McFadden had said he received between $60,000 and $70,000 and that the legal fees were a similar amount.

Gold turned his attention to the financial implications of Richard Oland's death. McFadden testified he had received $765,000 to date as co-executor of Oland's estate and $50,000 as trustee. Dennis Oland received $100,000 and $50,000 for the same roles, said McFadden. Gold did not ask him to explain the disparity. (On redirect, Veniot asked McFadden why he was paid so much more than his co-executor, and McFadden simply said they decided the amounts between themselves. Veniot didn't press the matter, either.) Neither the Crown nor the defence asked how much

McFadden earned as president and treasurer of Far End Corporation and Kingshurst Estates, or as secretary and treasurer of the main holding company, either. Dennis received about $50,000 a year from Far End and Kingshurst, he told officials.

"Richard Oland trusted you and his son when he created his will?" Gold asked.

"Yes," McFadden replied.

Any changes to his will Oland had considered making would not have cut anyone out or favoured one heir over another, Gold submitted. Rather, he reminded the jury, Oland wanted to set up a family trust to reduce the taxes payable upon his death and an auction process for his belongings to avoid any fights among heirs. McFadden concurred. "There's nice stuff, and there's not so nice stuff," he said.

Being executor comes with duties and obligations, noted Gold. McFadden said that he and Oland discussed his role in advance, and that part of his job was to "preserve the assets." He dismissed any implication that it was improper for him and Dennis to appoint themselves co-directors of the main holding company and its two subsidiaries. Trustees are responsible, so they appoint themselves as officers because they have that responsibility, he said.

On redirect, Veniot zeroed in on one of McFadden's answers. When Gold had asked whether there was any animosity between father and son when Dennis Oland missed a mortgage payment of around $10,000, McFadden responded, "It was refinanced, yes." Veniot pointed out that McFadden hadn't really answered the question, and he asked again: was there any animosity? McFadden paused, chuckled, rolled his eyes, held his hands out, and finally said that it was a long time ago. He told Veniot that he was testing his memory and noted: "If there was animosity, Richard could have foreclosed and taken the property. I would say perhaps he was disappointed, but he said, 'Fine, let's just document it and carry on.'" But Veniot did get McFadden to acknowledge that he had no idea that Dennis was borrowing against the home he had already refinanced with his father.

Justice Walsh also jumped in, seeking clarification on the financial arrangement. The $500,000 was an advance on his inheritance, and it was to be secured on a mortgage on 58 Gondola Point Road, he asked. Yes, McFadden affirmed. He asked McFadden if he had "personal knowledge" why Oland wanted a mortgage, an option to purchase, and a domestic agreement between Dennis and "his significant other," but none of those documents were ever executed. Legal papers were drawn up, said McFadden. Oland and his lawyer drafted the mortgage and option agreement, while Dennis and his lawyer drafted the domestic contract. But Dennis "had some concerns" about the documents, and Lisa Andrik needed time to find a lawyer to review the agreement. Time passed, and the documents just never seemed to get signed, said McFadden. Gold asked if Oland had ever expressed anger that the documents remained unsigned. McFadden said that he had not. "It was more fun building sailboats," he replied.

The defence also questioned Dennis Oland's former supervisor, John Travis, about the $16,000 advance on his pay. Travis acknowledged that he had been the first to suggest a cash advance. The markets were poor, and Oland's numbers were down, he said. Nor was it an unusual arrangement, Travis said. Wood Gundy had done the same thing for other financial advisers on occasion. Similar to clients, financial advisers can be victims to the market, he said, and he noted he would have offered Oland assistance "in some form" even if Oland hadn't told him that he expected to bring in between $10 million and $20 million between August and September.

During cross-examination of the Crown's forensic accountant, Gold continued to push the idea that Dennis Oland's money troubles were nothing new, blaming, in part, his job in an industry full of ups and downs. In fact, the defence asked Eric Johnson to spend his weekend reviewing Oland's financial records before returning to the stand. Johnson's review for the Crown had focused primarily on the six months leading up to the murder, but the defence asked him to take a broader view and examine 2009 and 2010.

Johnson found Oland's accounts were often overdrawn and over limit during those years, as well. On July 7, 2010 for example, Oland's main CIBC chequing account was $1,553.63 overdrawn; his line of credit and Visa were $35,098.04 and $23,128.07 over limit, respectively;

his investment account had only $650, and his RRSPs stood at $70. His spending exceeded his income by about $129,000 during the first six months of that year, in part because of a trip to St. Maarten that resulted in foreign currency transactions of nearly $9,000. In July 2010 Oland bounced a $1,666.67 payment to his father on the $500,000 advance—just as he had in July 2011, said Johnson; the court had already heard about that bounced cheque during Adamson's and McFadden's testimony. In addition, Johnson found $75,000 originally counted as 2008 income from CIBC Wood Gundy was actually a loan from his employer, to be paid back over ten years—meaning his debt was even worse than initially thought.

Gold suggested Oland could have solved his financial problems in 2011 by borrowing more. He asked Johnson if he found any evidence indicating Oland sought to increase his line of credit and been refused. Johnson said he did not. But the Crown maintained the accused's financial situation was particularly dire just before his father was bludgeoned to death. His line of credit and credit card debts were mounting, he owed $75,000 to CIBC Wood Gundy, and he'd received a $16,000 advance on his pay. But Oland's take-home monthly income was averaging only about $6,000, said Weaver. That meant that after the father of three paid his child and spousal support and the interest payment to his father, he had less than $100.33 a month to pay for everything else.

thirteen

THE BROWN SPORTS JACKET
THE CROWN'S CASE

It was Week 11, Day 40, when Crown prosecutors presented what they believed to be the coup de grâce in their case against Dennis Oland. Joy Kearsey, a scientist formerly with the RCMP's forensic laboratory services for seventeen years, most recently in Halifax, stepped into the witness box on November 23, 2015.

Between August 2011 and August 2013, Kearsey prepared eleven blood and DNA reports related to the Oland case, amassing 1,400 pages. Other courts across the country at the provincial, Court of Queen's Bench, and provincial Supreme Court levels had previously deemed her an expert, as had the Supreme Court of Bermuda. Kearsey had testified in forty-seven other cases, most notably one that she modestly described as "a homicide case at a pig farm." It was, in fact, the largest serial-killer investigation in Canadian history: the high-profile trial of Robert Pickton, the BC pig farmer charged with twenty-six counts of first-degree murder in the deaths of women who disappeared from Vancouver's Downtown Eastside. In that case, Kearsey developed DNA profiles of forensic evidence found during the twenty-month police search of Pickton's two properties in Port Coquitlam, a small city east of Vancouver. Those results were compared to at least 750 known DNA profiles, including victims, potential suspects, people with links to the properties, and those involved in the search.

Kearsey had given numerous lectures and written several reports over the years and received two commanding officer's commendations for her work. She was also awarded a Queen Elizabeth II Golden Jubilee commemorative medal, bestowed upon Canadians who have made outstanding and exemplary contributions to their communities or the nation. When the Halifax RCMP lab closed in 2014 as part of a national consolidation, Kearsey went to work for the Nova Scotia government's public health laboratory network as a biosafety officer. Walsh deemed Kearsey an expert qualified to give opinion evidence in the application of DNA typing procedures and results, and the calculation of frequency estimates of DNA profiles within the general population. But he gave his usual reminder to the jurors that it was up to them to decide how much weight to give any expert's evidence.

Kearsey started by giving the jury a daylong, university-style tutorial about DNA (deoxyribonucleic acid), complete with a forty-page PowerPoint presentation titled "What is DNA? Why is it useful in forensics?" that included colourful charts and graphics. She also delivered a presentation on the identification of blood and some of the strengths and weaknesses of the forensic tests scientists use. Throughout the complex crash course, Kearsey made regular eye contact with the jurors to ensure she wasn't losing them. None appeared to take notes, but they were attentive.

DNA is the genetic material inherited from parents, and it governs traits, such as eye colour and stature. Human DNA is 99.9 per cent identical from person to person, but no two people have identical DNA, except for identical twins, said Kearsey. Forensic analysis targets the 0.1 per cent that is unique, she explained; a person's "blueprint for life," she said. DNA is present in essentially every one of the estimated one hundred trillion cells that make up a person's body. It is identical in every cell, whether it's from blood, semen, saliva, urine, hair, teeth, bone, tissue, or skin, and it does not change with age.

DNA, Kearsey said, is organized into units called chromosomes. Humans have twenty-three pairs in each cell. One of each pair is inherited from the mother and the other from the father. Although siblings get their DNA from the same parents, it's a random combination, and they can end up with much different DNA profiles, she noted.

Scientists assist police investigations by comparing known DNA samples of people to unknown samples taken from crime scenes to determine if they match. If the two samples do match, scientists can use a DNA database to determine how common that particular profile is and then employ a mathematical calculation to estimate a frequency of occurrence, or what's known as the random-match probability. Based on the Canadian Caucasian database, for example, the estimated probability that an unrelated individual selected at random from the Canadian Caucasian population will have the same genetic profile as the test subject is one in ninety-seven billion, Kearsey said. The commercial DNA typing product she used, Profiler Plus, analyzes DNA in nine locations, called loci, for distinctive DNA elements. A minimum of 0.246 nanograms of DNA, a billionth of a gram, is required for analysis, she said. The ideal amount is 1 nanogram.

Kearsey also explained Locard's exchange principle, which states that whenever two objects come into contact, a transfer of material, such as cells containing DNA, will occur, which can be useful in crime analysis. But it's not as easy as it looks on popular TV crime shows, such as *CSI*, where something is always found. "In real life crime scene investigation," Kearsey stressed, "it is always more challenging."

The identification of blood involved two tests, Kearsey explained. The preliminary screening test, Hemastix, is a three-inch plastic strip with a special reactant at the tip that detects the peroxide-like activity of hemoglobin. If the test area changes from yellow to green within ten seconds, it's considered a positive result. Hemastix is very sensitive, but it's a presumptive test not specific to blood, and a wide range of other substances — certain metals and rust, suedes and leathers, dirt and moulds, and other bodily fluids, such as saliva and perspiration — can give a false positive for blood. A positive Hemastix result indicates only that blood may be present. It can also produce false negatives if what Kearsey called "environmental insults" have degraded the hemoglobin. Washing an item, for example, or warm and moist environments can create false negatives, she noted.

A confirmatory test called the hemochromogen test confirms the result of a Hemastix test. This test is less sensitive than the Hemastix and is specific for blood, so a positive result means the sample tested is blood. It is not known to render any false positives, said Kearsey, but like the Hemastix, it can produce false negatives in cases of "environmental insults," diluted samples, and old stains, she said. So if a stain tests negative for blood, that doesn't necessarily mean it wasn't caused by blood, just that blood was not confirmed. Kearsey also spent some time describing the various protocols that ensure the accuracy and reliability of test results. The RCMP labs are accredited by Standards Council of Canada, she noted, which ensures that samples are securely stored, equipment is properly maintained, and technicians receive standardized training. Proficiency tests, independent reviews, and the use of quality control samples ensure the accuracy of test results. To prevent contamination, exhibits from different sources — for example, a known sample and an unknown sample — are stored separately and handled individually, and technicians always wear gloves.

Although the exact number was never clearly stated during the trial, Kearsey tested eighteen stained areas found on the inside and outside of Dennis Oland's brown sports jacket. She also tested several other articles of clothing and bedding seized from his home, swabs of his car and the red grocery bag seized from its trunk, his smartphone, samples from the crime scene and autopsy, and the victim's clothing.

At the judge's urging, the Crown and defence spent several hours paring down Kearsey's results to a more manageable report to present to the jury. Walsh told them to work "into the night, if necessary." At fifty-two-pages, the final product was still "somewhat voluminous," said prosecutor Patrick Wilbur, but it included pictures.

As hard copies of the report were handed out to the jurors, Walsh thanked the lawyers for their "professionalism" in working together to reduce the material. He said he griped at them a lot, so it was good to give them a pat on the back every once in a while. But the brief levity did little to ease the tension. A chart on the courtroom monitor showed the exhibits tested, the exhibit numbers, the locations of the samples, a photo of the exhibit (if available), and the results.

No foreign DNA was found on the victim's pants or shoes, said Kearsey. Numerous samples taken from the crime scene matched Richard Oland's DNA with a certainty of one in 510 billion, other than one, which had a certainty of one in 57 billion. The blood found in the office washroom sink and on a paper towel in the garbage can predated the murder, the tests showed, and belonged to Galen McFadden, the son of Robert McFadden. Swabs of Oland's hands and fingernails and multiple nail clippings did not detect any foreign DNA; all matched his profile with a certainty of one in 510 billion, said Kearsey. Three hairs found between the fingers of his left hand and a fourth hair in his right hand could not be tested for DNA because they did not have roots with the required cellular material, she said.

The back of the Blackberry Dennis Oland used immediately after visiting his father was swabbed, along with the battery and battery housing, but no blood was confirmed. A cutting of a duvet seized from his bedroom, which had tested positive for blood with a preliminary test but tested negative in the follow-up test, had the DNA profile of an unknown female. A cutting of a pillow seized from the bedroom also initially tested positive for blood (no confirmatory test was done) that matched the accused's profile, said Kearsey.

A variety of tests done on Dennis's Volkswagen Golf, where police expected to find blood transfer, didn't turn up anything noteworthy, either. Swabs of the steering wheel, driver's door inside handle and latch, the headlight and turn-signal switches, emergency brake, front passenger seat, and trunk release all tested negative for blood, and none of the victim's DNA was confirmed. A swab of the front passenger seat headrest tested positive for blood during preliminary testing, but no confirmatory test was done. The DNA was of mixed origin, consistent with having originated from at least three people, at least one of them male, but no meaningful comparison could be made to any samples, she said.

The red reusable grocery bag police believed Oland had with him when he visited his father on July 6 produced nothing of evidentiary value. Several parts of the bag were tested, but no blood was confirmed, nor was any DNA identified as belonging to Richard Oland. Four stains on the shirt police believed Dennis Oland wore that night, which was subsequently laundered at the dry cleaner, came back negative for blood, and no DNA was detected. Two similar shirts seized from his closet produced the same results, Kearsey noted. Tests on his pants, which also had visible stains, matched his own DNA to varying degrees, ranging from one in ten thousand to one in 180 million. The shorts police believed were the ones Oland was seen wearing later that night in surveillance video also matched his DNA in varying degrees, from him being a "possible contributor" to a certainty of one in fifty-five million.

Then Kearsey got to the results for the key piece of evidence in the Crown's case against Dennis Oland: the brown sports jacket that he wore to his father's office on July 6.

The jury first saw the jacket on October 5, when forensic Sergeant Mark Smith submitted it into evidence. Smith didn't discuss the forensic test results on the jacket or any of the numerous other items he entered into evidence that day. His only role was to go over the police chain of custody to confirm continuity for the court. Some of the jurors appeared taken aback as Smith snapped on a pair of blue latex gloves to handle the clear plastic Ziploc-style bags containing the exhibits, some of which were preserved in a police refrigerator or freezer and were labelled as biohazards. Justice Walsh assured the jury that it was not an "unusual occurrence" for a witness to wear gloves when handling DNA exhibits.

Smith told the court the jacket, like the more than five hundred other exhibits collected in the case, had been carefully catalogued and secured to prevent any mix-ups or tampering. But the complex process involved proved almost as difficult to grasp as the scientific findings. The Saint John police and the RCMP each have their own numbering system, and the court assigns its own numbers. The jacket, for example, was labelled Crown Exhibit 23 by the court, but was previously known as Saint John Police Exhibit 221 and renumbered 405 by the RCMP. The four vials containing DNA extracted from clippings of the jacket were assigned individual RCMP numbers and four different Saint John police exhibit numbers. At one point, even the judge seemed to struggle to keep the various exhibit numbers straight.

The jury learned details about the jacket itself more than a week later, when Saint John forensic Constable David MacDonald and RCMP

Sergeant Brian Wentzell testified. MacDonald examined the jacket over two days, November 9 and 17, 2011. He visually scanned the jacket, up and down, left to right, using a bright light, and found "areas of discolouration," on both of the sleeves and on the chest area. The small "reddish" stains "appeared to be embedded in the material," he testified. He circled each one with a white wax pencil, numbered them, and photographed them beside a scale to indicate their size. He also took overexposed and magnified photographs of the stains to better illustrate them.

A screening test for blood came next. MacDonald tested the inside of the right cuff with a Hemastix, where "red and brown coloured" spots appeared "diluted," as though they "may have been exposed to liquid." MacDonald got what he described as a "weak positive" result from the presumptive test when the strip turned "greenish" after fifteen seconds. MacDonald did not test the other stained areas for blood. He wanted to leave them "pristine" for the RCMP lab to handle, he said. Swabbing "could take away substance that's in that area," he explained.

The Saint John Police Force normally sends items to the RCMP lab via Purolator but hand delivers "in serious cases," so MacDonald personally drove the jacket to Halifax on November 30. On December 6, five months after the killing, Brian Wentzell began his examination. Police attributed the delay to RCMP policy. The RCMP lab limited the number of exhibits the Saint John police could submit, and investigators had to receive results before sending any more. The jacket formed part of Saint John's eleventh submission to the RCMP.

Wentzell was the blood-spatter expert who assisted Saint John police with the analysis of the crime scene four days after the murder. "I was to determine if I could locate what stains were on the jacket and how they were deposited on the jacket," he told the court. The jacket bore no manufacturer's tag to indicate what fabric the garment was made from, he noted. Wentzell counted five areas: three outside, and two inside. The stains were visible without any special enhancements, just a strong light and magnification, he said. Like MacDonald, he circled, photographed, and measured them.

The first stain was on the outside right sleeve, about halfway up. It was "three millimetres or less in size," Wentzell said, showing the courtroom an enlarged photo of the area in question. But even when magnified twenty times, the stain was difficult to discern on the large display screen. "Red staining is noted in the fibres," he said. Wentzell was careful not to call it blood since he didn't conduct any of the confirmatory blood tests himself.

Another stain was just a few centimetres from the first, closer to the crook of the elbow. It also measured "three millimetres or less" he said. The third "reddish staining" was in the outside upper left chest area, above the breast pocket. It was about one millimetre in size—not quite the thickness of a dime.

On the lining of the right cuff was a "minimum of two stains, sub-millimetre in size," and "three areas of diluted-appearing stains" that spread out about two centimetres. Wentzell circled the areas on an interactive screen to help make them easier to see in the photo displayed on courtroom monitors. On the lining of the left cuff, he said he found a "minimum of four stains, sub-millimetre in size": two stains measuring one millimetre by five millimetres, and one stain measuring one millimetre by three millimetres. When Wentzell finished examining the jacket, he put it in the lab freezer and sent an email to another RCMP lab requesting the areas he had marked be tested for blood and DNA.

Joy Kearsey confirmed blood in four locations on the outside of the jacket: two on the right sleeve, one on the upper left chest, and one on the back, in the middle, near the hem. One of the bloodstains on the right sleeve did not contain enough DNA to meet the RCMP's minimum requirement for comparison with the known sample for Richard Oland obtained during the autopsy. But the DNA found within the other three bloodstains matched Richard Oland's DNA profile in all nine areas used for comparison, she said. The odds that the DNA could belong to an unrelated Canadian Caucasian individual chosen at random were one in 510 billion, she said. Canada's current population is about thirty-four million, and the estimated world population is between seven and eight billion, meaning it was virtually impossible the DNA could belong to somebody else. The courtroom was silent as those statistics settled in. Dennis Oland was following along, but he did not visibly react.

Richard Oland's DNA was also detected in three additional stained areas inside the cuffs that initially tested positive for blood but where blood was not confirmed with follow-up testing. Two stains found on the inside of the right cuff had a DNA profile of mixed origin, with the component matching the victim's profile in six of the nine areas of comparison. The estimated probability it could match someone else was one in 180 million, said Kearsey. The minor component matched the DNA profile of the accused. The third stain found on the inside left cuff also had a mixed DNA profile. In that case, the minor component matched Richard Oland's profile with a certainty of one in forty, she said.

Eight additional stained areas came back positive for blood with the preliminary test but had negative follow-up results. "We can't call it blood, but we also can't say it's not blood," Kearsey noted. "We can't really say one way or the other." The terminology the RCMP lab uses is "blood is not confirmed," she said.

Five areas of Dennis Oland's jacket matched his father's DNA, four areas tested positive for blood, and three areas were positive for both blood and Richard Oland's DNA.

On November 25, the forty-second day of the trial, prosecutors gave the jury still more to think about when they called their forty-fourth and final witness: Thomas Suzanski, a forensic specialist in the biology section of the RCMP forensic lab in Ottawa.

Suzanski had worked with RCMP forensic labs since 1987 and, like Kearsey, with whom he had worked in Halifax, he had previously testified in three levels of court in Canada as well as in Bermuda. He holds a master of science and served as a consultant in the Swissair disaster in 1998 and has done casework in several other countries. At the time of his testimony, he was a "team lead," undertaking administrative duties as well as maintaining casework activities. Walsh deemed Suzanski an expert.

Unbeknownst to the jury, the Crown had applied to the judge for special permission to conduct additional testing on extracts taken from Dennis Oland's jacket, which the defence opposed in a pre-trial hearing on March 30, 2015. The Crown argued for the retesting on the ground that Kearsey's tests used a program called Profiler Plus, which compared only nine areas of DNA. But in 2014, in the midst of Dennis Oland's preliminary inquiry, the RCMP switched to a "more discriminating" new program, Identifiler Plus, which compares fifteen areas of DNA.

One of the extracts, taken from the back of the jacket, at the bottom, near the centre, had been entered as an exhibit at Oland's preliminary inquiry in 2014. The other two, taken from the right sleeve and upper left chest, were not entered as exhibits at the preliminary but were in Saint John police custody, along with the known DNA samples of the victim and the accused needed for comparison. At the March 30 pre-trial hearing, the Crown also argued for the release of an extract taken from the inside left-pocket seam, which had been entered as an exhibit at the preliminary.

A judge's power to release exhibits is discretionary. The defence argued the Crown should have to satisfy Walsh before any of the six extracts were released for retesting, not just the two that had been formally marked as exhibits. Walsh agreed with the defence, but he felt the Crown made a "compelling case for release," as he wrote in the sixteen-page ruling he issued on April 7. The "appropriate threshold for guiding the exercise of judicial discretion," Walsh determined, "can be formulated as . . . whether it has been shown that there is an 'air of reality' that such production and retesting has a 'meaningful capacity to advance' the interests of justice."

Walsh noted non-identical siblings can share genetic markers at more than the nine sites compared by Profiler Plus. Retesting with the new program would "provide a further six loci to compare the samples, either giving a further discriminating match or possibly excluding what was previously a match," he wrote. Walsh cited the Crown's brief. "If a sample of a sibling's DNA is not available, retesting with Identifiler Plus would be the next best option in reducing any chance of a coincidental match between siblings," the brief stated. It would "significantly reduce the chance that DNA matching an individual would also match that of their unidentical sibling (as it is highly improbable that unidentical siblings would have matching DNA at all 15 loci)."

Thomas Suzanski had advised the judge that additional testing on the DNA extracts from the jacket would make it "likely there will be nothing left for any further retesting" of two extracts, one from the right sleeve and the other from the inside left-pocket seam. But Walsh said he was satisfied "policies and procedures are in place in the RCMP biology laboratory directed at quality control and quality assurance at each stage of the DNA analysis procedure, including documentation and internal peer review. In other words, reasonable safeguards appear to exist to protect the integrity of the DNA extracts and the results obtained." The "results of retesting have a realistic potential of contributing reliably probative evidence bearing on a critical issue in the case, namely identity," Walsh concluded, "identity in criminal cases, needless to say, being an issue of special and grave concern to all involved in the criminal justice system and to society as a whole." Walsh ordered the DNA extracts be released for further analysis "to be performed in a timely manner." He also ordered a copy of the results be provided to the defence "forthwith."

In May 2015 Suzanski retested the DNA extracted from the three confirmed bloodstains on the jacket. His method augmented the certainty of Kearsey's findings of one in 510 billion. He concluded the chances that the DNA extracted from the three bloodstains did not belong to Richard Oland or a blood relation were, he said, not one in a million or a billion or a trillion or a quadrillion, but one in twenty quintillion. People in the courtroom struggled to wrap their brains around the mind-boggling figure, which has eighteen zeroes. CBC reporter Robert Jones, who was live-tweeting from the courtroom, put it this way: "The equivalent: you have a one in 20 quintillion chance of winning two 6/49 jackpots in a row AND then being hit by lightning within seven years."

Suzanski described the samples used as "clean" and "easily interpreted" with no evidence of degradation. They produced a full, single-source DNA profile, he said. "Based on the RCMP Canadian Caucasian population [database], it is 3.4 million times more likely that the DNA evidence obtained would be observed if Richard Oland was the donor of the DNA obtained from [the three areas in question] rather than a full sibling," Suzanski testified. He had tested the cast-off DNA obtained from Derek Oland; the victim's brother was not the source of the DNA profile found in the three bloodstained areas of Dennis Oland's jacket.

At 9:08 on the morning of Friday, July 8, 2011, roughly ten hours after police questioned Dennis Oland about what he wore when he visited his father and told him they considered him a suspect and would execute search warrants against him, the brown sports jacket was dropped off at VIP Dry Cleaners in Rothesay. It was never made clear who brought in the Olands' dry cleaning that morning, but that person specifically requested next-day service.

Yang Hwan "Steve" Nam co-owns VIP Dry Cleaners with his wife, Jin Hee Choi. Nam testified through a Korean interpreter, who was also sworn in as a witness, and the defence had its own interpreter to verify the accuracy of the Crown's questions and Nam's answers. The Crown called Nam to prove that the jacket was cleaned shortly after Richard Oland's death, thereby diluting or degrading the DNA evidence.

Nam said it's up to customers to point out any stains, but he normally checks garments, too, in case customers forget. He marks any stains he finds with red tape and pre-treats them, he said. Items from different customers are cleaned together in the dry-cleaning machine, but they're marked with identifying tags. The hour-long process uses solvent and a detergent, but no water. Nam didn't know the chemistry of the solvent or detergent used, and he also couldn't say how hot it gets inside the dry-cleaning machine. He sets the temperature at 150 degrees, but he wasn't sure if that was Celsius or Fahrenheit. VIP advertises that it offers a gentler service because it uses mild, less toxic products, so Nam usually checks items for any stains after they've been cleaned. He then divides the items into piles of similar garments, irons them, and matches the tags to customers' orders.

Nam couldn't remember who dropped off or picked up the jacket and eighteen other items on the order that July morning, but it was under the name of Dennis Oland's wife, Lisa Andrik-Oland. The dry-cleaning tag attached to the collar of the seized jacket matched the tag on the store copy of the receipt, the court heard. That receipt also matched a dry-cleaning receipt seized from Oland's home. Nam confirmed VIP's normal turnaround time is two business days, but Andrik-Oland's receipt showed that next-day service was requested. As noted, Nam had crossed out the preprinted pickup date of Monday, July 11, at three p.m., and written "SAT" for Saturday instead.

VIP doesn't document stains, but Nam testified that, as far as he could remember, he had told police in July 2011 that he didn't notice any stains on the brown sports jacket or any of the other items in the Olands' order.

The Crown's contention that the brown sports jacket proved Dennis Oland's guilt hinged on whether or not he wore the jacket on the evening of July 6, 2011. Although Oland had told police he remembered wearing a blue jacket, Maureen Adamson testified that when she saw him arrive at the office that evening, his jacket was brown, and security video of him earlier that day showed him in a brown sports jacket. To determine if the brown Hugo Boss jacket seized from Dennis Oland's closet and the brown sports jacket in the security video were one and the same, Saint John police contacted Grant Fredericks, a forensic video expert. Fredericks, a former broadcaster, was previously an officer with the Vancouver Police Department, where he served as the head of the criminal investigation division's forensic video unit. He now operates Forensic Video Solutions in Spokane, Washington.

According to the background information he provided to the court, Fredericks has processed thousands of videotapes and computer discs containing multimedia evidence for both criminal and civil cases over the years, focusing on issues such as reflection of light, pixel tracking, digital-compression technology, colour measurement, and digital- and analog-error identification. He also teaches forensic video analysis at the Federal Bureau of Investigation National Academy, the University of Indianapolis, and for the Law Enforcement and Emergency Services Video Association, and he served as digital video adviser to the International Association of Chiefs of Police.

Saint John police contracted Fredericks to examine video of Dennis Oland, whom they identified only as a white male dressed in a brown suit jacket, light brown pants, and dark shoes, and to provide a comparative analysis of photographs of "known" items seized from Dennis Oland's home, including the brown sports jacket, the blue-and-white-check

J. Crew dress shirt police believed him to be wearing when he visited his father, and a pair of blue-grey J. Crew shorts police believed he wore in surveillance video at the Irving convenience store at 10:32 p.m. that night.

Fredericks advised the jury that most security videos compress data to maximize memory space, resulting in a loss of resolution and quality. Tools exist to enhance the data, but it's not like the "movie magic" often seen on televised crime shows, he said. Any analysis is limited to what was recorded. In reviewing videos of Oland taken near his CIBC Wood Gundy office on July 6, Fredericks observed the brown sports jacket he was wearing had two buttons on the right-hand side, a V-cut at the lapel, four buttons on the left sleeve, and a breast pocket. The seized jacket in the police photographs had the same four features, he said.

Fredericks also noted the top button of the seized jacket was broken, and the top button of the jacket in the video appeared smaller than the lower button. However, there was not enough resolution in the video to be able to say the top button was broken, only that it was reflecting less light than the lower button, which could be due to its position or size, he said. Asked by Crown prosecutor Patrick Wilbur whether the top button in the video image could have been broken, like the one on the seized jacket, Fredericks agreed it was possible. But Fredericks could not say with certainty the brown sports jacket Oland was seen wearing in the surveillance videos was the same one police seized from his closet.

"After carefully examining the Known [seized] jacket . . . with the Questioned jacket worn by Male #1, I have formed the opinion that the Known and Questioned jackets are of the same class," Fredericks concluded in his fifteen-page report. "The Questioned jacket is indistinguishable from the Known jacket. Since no unique characteristics are visible in the video that could uniquely identify the Questioned jacket, it is not possible to state that it is the same jacket. However, the Known jacket cannot be eliminated as being the Questioned jacket."

Fredericks reached the same conclusion about the shirt and shorts: he could not confirm whether the clothing items in the videos were the same as the seized articles, only that they had the same class features.

fourteen

THE BROWN SPORTS JACKET
THE DEFENCE'S CASE

When Alan Gold cross-examined the pathologist, Ather Naseemuddin, he asked him if Richard Oland's killer would have been covered in blood. "Certainly the weapon," Naseemuddin replied. "I don't know about the clothing." Gold reminded Naseemuddin that when asked at the preliminary inquiry if the attacker would have had a substantial amount of blood on them, Naseemuddin answered, under oath, "Yes." Gold put the question to him again. "I would agree that answer is true," Naseemuddin replied.

The defence had scoffed at David MacDonald's "weak positive" Hemastix result on the "red and brown coloured" spots on the right cuff of Dennis Oland's jacket, a result that, MacDonald said, took fifteen seconds to materialize. Gold asserted that the RCMP standard for a Hemastix test is ten seconds, and any reaction beyond that should be considered negative. But Gold's real attack on the DNA evidence and the brown sports jacket started with his cross-examination of RCMP Sergeant Brian Wentzell.

Gold pointed out that the blood tests the RCMP used didn't distinguish between human blood and animal blood. Wentzell confirmed that was true. Not all human blood is the same, Gold continued. There are four types: A, B, AB, and O. There is also the Rhesus (Rh) factor, the inherited protein found on the surface of red blood cells, to consider. Rh positive indicates the person's blood has the protein; Rh negative means they don't. Gold asked if anyone had tested the blood type on the jacket to determine if it matched the victim's. Wentzell said the lab does not test for blood type.

Gold submitted that Wentzell could say only if blood was present; he couldn't say if it was animal or human or if it belonged to the victim. Wentzell confirmed this was true. Gold stressed how small the stains were—other than the "diluted" areas, all were less than three millimetres in diameter. Wentzell agreed the drops were minute. "There's a small quantity there," he said.

The drops were so small, Gold suggested, they could easily go unnoticed by the wearer. In fact, Wentzell missed one of them himself, despite carefully examining the jacket "inch by inch" on two occasions, Gold noted. The sixth stained area, measuring five millimetres by five millimetres on the back of the jacket, in the centre, near the hem, was not found until November 2012, the court heard. Wentzell said the stains "were visible, but quite faint and varying in concentrations." He added: "Because of the colour of the jacket, they don't show up very well."

Gold asked if it was true that the blood drops close to a body would be larger in size than drops farther from a body. "Yes," said Wentzell. Shouldn't the killer or killers have larger spatter stains on them, since they would have been close to the source? Wentzell replied that air resistance and gravity can affect spatter size.

If the killer wore the brown sports jacket during the murder, Gold argued, a significant amount of blood would have stained the garment, not a few tiny specs. He had made the same suggestion earlier in the trial to Constable Duane Squires, the first officer to witness the carnage at the crime scene. The photographs of the crime scene, Gold argued, made it "obvious."

"Whoever had done this, you expected to see blood on them, didn't you?" Gold asked Squires.

"Yes," the officer replied.

"This wasn't a gun shot from twenty yards. It was up front and close, with a lot of blood flying through the air," Gold had said.

In questioning Wentzell, Gold posited that Richard Oland's attacker —"assuming there was only one," he said —"was the perfect target for spatter," given the amount of blood. Richard Oland suffered a "brutal, vicious beating," and the victim and "perpetrator or perpetrators" would have been in close proximity, he said. "The bloodstain evidence would support that," said Wentzell.

However, when Gold suggested the killer would have had "dozens and dozens" of spatter stains on him or her, Wentzell replied that it's "reasonable there would be some," but he could not say how much. Gold emphasized that the blood spatter radiated 360 degrees from the body. "Hundreds" of blood drops from the injuries and cast-off from the weapon or weapons flew around the room, some travelling up to three metres away. He led Wentzell through a series of the crime-scene photos, asking him to confirm the number of blood-spatter spots the defence had circled and counted in each area.

"To the right of the victim's body, fifty-four?"

"That's a reasonable estimate," said Wentzell.

On the front of Richard Oland's desk, Gold said, "our count was over one hundred and fifty." Wentzell agreed. The table surface where Adamson had set down the tray of coffee? Forty-six spots. "That's the exact number I had counted in my report," Wentzell confirmed.

When the running tally reached approximately seven hundred, Gold pushed again, trying to get Wentzell to agree that a similar volume of blood would have marked the killer. "Look at these numbers," he said to Wentzell. "Wouldn't it be in the same ballpark as the assailant?" But Wentzell wouldn't budge. "I'm not saying there wouldn't be [any blood]," he testified. "I'm just not able to say . . . that there would be a large amount."

According to Wentzell, several factors could affect the amount of blood on the killer. The first blows would not generate much blood. The pathologist had previously testified that forty of the forty-five separate wounds were sharp-force. Police believed a "linear-shaped weapon" caused those incised injuries. Such a weapon may have a small surface area, which tends to disperse blood to the sides, rather than back at the killer, or forward. A blunt-shaped instrument, Wentzell noted, would cause the spatter to travel in all directions. The court also heard there was no void in the spatter pattern; no area free of blood where the assailant or assailants' body would have blocked the spatter during the attack. There was less spatter in the south end of the office but no distinct void, Wentzell said.

Gold was unrelenting. He introduced a diagram illustrating the range of blood spatter in the crime scene. "Some of those dots actually represent hundreds of dots," he said, reminding Wentzell that he had previously stated unequivocally that there were "no less than one hundred separate, visible spatter" marks on the back of the victim's shirt collar alone. "Isn't the assailant just another location where, if we had him, we could draw fifty, seventy-five, or one hundred [spatter] circles?" Gold challenged. "In fact, the assailant would probably have more," he argued. He displayed a close-up photograph of Richard Oland's head wounds for the courtroom and urged Wentzell to look at "the bloody state of this man's head."

"By blow number twenty, or twenty-five, or thirty, do you agree there's a reasonable prospect of the assailant having spatter on them?"

"I'm not saying there wouldn't be any. I'm just not able to establish how much," Wentzell replied.

When Gold suggested that Wentzell's role as an RCMP officer biased his analysis, Wentzell, now into his third straight day of testimony, was unfaltering. He said he was giving his opinion as a blood-spatter expert, noting he had conducted experiments over the years comparing the blood spatter from knife-like and blunt weapons. Gold asked Wentzell to explain how the killer could avoid getting spattered, prompting Justice Walsh to interrupt. "He didn't say that," Walsh admonished. Wentzell "has been agreeing with you all along," Walsh told Gold. The only disagreement was over the adjective "significant," he said. Wentzell, the judge noted, "won't go there."

Gold told the court that Saint John police, acting on information Wentzell provided, swore to a judge that "significant" blood spatter would be found on the killer's clothes in order to obtain warrants to search Dennis Oland's home. Gold's counterpart, Gary Miller, had earlier raised this with forensic Sergeant Mark Smith. Smith confirmed that, yes, he told the officer who applied for the search warrant that "the killer would likely have had substantial amounts of blood on them" and that this justified the search warrant. But when Miller asked Smith if this meant he thought the killer "had substantial amounts of blood on him after the attack," Smith replied, "That's speculation." Now Gold cited Constable Stacy Humphrey's sworn affidavit, in which she stated that Mark Smith told her that he and Wentzell had examined the crime scene and reviewed photographs of the body, and in their "expert opinion," the assailant would "have significant bloodstain spatter on their person." Wentzell said he didn't recall using the word "significant" but acknowledged the possibility. Gold questioned whether Wentzell changed his opinion when police didn't find significant blood on Oland's clothes, or any of his possessions that police tested. Wentzell didn't waver. "My opinion is an unbiased opinion."

Gold turned his attention to Dennis Oland's brown sports jacket. If the stains on the jacket were blood, Gold put to Wentzell in a question that was really a statement, "you're unable to say how it got on there?" Wentzell agreed; he "was unable to determine how the blood was deposited." Gold also argued there was no way to know how old the stains were. They could have been on the jacket for weeks or months before the murder. Wentzell confirmed there was no way to verify the age of the stains. "So you can't say the bloodstains on the jacket are connected to the murder?" Gold asked. Wentzell acknowledged that he could not.

Police had not found any evidence, Gold noted, that the killer or killers tried to clean themselves up before leaving Richard Oland's office. Wentzell agreed. The lawyer then played the security video that the defence said showed Dennis Oland leaving his father's office at 6:12 p.m. on July 6, 2011. Nothing in the video suggested the accused had taken part in a bloody attack, Gold argued. Wentzell acknowledged that from what he observed in the video, this was true, but he added, "I can't see anything in that video." Even Grant Fredericks, the forensic video analyst brought in from Washington State, wasn't able to glean much from the grainy footage.

When Gold cross-examined Joy Kearsey and Thomas Suzanski, he argued that there was no way to know how Richard Oland's DNA got on Dennis Oland's jacket. It wasn't necessarily from the blood. Touching, sneezing, and coughing can all transfer DNA, he observed. "As far as how DNA got somewhere, you have no idea, correct?" Suzanski agreed that was true. The test allows scientists to determine only if there is a match and to calculate the frequency. "We can't say when DNA was deposited, how it was deposited, the order in which it was deposited, or how long it was there," he told the court. In his opinion, however, the DNA came from the blood. The extracts, he noted, came from three different locations on the jacket: the right sleeve, the upper left chest, and on the back. He considered it "rather unlikely" that any other possible DNA source, such as saliva or sweat, could occur in all three instances.

With Joy Kearsey, Gold reiterated that no one could say with any certainty how the blood on the jacket got there, how long it had been there, or how degraded it was. "They were tiny, tiny spots" that "could have been on the jacket for weeks or months," but went unnoticed because they were so small, said Gold. The third stain on the back, he pointed out, was missed during three previous careful examinations of the garment. Kearsey agreed there was no way to know how the blood was deposited or the age of the blood, but she said she would expect some would be removed every time the jacket was cleaned, depending on the thoroughness of the laundering or dry cleaning.

Gold went on to argue that the DNA extracted from the bloodstains did not necessarily come from the blood. He suggested it was possible the bloodstains were so degraded that the DNA came not from them but another source underneath or on top of the stains, such as saliva, perspiration, or tears. He even suggested that since the tests do not distinguish between human and animal blood, the blood could be animal blood, and the human DNA came from another biological source.

Kearsey acknowledged she could not say "for certain" the blood was the source of the DNA, but testified it was "more likely" it came from the blood than the other two possibilities. "I base that on my experience and knowledge of how the process works," she said. "I can't put a percentage or anything on it." The RCMP tests didn't distinguish between human and animal blood because that's generally considered a redundant exercise, Kearsey explained. When DNA is extracted from a blood sample, a quantification test determines how much human DNA is present, confirming whether the source is human or animal. She said she was aware of only one case where the RCMP tried to distinguish between human and animal blood, and that was a unique situation; she referred, of course, to the Pickton case. She found no indication of any animal DNA, she added.

Gold also referred to Kearsey's earlier point that DNA can be transferred by touch. Some people are "good shedders" who leave behind more DNA than others, he said. Richard Oland could have been one of them, said Gold. DNA can also "migrate" depending on how an item is packaged, he continued, referring to how the jacket had been stuffed into a small bag, where it remained for months. Some stains could be "offspring" of other stains, he suggested. Kearsey responded that she wouldn't expect a bloodstain to transfer if the blood was dry, but she acknowledged that flakes could potentially dislodge.

The critical question, Gold emphasized for the jury, was how the blood and DNA got on the jacket—a question Kearsey couldn't answer. "All you can say is, 'I did my work, these are the profiles,'" Gold put to Kearsey. "Everything else is for the triers of fact, the jury, to say. Correct?"

Kearsey agreed.

When Alan Gold cross-examined Yang Hwan "Steve" Nam, co-owner of VIP Dry Cleaners, about Lisa Andrik-Oland's July 8 dry-cleaning order, Nam revealed that Saint John police did not formally interview him until February 2015, almost three and a half years after the murder. During his in-chief testimony, Nam told the court that the police mostly talked to his wife earlier in the investigation. Gold also questioned Nam's wife, Jin Hee Choi.

She testified that VIP does not often receive bloodstained clothes. Gold pointed out that she had said the opposite at the preliminary inquiry, to which she responded that in the year since the inquiry, they had not received many bloodstained clothes. With that point clarified, Gold asked Choi if bloodstains require special treatment to remove. He suggested saliva works well because the enzymes help break down the protein. If a stain is not removed and gets heated up, it becomes permanent, he submitted. Choi agreed. (Walsh would later rebuke Gold for this.)

Gold asked her if the Olands' clothing bore stains. "I'm not sure," Choi replied. But she and her husband had both told police at the time there were no stains, Gold pointed out. "My husband received those clothes, and he said there were no stains," Choi said. She said she normally handles the administrative side of the business, dealing with customers, but her husband accepted the order that Friday and let it be picked up without payment on Saturday. Dennis Oland's wife came in to pay later that Saturday, sometime between two and three p.m., she said. Andrik-Oland came in alone, but Choi said she saw Dennis Oland outside, sitting in a parked vehicle.

Gold argued there was nothing unusual about the Olands' request for next-day service, and Choi confirmed that their previous order had also been dropped off on a Friday for Saturday pickup. VIP, Gold pointed out, offers two-day, one-day, and same-day service for the same price. If the Olands were anxious to get rid of any stains, they could have asked for the items right away, he posited. Choi agreed.

On redirect, Crown prosecutor Patrick Wilbur introduced into evidence VIP's customer information sheet for Lisa Andrik-Oland, covering the period between November 1, 2010, and July 9, 2011. It included 185 items and invoices totalling $1,103.85. He asked whether any of the other orders included any men's sports jackets. There were none, only one other transaction with a man's suit, she said.

In his bid to further discount the significance of the blood found on his client's jacket, Gold's cross-examination of Brian Wentzell raised questions about the absence of blood outside the crime scene, despite there being no evidence that the killer cleaned up before leaving Richard Oland's office. Joy Kearsey's in-chief testimony established that no blood was found on Dennis Oland's other clothing. Forensic Constable David MacDonald examined Oland's shoes using large halogen lights and chemical tests in 2011 on September 3 and 4, and again on November 2 and 18, the court had heard. Shoes are typically an excellent source for blood evidence, Gold noted, because blood can soak into the stitching and laces and get trapped in the eyelets and treads. If Dennis Oland wore the shoes in question during the murder, as the Crown alleged, wasn't it certain that blood would be on them? Gold asked. "If they're exposed to the blood source" and not altered in some way, Wentzell acknowledged. He noted that no identifiable footprints were found at the crime scene.

Gold handed Wentzell the camp logbook Maureen Adamson had left out on the office table that night for Dennis Oland to take to his mother so she could return it to his uncle. The book, which MacDonald processed on December 6, 8, 9, 12, 13, and 15, 2011, tested negative for blood.Could the book have been in the office "during the spatter event, if I can call it that," and remain clean? Gold asked. Wentzell replied that it would depend on whether the book sat behind another object that caught the blood first, like the typewriter observed in the crime-scene photos. "I can't conclusively say one way or another," he said.

Gold also inquired about the red reusable Sobeys grocery bag Oland reportedly had with him when he visited his father that night. William Adamson, Maureen Adamson's husband, testified to seeing a man matching Dennis Oland's description enter the Canterbury Street office with a red bag on the evening of July 6, and security video appeared to show Oland leaving the building with a red bag. As Joy Kearsey had testified, extensive tests on the bag came back negative for blood. If a bloody murder weapon were put into a container, such as the red bag, would the container have also gotten blood on it, asked Gold. "If it wasn't wrapped up in something," said Wentzell. "Whatever touched that weapon, it would have significant transfer of blood, wouldn't it?" the lawyer asked. Yes, Wentzell replied.

Nor did Dennis Oland's Blackberry test positive for blood, as Kearsey's testimony confirmed. Oland had sent forty-two text messages on the day his father was murdered, according to records submitted into evidence, including one at 6:12 p.m., at which time, he said, he was leaving his father's office, and he also said he took a call from his wife at 6:36 p.m., just as he was leaving, and yet no blood was found on the Blackberry, its battery, or the battery housing, Gold reminded the jury. Police also could not find any blood in Dennis Oland's Volkswagen Golf, despite running numerous tests, and the car did not appear to have been cleaned recently. If the killer had gotten into that car shortly after the slaying, Gold argued, there would be an "excellent chance" of blood being in the car. "The probability is yes, there would be blood transfer," Wentzell said.

"The killer would have a better chance of winning the New Brunswick lottery than not leaving any trace in that car. Is that fair?" Gold asked, eliciting a brief smile from Wentzell, who said he couldn't comment on the lottery odds. Gold persisted. "There's almost no chance of that being true. Isn't that the bottom line?"

"If the individual had clothing on and received blood on their person and went to that vehicle and the blood was still wet, there would be a good opportunity for transfer," said Wentzell. He added, however, that he did not know the "circumstances" of the case in question. Several other tests conducted throughout the investigation, from the lint trap in Dennis Oland's clothes dryer and bags of garbage seized from his home to swabs of the crime scene and hairs and fibre samples taken during the autopsy, failed to produce "fruitful" results, Gold told the court.

Gold argued that the "probabilities" of finding "some sort of evidentiary material" on the assailant's clothing, car, or other items would be "excellent." Wentzell, placid and firm, said he agreed, "based on those circumstances and assumptions you've provided to me, there could be... but it's speculative." Gold pointed out that Wentzell agreed with the proposition when it was put to him during the preliminary inquiry, quoting from the transcript. Wentzell countered that he had clarified his meaning at the preliminary inquiry, but Gold refused to read aloud his qualification, saying that the Crown prosecutors could bring it up on redirect if they wished. Veniot did indeed bring it up. "In order for blood to be transferred, it has to be in a wet, liquid state," Wentzell had said.

The defence's bloodstain pattern analyst, Patrick Laturnus, told the court he had conducted many blood-spatter experiments over the years, recreating blows to study the results. He had tested a variety of weapons, such as hatchets, hammers, and crowbars, he said. The number of blows in the Oland case, forty-five, was unusual, Laturnus noted. That many strikes would release more blood, he said, adding that it made for an interesting case.

Gold led Laturnus through some of the graphic crime-scene photos he had reviewed as part of his analysis, including ones with the victim's body still splayed on the floor. Laturnus said the photos showed the blood spatter travelled up and out from the victim's body, radiating 360 degrees. He suggested the jury visualize a fountain to imagine the blood flying off the victim's body as he was struck.

Blood travels in straight lines but resistance and gravity affect it, he said. If the blood source is close to a target surface, the stains are long and narrow. As the source moves away, the stains get wider until they become circular. The round blood spots on top of Richard Oland's desk indicated they originated from below, flew straight up, and then gravity forced them straight down to land on the desk, said Laturnus. If the victim had been standing, the blood would travel down and sideways and would not retain its circular shape, he said. That meant the victim was on the floor for at least some of the repeated blows, and the assailant would have been standing over him during part of the attack, said Laturnus.

What, if any, spatter would be on the assailant, asked Gold. "It follows the assailant would also have spatter on themselves," Laturnus told the crowded, attentive courtroom. He said the killer would have bent over the victim during the strikes, "so it follows and it's logical" to say a "significant amount." The blood could be anywhere, "from head to toe," he said, but likely primarily on the killer's hands, face, and upper body. If Oland's brown sports jacket had been worn during the slaying, it would have had "so much blood" on it, the blood would have been visible in the images the Crown showed the court, despite the jacket's dark colour, said Laturnus. Gold asked whether spatter or routine transfer caused the bloodstains found on the jacket. There "isn't any analyst that could say with any certainty how those stains originated," Laturnus said.

If the camp logbook had been on the table in the centre of office during the killing, it would have had spatter on it, too, he noted, and the weapon would have been "covered" in blood. "There's no doubt [it] would have a significant amount of blood on it," Laturnus said, adding he saw no evidence of any cleanup at the scene.

Gold asked Laturnus what he would expect to find if the perpetrator did not wash their hands and drove a vehicle right after the killing. Laturnus said he would expect to find blood transfer. What would he say was the probability of finding no blood? Anything was possible, Laturnus replied, but he expected the possibility of finding traces of blood was very good.

Gold dug Dennis Oland's Blackberry out of the exhibit pile and handed it to Laturnus. "What about on a Blackberry that was handled after the slaying?" he asked. Laturnus replied that he'd also expect to find traces on the phone. Skin is pliable, so if the blood on the killer's hands was wet, it would transfer, and if it was dry, it would flake off, he explained. A bag or wrapping used to conceal a weapon would also have traces of blood on it, he noted. Gold handed him the red reusable grocery bag seized from the trunk of Dennis Oland's car. Laturnus told the court that he'd expect to find traces of blood on it, noting that the texture of the bag's fabric would promote transfer.

When prosecutor P.J. Veniot cross-examined Laturnus, he asked how long blood continues to transfer from one item to another. Laturnus said that it depends, but transfers lessen over time because blood dries and gets worn away. Veniot asked if it was possible the blood on the killer's hands had dried by the time they got in their car and would not transfer to anything they touched. "It's possible," Laturnus conceded.

Veniot asked whether the cross-hatching pattern the pathologist noted in the blunt-force wounds could have affected the blood spatter differently than in other cases Laturnus had seen or in his experiments. Laturnus said he suspected it would. Was it possible the weapon may not have been lifted high enough to cause cast-off, Veniot asked. Laturnus replied that it was. And how did Laturnus know if a bloodstain resulted from impact spatter from a wound or cast-off from a swinging weapon? They typically create a different pattern, he said, but in this particular case the pattern was difficult to discern because of the volume of blood. Veniot noted that there were no bloody footprints or blood drips leaving the scene of the crime and asked Laturnus if the killer was covered with blood, would he expect to see footprints and/or a drip trail. Laturnus said it was possible the assailant didn't step in the blood pool because the blood pool may have been smaller during the attack. He also said the killer's clothing would have to be saturated with blood to leave a trail. A person can have a significant amount of blood on them but not be saturated to the point of dripping and leaving a trail, he said. Veniot asked if he was suggesting the killer would have been covered in blood to the point of being concerned about visible staining. Yes, Laturnus said.

Veniot displayed some of the crime-scene photos that showed numerous bloodstains similar to the size of the ones found on the jacket. He asked Laturnus if it was true that blood hitting fabric can be absorbed, and spots will appear smaller than they would on a hard surface. Laturnus agreed that it was. But when Veniot proposed that Laturnus was quite possibly wrong about the amount of blood that would have been on the assailant, Laturnus flatly replied: "No."

Veniot asked Laturnus if he reviewed Brian Wentzell's PowerPoint presentation on blood spatter. Laturnus said he had, and he had agreed with the content. Veniot pointed out that Wentzell's presentation had stated that spatter analysis is based on science and math, not conjecture, which Laturnus acknowledged was true. Venoit referred to a well-known article, "Absence of Evidence is not Evidence of Absence," published in the *Journal of Forensic Identification* in 1996, in which co-authors Paul Kish and Herbert MacDonell stress that conclusions should be based upon what is present, not on speculation about why something isn't present or on what one might expect to find.

Veniot prodded Laturnus. Wasn't he supposed to deal in facts, not theories? Didn't experts in his field argue against assuming that extensive blood at a scene means extensive blood on an attacker, and wasn't it true that the absence of blood spatter on the clothing of a suspect does not necessarily exonerate the accused? Laturnus agreed, but he said the article also states that if a suspect does not have blood on them, the analyst needs to ask more questions, such as whether the suspect may have been naked during the attack.

On redirect, Gold returned to the issue of the lack of bloody footprints or a blood trail. He asked Laturnus if that absence was, in any way, inconsistent with his opinion the killer would have significant spatter on their hands and face and clothing. Laturnus said it was not.

fifteen

DENNIS OLAND SPEAKS

Gary Miller moved the lectern into place, signalling he would deliver an opening statement and launch the defence's case. It was the morning of November 26. After forty-two days and forty-four witnesses, the Crown had wrapped up its case, and the jury was about to find out whether the defence would present any evidence. "If it can be said that there are ordinary murder cases, this is certainly not one of them," Miller began. Dennis Oland and his family had lived under "intense media scrutiny" for four years, he said. "It will soon be time for him and some of his family members to speak publicly for the first time about what they know about any circumstances in this long ordeal."

Miller said it was Oland's wish to testify in his own defence. He would "describe in considerable detail what he did and who he communicated with" on July 6 and July 7. Miller warned the jurors it could prove a bit tedious as they reviewed Oland's cellphone records, text messages, email, and security videos. Oland's wife, Lisa, would also be called to testify, he promised. She would tell them it was she who took the bloodstained jacket and several other clothing items to the dry cleaner on the morning of July 8, because Oland needed clean clothes for his father's visitation and funeral. Miller said that Oland's sister Jacqueline Walsh, who "saw him shortly after" he visited their father; his mother, Connie; uncle Jack Connell; and friend Mary Beth Watt would also testify on his behalf.

The experienced lawyer described the case as a "marathon trial" — the second longest of his career. Despite the duration of the trial, Miller argued, the Crown had not satisfied the legal burden of proving beyond a reasonable doubt that it was Oland who committed this "dastardly deed." He also dismissed the prosecution's two proposed motives of Oland's cash crunch and his father's affair. Neither situation was new, he said, and there was "no evidence whatsoever" of animosity between the father and son over either issue. "Apply your common sense in assessing all the evidence," Miller urged the jurors. "At the end of the day, you will see that the only verdict you can bring back is not guilty."

The burden of proof was on the Crown, so Oland did not have to testify to prove his innocence. But Anthony Moustacalis, president of the Criminal Lawyers' Association, said it was no surprise Oland would take the stand in his own defence. "It happens frequently" in murder trials in Canada. "Juries, in my view, tend to want to hear what the person charged has to say." Putting an accused in the witness box can come with pitfalls, however. Testifying can be stressful, so an accused may not "come across well," and "it's hard to judge someone's entire believability based on a few hours or days on the witness stand." The accused also runs the risk of filling in any gaps in the Crown's case, or inadvertently exposing and amplifying any inconsistencies.

A murder charge, Moustacalis pointed out, has two essential elements: the physical act and the intent. It may be important to have an accused explain his or her actions. Moustacalis cited the case of James Forcillo, the Toronto police officer recently convicted of attempted murder in the 2013 shooting death of a teenager on a streetcar, as an example. Forcillo testified in his own defence even though the incident was captured on video. Testifying also allows the defendant to argue that their good character — "reputation in the community for honesty, and integrity, and peacefulness," to quote Moustacalis — makes them unlikely to have committed the crime in question. On the other hand, that also permits the Crown to question the accused about any examples of bad behaviour, if any exist, he said, but disclosure rules mean the prosecution has to reveal any examples of bad behaviour it intends to raise, so the defence can minimize the risk.

The courtroom was crowded on December 1. National reporters, who had left after the first few days, were back in town, and a handful of Saint John police officers sat in the back row. Everyone was anxious to hear what the defence had to say. The noise level rose steadily until Justice Walsh arrived. He had to deal with a preliminary matter before bringing in the jurors. It took nearly an hour and Walsh apologized for the delay. "We had legal issues to address," he explained to the jury, without elaborating.

It wasn't reportable at the time, but the lawyers were arguing about a timeline the defence wanted to submit into evidence. The timeline covered from 6:55 a.m. on July 6 to 1:28 p.m. on July 7 — outlining Oland's movements in the hours before and after his father's murder. Gary Miller said the twenty-two-page document, which included text messages, emails, and phone calls Dennis Oland made and received on July 6 and July 7, 2011, as well as time-stamped security videos and store receipts, would help the proceedings "flow more smoothly." It would facilitate the presentation to the jury and save time by not having to pull out individual exhibits, he said. Prosecutor P.J. Veniot objected. "The sequence of events here, as I said in my opening, is entirely important," he said. "We had expected a witness would take the witness stand and be able to indicate to this court what it was they did and they said . . . not to have a script in front of them."

"If this can help the jury follow Mr. Oland's testimony, I'm inclined to want to do that," Justice Walsh said, noting the large amount of evidence involved. Oland was a "very important witness," he stressed. "Not literally but figuratively, the man's on trial for his life." Veniot maintained his objection. "It would certainly be an unusual situation if you were to allow this," he said, noting reports by some of the Crown's expert witnesses were not put before the jury. Other witnesses were only allowed to refer to any notes they had, if necessary, to refresh their memory, he said. Walsh countered a timeline was not the same as a report. "No other witness is in the jeopardy Mr. Oland is in," he noted. "That's the difference." Veniot stood his ground. "I think it's premature assisting him in remembering the sequence of events," he argued, and suggested the timeline be entered into evidence following Oland's testimony. But Walsh said waiting until the end would "remove a large part of the benefit" of the document, which he saw as speeding up the process and reducing the risk of the jury being "confused or misled." He told Veniot, "I haven't been told there's anything actually inaccurate in that particular document. . . . It's a timeline of July 6 and 7 that is otherwise not contentious," and ruled the document admissible. "If, Mr. Veniot, at any time you feel it's gone too far," he noted, "you pose an objection, and we'll reel it in."

Miller also requested that the judge advise the jurors that Oland's relatives, who were scheduled to testify in his defence, had been ordered excluded from the courtroom during his testimony. "We don't want the jury to think his family's abandoned him," he said.

The jurors were summoned, and Miller called Oland to the stand. He was sworn in, took his seat and said his name loudly and clearly. Nearly four and a half years after his father's death, he was about to tell his side of the story. A hush fell over the courtroom, and several of the jurors turned in their seats to face him. They had sized him up for the past two-and-a-half months, watching his every move, searching for any signs of his innocence or guilt in his demeanour. On October 28, one of the jurors submitted a note to the judge, questioning the appropriateness of Oland using his smartphone in court. Walsh assured the jury that Oland used the phone not for games but to send text messages to his defence lawyers. In "the old days," he explained, "defendants used to have to write a note, stand up, and hand it to their lawyers." The next day, however, when Oland had something to tell his lawyers, he got out of his seat and whispered in Miller's ear.

Walsh explained to the jury the absence of Oland's loyal family and told them the timeline was just a way for them to keep the order of events in mind, not a substitute for the evidence given. "It is a chart, a guide," he said, "nothing more, nothing less." Then Miller launched his direct examination in dramatic style.

"We'll start at the end," he said. "Did you kill your father?"

"No. No, I did not," Oland replied in a steady voice.

Miller circled back to the morning of July 6, leading Oland through the timeline. Oland appeared quite comfortable on the stand, looking directly at the jurors at times. He wears hearing aids, and a couple of times during his examination he had to ask Miller to speak up. The timeline painted the picture of an ordinary day dealing with family and work-related issues. His son, Henry, was invited to go to New River Beach that day with Oland's sisters, so early morning calls and texts passed between them to coordinate the excursion. Henry was eleven at the time and, given his age, "quite a handful. So I had to be on top of things," Oland said with a smile. His daughter Hannah had an invitation to a friend's cottage, but Oland wanted an apology from her first. "I am hoping she can [go]," he texted the friend's mother. "Right now she has herself in a bit of trouble with me and I am waiting for an apology. If I do not get it, and a good one, I will not be able to let her go. Hopefully she will swallow her pride and do the right thing. I'll let you know." To the court, Oland explained that he and his daughter were "having a bit of a squabble at this point." He didn't explain the cause, but the texts suggested that she had called him lazy. "I will not allow my children to speak to me the way that you have and get away with it without consequences. You will be grounded for this," he texted her. On the stand, he chuckled as he read her response: "Dude i said i was sorry." "Excuse me for laughing…she called me 'Dude.'…She's thirteen years old," he said.

Hannah called and they spoke for about twelve minutes, according to the timeline. Then he texted her again: "Can u do one more thing. You should call your grandfather to thank him for the donation that he gave to send u to NFLD," referring to the anonymous $1,000 donation Richard Oland made to her basketball team's trip. "Since u r prob a bit upset right now u can wait a bit or do it tomorrow. If u need help let me know." The exchange between them ends with Oland texting, "I love u and despite the crappy chat we just had to go through I do think you are wonderful ☺." "Love you 2 and thanks ☺," she replied.

Oland was also texting with his eldest child, Emily, who was hoping to get her braces off that day and needed a drive to her orthodontist's office. "Bet u can't wait til u get yer licence ☺," he wrote. "Yeah no kidding," she replied. Lesley Oland, Dennis's first wife and the children's mother, offered to take her to the appointment. There were also some messages about trying to arrange a summer job for Oland's stepson, Andru Ferguson.

At 9:12 a.m., Oland texted his wife, Lisa Andrik-Oland. "Do u hav my credit card?" He called her twice then texted at 9:18 a.m. to ask again. She replied that it was at the house. "Do u know where?" he asked. Three minutes later, when he hadn't received a response, he texted again: "Where at the house?" Three minutes later: "I cannot leave for work without the card. Where at the house is the card??" Twenty-seven seconds after that, he called her cellphone.

At 1:20 p.m., he sent an email to his father: "Subject: RRIF Trade." Oland said it was regarding a trade he did for him that day. The email indicates the number of shares, the cost, and the commission, he said. At 2:41 p.m., another email: "Subject: CPL Stock Split." It was a "very bizarre stock split...ten for one," he told the courtroom; in his police statement he described it as "hooky." Ten minutes later, he sent him another email about a separate stock issue. He said he also called and talked to his father about the matter. Miller put a photo of the crime scene on the courtroom monitor, showing a blood-spattered document and handwritten note about the transaction on Richard Oland's desk.

Dennis Oland said he was at his CIBC Wood Gundy office all day on July 6, except for when he got lunch at Tim Hortons — at "around two," he told police. Miller used a series of time-stamped surveillance video to lead Oland through the rest of his comings and goings that day. The first video showed him leaving his office at 5:08 p.m. and heading to the parking garage to retrieve his car. "Yes, that was me," said Oland. He was on his way to visit his father at his Far End Corporation office on Canterbury Street to show him some genealogy information he had uncovered during a recent trip to England and to pick up an old logbook to return to his uncle.

The next video showed the top half of a silver car driving by the clock at the bottom of King Street at 5:16 p.m. Oland said that was he in his Volkswagen Golf City. It was "exactly" when he would have been driving by there, he said. Another video showed a silver car driving east up King Street, by the clock again, two minutes later. Oland said he was having trouble finding a parking spot. "So what's happened is I've gone up and around. ... I've done a big loop." He turned right onto Canterbury, a one-way southbound street, and said he parked in the same lot his father used, at the corner of Princess Street. He got out of his car and started up the stairs to his father's second-floor office, toting the genealogy material in a red Sobeys grocery bag. "That's my—someone told me, my man purse," he said, prompting laughter from the packed courtroom. He doesn't like briefcases, he said, and carried the bag everywhere.

On his way up the stairs, he realized "gosh," he had left a book and some documents about an Oland cottage he wanted to show "Dad" back at his office. He said he couldn't remember how far up the stairs he got— maybe to the top, "I may have even gotten into the foyer"—before he went back to his car to go and get them.

Oland observed that people have asked why he didn't just walk the short distance to CIBC that evening. He explained it was easy to park on Chipman Hill and quickly access the elevator to his office in Brunswick House, at the corner of Chipman Hill and King Street. But he realized "en route" he didn't have the pass card required to operate the elevator after five p.m., he said. (The branch manager, John Travis, confirmed the need for a pass card after hours.) Oland had two choices: go back to his father's office, or go home. "I was happy that I could do my genealogy chat with my dad with the stuff that I had," he said.

He headed up King Street again. At 5:22 p.m.—four minutes after he passed the clock, parked his car in the lot near his father's office, got out and went at least partway up the stairs before returning to his car, driving to his office, and then coming back—video showed him passing the clock again. Oland turned down Canterbury. He found a parking spot on the west side of the street, across from the father's office, by the Thandi restaurant parking lot. "I was lucky that time," he said. Grainy black-and-white video from the parking-lot camera captured a small light-coloured car in the top right corner of the frame. The video was time-stamped 16:25, but the camera's clock was off by an hour, and the actual time was 17:25. "That is my vehicle," said Oland. He parked just north of the building, facing south, with the office building to the east, on the left-hand side of his car. The video showed he remained in the car for several minutes. "I think I went into the office after 5:30 p.m.," he said. Robert McFadden and his son had left around 5:31 p.m., according to another time-stamped video. Maureen Adamson was still at work, her husband parked in the loading zone out front.

Oland said his father greeted him with a handshake and a "'How you doing?' type of thing." They hadn't seen each other "for a long period of time," he said. Adamson left a few minutes later, leaving Oland and his father alone. Security video showed her husband's blue Saturn Astra pulling away at around 5:44 p.m. Oland said he and his father had "a great time," laughing together about his discovery of an illegitimate child in the Oland family tree. They pored over the information in detail. "When you're with Dad and you're into a document, it's a bit specific... He wants to dig into something very deeply," he said, speaking in the present tense. His father got a kick out of debunking the "elite," aristocratic notions of the Halifax Olands, who supposedly spent all their money trying to keep up appearances. "Dad wore that with pride. He didn't care for the hoity-toity type of stuff," he said. "It was just a really engaging, wonderful conversation." Later, during Oland's second day of testimony, Miller asked if he and his father had a drink together while they were meeting, alluding to the alcohol detected in Richard Oland's urine. No, replied Oland. They also had not discussed the bounced cheque (although at that point, as noted, the cheque had not been returned NSF) or talked about Dennis's finances. Nor had he asked his father about his affair with Diana Sedlacek.

Miller asked Oland what time he left. "I could say around 6:12 p.m.," around the time he sent a text message intended for his wife, Lisa, to his sister Lisa, by mistake. That text was also included on the timeline. "I am at my dads office doing history stuff," Oland wrote. "I shud not be too long." Oland said he walked out of the building and turned left and started to walk south on Canterbury Street by mistake, toward the lot he had parked in the first time, when he remembered his car was now parked on the street, across from the office, in the other direction. He said he crossed to the west side of the street, in front of Thandi, then crossed back to the east side of the street because his knee was bothering him and he was going to go to the nearby drugstore, the Lawtons in Brunswick Square mall, to buy an over-the-counter painkiller. He changed his mind, however. "I just decided not to do that," he said. Miller played for the jury a 6:12 p.m. video of the sidewalk in front of Thandi that showed Oland, carrying the red bag, walking northbound and crossing back toward his father's office, on the east side. "It really just confirms what I said," said Oland.

Miller asked a sheriff's deputy to turn out the courtroom lights to make the next security video easier to see. It was another one taken from the Thandi parking lot camera across from the office that showed a small light-coloured car in the upper right of the frame at 6:12 p.m. Miller played the approximately four-minute grainy motion-activated video. Then he played it again, asking the jurors to "pay careful attention" to what they might see at the hatchback and the driver's door. Justice Walsh suggested to Miller it might be appropriate to ask his client what he remembered doing. Oland said he remembered taking off his jacket and putting "things" in the back of car. Beyond that, he said, his voice trailing off momentarily, "I remember reading a text or an email message" at the back of the car. "That is what I remember." Miller played the video a third time.

The next video of Canterbury Street showed the bottom half of a light-coloured car driving away just before 6:15 p.m. "That is me. That is my car," said Oland. He pointed out some of the unique features of his City-model car that "make it look a bit funkier" than a regular Volkswagen Golf, such as the wrap-around tail lights, five-spoke rims, black guard on the hood, and low front bumper beneath the licence plate. "It's very clear to me that is my vehicle."

At this point, Justice Walsh called for a recess. During the break, without the jury present, Walsh noted that Miller was "going directly to the videotape and asking [Oland] what he sees as opposed to" what he remembered, which was one of Veniot's concerns. "A gentle reminder, if you would," he said.

The shock came after the break. Miller played another video of a silver car driving up King Street past the clock again at 6:19 p.m., and three others from around the corner on Canterbury Street that showed a small light-coloured car approaching Thandi's parking lot, passing in front of Thandi and continuing past Thandi, at 6:21 p.m. "That's me again," said Oland. "That is me driving by." Oland said he realized he had forgotten the logbook he was supposed to take to his parents' house for his uncle, so he looped back around to get it.

"You went back to your father's office?" asked Miller.

"Yes, I did," Oland replied.

For the first time, Oland testified to taking a third trip to his father's office. He had mentioned only two trips in his handwritten and videotaped statements to police on July 7, 2011, roughly twenty-four hours after the fact. He only remembered making the third trip "in the following days afterward," he said. Miller did not ask Oland when, or if, he told anyone once he remembered his third trip to 52 Canterbury Street. Nor was it clear whether the defence knew about the third trip earlier in the trial, when they had more than once played the video of Oland walking in front of Thandi at 6:12 p.m., stressing the lack of any visible blood on him, as though they understood it to show Oland's final exit from his father's office. Now, Oland revealed he had returned a few minutes later.

The logbook, Oland said, was for an old camp on his mother's side of the family, but members of his father's side had helped build it, he said. His father had borrowed the book from Oland's uncle, Jack Connell, about a year prior to scan it, and Connell was anxious to get it back, he said. Maureen Adamson had testified she needed to ensure Connie got the book so she could return it to Connell, who lives in Toronto but was visiting and was understood to be leaving soon. But an email Connell sent to Dennis Oland the next morning stated: "I'm around all summer — & the living is easy."

Oland said because of the importance of getting the book to his uncle, he decided to go back. He had trouble finding a parking spot again, so this time he turned the wrong way up Princess Street "about two car lengths" and pulled into the gravel parking lot at the corner of Princess and Canterbury. In his videotaped police statement, he had said he made that wrong turn on his second trip. He said he didn't take his phone or jacket with him when he went back up to the Far End Corporation office; he didn't expect to be long. Oland testified to walking to the long table in the centre of the office to retrieve the logbook from the end of the table, near the typewriter. In court, he marked an interactive diagram of the office layout to show where he found the logbook. His father was by Adamson's desk at the time, he said. "He made me stay and go through it with him."

The book included an entry about his father when he and Connie were dating. "Dick had to go home to shovel shit," it said— "There's a horse barn," Oland explained, generating laughter— "for only $20 a week." There were other entries about having to look for the "Goddamned well," drinking and playing cards, and making a grave marker for a dead rabbit. "It's just funny," said Oland.

When he got back to his car, his wife, Lisa, called at 6:36 p.m. The timeline showed she had also tried to reach him at 6:24 p.m., but that call went to voicemail because, he said, he left his phone in the car while he ran up to get the logbook. She was "a bit upset" because she never got the text message he had mistakenly sent to his sister, so "she didn't have a clue where I was," he said; in his police statement, he'd said his wife knew he was going to his father's office, "she just didn't know it was going to take me that long." She also had a cold and wanted to get some medication. "So I just said I'd be right home." But he didn't go straight home, the court heard. He made a stop at Renforth wharf. Miller asked him his purpose in stopping. Oland said his children hung out there a lot on hot summer days when they were staying at their mother's place just up the hill, as they were that week. "It's not easy when you go through a divorce and you don't see your kids half the time," he said. "If I can find a way to run into them, I do." He said he couldn't see to the end of the wharf to tell if they were there and had noticed two broken beer bottles (including "a Moosehead red label bottle") in a gap between boulders where people normally walk. So he got out of his car, put on his jacket, and retrieved the red Sobeys bag. He said he picked up the broken glass, walked to the end of the wharf, and looked over the edge to see if his children were in the water. The tide was low, he said, so he had to look over the side. Not seeing them, he "sat down on the end of the wharf, looking around to see if I could see any of their friends," and "put the beer bottles in the bag." Then he drove home. Oland told the court he couldn't remember if he disposed of the broken glass in the garbage at the wharf or at home. He was not asked whether he removed the genealogy documents from the bag before putting in the broken glass, but he had noted that the bag had "two sleeves on the side that are separate from the rest of the bag, ... [s]o I put the bottles in there."

Miller propped an enlarged map of the uptown Saint John area on a large easel at the front of the courtroom, with some difficulty. "That's why we became lawyers, eh? Not tech savvy," joked Justice Walsh. "You don't need any skill when you become a lawyer," replied Miller. He asked Oland to mark on the map what routes he took on each of his three trips to his father's office. Oland marked the first trip in blue, the second in green, and the third in orange. On another enlarged map of the Saint John and Rothesay areas, Miller asked Oland to mark the route he took on his way home. He travelled Lower Cove Loop to Crown Street and out to the highway on-ramp, took Highway 1 east to the Rothesay Road exit, and drove down to Renforth wharf. He drove back to Rothesay Road and then to his home at 58 Gondola Point Road.

Oland estimated he got home between 7:00 and 7:10. He said he went upstairs, changed into a short-sleeved shirt and shorts, left his other clothes on the bed, and went downstairs to look for his wife, who was in the sunroom. When she went upstairs and she saw his clothes on the bed, she told him to put them away, he said, describing her as a "neat freak." The couple went to Kennebecasis Drugs to get some cold medication for Lisa, he said. Security video showed them arriving at 7:38 p.m. Their receipt was for only one item, Buckley's Complete, for $10.99, plus tax. The receipt is time-stamped 7:42 p.m., although the time-stamped video showed them leaving the drugstore at 7:40 p.m. The next time-stamped video showed the couple at Cochran's Country Market from 7:38 to 7:42 p.m. The time discrepancy between the Cochran's video and the drugstore video remained unexplained but likely arose from inaccurately set clocks on the recording equipment.

After shopping, Oland said they went home, ate dinner, and then he did some gardening and put their hens away for the night. Then they watched part of *The Life Aquatic*, a Wes Anderson movie with Bill Murray. During the film, Oland went to buy milk at the nearby Irving gas station and convenience store on Marr Road. Video showed him walking in at 10:32 p.m. and driving away two minutes later. "I think the movie idea kinda petered out then," Oland observed. "We might have watched a little bit more of it, but then went upstairs to bed, or up to the bedroom. I probably read for a bit then went to sleep."

Oland did not deliver the logbook that night, the logbook he said he had made a third trip to his father's office to get, the court heard. His parents' house, where his uncle was staying, is just down the street and around the corner from his home, roughly a five-minute walk away, but he didn't drop it off until the following morning.

Oland's testimony occupied two full days. The courtroom was full the first day, even though it wasn't publicly announced he would be in the witness box. Once word got out he would testify in his own defence the following day, so many people showed up that some had to be turned away. Court proceedings are open to the public, but the posted occupancy limit for that courtroom is 124, under the New Brunswick Fire Prevention Act, and no one is allowed to stand "out of respect for the court," said George Oram, the regional sheriff for the southern district. His deputies brought in some extra chairs to put at the back of the courtroom, but once the maximum head count was reached, they had to start denying entry, he said. Oram believed it was the first time that had ever happened in the roughly two years since the Saint John Law Courts building opened.

The second day began with Miller's continued direct examination of Oland. A couple of courtroom sketch artists sat at the front of the crowded courtroom to document the proceedings. Miller led his client through some of the events of July 7, 2011, the day his father's body was discovered. The first entry on the timeline for that day was a security video from Kent Building Supplies on Consumers Drive on Saint John's east side at 8:08 a.m. Oland said he was searching for parts to jerry-rig a fix for a recurring problem on his wife's sailboat, *Loki*. The throttle becomes disengaged, he said. At 8:47 a.m., he picked up a sail cover for the boat from the Estey Group on City Road in Saint John's south central peninsula, according to a receipt submitted into evidence. At 9:22 a.m., he went to the Irving gas station on Millidge Avenue in the city's north end. Security video showed him, in the periphery of the frame, get out of his car, open the back door on the driver's side, and walk out of the camera's range and then get back in his car and drive away by 9:25 a.m.

Oland forwarded an email from a client to his assistant at 9:49 a.m., and emailed her again at 9:56 a.m. "I was in [the office] but I have now left to go do some work on the boat. Its too nice a day ☺," he wrote. His uncle, Jack Connell, emailed him at 11:10 a.m. to thank him for dropping off the logbook and to ask for a suggestion for what he could buy Maureen Adamson as a thank-you gift. Connell, who was another one of Oland's CIBC clients, also inquired about some stocks. Oland replied at 11:14 a.m. "I am not at the office right now. I was there for a bit but decided to go and do some work on the boat. Nice days like this are hard to pass up! ☺ If I get things done on schedule I do plan to go back to the office, if not, I'll have a look tomorrow morning." At 11:16 a.m., he sent Connell another email. "Oh, as for Maureen, I think she's just happy to do it." In the interim of those messages, Oland had driven back to the city's east side, to the Canadian Tire on Westmorland Road, where he spent roughly half an hour. A receipt showed he bought a wire rope clip, a 22-inch universal lawnmower blade, five "No Trespassing" signs and three "Private Property" signs.

He said he was at the Royal Kennebecasis Yacht Club working on the sailboat when his uncle called him shortly before twelve thirty p.m. and told him to go his parents' house. "Something bad had happened," he said. "It's your father." Oland said he drove there right away, arriving within fifteen minutes. The family was gathered in the family room, "emotionally distressed," when the police showed up at two p.m., said Oland. "All of us made inquiries as to what happened to our father. They [the officers] wouldn't provide any answers," he said. "We weren't getting any answers and we were all asking, sort of repeatedly."

Miller asked Oland about the statement he made to police early that evening. Why had he told police he was wearing a navy blazer when he went to his father's office, Miller inquired. "Clearly I was mistaken," Oland replied. He said he believed he might have said that because he had been wearing a navy blazer on the morning of the interview, as seen in the Kent Building Supplies video. "I wasn't wearing it very long, but I was wearing it." He tends to wear sports jackets in the summer, rather than suits, because it's too hot to wear ties, he said. Miller asked Oland if the police had advised him they would review security video to verify what he told them, and Oland said that they had.

Oland confirmed he was wearing the brown sports jacket when he visited his father: the jacket that had four small confirmed bloodstains on it, three of which matched his father's DNA profile. He was also wearing a checked dress shirt. As the jury had already heard, police found staining on a checked shirt they believed he was wearing, but it had been laundered and tests did not confirm the presence of blood. When asked what shoes he was wearing, Oland pointed to a photo of the brown shoes police had seized from his home and tested. No blood was confirmed. Nor was any blood confirmed on the red bag taken into evidence, the "man purse" Oland said he was carrying that day. What, if anything, did he have to do with clothes being taken to a dry cleaner on July 8? asked Miller. Nothing, Oland replied.

Oland said he had owned the brown Hugo Boss sports jacket for about two years. He bought it in Orlando, Florida, in April 2009, along with a suit, he said. The defence produced a Visa statement that showed a Hugo Boss purchase on April 27 for US$860.47. Oland testified that he wore the jacket regularly, more than once a week, and had worn the jacket in his father's presence many times. Miller revisited the theory that the blood on the jacket could have transferred through routine contact. He asked if there was any physical contact between Oland and his father. "There's always physical contact when you're in his presence," said Oland, again speaking in present tense. "The big handshake and the pat on the back sort of thing." Miller asked Oland to role-play his father and demonstrate for the jury. Oland stood in the witness box and shook Miller's hand while grabbing hold of his elbow. Miller asked Oland if he ever noticed blood on his father. Oland replied that he had; his father often chewed his cuticles. "He was a constant chewer," Oland said, and would sometimes have dried blood on his fingers. He said he also often saw scabs on his father's bald head. "He would scratch at them and pick at them," leaving "crusty blood" behind.

The defence had suggested earlier in the trial that if Richard Oland's blood was on Dennis's jacket, it could have been transferred through innocent contact. Maureen Adamson confirmed that her employer had a skin condition that sometimes made his scalp bleed, and he often had scabs on his scalp. Adamson also confirmed he had a hearing problem and would often lean in when speaking to someone. Miller asked if Oland was "touchy-feely" and Adamson agreed he was.

"He liked to get close to people," Robert McFadden concurred. "He would invade your space." John Travis of CIBC Wood Gundy, who had known Oland most of his life, said that when Oland shook someone's hand, he would also often put his hand on their shoulder, or put his arm around them. Oland acted the same way with his son, said Travis. The defence had introduced a series of photos of Oland socializing at the 1996 opening of the New Brunswick Museum at its Market Square location to illustrate their point. Travis said he had cautioned Oland about being such a close talker, particularly with clients. He advised him to give people their space, he said. Diana Sedlacek, however, had testified that his skin condition was never severe and had been cleared up for at least the eighteen months prior to his death, and the pathologist did not recall noting any open sores on Oland's scalp that were unrelated to the attack.

Dennis Oland said that his brown sports jacket had been stored in his father's closet for a few months in 2010. His parents were travelling in the Caribbean between February and April, and his home was being renovated at that time, so his family moved into his parents' home, he said. (Adamson corroborated this during her testimony.) Even after his parents returned, he kept his clothes stored in his father's closet for roughly another month, he said, until his father asked him to remove them. "He kept getting confused as to what was his and what was mine," he said, the implication being that his father may even have put on his brown sports jacket at some point by mistake. Oland also recounted an incident in August or September 2010, when he used his father's workshop to straighten a tractor steering arm that bent while he was doing some ditching on his farm. He said he was wearing the brown sports jacket when he stopped at his parents' on his way home from work. He took the jacket off in the workshop and ended up forgetting it, he said. When he returned a few days later to retrieve it, his father, who was "very particular about his workshop," grabbed the jacket and handed it to him, he said. Oland told the court he recalled seeing blood or a scab on his father's head at the time.

Miller touched briefly on some financial dealings between father and son. Oland said his father wanted him to buy his grandparents' house after they died and arranged the financing for him with a $10,000 annual payment. There were other arrangements over the years, where his father would put up the money, and he would pay him back. Some payments were missed, but there was no drama, he said. His father would refinance him and they "carried on."

They had an "old school" father-son relationship, he told the court. "It was a bit formal," a bit "father-knows-best." There was "a properness about it," he said. "He wasn't a guy that was gonna say every day 'I love you,'" but he would say it "from time to time." It might come across as cold, said Oland, but he suggested it was the same for many of his friends. They grew up addressing adults as "sir," or "mister," he said. "It's the type of thing that doesn't exist as much today as it did then." He is more of a friend with his children than his father ever was with him, he observed.

Oland described his father as being very particular and impatient. "Sometimes he wasn't nice about it, and so you had to deal with that." He could be hurtful sometimes, he said, but you just had to understand that was his nature. He said they never had "big fights." The biggest one he could remember was "the Christmas fruitcake, rum cake scenario." Any differences between them would blow over quickly, he said. He didn't recall any grudges.

Oland spoke admiringly of his father as an adventurer. "Probably one of the most interesting people I ever met... So engaging." He was glued to his side as a child, he said, and lately, their relationship was better than ever. His father seemed more interested and engaged in him and his life, he said. They skied together with Oland's children, talked politics, and their family history project was a "wonderful thing." "I think he stopped looking at me as being his child and started to see me as an adult," he said. Miller asked Oland if he loved his father. "Absolutely, yes," Oland replied. Did he miss him? "Yeah," Oland said, wiping his eyes with a tissue. "Yeah."

No more questions.

Miller might have been done, but Veniot was just gearing up. The punctilious prosecutor knew this cross-examination was critical, and he wasn't going to let Oland's sudden surge of emotion go unchallenged. He wasn't buying it—and his job was to make sure no one else did either. He was out to prove patricide, and he intended to use Oland's own words to help him do it. He pulled out the 114-page transcript of the statement Oland gave to police, just hours after learning of his father's death, when Oland shed no tears.

Didn't you say your relationship changed in your adolescence, asked Veniot; in Oland's statement, he had said, "My teenage years with him were very difficult." Yes, said Oland. That your father was harder on you than your sisters? That he expected more of you, just as his father did of him? Again, from the police statement: "I was the only son, so I think I took most of the pressure." Didn't you say you did not have a close father-son relationship? Oland responded that at times they were close, and at other times they were not. Veniot directed him to turn to page 8: "My father and I weren't close son, father and son." Oland had also told the police, "He and I didn't have that close father-son relationship.... He had this thing that you can't be friends with your son."

Is it fair to say in your family, you were not given things; you were expected to earn on your own? Veniot asked. "Somewhat true," said Oland. Veniot cited page 17: "In our family, you know, you don't get given stuff." Page 21: "He doesn't go out and buy you things, he doesn't take you on trips." Oland countered the comments were made in the context of his family's wealth. He was given a car as a graduation gift, for example, and trips. They were given stuff, he said, just not on a silver platter. But, Veniot pressed, there was definitely a nature of "provide for yourself and learn the value of money and hard work?" "Yes," Oland conceded.

Were all of the family members asked to give statements? Yes. Was the statement you gave—both written and oral—the best you could recollect? Yes. Nothing deliberately misleading? No. You had no reason to believe you were a suspect at that time? No. You were not under arrest? No. You were there as a witness? Yes. "No misleading on your part whatsoever?" Veniot pressed. "No, sir," Oland replied.

Veniot turned his attention to the mistress motive. He asked Oland how the news of his father's extramarital affair affected him. "I certainly couldn't say that I liked it," said Oland. "It was an odd situation for me, because I guess I'm a bit naïve. If I'm in a situation where there's a rumour, I tend to want to validate that rumour with fact." Because he had no direct knowledge or confirmed information about it, he said, he "put it in limbo." His sister, Lisa Bustin, was "more engaged in that topic," he said. "I sort of, in a lazy way, just let her carry that...I didn't want anything to do with it."

Veniot's questions about July 7 bounced around from Oland's trip to the office, the hardware stores, and the yacht club—hoping, perhaps that his story would shift and expose him as a liar. All Oland's answers were composed and clear; the courtroom was silent.

Then Veniot turned to the financial motive. It was an area Miller had avoided delving into in any depth, but Veniot drilled down. He emphasized Oland's escalating debt and mounting expenses. The $500,000 loan your father gave you, did he make you sign a promissory note for that money? Oland said he did, but his father told him there would be no obligation to make any principal payments. "If I were to receive an inheritance at some point in the future, it would be deducted from that," he said, as Robert McFadden had said. Would you have been able to get a loan for that amount, asked Veniot. Oland said he already had a mortgage on the house. "I didn't have to ask him. He offered," he said. "That's what surprised me, [which] was nice." It was important to his father "that I be able to keep the house," he said, "because during my divorce my ex-wife had attempted to list the house for sale."

Veniot asked Oland if, in August 2010, he got a collateral mortgage to secure a $75,000 line of credit? He said he had. Did you advise the bank of your monthly spousal and child support payments of $4,322? Oland said he had no recollection, but "they generally ask you to provide information." Did you advise the bank of the $500,000 loan from your father? No. In March 2011, when you increased your line of credit to $163,000, did you tell the bank about your spousal and child support payments? Again, Oland said he couldn't recall. "I certainly didn't provide any information about a loan," he said.

Asked whether he told his father he had gotten the increase by securing it against his $650,000 home, Oland replied, "I did not tell him anything." Veniot suggested the collateral mortgage was an encumbrance on the property his father was supposed to have a mortgage on and questioned whether Oland was concerned his father would "not be happy" if he found out. No, said Oland. Although there had been "initial discussion" about his $500,000 loan being secured against the house, it never went anywhere. In his police statement Oland had said, "So basically I have a mortgage with him." In court Oland testified that he did not believe his father was supposed to have a mortgage on the house.

Veniot also quizzed Oland about whether he misled his boss at CIBC Wood Gundy about the prospect of bringing in up to $20 million of new business from his father and another client in order to get a $16,000 advance on his pay. But Oland testified he wasn't suggesting the full amount of that money would come from his father and the other client. He was in the process of "building a prospecting list" and "had other people in mind." Veniot pointed out Oland never used the word "prospect" in the email, naming only his father and the other client. Oland said the request for the advance was unrelated to the millions mentioned. September is always a "wonderfully busy month" and all indicators were the stock market downturn was coming to its end, he said. How much of his father's investments did he handle, Veniot asked. Oland estimated it was about 10 to 20 per cent. He told police he was more of an order-taker on stocks for his father? Oland acknowledged he had said that. His father felt he could beat the markets, but he couldn't, he said. Part of his job as an adviser was to protect investors from themselves, so he tried to steer his father, he said.

Veniot also explored two automated-teller withdrawals Oland made on his overdrawn $27,000-limit CIBC Visa on July 6, 2011, the day police believed his father was killed: two withdrawals of $401.50 each. Oland told the court he didn't remember making them. Veniot expressed incredulity that on the same day he was texting his wife, trying to locate his credit card, he didn't remember getting cash advances. Veniot pulled out Oland's chequing account records, which showed an ATM deposit of $780 that same day. Did you have pre-authorized payments on your account for your spousal and child support payments and the $1,667 you owed your father each month? Yes. Did you ask your father's secretary to delay depositing a cheque to him because you knew it would bounce? Yes. So your chequing account was overdrawn the day of the murder? Yes. Your Visa was $5,000 over its limit? Yes. Your $163,000 line of credit was at its limit? Yes. Your income was less than what you expected, less than what you would have hoped for? Yes. Would it be fair to say in July 2011 you were not in a position to meet your monthly expenses as they were coming due? "That would be correct."

Your wife's credit card was also maxed out? Oland said he couldn't recall. Veniot refreshed his memory by showing him email exchanges between him and his wife about her overdrawn Visa and the email in which Oland had asked his wife if he could get $1,000 from her or her line of credit. Your wife was off work at the time? Yes, until September, Oland acknowledged. "We lived a tight existence," Oland said. And yet, Veniot pointed out, you took trips to England, Rome, Budapest, and Florida during that period. Oland confirmed that was true.

Had you requested an increase on your credit limit and been refused, asked Veniot. Oland said he couldn't recall. Is it fair to say it would have been tough to convince the bank to lend you more money? No, said Oland. In fact, he subsequently did borrow more, he said, noting his house is worth $650,000. (During his bail hearing in November 2013, the court heard he increased his line of credit by an additional $300,000 one year after his father's murder.) Would a bank lend you money knowing what you owed your father? Veniot asked. Oland maintained there was no reason to tell the bank about his father's loan, but Veniot persevered.

Is it reasonable that an option for your financial problems would have been to approach your father for help? Oland testified he could have asked his father for more money, but he did not. He wasn't overly concerned about his finances, he said. As an investment adviser, he had seen ups and downs in the market before, and things always eventually turned around. All indications were that the stock market downturn was coming to an end, he said. You did not tell your father on July 6 about the financial mess you were in? No. Even though he had the resources to help you, you didn't ask? No.

Veniot turned his attention to the video of Oland leaving his office tower on July 6 at 5:08 p.m. on his way to visit his father. He wanted to know what Oland was carrying in his left hand. "I've tried to figure that out," Oland replied. He said he thought it might be notepads. It appears to be white and several inches thick, resembling paperback books. So you remembered whatever genealogy material you had in your red bag, but not the important information you wanted to show him? Correct. How often did you visit your father? About once a month, said Oland. According to McFadden, Dennis would "drop in" about "four or five times a year," and the most recent visit he knew of, he said, was about a month prior. McFadden said he was unaware Oland was coming that night, and there was no record of a planned visit. Did you ever call ahead? Veniot asked. No. Did your father or anyone know you were coming? No. When you realized you had forgotten this important information, could you have gotten someone to let you back into your office? Possibly. Veniot noted the short distance between the two offices and questioned why Oland didn't walk. He said he never walked over, because then he'd have to come back and retrieve his car from the parking garage. Plus he had a sore knee that day, he added.

Veniot picked up on that, asking about Oland's zigzag movement after leaving his father's office, when he was captured on video at 6:12 p.m. crossing from the west side of Canterbury Street back toward his father's office on the east side before crossing back again to his car on the west side. Oland had said he was thinking of going to the drugstore to buy pain medication for his knee and then changed his mind. Veniot pointed out Lawtons closes at 6:00 p.m. and asked Oland if he knew the drugstore would already be closed. No, said Oland. Veniot noted the email Oland intended to send to his wife but sent to his sister by mistake at 6:12 p.m. indicated he was still at his father's office. "I believe I sort of bluffed it a bit to buy time, to say, 'I'm still here' when I'm not, I'm on my way out," he said. (Veniot did not ask him to explain that comment.) Oland said he wouldn't have texted in front of his father, so he would have sent the message either as he was leaving the office or as he was leaving the building. Not after? Oland couldn't say.

You told police you left around six thirty p.m., does that still hold true, asked Veniot. Yes, said Oland, because he received a call from his wife at 6:36 p.m. So you were alone with your father for roughly forty-five minutes, from 5:45 p.m., when Maureen Adamson left, until 6:30 p.m., when you left? Approximately, yes, Oland agreed. Was the back door open or closed? Oland said it was closed. If it was open, he would have taken note, he said. Your wife was not expecting you to be late? No. You had not mentioned you were going to be meeting with your father? No, she only learned that when we spoke. And when your wife called, you said you were heading home? Yes. Did you tell your wife you would be stopping at the wharf on your way? I did not, he said. How long is the drive to the wharf? Oland estimated it was fifteen minutes. You said you went to the wharf to see if your children were there, but isn't it true there was a better chance your children were not going to be there? Oland disagreed. Veniot reminded him his son Henry had gone to New River Beach that day, which is roughly a forty-minute drive, southwest of Rothesay. Oland's text messages also seemed to indicate his daughter Hannah had already been at the wharf kayaking earlier in the day.

Veniot noted Oland was wearing his jacket at the wharf. Oland testi-fied he had taken off his brown sports jacket after the second trip to his father's office and didn't bring it up with him on the third visit, but Veniot pointed out that witnesses said, and Oland confirmed, he wore his jacket at the wharf. Why? Veniot wanted to know. Oland described himself as a bit "old-fashioned" that way. If he's walking around, he wears his jack-et. He was not, however, wearing a jacket during his police statement, or at Canadian Tire on July 7. And you had the red reusable grocery bag with you on the wharf? Yes, to put the broken glass into. You sat down at one point: was that to put the bottles in the bag? Oland said he didn't think it was singularly for that. You were there about five minutes? Approximately, yes.

Phone records showed Oland called his wife's cellphone at 7:24 p.m., but they were calling each other at the same time, so the calls went to voicemail. Oland called his wife's cell again at 7:26 p.m., which also went to voicemail, and then she called his phone at 7:28 p.m., which connected. Oland said the calls weren't made on his way home, but after he was already there. He called her because he couldn't locate her in the house, he said. In his statement to police, he had also mentioned locating his wife through a phone call.

Veniot asked about taking the brown sports jacket to be dry cleaned on July 8, the day after Oland was questioned by police and was told he was a suspect in his father's death. You had nothing to do with the dry-cleaning decision? No, said Oland. The family had at least four visitations coming up and the funeral; "everybody needed clean clothes," he said. Did you wear the brown sports jacket to any of those events? Veniot asked. Oland said he didn't know. His stepson had tried it on, but it didn't fit, he said. Were you and your father the same size? No. His father wore 40/42, and he wears 38/40. Veniot argued that meant there wasn't much chance Richard Oland would have put on any of his son's clothes by mistake when they were stored in his closet in 2010, as implied by the defence's blood transfer argument.

During his cross-examination, Veniot also underscored discrepancies between Oland's statement to police and his testimony. Not only did Oland get which jacket he was wearing wrong and the number of visits wrong, the prosecutor said, but he also told police his father was sitting at his desk when he left the office and then testified he was standing near his secretary's desk. Veniot wondered how he could get that wrong, just twenty-four hours after the last time he saw his father alive. Oland told the court those were "two separate occasions." During their meeting, a news story on the TV had caught his father's attention, so he could tell the meeting was over and said goodbye. His father was sitting at his desk at that time. But when he returned to get the logbook, his father was by his secretary's desk, he said.

In his police statement, Oland said he may or may not have used the washroom in the foyer outside his father's office on his first trip; he couldn't remember. Yet more than four years later, Oland testified he was certain he did not use the washroom. Veniot wondered how that was possible. Oland said he now knew he didn't use the washroom at the office, because he remembered using the washroom when he got home that night, prompting Veniot to remark that Oland had a very peculiar memory; as time passed, he remembered distant events more clearly. (He did not ask Oland to account for his detailed memory of the 2010 incident in his father's workshop, when he said he observed dried blood on his father's head as he handed him his brown sports jacket.) Although Constable Stephen Davidson asked him repeatedly to carefully recount his comings and goings, he was better able to recall now, he said.

Would you agree there are inconsistencies with what you told police in 2011 and what you have told the court? Yes. He elaborated that his ability to remember events had changed with the passage of time. Now, he was "not under the same level of stress and sadness." Veniot played the end of Oland's videotaped statement, when he was tracing imaginary routes on the tabletop and mumbling to himself, seemingly utterly confused. Veniot then asked Oland to read the transcript of what he had said. Did you know you were on camera at the time? Veniot asked, pushing up the bridge of his silver Harry Potter–style glasses to look Oland directly in the eye. I would have assumed, said Oland. You were not attempting to mislead the police? "Nothing in this [statement] was an attempt to mislead anybody," Oland replied.

The morning after Oland's testimony ended, the defence abruptly closed its case. Miller informed the court that he and colleagues Alan Gold and James McConnell saw "no need to call any other evidence." Other than Oland, the defence had only called a bloodstain pattern analyst and a forensic computer expert. The jury would not hear from Oland's wife, mother, sister, uncle, and friend after all.

To Christopher Hicks, a veteran Toronto lawyer who specializes in murder cases, the surprise move demonstrated the defence team's confidence. "It's a wonderful gift for a criminal lawyer to have a client with no criminal record, an upstanding member of the community, well spoken, intelligent, and put him on the stand to say, 'I didn't kill my father.' He doesn't really have to go much further than that," Hicks said. Oland had "a few inconsistencies in the evidence" to address, but "nothing serious," in Hicks's opinion. Some observers cynically inferred the defence never had any intention of calling the other witnesses and that the sudden stop was meant to plant the impression of a strong case in the minds of the jurors. Hicks did not believe that was the scenario. "In an important trial like this, a jury trial, the defence counsel is recalculating all the time," he noted. "Dennis Oland must have done very well in his testimony and that just precluded any more testimony." The other witnesses would have been "superfluous," he said.

Asked whether the defence might have been concerned about evidence the Crown might have uncovered through its cross-examination of the other witnesses, Hicks said it was possible but "most unlikely." Knowing when to "shut up and sit down" is part of "the criminal law business," he said. Part of the strategy of closing immediately following Oland's testimony might have been to see it go to the jurors as soon as possible, so the defence could reinforce what he had said while it was still fresh in the jurors' minds, Hicks added.

Walsh announced an eleven-day adjournment. It was a "very long" trial with a "mass of evidentiary detail" and the lawyers needed time to prepare their closing arguments, he told the jurors. He also needed time to prepare his instructions to them. Walsh planned to give the jurors a written copy of his instructions. He had previously commented to the lawyers in the jurors' absence that it was "unusual," but he felt not doing so in this case would "simply be unfair."

"I told you at the outset, I don't blow smoke. I don't gild the lily, so to speak," Walsh reminded the jury when he told them about the adjournment. "My charge will be long," he warned, possibly up to two days. Walsh urged the jurors to make good use of their time off. "With the holiday season coming, if you have any decorating to do, or Christmas baking, or other arrangements, get all of that done," he said. They should also get some rest before deliberations, he advised. "You will find it will be tough duty. It's a tough task," said Walsh. It will be "mentally exhausting" and "emotionally draining." He reminded them only twelve jurors could deliberate, so one of them would be eliminated by a random draw. (The jury of fourteen had shrunk to thirteen on October 5 when Walsh discharged juror No. 7 because he "had a close association to someone" involved in the case.) As Veniot put it in their absence: "Unlucky juror number 13 gets booted at some point," to which Walsh said, "Given how long they've been together, it will not be a pleasant task." Once deliberations began, he told the jurors, they would be sequestered, "cut off from the world," until they reached a unanimous verdict. To the lawyers, he'd expressed it differently. "Once I charge the jury," he said, "they are together come heck or high water."

CLOSING ARGUMENTS

The evidence phase of the trial was over. The testimony of the nearly fifty witnesses covered everything from the father-son relationship to details about the police investigation, blood and DNA evidence, and cellphone technology. But there was no big reveal, no "aha moment." Around town, people continued to discuss the case, although conversations seemed to shift from problems with the police investigation to DNA random-match probabilities, cell tower pings, and the definition of reasonable doubt. Soon, Dennis Oland's fate would be in the jury's hands. But first, the defence and Crown would deliver their closing arguments, and Justice Walsh would give his instructions to the jury.

Walsh welcomed the jurors back from their eleven-day break, telling them he missed their "smiling faces" and that he hoped they were well rested; they still faced a long, difficult road. He asked them to stop discussing the case among themselves until they heard the closing arguments from both sides, as well as his instructions.

Both defence lawyer Alan Gold and prosecutor P.J. Veniot prefaced their closing arguments with acknowledgements of the importance of the jury's role and appreciation for the panel's service. The jurors, Gold noted, had "truly an awesome responsibility to sit in judgment of [their] fellow citizen." They were the "ultimate judges of his fate," and it was their responsibility to prevent the possibility of a wrongful conviction. The presumption of innocence is the "very cornerstone of our system of justice," he said. The burden of proof beyond a reasonable doubt rested with the Crown. It was not enough to think Oland was possibly guilty, probably guilty, or even likely guilty, he said. The standard was higher, more rigorous and exacting.

P.J. Veniot argued the identity of the person who killed Richard Oland was the issue before them. "It's Dennis Oland," he said. "The Crown submits it cannot be anyone else." Oland was the last known person to see his father alive and had "clear opportunity" when he was alone with him in his office between approximately 5:44 and 6:30 p.m. He only visited his father's office four or five times a year, yet he just "happened to be" visiting on the same day his father was killed, wearing the brown sports jacket later revealed to have his father's blood and DNA on it. The crime was not a robbery: police found no sign of forced entry and the victim's Rolex watch, wallet, and digital equipment were left untouched. The savagery of the attack indicated it was a "crime of passion," committed by someone Richard Oland knew. Dennis Oland's statement to police portrayed a strained father-son relationship, much worse than the one he depicted during his testimony, noted Veniot. Oland had matter-of-factly told police his father was not the easiest guy to get along with and they didn't have a close relationship, but in the witness box, he fought back tears as he told the court he loved and missed his father. "It was unclear he was still talking about the same relationship," remarked Veniot.

Oland also had motive, the prosecutor argued. His financial circumstances were the "polar opposite" of his father's, he said. Richard Oland was a multimillionaire who could afford the best but watched his money carefully. He would invite family on vacations and make them pay their own way. He even made his wife submit receipts to justify her monthly spending. Dennis Oland, meanwhile, spent with abandon and got himself into financial messes; none bigger than the one he faced on the eve of the murder, according to Veniot. Oland did not tell the bank about his father's loan against his house, he didn't tell his father about the bank loans against the house, and he borrowed heavily from his employer on a promise of bringing in new business. Oland had nowhere left to turn, Veniot posited. His father was his "last resort," and he asked him for more money on the night in question. "Why not? Richard Oland had more money than either he or Connie would ever be able to spend in their lifetimes. Why not take another bite out of the inheritance?" Had Oland asked the "Bank of Daddy" for "a few more thousand dollars" and promised "Dad" it would never happen again? "You can imagine how a conversation like that ended," he told the jury.

Gold rejected the Crown's proposed motive. Not "a shred of evidence" existed to prove that Dennis Oland's finances "would produce the kind of emotion that would lead to this brutal killing," he argued. Money troubles were nothing new. He normally spent more than he earned. He hadn't tried to borrow more money from his bank and been refused, although, Gold argued, he could have borrowed up to $300,000 more on the line of credit secured against his house. There was also no evidence Richard Oland was upset about Dennis's financial situation. "Richard Oland appears to have cared less," Gold observed.

Police found "not a shred" of evidence on Dennis Oland's computers that he planned or carried out the crime. Nothing in his email or Internet search history about his finances or his father's mistress; "nothing about iPhones, hammers, bloodstains — nothing." And his actions were "inconsistent" with him being the killer, he argued. Whoever killed "Dick" planned the attack before they went to the office and brought the weapon with them, Gold submitted. If Oland planned to kill him, why would he go when his father's secretary was still at work? He knew the office routine; he could have waited until everyone was gone for the day and no one would have ever known he was there, he said.

Oland, Gold noted, "was not afraid to take the stand, and tell you in his own words that he was not guilty." Some of his testimony may have "reflected his nervousness," but that's to be expected when you're defending yourself on a murder charge, said Gold. His testimony was "frank, straightforward, and honest," "candid and forthright," he said. Gold acknowledged "differences" between Oland's statement to police and his testimony. But "they are not important, and they do not affect his believability," he insisted. Gold pointed out that Oland believed he was giving the statement as a witness, not a suspect, and would not have realized how important every detail about his actions would become. He also urged jurors to consider Oland's state of mind at the time of the interview. He had just learned of his father's death but didn't know what had happened to him, and he had to break the "terrible news" to his three children. Mistakes, Gold suggested, would be understandable.

Oland told police he was wearing a navy blazer when he was actually wearing a brown sports jacket, and he told police he went to the office twice when he actually went three times. Both were "honest mistakes," said Gold. Police had advised him they could verify his story through security videos, he reminded the jurors, so why would he lie? Gold argued that Oland's inaccurate statement to police was actually a sign of his innocence. A killer would have had a "nice, easily flowing" story ready; Oland didn't. If Oland wanted to lie, he could have omitted any mention of the third visit.

Veniot said the timing of the third visit was "consistent with" the time prosecutors believed Richard Oland was killed, and his wrong turn up a familiar one-way street pointed to a "distracted and distraught" man. Oland told police he wore a navy blazer with "no equivocation, no confusion, no ambiguity," said Veniot. The Crown contended it was an attempt to mislead police, whose investigation ultimately showed the brown sports jacket had four confirmed bloodstains, and the DNA extracted from three of those areas matched his father's profile.

Science couldn't say how the blood and DNA got on Oland's jacket or how long they had been there, Veniot acknowledged, but he urged jurors to use their "common sense and logic" in determining how they were deposited. He also drew their attention to the additional red and brown stains found on the inside cuffs. Preliminary testing came back positive for blood, but follow-up testing was negative. Veniot advised the jurors to consider the colour and location of the stains and the fact that the jacket had been dry cleaned. The jacket was dry cleaned, in a bid to destroy evidence, Veniot argued. Destroying the expensive Hugo Boss jacket itself would be "more suspicious," he said. "It's the concept of hiding something in plain sight."

Gold downplayed the significance of the forensic evidence found on the jacket. The "true" killer, or killers, he said, would have had "lots" of blood spatter on them, "tons" after the "horrible bloodletting," not "minuscule" "specks." Officers expected, based on the crime scene, to find "significant" blood spatter on the killer. The defence's bloodstain expert said the potential for blood spatter in the case was "huge," and when the defence asked the Crown's bloodstain expert if the killer would have been a "perfect target" for spatter, he agreed.

To drive home his point, Gold displayed some of the graphic crime-scene photos on the large monitors for the jury. "See that photograph of Richard Oland's bloody body?" he asked, letting the image linger for dramatic effect. "That's the scene." He displayed a photo of the brown sports jacket. "That's the jacket. There is no way to go from that bloody scene to that jacket." Gold reminded the jurors two officers who examined the jacket "inch by inch" overlooked the fourth bloodstain subsequently located on the back by someone at the RCMP lab. "These were virtually invisible," he said, and no one could say how "those four tiny spots that the Crown is so fond of" got on the jacket or how long they had been there. They could have gone unnoticed for months. The tests also come with a "built-in bias," he said, because police check for DNA only in stained areas. Gold also suggested the increased sensitivity of current DNA analysis could result in picking up DNA unrelated to a crime. DNA could be elsewhere, and it could be perfectly normal for everyone to have the DNA of their relatives on their clothes, he suggested. The jury should not draw any inference about the significance of the jacket findings without knowing how common it was.

The blood and DNA on the jacket were the "simple result of some innocent transfer" through routine contact "wholly unrelated to Richard Oland's death," Gold maintained. Dennis Oland had other possible explanations for how his father's blood and DNA got on his jacket, explanations the Crown did not challenge. The fact that the jacket was taken to the dry cleaners was a "giant red herring," according to Gold. Oland's wife took the clothes in because they needed clean clothes for the visitation and funeral, he said. No stains were pointed out to the dry cleaners, and none were noted when the cleaners examined the jacket before cleaning. If Oland was the killer and cleaned the jacket to destroy evidence, why leave the tag on the jacket and the receipt lying around?

Police didn't seem to care about his clothes, suggested Gold. They didn't ask to seize the pants and shoes he had on during the interview, which he said he wore on July 6, so why not dry clean his clothes?

Gold underscored the absence of any other forensic evidence: no blood transfer in Oland's car, and no blood found on the pants, shoes, or shirt he wore that night. No drip trail at the crime scene, and no evidence of any cleanup, suggesting the weapon was likely put in some kind of bag and removed. The red reusable grocery bag Oland had with him tested negative. Even the Blackberry Oland handled after leaving his father's office, when his wife called him at 6:36 p.m., produced no evidence, said Gold, who doubted Oland would have answered that call if he had just bludgeoned his father to death. "If I could steal from Winston Churchill," he said, "never have so many searched for so long to find so little."

Gold attacked the police investigation, accusing officers of being cavalier about the crime scene. Police had not "properly investigated" the back door, although it would have been the "preferred exit route" of the killer. It was not tested for fingerprints or blood or DNA, Gold said, because whoever opened it contaminated it. If there was evidence on the door that could have helped the investigation, police did nothing to find it, said Gold. Police didn't even think to photograph the door until three years later. Police, he alleged, "lost the trail of the true killer or killers" on Day 1, just feet away from Richard Oland's office, he said.

Veniot defended the police investigation. "Certain things could have been handled better," he conceded. It would have been "preferable" if the number of officers in the crime scene had been limited. "Notwithstanding the number of officers who entered the crime scene, we suggest there was no contamination and no tainting of the evidence." That officers used the washroom in the foyer for two days before testing it was not disastrous to the case either, he proffered, because there was no indication of any cleanup by the killer. "No investigation is imperfect, ladies and gentlemen," said Veniot. "Pointing the finger at police for something that was not done is not a difficult task." But to suggest any evidence was missed or lost is "speculation." The notion some case-cracking forensic evidence was waiting to be discovered on the back door is doubtful, he said. The office itself, which was full of blood and signs of struggle, provided no clues, so it's doubtful the back door would have, he said. There was "no evidence the police acted in bad faith," said Veniot. And "solid police work" turned up important and valid findings, including the brown sports jacket and dry cleaning, financial records, and computer and cellphone evidence.

Gold suggested one of the most crucial pieces of evidence at the trial was the noise Anthony Shaw and John Ainsworth heard emanating from Richard Oland's office on the night of the murder, while they worked in the print shop downstairs. Based on the description and location, Gold argued, "Surely these noises related to the terrible beating death of Richard Oland." Shaw testified to hearing a loud crash, followed by eight to ten "swift" thumping sounds, "like rapid fire." The following morning, when they heard about the murder, Shaw and Ainsworth both immediately felt the noises were related and reported them to the police. Both men pegged the time as before a customer came in to have a document faxed via email, and that email was later found to be time-stamped 8:11 p.m.

Shaw told the court the noises occurred between 7:30 and 7:45, said Gold. The jury had seen security video of Dennis Oland shopping with his wife in Rothesay, about a fifteen-minute drive away, at 7:38 p.m., looking "perfectly normal and ordinary," showing no signs of being someone who had just bludgeoned his father to death, said Gold. "It could not be Dennis Oland killing Richard Oland at the time of the noises. It's as simple as that," he said. Ainsworth was less certain of the timing, saying only it was between 6:00 and 8:00, but Shaw's recollection remained clear and consistent since the day the body was discovered, said Gold, and the jurors had no reason to question his account. "Unless you completely reject Anthony Shaw's evidence, that is the end of the Crown's case right there." The Crown would have to convince them Shaw must be so badly mistaken about the timing of the noises that they would have to throw out his evidence. Otherwise, they must acquit Oland, he said. Noises heard coming from Richard Oland's office between 7:30 and 7:45, when Dennis Oland was seen on security video in Rothesay, "cries out innocence," declared Gold. At the very least, he said, it cries out reasonable doubt. "It cries out that your verdict has to be not guilty."

Veniot stressed Shaw and Ainsworth were uncertain about the time; they made "guesstimates." There was no evidence either man checked the time, and it's easy to lose track, he said. Veniot argued that Richard Oland's missing iPhone was "crucial" to the time of death. The iPhone, which went missing from the crime scene and was never recovered, was backed up on his office computer at 4:41 p.m. and disconnected at 4:44 p.m. The last registered human activity on his computer was at 5:39 p.m., right around the time Dennis Oland arrived, and the last message received by the iPhone was a text message from Diana Sedlacek at 6:44 p.m. Richard Oland never responded to that message, or any other texts or calls that night, Veniot submitted, because he was "already dead."

A cell tower in Rothesay transmitted that final text. "You know why this cell tower's important," Veniot told the jurors: it was located near the wharf where Oland had stopped on his way home after visiting his father, even though he said he knew his wife was sick and anxious for him to get home. Two witnesses described seeing Oland pick something up near the wharf, walk to the end of the wharf, sit down, put the mystery object he had picked up in a reusable grocery bag, walk briskly back to his car, and drive away. Oland testified he put on his jacket, took his reusable grocery bag out of his car, picked up broken beer bottles, walked to the end of the wharf, and sat down, recounted Veniot. Oland couldn't remember what he did with the broken bottles. It was up to the jury to determine what the actual purpose of his stop at the wharf was, Veniot said. The Crown's cellphone expert testified the general rule is cellphones generally communicate with whatever tower provides the best reception, which is usually the closest. Richard Oland's iPhone had communicated with the tower in uptown Saint John earlier in the day, but accessed the Rothesay tower at 6:44 p.m. because it had left his office and was moving east, "coincidentally" at the same time as Dennis Oland, submitted Veniot.

Gold discounted the significance of the computer and cellphone evidence. The Crown's computer expert wasn't asked to establish Richard Oland's normal computer usage to determine whether it was unusual for computer activity to stop at that hour, but the defence's witness did and found no evening use, he said. The last activity on July 6 being at 5:39 p.m. "proves nothing," Gold argued. Nothing could be inferred from Richard Oland not responding to the text message from Sedlacek at 6:44 p.m. either, said Gold. His phone records showed that he didn't respond to many messages when he was alive and well. He often took hours to respond to Sedlacek, Gold noted. Cellphone inactivity after Dennis Oland left the office did not mean Richard Oland was dead. A murder after 7:30 p.m., when Dennis Oland was in Rothesay, was not inconsistent with no registered computer use after 5:39 p.m. or no response to the 6:44 p.m. text, Gold asserted.

Oland told police he went to the wharf, Gold pointed out. Why would he do that if he had anything to hide? He also noted the witnesses at the wharf did not see Oland discard anything. Gold suggested the victim's iPhone might have communicated with the Rothesay cell tower because Richard Oland may have headed that way himself after his son left. That might also explain the presence of alcohol found in his urine during the autopsy, even though witnesses testified they didn't believe he'd left the office that day and didn't keep any alcohol there, said Gold.

It's also possible he was still in his office and his iPhone just happened to connect to that cell tower for technical reasons, he said. It's impossible to say it didn't. The Crown's expert said cellphones usually communicate with whichever tower provides the best service, which is usually the closest, but that's based on prediction models of a cellphone ring being at street level, stressed Gold. Oland's iPhone might have been in his second-storey office.

Veniot countered that was the "least plausible" of all explanations. The Crown's cellphone expert testified the chances of the iPhone being in Saint John and connecting with the Rothesay tower were "minimal." It was "more likely" the iPhone was in Rothesay, near the tower that transmitted the text message, the witness said. And not one of the more than one hundred test calls made by police east of Saint John used the Rothesay tower, Veniot pointed out. If the jurors accepted that the killer took the iPhone and that it was in the Rothesay area at 6:44 p.m., just minutes after Dennis Oland left his father's office and was headed that way, only he could be the killer, suggested Veniot. There wouldn't have been enough time for a "third party phantom killer" to enter the office after Dennis, inflict forty-five wounds, and be near the Rothesay tower by 6:44 p.m.

Although Gold declared: "You are no closer to knowing who killed Richard Oland today than you were when you all walked into Harbour Station for jury selection that first Tuesday after Labour Day," Veniot asserted that the "only logical, inescapable conclusion" was that Dennis Oland killed his father. He urged jurors to find him guilty.

The following morning, Justice Walsh began to deliver his instructions to the jury. He had spent weeks preparing his remarks, consulting with the lawyers for both sides in a bid to ensure his charge to the jury wouldn't form the grounds for a future appeal. Walsh reminded jurors that they would now be sequestered until they reached a verdict, and he swore in the regional sheriff and five deputies to take charge of the jurors. His instructions would be lengthy — the written version was 204 pages long — but he promised to break it into fifty-minute sections, having learned in law school that was the longest anyone could listen to someone speak about the law and evidence in a single sitting, he said.

Walsh told jurors his job was to review the evidence and instruct them on the law. Their job was to assess the evidence impartially and decide the facts. They should rely on their own memory of the evidence over whatever he or the lawyers said, he advised, but they must follow his instructions on the law. He noted that if he made a mistake, the Court of Appeal could correct it; everything he said was on the record. "Justice will not be done if you wrongly apply the law," he cautioned them. "Your decisions are secret. You do not give reasons. No one keeps a record of your discussions for the Court of Appeal to review." They should make their decision without sympathy, prejudice, or fear, he said. Nor should public opinion influence them.

Dennis Oland, he said, did not have to prove anything; he was presumed innocent. The Crown had to convince them beyond a reasonable doubt that he had killed his father on or about July 6, 2011, that he did so unlawfully, and that he meant to kill him or cause him bodily harm he knew was likely to cause his death. Walsh reiterated Gold's observation that it was not enough to believe Oland was probably or likely guilty, but it was "nearly impossible to prove anything to an absolute certainty," and the Crown was not required to do so.

Walsh cautioned jurors about the circumstantial evidence. They must distinguish between inference and speculation, he said. He defined an inference as a deduction of fact that may logically and reasonably be drawn from another fact or group of facts. If they saw someone come in wearing a wet coat and carrying a dripping umbrella, they might infer it was raining. Speculation was different. The police suggested a drywall hammer might have served as the murder weapon, but for the jury to conclude that was the case would be "pure speculation and conjecture." Indeed," he added, "you do not even have before you in evidence such a kind of instrument or even a picture of one."

After a break, Walsh began to review the blood and DNA evidence. All the jurors turned to face him, their brows furrowed in concentration. They should ignore any preliminary positive test for blood that was not later confirmed, he instructed them. With regard to witness testimony about the brown sports jacket, he suggested they consider the size, extent, and location of the staining, the DNA results, and other possible explanations for the findings.

It was up to the jurors to assess the credibility of Oland and every other witness to determine how much or how little of their testimony to accept. "You must remember that just because an accused was not cross-examined on something he or she said, [that] does not amount to acceptance by the Crown of what the accused said," Walsh noted. "If you believe Dennis Oland's statement and testimony that he did not commit the offence charged, you must find him not guilty. Even if you do not believe Dennis Oland's statement and testimony that he did not commit the offence charged, if it leaves you with a reasonable doubt about his guilt, you must find him not guilty. Even if Dennis Oland's statement and testimony does not leave you with a reasonable doubt of his guilt, you may convict him only if the rest of the evidence in the case as a whole that you do accept, including any portions of the statement Dennis Oland made to the police and/or his testimony that you do accept, proves his guilt beyond a reasonable doubt."

The dry cleaner's testimony that a bloodstain that isn't broken down before it's heated in the dry-cleaning process would become fixed in the fabric should "carry very little, if any, weight," Walsh cautioned, because the court had not declared her qualified to give an opinion. It was unclear from the evidence what effect, if any, dry cleaning would have on bloodstains, and Walsh said he personally would not rely on the dry cleaner's answers on that subject.

The proceeding was unexpectedly interrupted by a power outage and related technical issues with the recording equipment. A sheriff escorted the jury to the judges' lounge, and the crowded gallery was cleared. Sheriffs directed everyone — Oland, his family, the lawyers, reporters, and the public — to take the stairs down to the lobby. When court resumed approximately ninety minutes later, Walsh summarized the Crown's and defence's cases. "At the time of his death, Richard Oland was a very wealthy man, by anyone's standard," Walsh said. "But you might also find from the totality of the evidence given that, generally speaking, he did not give his money away, even to his own family, and that it seems he was a very demanding, narcissistic-type person when it came to his family — a difficult person, you might conclude. But all of that is for you alone to say. Although I am entitled to express my own views on occasion, and I have done so here, it is your view and only your view that counts." The jury was not required to find that Dennis Oland had a motive in order to convict him, he added.

Walsh reminded the jurors of some of the evidence they'd heard that suggested the police investigation was "inadequate." Police failed to secure the crime scene against too many unnecessary entries, thereby increasing the risk of scene alteration and/or contamination. They also failed to secure the second-floor washroom, resulting in the possible loss of evidence, and failed to ensure that the exit to the alleyway was untouched until it could be properly examined. Finally, police never asked the pathologist to consider whether a drywall hammer could have been the weapon that inflicted Richard Oland's fatal injuries. If a drywall hammer was used, the defence had no opportunity to exploit the fact that no evidence connected Dennis Oland to the use or possession of a drywall hammer at any time in the past.

During a pre-trial hearing, the defence requested that Walsh include the police's investigation, or lack thereof, of Jiri Sedlacek, the husband of the victim's mistress, among the possible inadequacies. Police interviewed Sedlacek twice but did not ask to see, or apply to seize, his phone or bank records or make any neighbourhood inquiries as to whether he knew about the affair. The defence stopped short of suggesting Sedlacek was the actual killer but argued that it was possible he might have "contract arranged" the murder. Walsh concluded the police's decision to accept Jiri Sedlacek's denial of any involvement was a reasonable one and not proof of negligence. The "horrific" and "emotion-laden" murder of Richard Oland "flies in the face" of a contract killer, he added.

Walsh spent some time reviewing the testimony of John Ainsworth and Anthony Shaw about the noises they heard on the evening of July 6. The pathologist who conducted the autopsy testified the egg-like fracture to Richard Oland's eye socket could have occurred if he had fallen to the floor face first. Naseemuddin also found some sharp-force injuries behind the victim's right ear appeared to have been made in rapid succession, because they were parallel, on the same plane and axis. Something solid striking the skull would make some noise, he testified. "In other words," Walsh said, "there is evidence from which you could reasonably infer that the noises that John Ainsworth and Anthony Shaw heard on the evening of July 6 were the sounds of Richard Oland's death. Whether you draw that inference is entirely up to you." If the noises were related, and if Shaw's evidence that they heard the noises between 7:30 and 8:00 was accurate, why didn't Oland answer the text sent at 6:44 or subsequent phone calls? Or was Shaw's evidence as to the time inaccurate? If the jurors concluded the noises were related and accepted Shaw's estimated time, "which would mean that Dennis Oland was elsewhere when the offence was committed," Walsh said, they "must find Dennis Oland not guilty." Even if they didn't accept Shaw's evidence but it raised a reasonable doubt, they must find Oland not guilty.

"This case is in its totality a circumstantial one," Walsh said. "In order for you to find Dennis Oland guilty of the offence charged on the basis of circumstantial evidence, you must be satisfied beyond a reasonable doubt that his guilt is the only rational conclusion that can be drawn from the whole of the evidence."

Walsh's instructions took roughly ten hours over two days. He then held a random draw to determine which member of the jury would be excused from deliberations. He shook the selected juror's hand and offered his "personal, heartfelt thanks" before sending the remaining members to the jury room. "We will await the jury's decision."

seventeen
VERDICT AND SENTENCE

By the time the jury began deliberations at about three thirty on the afternoon of December 16, 2015, the city was firmly divided into three camps: those who believed Oland was innocent, those who believed he was guilty, and those who believed he was guilty but were convinced he would never be convicted due to lack of evidence, police bungling, or the family's prominence.

The ban on Judge Ronald LeBlanc's decision at the preliminary inquiry was lifted once the jury at Oland's trial was sequestered, and it concisely listed the six key points he felt could lead a jury to conclude Oland killed his father. They included: opportunity, his apparent lie to police about which jacket he wore when visited his father, the blood and DNA found on his brown sports jacket; the jacket being dry cleaned, the attack appearing to be "a crime of passion," and his arrival at his father's office coinciding with the cessation of Richard Oland's computer and phone activity.

But LeBlanc also expressed reservations about the Crown's case. He said prosecutors had failed to establish a motive and police were too quick to target Dennis Oland as the suspect based solely on inconsistencies in his statement. Their conclusion was "totally unjustified and, indeed, irrational," he said. "The police merely had a hunch, and an unsubstantiated one at that." LeBlanc questioned the Crown's theory that Oland dry cleaned his jacket to destroy evidence when he left the tag attached and receipt out. "Surely the more logical thing to have done would be to get rid of the jacket altogether." A "serious setback" to the Crown's case, he said, was the timing of the noises two witnesses heard coming from Richard Oland's office at a time his son was in Rothesay. He found the timing of Richard Oland's last computer and cellphone use "significant."

Dennis Oland's family and supporters thought it was only a matter of time before he would be acquitted. "I sat through the preliminary hearing and a good portion of the trial, and I didn't hear one thing through all of that that would shake my belief in his innocence. There was nothing," said Kelly Patterson. "And in fact, what happened was, day after day of the testimony, you realize, this is really ridiculous. Of course he's going to get off." Oland's long-time friend Larry Cain agreed. "That's exactly how we all felt," he said. "We expected to be at someone's home celebrating that night."

But the jury stayed out, dinner was brought in, and at around nine p.m., the jury members were sequestered for a second night at an undisclosed hotel, where the Department of Justice had reserved an entire floor. Jury members each had their own room, and sheriff's deputies stood guard at both ends of the hallway until they escorted the eight men and four women back to the courthouse the following morning, shortly before nine a.m. The jurors put in close to a twelve-hour day deliberating behind closed doors on December 17, and another twelve hours on the eighteenth. As the deliberations stretched into a fourth day, without any questions from the jury, Oland's supporters became all the more convinced he would be exonerated. Others, though, speculated the extended deliberations signalled discord and predicted a deadlock. If the jurors were unable to reach a unanimous verdict, the expectation was Walsh would urge them to try again and send them back to the jury room. But with Christmas just days away, no one knew how long Walsh would compel the jurors to persevere. If they could not reach a consensus, Walsh would likely declare a mistrial and discharge them. It would then be up to prosecutors to decide whether to pursue a new trial—and no one wanted that.

The courts have ruled that mistrials should be "a remedy of last resort." They "often create huge and wasteful cost in terms of both time and money and can be profoundly unfair to the jurors, to witnesses, to victims and their families, and on occasion, to the accused," according to the British Columbia Court of Appeal. The Oland trial was already one of the longest — and likely one of the most expensive — trials in New Brunswick history. Jury fees and expenses alone totalled more than $205,000, a right-to-information request to the Department of Justice showed.

Hung juries are uncommon in New Brunswick, although oddly enough there was one in Fredericton on December 18, while the Oland jury was still deliberating, in the case of a man accused of four sex-related offences involving a fourteen-year-old boy who had posted a classified advertisement, claiming to be eighteen, and seeking sexual encounters with men.

The duration of jury deliberations varies widely. One Fredericton jury needed only two hours to convict a New York man of second-degree murder in the shooting death of a police officer in 1987. The jury in the second-degree murder trial of aboriginal rights activist Noah Augustine in 1999 took about two hours to reach its not guilty verdict. And in 2008 a Saint John jury deliberated for seven hours over two days before acquitting Scott Taylor of second-degree murder in the sword death that Constable Duane Squires attended as a rookie. (Taylor disappeared late in 2011; his body was found in the woods off Old Black River Road, outside Saint John, in May 2016. Typically, juries deliberating on cases involving multiple charges or multiple defendants take longer. But in Oland's case, there was only one issue to be decided: guilty of second-degree murder, or not guilty.

It was, however, a complex, largely circumstantial case, with testimony from forty-seven witnesses and 236 exhibits to consider. The jurors also knew the eyes of the province, the Atlantic region, and the country were watching. How long they would take was anyone's guess. And many were doing just that, with wagers between drinking buddies, teetotallers, and seasoned lawyers alike.

Deliberations resumed for a fourth day on Saturday, December 19, at nine a.m. About a dozen reporters trickled in, lugging laptops, video cameras, and audio equipment, and gripping extra-large coffees. For many, it was their sixth straight day on the job, and long days at that. One reporter from Fredericton was still wearing the same clothes as the day the jury was sequestered. The early sequestering amid Walsh's instructions had caught her off guard. She couldn't drive home or even shop for new clothes, lest she miss an important development. Those from out of town or out of province did have one advantage: their hotels were just a few minutes' walk from the courthouse. They were the same hotels where the jurors were sequestered, and where Oland, his family members, and his lawyers were staying, as the reporters awkwardly discovered when they crossed paths with them in the hallways or at buffet breakfasts.

The reporters slowly settled into what had become their usual spots on the fifth floor of the Saint John Law Courts. Most were just a few hurried strides away from the locked courtroom doors, seated around the massive rectangular wooden table, a century-old jury table from the historic Sydney Street courthouse, and the place where Oland and his supporters congregated during court recesses, drinking coffee and chatting in the daylight beaming in from the floor-to-ceiling windows. A few reporters were holed up in a bathroom-sized office at the other end of the hallway, ordinarily used for confidential lawyer-client conversations. During the trial, members of the media used a larger room to store their gear and work in private, but it was adjacent to the jury deliberations room, so the media were relocated to ensure they wouldn't overhear anything through the common wall. Now, some reporters pored over newly released information regarding the preliminary inquiry and pre-trial hearings, hoping to find a scoop. Other reporters scrolled through their Twitter feeds, caught up on email, and made small talk.

At around a quarter to eleven, members of the media were notified the courtroom would be opening shortly. Had the jurors reached a verdict? Were they at an impasse? Or did they just have a question? No one knew, but it was the first contact from the jury after about thirty hours of deliberations, and it caused a stir. Adrenaline-fuelled reporters scrambled to gather their gear and stake out a seat in the courtroom. The Crown prosecutors and defence lawyers must have been in the building or nearby because they were already donning their trial robes. The former lead Crown prosecutor on the case, John Henheffer, arrived and took a seat in the back row. Investigators Stephen Davidson and Sean Rocca were also present.

Dennis Oland ambled toward the front doors of the courthouse as he had so many times before, accompanied by his wife, mother, uncles, and family lawyer. He looked at ease, unflappable, with his back straight and head held erect. Lisa Andrik-Oland's face was pinched with worry, though. She snuck a side-glance at her husband's studied self-confidence and tried to put on a brave face, her hand firmly in his, their fingers interlocked. Oland whispered something into her ear before heading to his seat at the front of the courtroom, near his defence lawyers. Gary Miller walked over to him, shook his hand and they exchanged a few words as reporters looked on, their notepads, smartphones, and laptops at the ready to document the development, whatever it might be. Oland sat with his head down, not showing any emotion.

His sister Jacqueline Walsh and uncle Jack Connell, who had both been prepared to testify in his defence, arrived and sat near Derek Oland. A few interested members of the public, alerted by reporters' tweets about court reconvening, also managed to make it in time. One man abandoned his loaded grocery cart at Costco to witness what could be the conclusion of one of the most riveting trials in the city's history.

The court clerk, Amanda Evans, took her seat in front of the judge's bench, facing the gallery. The judge soon followed. "I am told the jury has reached a verdict," Walsh announced. The tension in the room was palpable. More than four years after Richard Oland was bludgeoned to death, there would finally be closure. "I realize the stress is enormous," Walsh said. He urged everyone to control their emotions.

"All rise," a sheriff's deputy instructed as the jurors entered. The court clerk asked the jury foreman if they had reached a unanimous verdict. They had, he said. "Guilty."

There was a moment of stunned silence as the word reverberated through the courtroom. Reporters' thumbs hovered over their smartphones, hesitant to post their tweets, unsure whether they had misheard. Then the heaving sobs began. At first, it seemed as if the noises were coming from Lisa, who was hunched over, weeping. But as the cacophony intensified, Oland collapsed into his chair, and it became clear he was the source.

"Oh no! Oh no!" he wailed, his head in his hands.

At Miller's request, the court clerk polled each juror to verify agreement with the verdict. "Do you find the accused guilty or not guilty?" she asked. One after the other, the jurors all replied, "Guilty," but their responses were drowned out by Oland's anguished cries.

"Oh God! Oh my God! My children!"

Miller rushed to the side of his client, the father of three and stepfather of one, to try to comfort him, but Oland was inconsolable. He clung to Miller and buried his face in his long black robe, howling like a wounded wild animal. The jurors sat transfixed, their faces ashen. Spectators were equally horrified, mouths agape. It was chilling, as if someone had flicked a switch and the meek, mild Oland who sat placidly throughout the trial vanished, replaced by an entirely different person. For some, it was an illuminating glimpse into how he might have snapped that night in his father's office four years earlier.

Some would later suggest those guttural, gasping sobs that filled the room were the sounds of an overconfident killer who believed he'd get away with it. Others would argue they were the lament of an innocent man, wrongly convicted. And still others speculated it was nothing more than theatrics, all part of a show intended to demonstrate his innocence for the appeal that would no doubt follow.

"Sheriff's officer, please take Mr. Oland into custody," said Walsh. Oland was led out of the courtroom, still wailing uncontrollably. "How could you do this?" his wife demanded through tears before rushing out to the hallway. His mother was silently doubled over under the weight of the verdict. "I don't understand it," someone in the hallway shrieked.

None of the jurors looked as if the heavy burden they had borne for the past three months had been lifted. Walsh thanked them for taking on the solemn responsibility of sitting in judgment of a fellow citizen, and for the long hours they put in. He also acknowledged the "mental and emotional toil" they had been through. "It is my honour to have you as my fellow judge," he said, dismissing them. The jurors were on their way out when the lead Crown prosecutor reminded the judge he had forgotten to ask them for a recommendation on sentencing. Although second-degree murder carries an automatic life sentence, parole eligibility can vary between ten and twenty-five years. It seemed Walsh, too, was rattled by the spectacle he had just witnessed.

The jurors were recalled, as was Oland. He had to be present for the jury's recommendation. Miller requested a moment alone with his distraught client first. When Oland was brought back into the courtroom, now a convicted murderer, he was directed for the first time to the prisoner's seat, rather than his former spot beside his lawyers. He rocked back and forth, flanked by two sheriff's deputies. His body was rigid, his breathing rapid and shallow. His wife returned to her front-row seat and their teary eyes locked. She mouthed something that appeared to help calm him.

A sheriff's deputy led the jurors back in. Many were visibly shaken, their eyes welling, or lips quivering. All of them avoided making any eye contact. Walsh asked the jurors if they had a recommendation on when Oland should become eligible for parole. Unlike their verdict, any parole recommendation did not have to be unanimous, he said. "It's a decision for each of you to make." They were not required to give one, he said, but if they did, he would be obliged to consider them in sentencing. He was not, however, bound to follow them. Some of the factors they should take into consideration, he said, included Oland's character, the nature of the offence, and the circumstances surrounding the commission of the offence. The jurors retired to the jury room to fill out a form with their individual recommendations, and Oland was escorted out again.

Within minutes, the Oland family's lawyer emailed a statement on behalf of Oland's mother, Connie. The speed with which the statement was issued suggested two statements had been prepared, one for a guilty verdict and the other for an acquittal. To judge by the family's dramatic reactions in the courtroom, they had been lulled into a false sense of hope for the latter outcome.

> We are shocked and saddened by the outcome of the trial.
> Our faith in Dennis's innocence has never wavered and the
> jury's decision has not changed that belief. We will now

discuss our options with the legal team. We sincerely believe justice will eventually be served. I am extremely proud of my son Dennis and he will continue to have our love and support in the difficult days ahead. We wish to thank our family and friends for their love and tireless encouragement and respectfully ask that everyone continue to respect our privacy.

Derek Oland and his family were also prompt to issue a statement that expressed similar sentiments.

We are disappointed and dismayed by the outcome of the trial. We continue to believe our nephew and cousin Dennis is innocent and we will support him and his family members through the course of whatever legal actions will unfold. We want to reiterate that all Oland family members are certain Dennis had nothing to do with the death of his father. We are proud of Dennis and we continue to place our trust in the expertise of his legal team. We have nothing else to say at the moment, other than we have faith that the process of law will eventually find Dennis innocent, as we all believe him to be.

The deliberations had taken some thirty gruelling hours, but the jurors needed only fifteen minutes to come up with their parole recommendations. Court resumed with Oland slumped in his seat, composed but crushed. All twelve jurors recommended Oland serve the minimum ten years behind bars before becoming eligible to apply for parole. "Thank you. You are now excused," Walsh told them, and they filed out at a brisk pace, eyes downcast.

Walsh ordered a pre-sentence report, a report prepared by a probation officer to assist a judge in deciding on an appropriate sentence. A probation officer compiles information about an offender's background and his or her willingness to change, based on interviews with the offender, family members, and sometimes other individuals, such as an employer. Crown prosecutor Patrick Wilbur told the judge the report would probably take six to eight weeks to complete. Walsh scheduled sentencing for February 11 at nine thirty a.m. and told Oland he would remain remanded in custody until that time. Oland nodded in response. He appeared disoriented, almost child-like, as sheriff's deputies ushered him out of the courtroom. He raised his right hand and offered a weak wave to his family members and supporters, who lingered behind in astonished disbelief, wiping away tears and embracing.

Lisa Andrik-Oland, still reeling, remained motionless, clenching a tissue, her eyes puffy from crying. When consoled by an older woman, she broke down again. "Shh," the unidentified woman murmured. "Shh."

Some reporters hurried off to file their breaking news stories. Others huddled outside the courthouse in the frigid, blustery conditions, waiting for someone, anyone, to offer comments. Oland's lawyers were among the first to emerge, stone-faced yet seething. They brushed past the cluster of cameras and microphones, ignoring all media requests.

Oland's devastated family members did not offer any additional comments as they made their way to their waiting vehicles. Just putting one foot in front of the other seemed a gargantuan task in their dazed state. Connie was guided out by her brother, his arm around her shoulders as she clung to a fistful of the back of his jacket. Lisa was shepherded to safety by Oland's childhood friend, Val Streeter, who looked like an offensive lineman, ready to take down anyone who got in their way. Dark sunglasses hid Lisa's puffy, bloodshot eyes. She carried her husband's overcoat over her arm.

Other supporters were equally dismayed, said Kelly Patterson, who was among those who gathered later that day at the home of the Oland family's lawyer, William Teed. "We were in a fog. Totally stunned," said Patterson, becoming emotional at the memory of that day. "It was surreal. You couldn't really grasp that this had happened."

"We were in shock for several days," said Oland's friend Larry Cain.

"Still," Patterson interjected.

"Still," said Cain. "You just can't process it."

The triumphant lead Crown prosecutor was measured in his first and only public address on the case. Veniot offered no comment on the verdict itself, but he thanked the jurors for "their careful and complete consideration of all of the evidence placed before them" in a prepared statement which he read aloud, Patrick Wilbur and Derek Weaver at his side.

"They have completed their duty as the law requires and as explained to them by Mr. Justice Walsh," Veniot said. He declined to take any questions from reporters. "We will be making no additional comments at this time with regards to the outcome of the trial."

Constable Stephen Davidson also declined to comment outside the courthouse. Chief John Bates, however, soon issued a written statement on behalf of his beleaguered force. "I do take some solace in the fact that our investigative team and the force, as a whole, which have been under some intense scrutiny and assailed with criticism ... will have realized a degree of validation," Bates said. "Not for a second did I waver in my belief or faith in their integrity, effort, or investigative skills." Bates also noted, "no winners emerge from such a tragic event. A man is deceased, and his immediate and extended family remains devastated."

The chief's carefully scripted statement did not go over well with many people in the city. It came across as misguided, at best, and unjustifiably smug, at worst, given the police missteps that came to light during the trial. Bates said he would address criticisms of the murder investigation by police "at a later date." In the weeks following the verdict, the jury faced an unprecedented backlash on social media. Many argued justice had not been served, that enough reasonable doubt existed to acquit. A poll on the website Vote Canada asked, "Was Dennis Oland proven to be the murderer of his father?" Of the 110 people who responded, 99 answered no. Critics accused the jurors of being more concerned about Christmas shopping than justice, of not understanding their instructions, and of a bias against wealthy people. Judith Meinert Thomas, one of a handful of people unconnected to the case who attended the trial daily, was "appalled" at the criticism. "I thought, this is the cornerstone of our justice system and people are slagging them online," she said. "They're questioning their integrity, their intelligence."

The Department of Justice "reached out" to the Oland jurors and "offered support," said spokesman Dave MacLean, but he declined to elaborate "out of respect for the jurors' privacy."

The case raised questions about whether the secrecy rules surrounding deliberations should change. It is a criminal offence in Canada for jurors to disclose anything about how or why they reached a verdict. The gag order is designed to protect those on trial who are ultimately found not guilty and to allow jurors to speak freely without fear their opinions will later be disclosed and subject to scrutiny. But Toronto lawyer Allan Rouben contends it's a disservice to jurors who might want to speak, to the public who want to know more, and to the justice system itself. "I think if jury members chose to come forward voluntarily — which they are not permitted to do in any way, shape, or form now — and explained the basis for their decision, then that would serve to enhance the validity and legitimacy of their verdict," he said.

On January 20, 2016, before Oland was even sentenced, his lawyers filed a notice of appeal and an application for bail with the Court of Appeal of New Brunswick, and a campaign was underway via email, Facebook, and telephone to ensure a large turnout for his sentencing hearing. "Our goal is to demonstrate the enormous level of support for Dennis," the email stated. Larry Cain, one of the organizers, booked a room at the Delta Brunswick Hotel and asked supporters to start gathering at seven thirty a.m. Coffee and tea would be served. The group would then march straight up steep Chipman Hill to the Saint John Law Courts for its eight a.m. opening. "Our goal is to have as many of you gather together so that we can arrive as a large group," the message said.

No one knew how many people would show up that Thursday morning, but no one expected the throng that did. About two hundred people, including many of the same upper echelon who attended Richard Oland's funeral, braved a heavy snowfall, sporting cashmere coats and fur-lined hoods. The lineup extended down the courthouse steps, onto the sidewalk, and into the street a full hour before the hearing was set to begin.

More than one hundred people quickly filled the courtroom beyond capacity, leaving another estimated forty milling about in the hallway as still more made their way through security, including his sister Jacqueline and cousin Patrick, the chief financial officer of Moosehead Breweries. It seemed doubtful they would be able to get in, but others let them pass.

Sheriff's deputies set up extra chairs, and even ignored policy to allow some people, including Senator John Wallace, to stand at the back. Nevertheless, deputies had to turn many would-be onlookers away, saying they had to clear the area. Despite the large crowd, the courtroom chatter remained at a respectful low hum while everyone waited for the proceedings to begin. Once Oland was led in, the courtroom fell completely silent, other than the sound of reporters typing or scribbling in their notepads.

He wore a taupe suit, a blue dress shirt, and a navy tie with red, blue, and yellow diagonal pinstripes. He was not cuffed, but his feet were shackled, and for the first time he shuffled his way to the prisoner's box, which had been removed from the courtroom during his trial. A sheriff's deputy sat beside him in the box, while another stood beside the box, blocking the doorway.

Oland quickly scanned the courtroom, packed shoulder to shoulder with family, friends, and other supporters. His gaze lingered on the front row, where his seventeen-year-old daughter Hannah was wedged between his wife and mother. His twenty-two-year-old stepson, Andru Ferguson, was also present. There was a hint of smile on Oland's lips and in his eyes. Maybe he was thinking about the fact his lawyers would be trying the very next day to get him released on bail pending his appeal, and he might soon be home with them. Or maybe he was just putting on a brave face for them. None of his children had attended the lengthy trial, although at one point early in the proceedings, during a recess, a polite and soft-spoken Oland approached the media and asked if they'd agree not to film or photograph his children if they came to court. Before the reporters could answer, Gold swooped in and pulled his client away. "The press conference is over," he said. Whether Oland was asking because he wanted his children to be with him, whether they had asked to attend, or whether having them present was part of a defence tactic intended to tug at the jurors' heartstrings was unclear. Whatever the reason, it never transpired.

Oland sat quietly as he waited for court to begin. The only issue was how long he would have to serve behind bars before becoming eligible for release. Walsh was not bound by the jury's recommendation of ten years. Would Oland be fifty-seven years old when he could apply for parole, or seventy-two?

Walsh informed the court he had received the pre-sentence report he requested, as well as victim-impact statements from Preston Chiasson, who was one of the first to discover Richard Oland's body, and John Ainsworth, the owner of the building where the murder occurred. Maureen Adamson, Robert McFadden, and Diana Sedlacek declined the opportunity to submit a statement. Oland's family members also declined, including his mother and sisters, his wife and children, his stepson, his ex-wife, his uncle Derek Oland, and his aunt Jane Toward. They, who lost a husband, father, brother, and grandfather in brutal fashion, seemed to believe the accused was more a victim than they.

Instead, his immediate and extended family members opted to write character reference letters in support of Oland, as did several of his friends, neighbours, business associates, clergy members, and even two of his former babysitters. A total of seventy-three people submitted letters, urging the judge to impose the minimum sentence, including some of the victim's closest and dearest friends, like Pat Darrah, who delivered his eulogy. The lack of a letter of endorsement from Oland's sister Lisa Bustin, however, was perhaps the most striking and later set some chins wagging. She was conspicuously absent during the trial, although she had attended some of the preliminary inquiry. Oland's aunt Jane Toward, the victim's sister, also failed to submit a letter of support.

Before beginning his submissions on sentencing, Crown prosecutor Patrick Wilbur challenged the admissibility of ten of the letters because they called into question the decision of the jury, referring to the verdict as a "travesty" and "miscarriage of justice." He cited a letter from Larry Cain's wife, Helena, as an example. She expressed "dismay and disappointment" with the guilty verdict due to, what she called, an "overabundance of reasonable doubt." It was "beyond" her how the jury could convict, she wrote, given the small amount of blood found on Oland's jacket and the noises witnesses heard coming from his father's office when he was shown on security video shopping in Rothesay around that same time.

Wilbur argued the letters were "objectionable" and should be "struck from the record," not merely edited. The accepted letters would form part of the official court record, including future proceedings, such as the appeal, so striking them altogether would be the most appropriate way to deal with the issue, he explained.

Walsh said he had read all of the letters the day before and had already marked all of the questionable sections. He said it was "extremely upsetting" some people "took advantage of the opportunity to file a character reference and used it as a Trojan horse in which to express their personal opinion" about the verdict. The purpose of the letters was to assist him in sentencing, "to speak to this man's character, so I can have a sense and assess," he said. "For people to go to the extent some did is offensive." Walsh's face was flushed, his folksy friendliness gone. "The only opinion that counts are the ladies and gentlemen that sat [on] that jury," Walsh stressed, as Oland listened attentively from the prisoner's box, his brow furrowed. "I am required by law to impose a sentence that verdict now demands," Walsh noted. "I'll say no more. I'm not pleased."

Oland's lawyers requested a recess to reread the character reference letters in question and discuss the matter with the prosecutors. Walsh agreed. Nobody left the courtroom during the break. They didn't want to risk losing their seat. The noise in the courtroom increased exponentially as people grew more restless. It didn't take long before the lawyers agreed to pull seven of the letters and redact the other three to remove comments about the outcome.

Walsh raised concerns about the letters from Oland's children—aged fifteen, seventeen, nineteen—and his adult stepson becoming part of the public record. "The privacy of the children far outweighs any other interests to be met by the freedom of the press," he said and imposed a "provisional" publication ban. He would give the media an opportunity later in the day to oppose the ban, he said.

The Crown began its submissions on sentencing by referring to the two victim-impact statements. They reflect the "collateral damage" that occurs with murders, said Wilbur. Chiasson told the court his "plight pales in comparison" to that of the Oland family, "But nonetheless I suffer." The image of Richard Oland's battered body sprawled on the floor "haunts me still," Chiasson wrote. It is "always present in my peripheral." He suffered from depression and was diagnosed with post-traumatic stress disorder, he said. His overall health declined, he turned to alcohol, and his marriage ended.

Ainsworth also expressed sympathy for the Oland family over the "devastating...impact" of "this tragedy," as well as for Richard Oland's secretary and business associate over how "tormented" they must be and "what they endure." He wrote, "I am especially emotionally shaken by the most undeserved horror Richard Oland must have experienced." Ainsworth said he cringes "envisioning the brutality of his death." Richard Oland "after all, was a person to me," with whom he had shared "amicable interactions," he said. "Someone else's actions have forced myself, my family, my employees, and affected friends to endure so much insidious, emotional upheaval." He talked about the "inordinate amount of time," the "most precious of commodities," consumed by "dealing with the consequences of another's terrible deed." The notoriety of his building has also been "detrimental" to his business, his livelihood, he said. "It is so demoralizing that thirty-plus years of my toil has been relegated to being inextricably linked to someone else's brutal actions."

The Crown argued allowing parole eligibility after the minimum of ten years "is the exception" in murder cases. Oland's case demanded more than the minimum, given the "brutal" and "heinous" nature of the slaying, said Wilbur, reminding the court the victim had been hacked and beaten to death. He recommended Oland have no chance of parole for at least twelve to fifteen years. "We respectfully submit that is the appropriate range," he said. Oland should also be prohibited from owning or possessing any weapons and be added to the national DNA database, he added.

"The jury's recommendation shouldn't be displaced very easily, without very sound reasons," Gary Miller countered. The jurors "heard all the evidence; they saw what a violent attack it was. The photographs showed the brutality," he said. In addition, there was no evidence of any planning, said Miller.

Walsh asked Miller about Oland's post-offence conduct, noting no murder weapon was ever found, and the victim's cellphone went missing. He also referred to Oland's apparent lie to police about what jacket he was wearing when he visited his father on the last night he was seen alive, and the fact his bloodstained brown sports jacket was taken to the dry cleaners the morning after he was told he was a suspect. If the jury found Oland lied about the jacket, Miller replied, "I don't know how they got there."

Miller quoted extensively from the character references that described Oland as kind, devoted, and non-violent. Miller said the show of support "overwhelmed" him. "I couldn't find three people to write a letter like this for me," he remarked, prompting laughter from the gallery and even a smile from Oland. The letters from Oland's children "brought tears to this old hard-ass's eyes," Miller said.

The publication ban on those letters was subsequently lifted. Oland's stepson Andru Ferguson wrote about how the family's lives will never be the same. "It deeply saddens me that the result of this case — regardless of what is to come in the future — has changed my family," he wrote. "It's hard to imagine fun times ahead without Dennis."

Oland's eldest, Emily, wrote that her father had "provided the best life he could have possibly given" for her and her siblings. "He has always tried to be a positive role model in our lives and has done so much for the community. My father has given us everything we could have asked for and more." Oland's kindness had also extended to many others, she said, citing as an example how he helped get treatment for a close friend's father who was diagnosed with terminal cancer.

Oland's wife, Lisa, told the judge she would switch places with her husband if she could. "He is my best friend, my strongest supporter, and my partner in every sense you can think of. He has taught me to be a better person for myself and for those around me," she wrote. "He is my husband and I love him more than life itself." Her four-page, handwritten letter continued: "Dennis is a good person, he is not the spoiled boy who was born with a silver spoon in his mouth, that some people have tried to portray him as. I have always known Dennis to see the good in people, to be the one to help people when they need it and to speak out for people who may have been misunderstood." She pleaded for the minimum sentence. "Our kids need their dad."

Miller observed that over the years, Oland had expressed concern about the impact of the case on his children. "I don't want this to turn them into something less than they are," Miller quoted Oland as having said; some of his supporters in the packed courtroom cried softly. Justice Walsh leaned back in his chair and stared at the ceiling as Miller spoke. Oland and his family "have suffered more than most accused do," Miller said. "I beg your Lordship, give him the kind of sentence where the law allows him to get home as soon as possible."

Walsh asked Oland whether he had anything to say before sentencing. Oland stood and quietly replied, "No, sir, thank you," with a polite nod. Walsh said he needed some time to "absorb" everything and adjourned for two hours. He could not guarantee he'd have a decision by then, but he said he expected to have one before the day's end.

A solid hour before court was set to resume, people had started gathering outside the locked door in a bid to get a seat. The packed courtroom was quiet as everyone waited for the proceedings to begin. When a sheriff's deputy led in Oland, Miller went over to him and whispered something in his ear. Oland nodded and smiled in agreement as he looked around the courtroom, filled, as usual, with family, friends, and other supporters.

Walsh thanked everyone for their patience. Sentencing, he said, is a "case specific exercise of judicial discretion." A judge must consider the character of the offender, the nature of the offence, the circumstances surrounding the commission of the offence, and the recommendation of the jury. While no two cases are identical, a sentencing judge must still compare like cases and ensure sentences are proportional to the gravity of the offence, he noted. Parole ineligibility is less about denunciation and more about promoting public safety and instilling confidence in the administration of justice, said Walsh. He also noted that eligibility for parole does not guarantee parole. Ultimately, it is the parole board that determines, when the time comes, whether an offender is suitable for release. No matter what, Oland's automatic life sentence meant he would, for the "rest of his days," be "under the eyes and control of the state, whether behind bars or, if and when permitted, in the community."

The range of parole eligibility is ten to fifteen years for those where the "prospects of rehabilitation are good," he said. Oland's pre-sentence report seemed to suggest he fit the bill. It described him as a well-educated, forty-seven-year-old husband and devoted father with no criminal past, said Walsh. Oland had told the parole officer who prepared the report that he could not express remorse because he did not commit the murder. Walsh said that was neither a mitigating, nor an aggravating factor for him in sentencing, but pointed out the identity of the killer was the central issue at the trial, and the jury obviously rejected Oland's claim of innocence.

Walsh noted Oland's family members declined to submit victim-impact statements, but did submit "glowing" letters attesting to his character. The judge singled out the letters written by Oland's three children and stepson, describing them as "simply heart-wrenching to read." They "love him dearly," a "high tribute to their father's character," he said. The victim, meanwhile, was "regrettably . . . a very difficult man," who created a "long-standing, highly dysfunctional family dynamic, hall-marked by a lengthy extramarital relationship," the judge said. "Dennis Oland simply lost it, snapped or exploded," he said, suggesting he must have been under "immense stress" at the time of the murder, given his "desperate financial straits."

Still, Richard Oland did not invite violence upon himself and did not deserve to be slaughtered on the floor of his office, he said. Walsh also had to consider the consequences of the crime on others. Ainsworth and Chiasson are both "haunted" by the murder and "struggling" to deal with it, he said, referring to their victim-impact statements. "Such are the wide and insidious consequences of murder."

"In the end, the tipping point for the court has been the unanimous jury recommendation" of the minimum ten years, said Walsh. All eyes turned to Oland to watch for a reaction, but he showed no emotion—a sharp contrast to his uncontrollable wails when the jury found him guilty.

The reaction in the courtroom was also limited. It was, after all, the best possible outcome anyone could have hoped for.

The jurors saw all of the evidence in the "complicated and convoluted" case and were aware of the "egregious brutality" of the killing, said Walsh. Their recommendation for the minimum was "not an apology for the conviction" but rather "a window into the basis of their verdict; that is, it reflects recognition of the long-standing dysfunctional family dynamic," a "perfect storm" of sorts that led to such a tragic end.

The case was, he noted, "a family tragedy of Shakespearean proportion."

eighteen

WHAT THE JURY DIDN'T HEAR

The jurors sat through fifty days of testimony, evidence, closing arguments, and instructions from the judge, but volumes of evidence were
never presented to them. The court dealt with much of this information
during pre-trial hearings, and it remained under publication bans until
the jury began its deliberations. The revelations range from fascinating
to perplexing and disturbing, including the fact something other than
Richard Oland's iPhone went missing from the crime scene, that the
iPhone was potentially in the United States three days after the murder,
and that Saint John police violated Dennis Oland's Charter rights.

Jurors did not see Dennis Oland's full police interview, which started
at approximately six p.m. and did not end until five hours later, at eleven
o'clock. Only the first half of the interview was played at the trial, but the
entire interview was submitted into evidence at his preliminary inquiry.
Although such evidence normally becomes public once a trial ends, in
the case of the interview video, CBC News had to petition the court for
its release. Both Crown and defence opposed the video's release on the
grounds that it had "no relevance in law." But the defence ultimately
decided that the public needed to see how the police "harangued" Dennis
Oland. The Crown also dropped its challenge.

The second half of the video starts at around 8:25 p.m., the point
when police stopped looking at Oland as a witness and began to consider
him as a suspect, according to Constable Stephen Davidson's testimony.
Davidson returned to the small interview room and told Oland that he'd
detected inconsistencies in his story. He advised Oland of his right to

contact a lawyer and asked him if he wanted to exercise that right. "Given how uncomfortable I'm feeling, yes, I would, sure, like to exercise my right," Oland replied. He and Davidson left the room together, Oland called family lawyer and friend William Teed, and Oland and Davidson returned to the interview room.

"Dennis, given our conversation, there's no doubt in my mind that you did this," Davidson said in an even voice.

"Did what?" Oland asked, blankly.

"You had involvement in this death. And I want to know why." Oland did not respond. He looked down and then used his hands to boost himself upright in his chair. "OK?" Davidson asked. "I want to know the reasons why."

"You just told me on a piece of paper [a reference to a form the police gave him to sign] I should be talking to a lawyer and, you know, shouldn't say anything, do anything, unless I talk to a lawyer," Oland replied. "I've done that, and now you're at me."

"I'm not. We're having a conversation here," Davidson replied.

"But I think the conversation probably should end because I don't like it, OK."

"But it's your opportunity to talk to us, OK, and to find out reasons why."

"Because of your tone and what you just said, I choose not to take advantage of that opportunity," Oland replied.

"But this is an opportunity for you to talk to me about why that offends you."

"You just accused me of being the cause of the death of my father, so I don't like that at all."

"OK. Did you?"

"No."

"Did you do it?"

"No."

Oland said he wanted to wait for his lawyer, but Davidson suggested the brief telephone conversation he had with Teed *was* his opportunity to speak to a lawyer and persisted, telling Oland that he wants to "just talk" and "know the reasons why." Oland repeatedly said he wanted to speak with his lawyer. Davidson kept talking. Oland crossed and un-crossed his legs, turned to his right and left, and stared at the ceiling, his arms crossed. After roughly seven minutes of this, appearing increasing-ly agitated, he told Davidson, "I'd like you to back off." Davidson rolled his chair closer.

"Listen," he said. "I understand the relationship you and your father had wasn't a good one. He was hard on you. You never amounted to what he wanted. That bothered you. I'm sure that resentment you carried through your whole life, even till now."

"I never said that," Oland bristled. "He was very proud of me."

"OK," Davidson conceded. "You guys had a strained relationship. It wasn't a regular father-son relationship." He then asked Oland what it was like to grow up feeling "belittled" and "embarrassed" all the time. Oland ignored Davidson. He sat turned away, his right arm across the back of his chair, eyes downcast, legs crossed, slowly tapping his left foot up and down in the air. Davidson suggested that Oland was a "good person" but noted that resentment can build up over the years. "We've all got breaking points," he said. He asked Oland if "it" was spontaneous or planned. Oland didn't respond. "I don't think you're a bad person; I think bad things happened," Davidson continued. He didn't feel Oland was "cold" or "heartless," he said.

At about 8:55 p.m., there was a knock at the door, and Davidson left without saying anything. Oland yawned loudly, scratched his head, and exhaled deeply. He turned to the narrow table attached to the wall at his left, crossed his arms, tilted his head, and appeared to close his eyes as he rotated his foot in the air.

Constable Keith Copeland of the major crime unit entered about a minute later. The twenty-eight-year veteran introduced himself to Oland, shook his hand, took a seat, and began to interrogate him in classic "bad cop" fashion, perhaps hoping the change of technique from Davidson's seemingly sympathetic "good cop" approach might get Oland talking. Copeland was not assigned to interview Oland, former lead investigator Rick Russell testified at the preliminary inquiry. His decision to enter the room was "something he would have done on his own volition," Russell said.

Copeland told Oland that he'd been observing the interview from the beginning. He was in "way over" his head, Copeland said, and his body language suggested he was guilty. What Oland told Davidson about the events of July 6 differed from what he put in the statement he wrote before the interview started, Copeland asserted. "An honest person remembers their story clearly, from start to finish, because it's honest, it's true, it's cohesive, it's the way it happened," Copeland said. Oland's story, he alleged, was "full of holes." Copeland reviewed some of the inconsistencies in Oland's account and told him his "story could easily be disproved" through the security cameras that are "everywhere."

Then Copeland seemed to drop the "bad cop" approach. "You didn't plan this Dennis. 'Cause if you would've planned this, you'd have planned this a much better way than you did," said Copeland. He pulled his chair closer to Oland and leaned in, staring at him, trying to force eye contact. "Did you just go there and get into an argument with him about money?" he asked. Oland remained unresponsive.

Copeland feigned empathy with Oland, another investigative tactic. "If I grew up in your circumstances, with money all around you, at this stage of my life, I would expect to be sharing in some of that, not battling with that son of a bitch every single day and having him control every aspect of my life because he wouldn't give up any of his goddamned money," he said, raising his voice. "You didn't plan this, Dennis. He brought this on. Pushed you, pushed you, pushed you. Squeezed you. Rubbed your face in the fact that he controls it all." Copeland described Richard Oland, the murder victim, as a "mean son of a bitch" who was controlling and tight with his multimillions, "a dirty pig" who "disrespected" his family with his extramarital affair. "I don't see any remorse," he told Dennis Oland. "The old man's gone. The tyranny is over." No one in the family seemed "overly upset about the passing of the old man," Copeland argued. He floated the theory that either Lisa Andrik-Oland or even Connie Oland was in on the murder. Oland greeted the suggestion with silence. Copeland, having switched back to "bad cop" mode, warned Oland that if he didn't "man up," he would force police to dig into the lives of everyone in the family, including his "long-suffering" mother, and leave "no stone unturned." Copeland berated and badgered Oland, sitting so close that their knees almost touched. Oland remained taciturn.

"Did Dennis finally get sick and tired of being browbeaten and abused? And watching his family be abused by this guy who sails all over the world racing expensive yachts, doing whatever he wants?" Copeland asked. "This was about ending the tyranny. 'I've had enough of this. You're not treating me like this anymore,'" he roared. "Or maybe there was no conscious thought. Maybe it was just like, 'Ahh!' Was it just a moment of, a flash of, whatever, just no plan, it just happened?" Again, no response. Copeland suggested that the reason Oland left 52 Canterbury Street without going into his father's office on the first trip was not because he forgot a genealogy document but because he planned to confront his father, likely about money, and "chickened out." It was implausible, he asserted, that Oland would drive back to an office a mere "stone's throw" away to retrieve forgotten genealogy documents. "Can you not throw a stone from there? Pretty darn close, that's for sure. A good pitcher could, that's for sure. Make no bones about that." Copeland also disputed Oland's explanation that he stopped at the wharf to see if his children were swimming after kayaking because, according to Copeland, kayaking is done much earlier in the day.

For nearly forty-five minutes, Oland said next to nothing, other than asking Copeland, shortly after nine, to tell his family members "that maybe they should go home." Copeland offered him water or coffee. "Water would be nice," replied the ever-polite Oland, who had earlier excused himself for yawning and tolerated Copeland referring to him as a chartered accountant four times before correcting him. Oland yawned again after Copeland left. "Oh, geez," he muttered to himself, or possibly to the officers he knew were watching him. Copeland returned even more insistent about Oland's guilt. He kept digging, trying to box him in. Oland rubbed his eyes and at times sat doubled over, arms crossed in his lap. He reiterated that he was following Teed's advice not to say anything until a lawyer arrived.

"How did you get that scratch on your left arm? Was there a struggle last night?" Copeland asked.

Oland glanced at his forearm. "No, I just did that now," he replied.

Copeland contended he noticed it earlier and said he could also see scrapes on Oland's throat and chest. He tilted his chair back, hands on top of his mop of grey curls. "I know that what you told us is untrue, is bogus, and it doesn't stand up to the light of day," he alleged. He left a pregnant pause, hoping to compel Oland to fill the space. "Even if you never tell me the truth, you'll have to face your mother and tell her the truth," Copeland said. "There is no way that you can't do that." Another pause. He counselled Oland that people have more respect for those who can admit that what they've done is wrong. "Do you want the evidence to show that you sat in a chair and closed your eyes and, for all intents and purposes, appear to be sleeping while I'm trying to talk to you about this?" Copeland demanded. "Is that the image you want to project? No remorse? 'And guess what, copper, I'm gonna have a snooze while you're talking to me about being a cold-blooded killer.'" None of his tactics worked.

At approximately a quarter to eleven, Copeland asserted, "The whodunit is gone; it's out the window. We know whodunit. So it comes down to ... Really, Dennis, all it is, is [it] a question of greed, or passion?" No response. "You are without a doubt the person that's responsible for your father's death," Copeland declared. He told Oland that he strongly believed him to be "a good honest person who reacted very badly" and urged him to take advantage of the opportunity to "tell the unvarnished truth." He identified "two ways out" of a "mistake": "one is to acknowledge it and to move on with it, and the other is to deny it."

"If I did anything wrong, the lawyer will likely tell me to fess up," Oland replied. "If I didn't do anything wrong, the lawyer will—" But Copeland cut him off. He warned Oland that he was on the verge of losing the opportunity to ask investigators to listen to his side of the story and "try to understand how and why this situation developed." Oland appeared to swallow hard. He rubbed his chin and the back of his neck. "Will you take advantage of that opportunity? Will you tell me what happened? It's a yes or no."

"No," Oland replied.

"We're done," snapped Copeland.

Despite their stated certainty that he was the killer, police let Dennis

Oland leave the interview without even attempting to seize his pants and shoes, the same ones he said he wore when he visited his father the previous night. At the preliminary inquiry, this omission was something that Judge Ronald LeBlanc commented on with incredulity. "The police did not seek to obtain his consent to providing his clothing, nor did they seek judicial authorization for their seizure," LeBlanc pointed out in his fifty-three-page decision to allow the Crown to proceed to trial.

The jury also didn't hear evidence that suggested Richard Oland's missing cellphone was alive and well, possibly in the United States, three days after his death, a time when the police had Dennis Oland under surveillance. Claudio Cusin, an investigator with Rogers Communications, testified that on July 9, a colleague, Tagie Polo, performed a forced registration on the phone for Sergeant David Brooker of the major crime unit to update its physical location. Polo "pinged" the phone three times that day and each time got a roaming error message, according to Cusin. He testified that meant the phone in question was registering, not within the Rogers distribution network but with a network outside Canada. Although the Crown argued Rogers mistakenly pinged the mobile "rocket stick" Richard Oland used for Internet access on his sailboat, which was moored in Rhode Island on July 6, 2011, Cusin testified the number pinged was the cellphone number. And although Brooker maintained his discussion with Polo about the roaming effort was on July 7, not July 9, leading him to conclude the iPhone was in the water at Renforth wharf, Cusin testified no forced registration was performed on July 7 or July 8. The defence had also argued police didn't even know the phone was missing until July 9 when they searched the office and asked Oland's secretary to identify anything out of the ordinary.

"The disappearance of Richard Oland's iPhone continues to be a mystery," wrote LeBlanc. "The phone ostensibly left the country within three days of Richard Oland's death at a time when Dennis Oland was still in the country. The tests done by Rogers Communications established that the iPhone had registered on a network outside of Canada and was still alive, in the sense it was not destroyed," he said. "This of course does not exonerate Dennis Oland in his father's homicide as there can be any number of means used to send the phone out of the country, but certainly it is a factor the justice presiding at the preliminary inquiry must consider in determining the identity issue."

Nor did the jury hear that the iPhone was not the only item that disappeared from the crime scene. Oland's mistress, Diana Sedlacek, had apparently left him a note. "Did Zu find note?" she texted him on the morning of July 6. "Have in [office]," Oland replied. "This note, in whatever form it may have been in, was never found by the police or by anyone at the Far End Corporation office," said LeBlanc.

A second pathologist offered evidence at the preliminary inquiry but was not asked to testify at the trial, so the jury had no idea of his findings. Saint John police asked Dr. Matthew Bowes, chief medical examiner for Nova Scotia, to review Dr. Ather Naseemuddin's post-mortem report as well as photographs, the toxicology report, and blood-spatter report and provide an opinion on how long it would have taken Richard Oland to die. Bowes agreed with Naseemuddin that Oland would have survived only "a matter of minutes." But he concluded that Oland was alive during all forty-five blows to his body. "I don't see any injuries that are clearly post-mortem," he testified, and Oland's heart did not stop beating until shortly after the attack.

Police did not ask Bowes to opine on the murder weapon. During cross-examination at the preliminary inquiry, however, Bowes said it was "most likely two instrumentalities" that caused the sharp-force and blunt-force injuries, but they could have been combined in one weapon. A combat, or tactical, knife could have killed Richard Oland, using the blade and butt-end, he said. Bowes agreed with Alan Gold that whatever weapon was used, both it and the assailant would have had "a lot of blood" on them. He also agreed with Gold that the time of death could have been well after eight p.m.

Just months before Oland's trial was scheduled to start, high-stakes legal arguments between the Crown and defence about the admissibility of his brown sports jacket—the Crown's key piece of evidence against him—took place. The wrangling, which was under a publication ban until the end of the trial, started during the pre-trial hearing on March 30, 2015, when Justice Walsh granted the Crown special permission to conduct additional testing on the DNA extracts from the jacket using the more discriminating Identifiler Plus program. Oland's lawyers urged Walsh to at least delay the retesting until he heard their Charter rights application in May. The defence planned to argue the bloodstained jacket should be thrown out as evidence because, they submitted, police had violated Oland's Charter right to be "secure against unreasonable search or seizure." Alan Gold argued that the Criminal Code allowed police to detain exhibits but not to test them. "It may be that people have always assumed that the police could do whatever they want with seized items, but there's no lawful authority for that assumption," he said. Gold pointed out that police records showed various officers "agreeing that they needed further judicial authority for certain testing." If the judge ultimately excluded the brown sports jacket as evidence based on the Charter argument, "it would be somewhat unseemly for the court to have taken part in what is essentially a further Charter violation by allowing, by its order, the Crown to retest the exhibits," Gold submitted. The DNA retesting would only serve to produce more evidence that would be excluded, and there was no evidence of urgency to conduct the retesting. John Henheffer, lead Crown prosecutor on the case, advised that if the jacket was not admitted, the Crown would have to "take a very, very hard, strong look" at its case. "I would be surprised it if proceeds further," he said. "It's crucial to the Crown's case."

Walsh described the defence's argument as legally compelling "in theory" but said the court must also "view the matter pragmatically." The reality was the lengthy trial was already scheduled to begin in September, and holding off on any additional tests until he ruled on the Charter application created a "real risk" of delaying the trial. It wasn't just a matter of waiting until the Charter hearing in May, he said, he also had to allow himself time to make a ruling. If he did rule in favour of the accused on the Charter application, any retesting "could be viewed in the rear-view mirror as having been unnecessary," he said. But he wasn't prepared to accept that any violation of Oland's Charter rights would be "magnified" by the retesting. It was possible the additional test would furnish results that worked in the defence's favour, he noted. Walsh ruled for the Crown; the testing would proceed.

The Charter argument began in earnest on May 5 and took three days. The defence challenged the validity of the search warrant for Dennis Oland's house under which the brown Hugo Boss sports jacket was seized. Oland's lawyers argued that police provided insufficient information in their application (known as an ITO, or information-to-obtain) to establish the reasonable grounds required for Judge William McCarroll of the provincial court to grant the warrant. Even if police established reasonable grounds, the defence submitted, "material errors and omissions" in the ITO would, if corrected and included, have negated those grounds. The defence also asserted that the general warrant police obtained on August 4, 2011, to examine the items seized during the search did not, on its face, authorize any DNA testing of the jacket, and all the DNA testing took place after that warrant expired on November 2. Moreover, the detention order granted for the seized items and subsequent extension orders stated the items were to be held in the custody of the Saint John Police Force's exhibit control office, not sent away to the RCMP forensic labs. Police needed additional judicial authorization for that, the defence argued.

The Crown countered that the search warrant was validly issued. Prosecutors argued the general warrant was not required, because the search warrant gave police the "inherent authority" to conduct the forensic examinations and analysis on the jacket, and the post-execution detention orders did not prohibit that testing. Again prosecutors told the court that excluding the jacket would "gut" their case against Dennis Oland. Walsh ruled on June 10. He noted that the fundamental statutory demand for a search warrant to be issued is that reasonable grounds exist to believe that an offence has been committed and that relevant evidence is in a particular building, receptacle, or place. The police officer who applies for a warrant must not only demonstrate through the ITO that he or she subjectively believes the necessary reasonable grounds exist but also present information to satisfy the authorizing judge there is an objective basis for that belief. Walsh stressed the issue before him was not whether the court would still have issued the warrant but whether the authorizing provincial court judge could have done so in the eyes of the law, based on the information he had at the time.

Of all the information provided in the sworn document, Walsh found "probably the most persuasive to the authorizing judge, taken in the entire context of the ITO," was the discrepancy between what Oland said he wore on July 6 and what security video and witness testimony proved he wore. Oland's "unqualified" answer might "in isolation" seem "a simple mistake," Walsh wrote, "However, that answer, taken in context of the evidence that [Oland] was the last known person to see his father alive, taken with the evidence of his father's iPhone being in Rothesay most probably at the same time he was, mere minutes after he left his father's office, and taken with the crime-scene evidence that the attacker or attackers would most probably have been blood-spattered, speaks to another logical inference that could be drawn — that Dennis Oland was lying, that he was attempting to mislead the investigators for a patently obvious reason." Walsh also noted that Dennis Oland went straight up to his bedroom and changed his clothes before seeing his wife that evening, even though she had asked him to come home because she was sick, "the inference being open to the authorizing judge" that it was "because of his condition and/or that of his clothes."

All of this, combined with evidence of the strained relationship between father and son and the possibility of a financial motive for the crime, convinced Walsh that the search warrant was valid. Walsh did agree, however, that the police ITO contained errors and omissions. The ITO failed to mention that police told Oland they intended to review security video before they asked him what he was wearing on the evening of July 6. If the judge who issued the warrant knew that Oland was aware police could verify what he told them, he might have questioned whether Oland's claim to have worn a navy blazer was an intentional falsehood. The ITO also did not include Oland's explanation that when he didn't see his wife as he passed through the living room of their open-concept home, he assumed she was upstairs. When he didn't find her in their bedroom, he changed his clothes and then went back downstairs to find her. Walsh agreed this was a material omission. "Fairness required that both versions be submitted," he said.

The more significant and "misleading" material error, Walsh said, concerned the information police provided in the ITO about the missing iPhone. As noted, police reported that a forced registration performed on the iPhone on July 7, 2011, produced a roaming error, starting on July 6, at 6:46 p.m. — two minutes after the cellphone pinged off the Rothesay cell tower located near the wharf where Dennis Oland stopped on his way home. The implication was that the phone, although still operating, appeared to suddenly drop out of sight of the Rogers Communications network. According to the ITO, the cellphone was within the cell tower's radius, which measured approximately half a kilometre west, four kilometres north, and five to six kilometres east. Walsh believed the authorizing judge could have inferred on a "common sense, practical, non-technical basis" that Dennis Oland disposed of the iPhone at around that time and in that place. But in 2013 Constable Sean Rocca discovered that the forced registration was performed on July 9, not July 7. And when David Brooker asked the Rogers analyst for an example of a roaming error, he was told that a roaming error could result if a Rogers phone was in the United States where it could not use the Rogers network.

"Somewhere in the telling between a Rogers Communications analyst, a Saint John police sergeant, and the deponent Saint John police officer, the import of the information regarding the 'roaming errors' revealed by that 'forced registration' of Richard Oland's iPhone got seriously misconstrued," said Walsh. The defence argued if Brooker had understood what he'd been told, police might have been able to work with an American network to track the phone, but no further investigation was done, Richard Oland's cellphone service was cancelled at the end of the month, and the killer may have escaped. "The defence is not alleging that what was involved was a deliberate attempt to mislead (nor would the evidence support such a finding) and attempting to pinpoint blame for the misinformation would be an exercise in futility," said Walsh. Still, he said he had "no doubt" the information in the ITO about the roaming error would have misled the authorizing judge.

The "corrected evidence," said Walsh, was that the phone was found to be operating on July 9, but its whereabouts was unknown to Rogers because it was not connecting to its network. Many months after the ITO was obtained, a Rogers analyst theorized in an email to the police,

"It is very possible that the person who took the phone went near the [United States] border and/or crossed the border between July 6 and July 9, 2011." Dennis Oland was under surveillance from the time he left the police station on July 7 until his home was searched on July 14, the jury heard—although the Crown pointed out that surveillance only started about fourteen hours after Richard Oland's body was discovered. Prosecutors argued again that Rogers pinged the mobile rocket stick on Richard Oland's yacht in Rhode Island instead of his cellphone, but Walsh, like Judge LeBlanc, noted no evidence of such a mistake was presented. But even if the corrected roaming error information had been provided in the ITO, Walsh found the other evidence about the missing iPhone "remains untouched." The phone registered with the Rothesay cell tower at 6:44 p.m., "probably at the same time Dennis Oland was in Rothesay."

Walsh also identified two erroneous statements in the ITO attributed to Dennis Oland about his relationship with his father. The ITO claimed that Oland said he had failed to live up to his father's high expectations, but in fact while Oland acknowledged his father's high expectations, he denied that he had failed to live up to them. Walsh noted, however, that any influence the error might have had on the judge would have been "muted" by Lisa Andrik-Oland's statement that her husband was always seeking his father's respect and had "never been able to live up to his standards." The second error concerned the ITO's statement that "Dennis felt as an adult the relationship generally improved but described it like a blanket." Walsh said the Crown agreed that the ITO's portrayal of the metaphor was inaccurate and should have been excised.

The defence also complained that the ITO misrepresented what Diana Sedlacek told police about Richard Oland's awareness of his son's financial issues by attributing her comments to Richard Oland. Walsh agreed; Sedlacek had not said Oland told her that Dennis was under financial strain. The defence went further, arguing that the ITO falsely and intentionally attributed these remarks to Richard in a bid to mislead the authorizing judge. Walsh reviewed Sedlacek's entire interview. Among other things, Sedlacek told the police: "Dennis Oland had no sense of work ethic and was babied by his mother," "Dennis was a financial analyst and was not making very much money," "Dennis is under a lot of financial constraint," and "Richard would never have given money to Dennis if he asked for it. Richard always complained about Dennis's work ethic. I know Dennis has gone to Richard looking for money and jumped up and down and screamed and cried for it. Dennis is like a wild kid. He just loses it." Walsh did not feel it was surprising the police inferred that Richard Oland was the original source for these statements and was unconvinced that police intended to mislead the authorizing judge.

The defence argued that police should have included Robert McFadden's information that Richard Oland's death did not relieve Dennis of the obligation to make monthly interest payments on the $500,000 debt and that the terms of the will meant he and his sisters would inherit nothing until their mother's death. "Having reviewed the entirety of the police narrative of the interview with Robert McFadden as to the composition and likely disposition of the deceased's estate (against the backdrop of the father-son relationship in contrast to the mother-son relationship), suffice to say," Walsh concluded, "the defence is out on a very thin limb to suggest that Dennis Oland would not have financially benefitted from his father's death."

Finally, the defence argued that police should have revealed Anthony Shaw tied the timing of the noises he heard emanating from Richard Oland's office to the fax sent at 8:11 p.m. and disclosed the time-stamped security footage of Dennis Oland in Rothesay at 7:38 p.m. But Walsh noted the timing of the fax was not confirmed until seven days after the search warrant was issued; Oland's wife had already provided an alibi, which is what the defence was seeking through the time-stamped video; and the deponent officer specifically stated she believed her. The ITO, Walsh noted, did not "overly emphasize" that Shaw made a guess as to what time he heard the noises. Walsh concluded that the ITO did not "pitch" the information one way or the other.

Despite the ITO's material errors and omissions, Walsh concluded two key pieces of information would, in his opinion, "compete for the authorizing judge's attention, like sign posts marking the entrance to paths running in opposing directions," one leading to Dennis Oland,

and the other away from him. On the one hand, Oland was the last known person to see his father alive at approximately six thirty on the evening of July 6, 2011, and minutes after he left 52 Canterbury Street, both his father's cellphone and he were most probably in Rothesay at the same time. On the other hand, two witnesses heard noises coming from Richard Oland's office at around eight o'clock that night. "A pathway of sufficiently credible evidence and reasonable inference leaning towards Dennis Oland," Walsh concluded, "remains open."

Next, Walsh turned his attention to the defence's submissions that the police were not entitled to subject the seized jacket, or any other items, to examination, particularly forensic DNA testing, without additional, specific judicial authorization. "The fact is that every day across this country for well over a century all kinds of 'things' 'seized' have been forensically examined in all manner of fashion by the police, or by others at their request on nothing more or less than the strength of having been obtained under a search warrant issued under the Criminal Code," he said. "Simply put, it has been the way of the law in employing search warrants. Of course, established practice can be a poor justification." As the defence put it, "You do not get judicial authority by implication." Clearly the police believed they needed judicial authorization to examine the jacket; they obtained a general warrant to permit examination and testing of the items seized during the search, said Walsh. But then they "inexplicably, allowed it to lapse before conducting the examinations contemplated."

After the seizure, the defence argued, the jacket was no longer the thing to be searched for, but rather the thing to be searched, and that should trigger additional Charter protection. Walsh disagreed, saying in this case, the opposite was true. "To prove that Dennis Oland was wearing that jacket, or even something similar, is evidence of nothing, unless there is evidence connecting the jacket to the homicide," he said. The evidentiary value of the jacket lay in "what might be splattered on it" and "the authorizing judge could have inferred that the jacket would be subjected to trace examination and/or forensic analysis, in particular DNA analysis, for the purpose, inter alia, of detecting and identifying Richard Oland's blood." If the defence position were to be accepted,

Walsh noted, police wouldn't even be permitted to look in the pockets of the jacket that was lawfully seized. "This cannot be the law following lawful seizure of an item by search warrant," he said. No other judicial authorization was required, he ruled.

The report to the judge stated that the items in question were "required for the purpose of a preliminary inquiry, trial or other proceeding, or for the purposes of further investigation." On August 18, 2011, the provincial court judge ordered the fifty-seven seized items be "detained in the custody of the exhibit control office of the Saint John Police Force" for a period not to exceed three months. The Court of Queen's Bench subsequently granted five extension orders for some of the items, up to December 2, 2013. The defence argued the wording of the detention orders permitted only detention of the items, nothing more, and that the Saint John police could not send the items off-site. Walsh dismissed both propositions. The original detention order and some of the extensions were very specific about what police would do with the seized items, and Walsh could not accept the defence's interpretation that Saint John police had to retain the items.

The jacket was not obtained contrary to the Charter, Walsh ruled. But something else was. Police had obtained a search warrant for Oland's work computer at CIBC Wood Gundy on August 11, 2011. The ITO content was much the same as the house warrant, with additional information about Oland's financial situation, the results of some preliminary forensic examinations of his car and home, and the results of the execution of the house warrant. Again, the defence argued the ITO suffered from material omissions, including that police had security video showing Dennis Oland at Kent Building Supplies on the morning of July 7 wearing a navy blazer. The defence suggested it bolstered the likelihood Oland made an innocent mistake when he told police he was wearing a navy blazer the night before. Walsh agreed it was material information, but the authorizing judge "could still have drawn an adverse inference in the context of the totality of the evidence," he said. In fact, the information could "just as equally and plausibly discount the probability of [an] innocent mistake given the fact it would have been even more recent in his memory," he said.

The defence further argued that police failed to comply with the terms of the search warrant. Investigators obtained additional personal information — including two letters Oland wrote to his father in May and October 2003, documents about his divorce, and two pay stubs from 2010 and 2011 — from a CIBC network drive after the warrant expired on October 9, 2011. The Crown contended the warrant was executed within the time limit and allowed CIBC to continue to examine the seized material for the information sought. Investigators didn't know the additional information existed until October 26, when they called CIBC corporate security to inquire why the data they'd received, including Oland's Internet activity and emails, did not have any personal files, and CIBC advised that its policy was for employees to save personal information on the network drive, not the hard drives on their computers. CIBC copied Oland's personal information onto a CD that police viewed on November 4, 2011.

Walsh ruled police obtained this evidence outside the authority of the search warrant, wrongly assuming that if CIBC corporate security had possession of the drive or access to it, then it was somehow in their hands, as though "corporate security for Wood Gundy was the alter ego of the police." As a result, Saint John police violated Oland's Charter right to be free of unreasonable search and seizure. "Police, seemingly without pause or concern for the limits of the authority given to them, went ahead and retrieved additional evidence, ostensibly seen at the time as very personal information related to Dennis Oland," he admonished. "Judges oftentimes in other contexts have to remind citizens that an order of a court means what it clearly says. Such a reminder should not be required to be given to the police. I find that the Charter-infringing state conduct was serious." Walsh deemed the evidence seized inadmissible at the trial, saying it was required to maintain the public's confidence in the criminal justice system. To do otherwise would send the message that individual rights count for little, he said.

Not everything undisclosed to the jury threatened to undermine the Crown's case, however. The preliminary inquiry heard additional forensic findings about Oland's brown sports jacket in favour of the Crown's case, findings not presented at trial. The fourth stain tested positive for blood but could not be tested for DNA because it did not meet the RCMP's minimum required amount for processing. But a private lab that works with less material analyzed it. Police forwarded a sample of the stain identified as AB, located on the right sleeve, to Maxxam Analytics. Stephen Denison, the DNA technical leader and forensic biologist, determined Richard Oland could not be excluded as the source of the "low-level" DNA profile. The probability that a randomly selected individual from the Canadian Caucasian population unrelated to Richard Oland would coincidentally share the observed DNA profile, Denison found, was estimated to be one in 2.5 billion.

Dennis Oland's lawyers sought to have his conviction quashed and either an acquittal entered or a new trial ordered. They also sought to have him released on bail pending his appeal, an application that Justice J.C. Marc Richard of the Court of Appeal rejected in February 2016. Had it succeeded, it would have been the first time in New Brunswick that a convicted murderer was granted bail. Oland's lawyers promptly appealed the bail denial, and when that failed, they applied to the Supreme Court of Canada for a reversal of the decision.

Dennis Oland began serving his sentence in an undisclosed federal penitentiary. About five months into his sentence, two violent offenders assaulted him. The attack took place in the maximum security prison's visiting room, in front of two people visiting Oland (their identities have not been disclosed) who tried to intervene. The two attackers, both in their mid-twenties, punched and kicked him, knocked him to the floor, and then continued to beat him. The assault ended when guards broke it up. Oland suffered injuries to his face and was treated at the prison. His attackers (who are serving life for first-degree murder and fifteen years for attempted murder respectively) eventually pled guilty and were each sentenced to serve four months concurrent with their original sentences. William Teed made it clear that Oland himself had not filed a complaint, did not participate in the investigation, and declined to submit a victim impact statement.

The Saint John Board of Police Commissioners announced the New Brunswick Police Commission would review how police handled the investigation. Soon after beginning his examination of Glen McCloskey's conduct, investigator Barry MacKnight recommended the commission ask Halifax Regional Police to conduct a criminal investigation. The investigation lasted eight months and cleared him of criminal wrongdoing. MacKnight's subsequent professional investigation however, found McCloskey "wilfully or negligently" made statements he knew to be false — both during his 2015 testimony and the subsequent investigation — "with intent to deceive, falsify or mislead." McCloskey and King did have the conversation that King described, MacKnight concluded, and McCloskey had used words to the effect of "you don't have to tell them that." He found that McCloskey acted in a manner that would likely hurt the reputation of the force, failed to perform his duties diligently, and counselled another member to commit a breach of the code of conduct. McCloskey was scheduled to face an arbitration hearing but retired in April 2018, and the matter was dropped. The police watchdog only has the authority to discipline active officers. The commission suspended its investigation of the rest of the police investigation once Oland's lawyers appealed his conviction, saying that it didn't want its review to affect the ongoing criminal proceedings.

When Bill Reid, then chief of the Saint John Police Force, announced that Richard Oland's death was a homicide, he told the assembled reporters: "We do not want to make a mistake. We want to be able to prove this case without a shadow of a doubt." By the time the Crown and the defence wrapped up their respective cases, public opinion was divided. Some were convinced Dennis Oland was guilty; others believed equally strongly in his innocence. Still others were not so sure. To some of those who believed Oland was most likely the killer, the trial's disclosure of procedural errors on the part of police left room to doubt the integrity of the Crown's case. To others to whom Dennis Oland just didn't seem like a murderer, his inexplicable lapses of memory raised uncomfortable questions about his claims of innocence. Despite the purported finality of the verdict and sentence, a shadow of doubt hung over the case.

In theory, the verdict is the last word in a criminal trial, and sometimes it is. But in the Oland case, nothing is simple. Was the protracted investigation the result of police reluctance to investigate a member of one of New Brunswick's most prominent families, as many assumed, or did the police's single-minded focus on Dennis Oland botch the investigation? Could the man who completely lost control when he heard the guilty verdict have committed such a violent and impulsive crime and then betrayed nothing to the people who saw him immediately afterwards, including his wife and aunt? Was the defence so focused on exposing the flaws in the investigation and confident that jurors would believe Anthony Shaw heard the sounds of murder between seven thirty and eight p.m. — *after* Dennis Oland left the office — that it failed to mount a decisive challenge to testimony that placed the missing iPhone in Rothesay when Dennis Oland admitted he was at the Rothesay wharf? What might have happened if the defence had called other witnesses to support its case?

Despite the presumed finality of the jury's verdict, more twists and turns were still to come.

nineteen

AN APPEAL AND A MISTRIAL

Oland's lawyers filed their written arguments to have the Supreme Court of Canada overturn his bail denial at the end of August 2016, arguing that Oland was a "model candidate" who posed no threat to public safety. "Even if it can be argued the appellant's success on appeal is not virtually assured, a reasonable member of the public would appreciate that this case was a very close one, that the grounds being raised could well be successful, and that the defence position that a wrongful conviction of an innocent man has occurred may well turn out to be the case," they wrote in their forty-eight-page factum. Oland's case provided an opportunity for the Supreme Court to clarify the legal test for granting bail pending appeal. "At present," they noted, "there is surprisingly no consensus."

The case drew the attention of the attorneys general of Ontario, Alberta, and British Columbia and the Criminal Lawyers' Association of Ontario, all four seeking intervenor status. Ontario argued that "very serious offences demand very strong grounds of appeal before bail will be considered" and that any reconsideration of the framework would significantly impact a populous province with a high volume of post-conviction applications for release. Alberta argued that, if Oland were successful, it would mean "a convicted appellant's entitlement to bail is essentially the same as an untried accused's." British Columbia noted it was appropriate to "[place] the onus on the now-convicted murderer, who is presumed validly convicted unless and until an appellate court says otherwise."

But the Criminal Lawyers' Association of Ontario, which repre-
sents more than a thousand lawyers, argued against what it saw as the
"reluctance" of the Court of Appeal of New Brunswick to grant bail
pending appeal in homicide cases. Michael Lacy, the lawyer who served
as vice-president of the association, called that "inconsistent with the
robust bail pending appeal tradition in Canada." If the three attorneys
general were granted leave to intervene in the case, it would be important
for the Supreme Court to hear from his organization "to have a balanced
perspective."

Oland's lawyers opposed the three provinces' motions. Intervenors
are intended to provide additional perspective, they argued, but the
three attorneys general were "mainly repetitive" of the New Brunswick
attorney general and their intervention could create an "imbalance of
representation" in favour of the Crown. The Supreme Court granted the
four intervenor requests.

Two and a half months later, Oland climbed out of the back of a
sheriff's van, ready to appeal his conviction. He wore a suit and tie and
shackles for his appearance at the Court of Appeal of New Brunswick.
Given the high level of public interest and limited seating in the
Fredericton courtroom, the court asked CBC to livestream the proceedings. It was — and is — very unusual for New Brunswick courts to allow
cameras. One of the conditions was that only the bench and the lawyers'
tables could be shown — not Oland, and no members of the public.

The court limited the time for oral arguments. Both sides had
previously submitted "exceptionally lengthy written submissions of high
quality," noted Chief Justice Ernest Drapeau, who would decide the case
with Justice Margaret Larlee and Justice Kathleen Quigg. "If it takes a
day to make an argument, maybe it's not very strong."

The oral arguments focused largely on the trial judge's instructions to
the jury regarding Oland's alleged "after-the-fact" conduct: his incorrect
statement to police about which jacket he wore on the night his father
was killed. The defence maintained he'd made an innocent mistake.
The Crown maintained it was a lie intended to mislead investigators.
Justice John Walsh had cautioned the jury on the issue. "You must not
use the evidence about what Dennis Oland said about the colour of the

jacket in deciding or helping you decide that Dennis Oland committed the offence charged unless you reject any innocent explanation you may find for it." Defence lawyer Alan Gold argued that Walsh wrongly suggested that Oland's "erroneous statement" could be considered the actions of a guilty man. He should have instructed the jury to ignore the statement because there was "no reasonable inference of guilt" unless the jurors fell into "circular reasoning" and "guilt was first assumed." The issue wrongly left Oland vulnerable to being thought a liar by the jury and contributed to the guilty verdict, said Gold. He described Oland's statement about the jacket as a "lynchpin" in the Crown's case: "The case may not have been as persuasive without it. There has to be a new trial." Gold didn't blame the jurors. Post-offence conduct was, he said, "too tough an area for a jury of lay persons."

"The case law seems to suggest that it's too dangerous; that if you have ordinary people sitting on a jury and they make a finding of a lie, they leap to guilt," observed Drapeau. "A jury must be told that before a false statement can be treated as incriminating evidence, there must be a reasonable evidentiary basis for inferring that the statement is not only false but fabricated and that the accused has been complicit in that fabrication in order to conceal his involvement in the offence." Drapeau didn't see "those magical words" in Walsh's instructions. In fact, Walsh appeared to have done "precisely the opposite," he said, telling the jury, "To decide the reason why Dennis said he was wearing a navy blazer, you should consider all of the evidence."

The Crown, of course, urged the appeal panel to accept Walsh's instructions to the jury and uphold the guilty verdict. Prosecutors argued that although Walsh did not explicitly tell the jurors, "Here is independent evidence of fabrication," he did point them to other evidence they could consider in weighing Oland's statement about what he was wearing, including that he answered the question less than twenty-four hours after the fact and without hesitation; he accurately described the shirt he wore, even though he has many more shirts than jackets; and blood was found on the jacket. Prosecutor Kathryn Gregory also pointed out that Walsh sought input, over several days, from the Crown and the defence before he compiled his instructions, and the defence didn't raise concerns about the issue at that time. If the judge made a mistake, "it was a harmless error," she said; Oland's statement about the jacket "was not a critical aspect of this case." Drapeau countered that he found that hard to believe. Oland's statement was not a "smoking gun," but it's "not peripheral," either, he remarked. "I would have tended to say it was significant on the scale of conviction," he said. "But that's me."

Gold also argued that prosecutor P.J. Veniot may have crossed a line in his closing remarks to the jury when he speculated about what transpired between Dennis Oland and his father on the night of the killing. "The Crown told the jury that what they would hear is 'what we believe actually happened,'" said Gold. This was improper and unfair to Oland, he said, describing it as "highly prejudicial speculation" combined with "a failure to put these allegations to the appellant," and lawyers should never express personal beliefs. Drapeau agreed, noting that Crown counsel have "special obligations" that defence lawyers don't. But he stopped short of saying his concerns would be enough to overturn Oland's conviction.

Drapeau did not agree with Gold's assertion that no evidence of animosity between father and son was presented to the jury, quoting heavily from Oland's statement to police. And he grilled Gold about why he and his colleagues didn't ask Walsh for a "directed verdict" to acquit Oland following closing arguments. That's a motion defence lawyers are entitled to use when they "know in their heart of hearts" a case is weak and should not go to the jury, Drapeau said. Gold said the defence felt asking for a directed verdict would be "essentially a waste of time" but maintained throughout that the Crown didn't have a case. "You have an objection, you make it," and get it on the record, Drapeau replied. "That's the law." Drapeau also challenged Gregory on why the Crown didn't make use of Oland's surprise testimony about the third trip to his father's office. Gregory said it was simply a prosecutorial decision.

In closing, Gold asked the appeal panel to consider which of "two competing" hypotheses was "more reasonable": that Oland was a "singularly unlucky innocent person whose father in the past happened to leave minute stains on a jacket, and he happened to visit his father the day that he was murdered," or that he is "an incredibly lucky, completely amateur killer who, within fifteen minutes, was able, with some mysterious weapon of unknown origin, to brutally batter his father to death without getting any significant spatter stains on his clothing, take his clothing to cleaners...who check for bloodstains because they use a bloodstain remover, which is not done because there's no stains found." Oland was "so lucky" that he disposed of both the weapon and his father's iPhone without being seen and left no traces of blood in his uncleaned car or on the Blackberry he used to take a call from his wife just minutes after "supposedly" having killed somebody. He spoke and shopped "normally" with his wife. He withstood hours of police questioning "that turned into interrogation" without making any admission of guilt. "And then, the ultimate unlikely event: a completely independent alibi by persons who hear the killing and immediately come forth to the police and put the killing noises at a time when his innocence had to be undoubted." (Security video showed Oland shopping with his wife in Rothesay around the same time.) "It is the inference of innocence that we submit is the only reasonable inference."

The panel pledged to do its best to render its verdict "sooner rather than later." If the judges could not reach a unanimous decision, the losing party would have an automatic right to take the case to the Supreme Court of Canada. On October 24, the panel's decision was ready. If the judges overturned the conviction, Oland could walk out of the Fredericton courthouse a free man.

In a unanimous decision, the appeal panel quashed Oland's conviction and ordered a new trial, ruling that Walsh erred in his instructions to the jury on whether or not Oland "lied" to police about the jacket he wore on the night his father was killed—a "key piece of the evidentiary puzzle." Walsh should have instructed the jurors to disregard Oland's incorrect statement, unless they had independent evidence that it was a lie concocted to conceal his involvement in Richard Oland's death. However, the jury's verdict was not unreasonable or unsupported by the evidence, so an acquittal would be inappropriate, the panel said, thus a retrial. Gasps from Oland's family and friends filled the courtroom. Oland himself showed little emotion at first, but later he appeared to be smiling and fighting back tears.

A bail hearing was scheduled for the next morning. Justice Marc Richard heard the matter. He'd denied Oland bail just eight months earlier, when Oland was still a convicted murderer. This time he ruled that "any reasonable member of the public would understand that Mr. Oland has reacquired the presumption of innocence" now that his guilty verdict had been overturned. A $50,000 surety from Derek Oland was required. Oland had to keep the peace, be of good behaviour, surrender his passport, notify police of any travel outside New Brunswick, reside at his home in Rothesay, and advise police of any change of address.

The Supreme Court of Canada hearing on Oland's bail appeal proceeded on October 31 as scheduled, even though it was now a moot point for him. The defence team wanted the court to declare the appeal court's decision to twice deny Oland bail while he waited to appeal his conviction "an error in law." Oland had been released, but the question of when convicted murderers should be granted bail pending appeal remained "ripe" for discussion, Gold told the nine-justice panel. The Crown and the four intervenors agreed. Dennis Oland attended the hearing in Ottawa in person, watching from the public gallery with several of his supporters. Oland had spent ten months in prison awaiting his appeal but, Gold noted, it could take up to three years for appeals to be heard in some provinces. Thus bail refusal could result in a "serious and lengthy incarceration." Kathryn Gregory argued on behalf of the New Brunswick attorney general that presumption of innocence no longer applies post-conviction. Murder is the most serious offence, she argued, and unless the court denying bail makes an error in law or in principle, deference should be given to the initial bail decision. The Supreme Court ruled on March 23, 2017, issuing a unanimous, precedent-setting decision that Oland was wrongly denied bail. The Supreme Court justices said they would have set aside Oland's detention order. Oland's defence team was "very happy" with the decision, Alan Gold wrote in an email to CBC News, "But that sentiment is considerably tempered by our regret that Dennis Oland had to spend so many months in custody unnecessarily."

—

Nearly two years after he'd been released on bail, and more than seven years since his father's murder, Dennis Oland arrived at Harbour Station for jury selection. Now fifty, he was slightly greyer but appeared tan, trim, and well rested. He held hands with his wife, Lisa.

A steady stream of more than one thousand prospective jurors filed into the arena. An hour and a half later, the line still stretched the length of the building and well out the door. The formal proceedings didn't get underway until mid-afternoon, after everyone got through security, registered, and was served complimentary submarine sandwiches. Patience wore thin for some as they muttered about cancelled plans, hard seats, and the cold.

Scheduling the retrial had been a protracted process. The Office of the Attorney General and the defence both failed to have the country's highest court review the New Brunswick Court of Appeal's decision to overturn Oland's conviction. Prosecutors hoped to have the guilty verdict reinstated; the defence sought an acquittal instead of a retrial. The Supreme Court of Canada dismissed both requests without providing reasons, as is the court's custom. A retrial date was tentatively scheduled to be set on August 8, but both sides wanted more time to prepare.

Only two of the three Crown prosecutors who handled the first trial were assigned to the retrial—P.J. Veniot and Derek Weaver—but the Crown anticipated a third would join them. Oland was expected to have the same defence team: Alan Gold, Gary Miller, and James McConnell. Court of Queen's Bench Justice Terrence Morrison, highly regarded in the legal community and widely considered a competent choice for the complex case, was tapped to come in from Fredericton to preside. During his ten years on the bench, Morrison had dealt with a variety of criminal trials, including at least one brutal murder, the case of a man who bludgeoned an elderly woman to death. "Patient is the word that first comes to me," lawyer Peter Hyslop observed. "He's very thorough and takes his time."

Jury summonses started showing up in area mailboxes in July 2018. The day before jury selection began, Gary Miller confirmed to CBC News that he was stepping down from the case. Miller, 70, thought the case would benefit from "a fresh set of eyes." He would, however, follow the proceedings "with keen interest." Toronto-based lawyer Michael Lacy replaced Miller; as vice-president of the Criminal Lawyers' Association of Ontario, he'd had intervenor status in Oland's appeal before the Supreme Court of Canada. Lacy had trained under Gold and worked with him on various cases over the years, including Oland's first trial (although he never appeared in court). Among the many homicide trials and appeals Lacy has handled, the most notable may be the case of Toronto police constable James Forcillo, convicted of attempted murder in the shooting death of Sammy Yatim on a streetcar. Lacy had also done some high-profile work in New Brunswick. In August 2018 he helped win a new trial for former Esgenoôpetitj First Nation Chief Wilbur Dedam on six sex-related offences against three girls between 1977 and 1985.

Jury selection for the retrial was no less lengthy and tedious than in the first trial. Prospective jurors were each assigned a number, and the court clerk drew the numbers at random. The prospects were divided into groups of fifty, assigned a group letter, and given a tentative date and time to attend the actual selection process at the Saint John Law Courts between October 29 and November 9. The final group wasn't dismissed until around eight thirty p.m. During the proceedings, Oland slowly spun his chair around and glanced at the crowd in the stadium seating, some of whom were expected to soon determine his fate.

On October 29 one hundred potential jurors from the first two groups entered courtroom 12. Morrison gave some preliminary instructions: sheriff's deputies would escort the prospects one at a time into courtroom 14 to face the multi-step selection process. Each side had sixteen peremptory challenges (i.e. the right to reject a potential juror without stating a reason).

"I'm going to put my cranky face on now, because I have to give you a very stern warning," Morrison said. "You must not under any circumstances tell anyone, in particular any panel member ... about the questions which were asked of you." He also warned them against posting on social media. Violation, he said, would place them "in very serious jeopardy. That is how serious we take the fair selection of a jury for any criminal process." What questions they should be asked was the focus of a pre-trial hearing. Gold later told reporters that Morrison's "fine decision on the challenge for cause [process] will stand as a precedent across Canada. Based upon the evidence we presented, the court allowed a much more fulsome challenge for cause than has ever been allowed in a Canadian court."

Some prospective jurors were dismissed within minutes. Others took much longer. Oland looked directly at each candidate, listened attentively to their answers using a headset that amplified the audio, and then huddled with his lawyers as they quietly discussed the individual's acceptability. By the end of the day, five jurors were chosen. The process moved more quickly the next day and brought the total to twelve, although one man was later dismissed for reasons that were under a publication ban. On the third day, the final three and two alternates were sworn in by mid-afternoon.

Morrison announced that the retrial would begin on November 6 and was expected to last sixteen weeks, sitting primarily Tuesdays through Fridays, from nine a.m. until four thirty p.m.

And then, the day before the trial was to begin, Oland and his lawyers were spotted at the courthouse. The doors to the courtroom were not only closed, which is unusual, but locked, which is almost unheard of. Morrison eventually opened the courtroom just long enough to advise that an "unanticipated legal issue" had arisen that needed to be dealt with in camera.

The next morning, only a few people waited in the rain for the courthouse to open, and most of them were members of the media—a far cry from the throng that showed up for the first day of Oland's trial in 2015. Judith Meinert Thomas had attended the original trial and was present again. "I was so fascinated by the justice system last time and so impressed by it, I just wanted to be here," she explained. The crowd slowly multiplied before the scheduled start.

When Morrison called for the jury, only two women entered. Court staff had managed to reach the other fourteen in advance to tell them they needn't attend. An "unexpected legal issue" needed to be resolved, Morrison said. He urged the two jurors to ensure staff had their correct contact information and adjourned the public proceedings for the rest of the day. On November 7, the legal issue remained unresolved, and Morrison postponed the start of the trial another two weeks.

Finally, when Oland returned to court on November 20 for what was supposed to be the start of the presentation of evidence, he appeared cheerful. Only a scattering of people were in the public gallery, including a few of his supporters and eight reporters. Lead investigator Stephen Davidson; the head of the major crime unit, Jay Henderson; and the head of forensics, Mark Smith, sat together in the back row.

The jurors took their seats, completely unaware of what was about to happen. Morrison addressed them. He told them that after jury selection was complete, the Crown became aware of "improprieties" related to the selection process. "I have determined that it's in the best interest of justice that a mistrial be declared, thereby ensuring that any further trial of this matter will not be tainted." He discharged the jurors and announced he would preside over a judge-alone trial that would begin the next day. Some of the jurors looked perplexed; others seemed disappointed or relieved.

The legal issue that prompted the locked-door hearings, delayed the start of the trial, and ultimately led to the mistrial was that a Saint John police officer had conducted "improper" background checks on prospective jurors during the selection process and on the sworn-in jurors afterward. The Crown and police are allowed to conduct limited background checks to determine if a potential juror has a criminal record, which would make that person ineligible to serve unless they had obtained a pardon. But Constable Sean Rocca, who had served as an investigator since the day Richard Oland's body was discovered and the file coordinator since October 2011, used the force's internal database, the Crime Management System, which shows any contact a person has had with city police, whether as a witness, complainant, victim, suspect, or accused.

Oland's lawyers argued this could be perceived as "juror shopping," screening for any negative interactions with police that might cause someone to look unfavourably upon the Crown's case. They noted the Crown objected to seven prospective jurors the defence was happy with and questioned if it was because of "improper input" based on information the officer had gleaned. Rocca, who sat with the Crown during the selection process, had offered prosecutors his "opinion from time to time," according to court documents.

Prosecutors said they were unaware of Rocca's searches, and the defence accepted that. Still, Gold argued, seven prospective jurors had been improperly excluded, calling the integrity of the trial into question. Morrison agreed. "In my view, the appearance of justice was fatally wounded," he said. The Supreme Court of Canada condemned "in no uncertain terms" the use of "police databases to conduct inquiries of potential jurors outside legitimate permissible checks for criminal records," he wrote in his decision. Some of Rocca's searches "went beyond looking for 'arrest flags.'" Morrison noted the way police handled the homicide investigation was central to the case and police would be under scrutiny at trial. "The fact that a member of the SJPF was engaged in the searches in question relating to potential jurors' contact with police amplifies the appearance of unfairness," Morrison noted in the written decision. Case law dictates that mistrials are a last resort, but he worried the wrong choice could become subject to an appeal. "The last thing any of us wants is to have a verdict in this case with an asterisk," he said.

(A redacted court transcript of Rocca's testimony during the locked-door hearing suggests that he stands by his actions. "I didn't see anything wrong with that whatsoever," he said. He'd performed similar searches for other jury trials he'd been involved with over his sixteen years with the force, he said, including Oland's first trial. He explained the provincial database only shows provincial charges, and the federal database only shows convictions that require fingerprinting. Saint John police routinely use all three, he said. Prosecutors only found out about Rocca's searches when he alerted them to "issues" he had discovered regarding two of the sworn-in jurors. The Crown immediately instructed him to stop conducting searches and, as required by law, disclosed his searches to the defence. What Rocca discovered about the jurors was never made public.)

The defence held a news conference after court. Saint John police "engaged in totally improper conduct" and "violated clear law," Gold asserted. The defence was particularly "aghast" and "gobsmacked" to discover Rocca used the same search practices during jury selection for Oland's first trial. Gold called for the matter to be "added to the list" of issues the New Brunswick Police Commission's review of the investigation should cover. He also called on the commission to immediately resume its probe. "The inquiry was put on hold to allegedly avoid any possible impact on the jury trial," Gold said. Now that the case was proceeding by judge alone, "that reason is now gone."

Oland's defence team had tried unsuccessfully for more than a year to get a judge-alone trial—likely the reason for Oland's cheerfulness when the mistrial was declared. They also initially sought to have the trial moved to another city, such as Fredericton or Moncton, arguing Oland couldn't get an impartial jury in Saint John given the publicity the case had garnered. It is "very likely the most highly publicized criminal law case in New Brunswick's history," they wrote. Normally, homicide trials in Canada are heard by a judge and jury. An accused can request a judge alone, but the attorney general must agree. In Oland's case, the attorney general refused to consent and refused to provide reasons, according to the defence. Oland's lawyers wanted Morrison to overrule the Crown's refusal. To support their argument, they sought permission at a pre-trial hearing to survey prospective jurors from Oland's first trial who weren't selected or panel members dismissed from other trials. Morrison denied the application, saying it would violate the Jury Act. Instead, the defence commissioned a telephone poll to gauge the level of bias against Oland. A psychology professor helped write the questions, with input from the Crown. In all 38,428 calls were attempted and 1,203 interviews with jury-eligible residents were completed in the judicial districts of Saint John, Fredericton, and Moncton. In the end, the results showed a slightly higher percentage of people in Fredericton and Moncton felt Oland was guilty (28 per cent in both compared to 27 per cent in Saint John), and Oland's lawyers abandoned their request for a change of venue.

They continued to push for a judge-alone trial, preparing a supplemental report that showed 45.7 per cent of Saint John residents who wanted to serve on Oland's jury believed he was guilty (18 per cent believed he was not guilty; 36 per cent said they didn't know or pre-ferred not to say). This suggested a significant risk of selecting jurors with pre-existing opinions of guilt, the defence argued. The Crown countered that the 45.7 per cent was not a percentage of the 401 people polled in Saint John but of the subset of 41 who said they would "very much" like to serve on the jury. Of the 401 polled, prosecutors argued, only 4.67 per cent were both eager to serve on the jury and believed that Oland was guilty. Both the Crown and defence called academics to weigh in. All agreed that how the data is presented is "determined by what 'story' one wants to tell." The results were "subject to a great deal of interpretation," Morrison noted, and he had to exercise caution. He wasn't convinced a fair and impartial jury couldn't be empanelled in Saint John. Seventy per cent of respondents said they could keep an open mind, he noted, and there are "safeguards embedded" in the system to address bias. Accordingly, he denied the defence's request. "There is a strong societal interest in having an accused tried by a jury of his peers which reflects the values and concerns of the community where the offence occurred," Morrison wrote. "The very strength of the jury lies in the determination of guilt or innocence by ordinary citizens who, although not legal experts, bring a healthy measure of common sense to the trial process."

Once Morrison declared a mistrial, the Crown consented to the trial proceeding without a jury. The defence suggested prosecutors had little choice. Going through the selection process again could bump the trial back several months, raising the possibility of an unconstitutional delay. The Supreme Court had set a time limit of thirty months from the time a charge is laid to the conclusion of a first trial. The limit for retrials is still "a little grey," Alan Gold said, but they should be completed even sooner. "Dennis and his family have endured the criminal process for over half a decade," he declared. "All Dennis and his family want is a fair trial as soon as possible, without further delay, a trial at which they are confident of Dennis finally being vindicated and his innocence declared."

twenty

RETRIAL

After weeks of delay, the retrial began on November 21, 2018. Oland was rearraigned, and again he pleaded not guilty to killing his father. Again he sat at a small table outside the dock, near his defence team's table, a request Justice Morrison granted because of Oland's hearing impairment. The defence had also argued that requiring Oland to sit in the prisoner's box could result in "prejudicial speculation," since the media had reported that he sat outside the box for his first trial and subsequent proceedings. "Jurors who have been exposed to this media coverage might reasonably conclude (albeit incorrectly) that the Applicant has had his bail revoked or otherwise engaged in conduct which has caused him to become a security concern." The table was on the right side of the courtroom, directly in front of the first row of the public gallery where his family and other supporters sat. A monitor on the table largely concealed him from scrutinizing eyes.

Jill Knee, the newest member of the prosecution team, delivered the Crown's opening remarks. She competently and briskly laid out the Crown's case in less than twenty-three minutes, not straying far, if at all, from P.J. Veniot's 2015 script. She described the "strained" father-son relationship and portrayed the victim as a demanding man of "considerable wealth." She contrasted that with Dennis Oland's financial situation at the time of the murder: his bank account overdrawn, his line of credit maxed out, his credit card over his limit, his expenditures (roughly $120,000) far exceeding his income (around $34,000) in the first six months of 2011. He owed his father an interest payment each month, and his latest cheque to him had bounced. He also knew his father was engaged in a long-term extramarital affair, and he did not approve, Knee told the court. She stressed the brutality of the "rage" killing. "The accused was the last person to see his father alive," she said.

Knee acknowledged some gaps in the evidence. The weapon (or weapons) was never found. The exact time of death was unknown. The victim's missing iPhone was never found. The Crown could not say why it was removed from the scene, but prosecutors contended the cellphone evidence was "critical." At 6:44 p.m., approximately eight minutes after Dennis Oland told police he'd left his father's office and headed home to Rothesay, his father's iPhone pinged off a cell tower near the wharf where Oland stopped. Knee also reviewed Oland's statement to police about what he was wearing and noted the blood and DNA found on the brown sports jacket he actually wore. "We submit that the evidence will support beyond a reasonable doubt that Dennis Oland killed his father," she said.

Unlike the first trial, when the defence waited until after the Crown had wrapped up its case to deliver an opening statement, the defence addressed the judge at the beginning of the retrial. Alan Gold got to his feet. "The Crown pointed out pieces of evidence that raise a suspicion and in isolation may point towards guilt," he said, "but there has to be some of that, otherwise we wouldn't be having a trial. We wouldn't even have a charge." But, he said, the "abundant evidence of absent, missing, incriminating evidence," meant the Crown's case failed to meet the burden of proof.

Gold pointed to the evidence of two witnesses who heard thumping noises coming from Richard Oland's office at around eight p.m. on July 6, when Dennis Oland and his wife were known to be running errands in Rothesay. Those were the sounds of "the horrible beating of Richard Oland." Gold drew attention to Oland's demeanour in the security video of him in Kennebecasis Drugs and Cochran's Country Market. "Would even a professional killer be able to be so calm and normal after a brutal, bloody, bashing murder?" he asked.

Richard Oland's body was discovered at around nine a.m., and by one p.m. police were discussing putting Dennis Oland under surveillance.

He *was* the last known person to see his father alive, "but to the police that word *known* evaporated very quickly," Gold alleged, pointing out that Knee had omitted it in her opening statement, demonstrating, he argued, "a disrespect for the presumption of innocence." Saint John police investigated Oland for more than two years and yet had "little evidence pointing to his guilt," Gold asserted. He challenged the Crown's claim that the father-son relationship was strained, noting the word came from police, not Dennis Oland. Their relationship, Gold suggested, was typical of Richard Oland's generation: "Fathers from that generation and families like that did not become friends with their children."

Gold also dismissed the money motive. Oland was not an immediate beneficiary upon his father's death. The money went to his mother. His financial situation was "difficult" but nothing more than that. The Crown had no evidence that Richard Oland had been asked for assistance, "much less refused in such a way as to occasion this rage leading to the homicide" with a "mysterious weapon" that somehow appeared from "who knows where." The computers of both father and son were examined and produced no evidence that Richard had ever complained about his son's financial situation.

As for the other leg of the alleged motive, Gold suggested it would be "normal for a son who loves his mother to disapprove of a father having a mistress for years." But the evidence showed Oland mentioned it only once to his father's business associate, approximately eighteen months before his father's death. "The financial and relationship evidence exemplifies, the defence submits, prejudicial evidence," Gold argued. "It paints Dennis in a bad light but logically fails as evidence of motive."

Why would Oland take his father's iPhone? Nothing was found on the phone's computer backup that would incriminate him. Yes, the phone connected with the Rothesay tower at 6:44 p.m., but "it is not impossible" the phone was still in Richard Oland's office, "along with a live Richard," at the time. "Agreed, the evidence will be it's unlikely," Gold acknowledged, "but it's not impossible, and unlikely happens all the time." He noted that the victim had a meeting to discuss his life insurance on the same day he was killed: "Surely that is far more unlikely than a random connection with a cell tower." (Oland's life insurance policy was worth about $8 million, Robert McFadden testified, payable to the Far End Corporation; Oland had the policy for tax reasons, he said.) As for the brown jacket, the bloodstains were "barely visible to the naked eye" and the Crown could not say how they got on the jacket or when. Gold dramatically displayed photographs of the bloody crime scene and a diagram illustrating blood spatter 360 degrees around the body "at considerable distance" and contrasted those with a photo of the jacket to challenge the Crown's contention that the killer had worn the jacket. No blood was found on Oland's other clothing or belongings, and the crime scene bore no signs that the killer had cleaned up before leaving.

Gold compared the evidence to a jigsaw puzzle "with missing pieces and pieces from a different puzzle," the Crown's puzzle that Oland killed his father, and the defence's puzzle that his visit was innocent. "With circumstantial evidence, all the pieces have to fit the Crown's puzzle and not some other, reasonable puzzle," he argued. "It's not whether you can see a picture or think you know what the puzzle will show when only some of the pieces are put together. It's that all the pieces fit. On our puzzle table, we've got a bunch of pieces that don't fit. You can't ignore those and claim you have enough pieces to show Dennis murdered his father."

The case called for "heightened vigilance" in assessing the evidence, Gold urged. "It is only through a rigorous application of the burden of proof and the presumption of innocence that the proper questions can be identified and answered without risking a miscarriage of justice."

The retrial largely mirrored the first trial. The parties agreed to use the 2015 videotaped testimony of eight witnesses, including Diana Sedlacek, rather than recall them. Her husband at the time of the murder, Jiri Sedlacek, was not called to testify again. At the first trial, the defence questioned whether or not police had investigated him thoroughly, but they objected to his appearance this time. They had a new angle to pursue.

But despite the familiar terrain, surprises and unexpected moments of drama lay ahead. The court heard about four Post-it notes found in a wooded area on the city's west side more than a month after the murder. The names Dick, Philip, and Derek were handwritten on them, along with "policemen Mike Stephen and Mark." A jumble of other scribblings referred to "Susannah Old" [*sic*], "Transfer $429," "alcoholic," and "Jon insured." Police searched the area for other evidence but did no other follow-up. Nor was the mystery resolved of what Gold described as "a note from Dick Oland's mistress" that apparently went missing from the office: "Did Zu find note?— re Our Trip?" she had texted the morning of July 6. Police never found the note, and none of the papers on Oland's desk were seized or inventoried. (Sedlacek's text appears to be the only evidence the note ever existed. McFadden came across her text when he went through the iPhone's backup data and asked police if they'd found the note referred to.)

In the midst of the retrial, the defence sought new disclosure about a claw hammer discovered in a garage near the victim's office the day after the discovery of his body. The hammer came up during testimony about police responding to a break-and-enter on Germain Street where blood was found in a sink. It turned out the incident was unrelated.

The Crown planned to call a new witness, Ron Ferguson, the ex-husband of Dennis Oland's wife, Lisa, to testify, but after prosecutors reviewed some information provided by the defence, who objected to Ferguson's appearance, they dropped him. What evidence he would have provided and why the defence objected remains unclear, but family court records revealed the couple, divorced since 2003, were in the midst of a legal battle. Ferguson was seeking sixteen months of retroactive child support for their twenty-five-year-old son. He filed the motion the day before the retrial was originally scheduled to begin. In the documents, Lisa Andrik-Oland called the timing "an attempt to bully" her.

Greg Oram, the officer who accompanied Glen McCloskey during his unauthorized second visit into the bloody office but who did not appear at either the preliminary inquiry or the first trial, was called to testify. Oland's lawyers had accused the Crown of "hiding" Oram, pointing to an email from prosecutor Patrick Wilbur to McCloskey: "I will try to limit/contain Oram's testimony so that the [defence] does not know to go there. As you know, Oram's Narrative...is short and lacks any specific details and he has no notes, so maybe we will...get away with it?" In subsequent emails to his supervisor, Wilbur insisted he meant he would ask only the questions necessary to establish Oram's role and presence.

If Oram said he had gone beyond the "authorized" area at the crime scene, "then I could not nor would I try to prevent him from testifying to same." The last phrase of the email referred to not calling McCloskey at the preliminary inquiry, "Period. Nothing more."

Oram testified that he asked McCloskey if he was allowed to enter the office, and McCloskey told him he could only, "go in so far, just prior to the body." Oram, who has been with the force for 30 years and is now a sergeant, told the court he entered the office alone and "made a conscious effort" not to disturb any evidence. He said that he was crouched about two or three feet from Oland's shattered skull when he heard McCloskey say he hoped it was a suicide because "it would be easier." Oram said he looked up and saw McCloskey "half-sitting" on a desk, table, or credenza on the left side of the office, one foot on the floor and the other dangling. Oram resumed observing the body. When he next looked up, McCloskey was on the opposite site of the office, standing in the doorway of McFadden's office. He joined him, and then, Oram alleged, they both wandered over to the front of Oland's desk, deeper into the crime scene than other witnesses had testified to travelling. Sergeant Mark Smith, the forensic officer, arrived shortly afterward and "asked" them to leave. (Smith said he "sternly ordered them to get out of my crime scene.") Oram marked their routes of travel on a diagram of the office, using multiple colours. The lines zigzagged almost the entire length, along both sides of a table in the centre and both sides of the desk where the body was found. He estimated they spent five to ten minutes in the office, and neither wore any protective gear.

Former Staff Sergeant Mike King repeated his allegation that either before or during the preliminary inquiry, McCloskey referred to Oram as "idiot Oram" for disclosing McCloskey's presence at the scene. "My immediate response—because I know that he was in there—was, 'Well, you were in there.' And right away he said, 'Well, you don't have to tell them that.'" King also recounted an earlier occasion when McCloskey called him into his office. He saw a box of exhibits related to the case on McCloskey's desk. McCloskey, he said, asked him to assign someone to deliver the box to the RCMP in Fredericton. King said he didn't know what was in the sealed box, but it "wasn't normal" procedure. King broke down when Alan Gold asked if it was easy for him to come forward with his allegations.

McCloskey, for his part, testified that Sergeant Mark Smith "invited" him, King, and Brooker in for a visit that lasted thirty seconds to one minute. (Smith had testified he grudgingly gave in to several senior officers. "Nobody actually pulled rank," he said, but "I've been on the police force long enough that, if the staff sergeant and inspector and whomever else asks to view the body, you just stop saying no.") Smith pointed to a spot on the floor and told them not to walk past it. Asked about his second trip into the office with Oram, McCloskey replied, "I said it was out of curiosity at the last trial." He explained that he meant, "professional curiosity in terms of what had transpired inside. We went in to try to figure out what happened. But having said that, my judgment was one hundred per cent totally wrong. I should have never been in the scene." McCloskey described following Oram; Oram had said he followed McCloskey. ("Everybody's memory's different, I suppose," McCloskey said when Gold confronted him with the contradictions between his testimony and Oram's.) When presented with a diagram he'd marked at the first trial to show his movements, he said, "I would say we went farther than what I had put here, that we were closer to the body." McCloskey told the court he did not sit on anything in the office and vehemently denied asking anyone to lie or alter their testimony, and he said he had "no knowledge" of a box of evidence being in his office. (Constable Shanda Weir testified that King asked her to transport a box to the RCMP on September 9, 2011. She couldn't say for certain, but she believed she picked it up from King's office. Acting Inspector David Brooker testified that he had a sealed box of evidence in his office, and he contacted King on September 9 to arrange for its transportation to the RCMP. "Weir came up to my office and transported it to Fredericton," Brooker said.)

One of the most dramatic points was when Mark Smith admitted he kept silent about finding McCloskey, his supervisor, and Oram in the office, not mentioning it in any of his notes or reports. In court, Smith explained that he knew he was going to testify and expected it would come up at trial. Michael Lacy challenged him, pointing out that Smith testified at Oland's preliminary inquiry and first trial without disclosing this information.

"I was waiting for the question," Smith said.

"So your claim...that you were going to testify and it would all come out that was only if someone happened to ask you a question about it, correct?"

"It was discussed . . ." Smith began before trailing off. After a long pause he said, "You're right." Smith said that when he was previously cross-examined by the defence, he was only asked about a specific time period. He expected the defence would follow up, but they didn't. Lacy pointed out that Smith could have raised the issue himself. "Correct," replied Smith, "and I should have." He didn't realize how deep into the scene the two officers travelled or the extent of their movements, he said. He never intended to mislead the court, he told Morrison. He said he'd discussed the McCloskey-Oram "situation" with the Crown and thought that either the Crown or defence would bring it up. "I admit to making mistakes at the crime scene, but I'm not a liar!"

Clearly the defence maintained that errors on the part of the police compromised their investigation and contributed to the wrongful prosecution of Dennis Oland, but would Justice Morrison feel the same way?

The mystery of Richard Oland's missing iPhone was arguably the most intriguing part of the retrial. It was also the most confusing. "You have lost me completely," an exasperated Morrison eventually interjected. "I, quite frankly, have no idea what a roaming error is." Dennis Oland's high-priced legal team admitted they misunderstood some of the cellphone evidence at the first trial but, Gold assured Morrison, "We now understand *roaming error* correctly."

Rogers Communications had performed a forced registration to try to "ping" the phone's GPS coordinates but got a roaming error message. When the forced registration was performed remained debated. David Brooker of the major crime unit had testified that it took place on July 7, mere hours after the discovery of the murder. At the first trial, the defence said it was July 9, arguing police didn't even know the phone was missing before then. Now, at the retrial, the Crown and defence reversed their positions. The Crown said Brooker was mistaken: the search occurred on July 9. The defence unexpectedly defended the officer, arguing that he was correct about the July 7 date. Gold objected to the Crown's attempt to enter into evidence emails that purported to show Rogers had performed three pings on July 9, all producing roaming errors, even though the emails had been a defence exhibit at the first trial. The Crown wanted the document marked as an exhibit because, without it, prosecutors were concerned Morrison would be left with the impression that there might have been a roaming error on July 7. Gold argued the document was not an official report but rather a "cut and paste" in an email that Sylvie Gill, the witness from Rogers, could not authenticate. Morrison sided with the defence but said the Crown could try to submit it later through another witness.

Gold wanted the court to accept as fact David Brooker's testimony about what he said a Rogers employee told him over the phone on July 7. As a rule, courts can't accept one person's account of a conversation as true, but the defence argued the verbal report met the common-law exception because it was an exchange between two professionals. Gold acknowledged he was making a novel argument. Brooker had testified that on July 7, 2011, he spoke to Rogers investigator Claudio Cusin about locating the victim's iPhone and its records. Brooker said Cusin told him Rogers couldn't locate the phone, using a "particular term" that Brooker could not recall and had not written down. "Could not locate cellphone," Brooker's notes read. During cross-examination, Gold suggested the term was *roaming error*. Brooker agreed. On July 9, Brooker spoke with a different Rogers employee, analyst Tagie Polo. According to a manual log Polo created, Polo pinged the missing iPhone three times that day. Cusin had no recollection of pinging the phone on July 7, and the digital record such a search would have created would have been automatically deleted before the police asked Rogers for its records, nineteen months later. In the end, both Crown and defence agreed to disagree: the Crown maintained the phone was pinged only on July 9, and the defence maintained it first happened on July 7. The relevance of this issue in the case against Dennis Oland, however, remained unclear.

The Crown once again called Payman Hakimian, a computer forensics expert with the RCMP, to try to pinpoint the time of Richard Oland's murder through his electronic activity. Hakimian testified that the iPhone was connected to Oland's main office computer at 1:50 p.m. on July 6, backed up by 4:41 p.m., and disconnected at 4:44 p.m. The phone's battery would have been charging during that time, he said. The last detected human interaction was with the Southern Ocean Racing Conference website at 5:39, around the time Dennis Oland arrived. Emails that arrived at 5:47 and 6:35 went unopened and unread. Under cross-examination, Hakimian revealed that Saint John police were scouring the iPhone's backup data for evidence as recently as August 20, 2018, when he produced a "data dump" using newer technology than the data dump a colleague produced in 2012. The raw data totalled 1,260 pages, according to Alan Gold: all call logs and text messages—everything that was on the cellphone at the time the backup was created. The last outgoing call was at 10:02 a.m., when Richard Oland called his office while driving to work. The last outgoing text message was to Diana Sedlacek at 12:01 p.m. regarding their travel options for their trip to Maine. The final incoming message was a text from Sedlacek at 6:44:33 p.m. A phone call from her two minutes later went directly to voicemail. Sedlacek tried calling eleven more times that night; every call went to voicemail. She also texted at least twice, but neither message was delivered. Two calls she placed to his office phone that evening went to voicemail. But no one could say why Richard Oland wasn't responding to his phones, and Michael Lacy pointed out that every incoming call to the iPhone, from morning until night, went to voicemail.

The records didn't indicate why the calls went to voicemail, but they did indicate which cell towers the iPhone communicated with. In the morning, when Oland was in Rothesay, his cell pinged off a nearby tower known as the Fairvale tower. When he called his office during the drive to work, his phone connected with the Fairvale tower, but as his vehicle got closer to Saint John, the cell switched to the tower on top of the Brunswick Square complex. That nearby tower continued to transmit all his calls and messages throughout the day. But at 6:44 p.m., the final text was transmitted by the Fairvale tower, near the wharf where Dennis Oland stopped on his way home between six thirty and seven p.m.

But at a pre-trial hearing the defence had presented new evidence related to a problem with the program Rogers used to extract text message records, evidence that only came to light about two years after Oland's first trial and that they contended called into question the reliability of Richard Oland's call detail records. The defence became aware of a letter Rogers sent in August 2011 to all law enforcement agencies, advising them of a previous problem with the software program, Cognos, which may have led the company to provide incomplete text messaging records. A software fix had been developed by July 2011, the letter said, and revised reports were in the works. The Saint John Police Force received the letter in relation to an unrelated investigation, and it was only brought to the attention of the lead investigator, Stephen Davidson, in November 2017. Davidson asked Rogers if there was any impact on the call detail records in the Oland case and was told that Sylvie Gill had checked to ensure the call detail records contained all the data before she sent them to police on July 13, 2011. The defence argued that Rogers's failure to disclose the problem earlier and Gill's failure to mention it during her testimony at the first trial undermined the integrity of the documents, but Morrison rejected the argument, ruling that the problem was identified and corrected before the records were provided and therefore had no impact on the case. He also rejected the defence's argument that one identified problem raised the question of other, undiscovered problems with the software, and ruled the call data records admissible.

Joseph Sadoun, the radio frequency engineer who helps design and test cellular networks, testified, as he had at the first trial, about the likely location of the missing iPhone when it received the final text message at 6:44 p.m. Based on prediction models of site coverage, Sadoun stated the phone was most likely in the vicinity of the Fairvale tower in Rothesay, about two kilometres from the Renforth wharf and fourteen kilometres from Richard Oland's office. During the first trial, the defence had argued that prediction models are typically based on a cellphone being at a height of 1.5 metres, the equivalent of a person standing at street level.

If the iPhone was with Oland in his second-floor office, that assumption wouldn't apply. Sadoun testified that before the new trial, he recalculated his prediction model based on the iPhone being six metres high, the equivalent of a second storey. His opinion about the likely location of the cellphone remained unchanged. He agreed it was possible the iPhone could have been in or near the Saint John office when the final text was delivered, but the chances were "very small," he said, citing the hilly terrain and various obstacles and the fact that other, closer towers would provide stronger signals, including the one on top of the Brunswick Square office tower. But Michael Lacy pointed to a series of test calls that police conducted at various locations to prove the propagation maps didn't always accurately predict which tower would transmit a call or text. The software predicted calls made from the Renforth wharf would be transmitted by the Fairvale tower. Twenty calls were made from the wharf; fifteen went through. All fifteen connected with a tower on Mount Champlain, more than twenty kilometres away. Sadoun agreed that he would have assessed the likelihood of that happening as low.

Lacy introduced new evidence in a further attempt to discredit Sadoun's probability assessment. The defence obtained from Rogers a purported list of the so-called neighbour cell towers — designated backups that could take over for the uptown tower during peak periods or technical problems. The list indicated the Fairvale tower was considered a neighbour tower. Neighbour towers aren't necessarily the closest ones. They're selected based on a host of technical requirements, not proximity. Derek Weaver also revisited the police test calls. Stephen Davidson had made ninety-six calls from locations west of the government garage on Highway 1; none of them connected with the Fairvale tower, suggesting the signals from the two sectors of the uptown tower and the tower on the city's east side were stronger. Although some calls didn't connect with the expected tower, they always connected with the next closest one. None bypassed an adjacent tower to jump two or more away. The Crown and defence later entered an agreed statement of facts: Although Rogers Communications was unable to confirm whether the Fairvale tower was on the neighbour list of the uptown tower on July 6, 2011, given the limited number of towers in the area and the fact no towers had been decommissioned since then, it was "highly likely" the Fairvale tower would have been.

The defence called its own cellphone expert for the retrial: Gregory Baumeister, a core network specialist with Ericsson, a global provider of mobile telecommunications infrastructure. As Gold put it to Baumeister, "Rogers operates the network; you supply all the gadgets that make it work." But the Crown wanted to expand the scope of Baumeister's testimony, arguing that as a former Rogers employee with "intimate knowledge of the workings of the Rogers cellular network," he should be able to give opinion evidence on its design and operation. The defence objected, noting they would not have called Baumeister if they knew the Crown's intentions. "How can we present a witness where the Crown apparently feels they're going to obtain favourable evidence of which we have no notice?" Gold asked, and the defence withdrew Baumeister as a witness. The much-anticipated reveal that would clarify the cellphone evidence and establish its significance failed to materialize.

The defence still argued that even if the iPhone was out of the office at 6:44 p.m., it could have been with Richard Oland. Earlier, the court heard from a new witness, the Crown's forensic toxicologist, that a small amount of alcohol was found in the victim's urine. Maureen Adamson and Robert McFadden testified that they had not seen Oland consume any alcohol, nor did they keep any alcohol in the office, other than an old souvenir can of Alpine that remained unopened after his death. Adamson did not see Oland leave the office all day. She had left only briefly at around noon to pick up a pizza and can of Coke for her boss. McFadden didn't see Oland leave, either, and went out himself only for a few minutes to go to the bank. The defence argued the only logical inference was that Oland went out for a drink at some point after his son left (taking his phone with him) and then returned to his office, where he was killed.

Forensic toxicologist Dr. Albert Fraser, now retired, had produced a report in 2011 based on the fluid samples collected during the autopsy. When alcohol is consumed, it goes to the blood first, then the vitreous humour (the clear gel in the eyeball between the lens and the retina), and finally the bladder. Fraser testified the level of alcohol in Oland's urine was 23 mg/dl. The reporting threshold is 16 mg/dl. He found no alcohol in Oland's blood or vitreous humour. He testified this was consistent with alcohol consumption several hours prior to death. A few doses of cough syrup containing alcohol could produce a positive result, alcohol can occasionally form in the bladders of diabetics, and body decomposition can sometimes produce alcohol, but consumption of alcohol was the most likely explanation, he said. Gold introduced a series of emails that the Crown had sent to Fraser between 2014 and 2017, noting the absence of evidence that Oland had consumed any alcohol and asking about other possible explanations, which Fraser subsequently provided and testified to. Gold alleged the Crown's emails had tainted Fraser's testimony (Fraser said during redirect that nothing the Crown said affected his opinion). Gold also asked Fraser if the results were consistent with Oland consuming alcohol an hour before he was killed. It would be more than an hour, Fraser said, noting it takes about three hours for the blood results to come back negative.

The defence called on forensic toxicologist Dr. Joel Mayer, an adjunct professor at the University of Toronto who also operates a forensic science consulting service. He stated that the small amount of alcohol in Oland's urine but nowhere else was consistent with the consumption of a standard drink about an hour prior to death. But Jill Knee countered that Mayer formed his opinion based on a set of assumptions presented by the defence. She argued that trying to determine when consumption took place through a reverse calculation is difficult. What if a person failed to void for several hours, or only partially voided? Mayer testified that he was never asked to determine when alcohol consumption took place. The defence had asked him whether it was possible for alcohol to show up in the urine before it shows up in the blood immediately after a drink, and he said yes, it was possible. And while his opinion was that the urine concentration was "consistent with" consumption shortly before death, that was only one possibility. It could also be consistent with consumption of a larger amount of alcohol several hours prior to death.

The alcohol evidence did little to zero in on the time of death. But the judge had the testimony of two possible "earwitnesses" to weigh and the atmosphere in the courtroom would become thick with tension.

Anthony Shaw says he recalls July 6, 2011, "because nobody will let me forget." Shaw was one of two men who heard "thumping" noises coming from Richard Oland's office on the night he was killed. Although Shaw was a Crown witness, he was crucial to the defence, who argued that his evidence provided an alibi of sorts for Dennis Oland. Video showed Oland shopping with his wife in Rothesay at 7:38 p.m. Shaw had testified in 2015 that he heard "a loud crash and then many thumping sounds thereafter," "maybe eight or ten repeated sounds," before 8:00 p.m. — sometime around 7:30 or 7:45. He believed, in hindsight, that the noises he heard were the sounds of the killing. Now, Shaw recounted that night for Morrison. It all started at around 6:00, when he stopped to visit John Ainsworth at Printing Plus. Shaw, a former long-term employee, sporadically dropped in a couple of times a week to socialize. Ainsworth was working on a brochure and having problems with his computer. Shaw, a former IT consultant, agreed to help.

They were sitting beside each other at a computer desk facing the south wall of the shop when Shaw heard "a loud crash. A really hard crash. And then... quick thumps thereafter." He estimated he heard between ten and fifteen thumps, all coming from the middle of the second-floor office. He and Ainsworth looked at each other, and then the noises stopped. He assumed someone in the office had dropped something or was hanging something on the wall.

Ainsworth's account was similar. "I heard like a thump with a lag and then rapid-fire thumping, like eight or ten times," he testified. "It'd be like somebody hitting something, and then a pause, and then whack, whack, whack kind of thing." The sounds were stationary and lasted ten to twelve seconds, he said. "It was so short lived... It didn't seem all that disconcerting in the scheme of things at the time." If the noises had been prolonged, Ainsworth said, he "more than likely" would have investigated. But he didn't hear any yelling or footsteps. Neither of them made note of the time and relied on "benchmarks" to estimate when they heard the noises, the court heard. Shaw said it was "a while" after he arrived at 6:00 and "quite a while" before he left at 9:00. An "Asian or Middle Eastern" man came in at around 8:00 to send a fax, Shaw remembered. "So I would guesstimate it to be around 7:30 p.m.," he said. "It's my best guess." Ainsworth testified that he couldn't pinpoint the time because he was "hyper-focused" on his troublesome project. It was sometime between Shaw's arrival at 6:00, he said, and 8:11, when the "Persian-looking" customer sent a time-stamped fax. Items piled on top of a filing cabinet blocked the large wall clock from view — "The supreme irony of it," Ainsworth said.

During cross-examination, Gold asked if, when Ainsworth heard the news of Richard Oland's death, he immediately tried to figure out what time he'd heard the noises the night before. Although Ainsworth said he didn't think it was all that critical at that point, Gold immediately quoted from his 2015 testimony in which he said exactly the opposite.

"Obviously it was critical to note time, right," Ainsworth said. "But it became even more critical how accurate that time was once it was related to a homicide and something devious being done." Ainsworth said that when he spoke to police at the scene and then later at the station, he was under the impression that Oland had died of a heart attack. He thought the initial thump was Oland falling to the floor, and the subsequent "rapid fire" sounds were him banging for help as he took his last breaths.

Gold asked if Ainsworth was being forthright and truthful when he spoke to police at the scene and put the timing of the noises at around eight p.m. Ainsworth revealed, for the first time, that his initial time estimate came from Shaw. "I asked him what time it was, 'cause I didn't remember what time it was," he told the court. "So I said to him when I got a chance, 'My God, those noises, what time...' He's the guy that gave me the eight o'clock."

Gold pounced. "So you agree that whatever time Anthony Shaw heard the noises, you agree with that time?"

"No, I didn't agree. I just put it out there. I didn't agree with it absolute." He said once he learned it was a homicide, he put more thought into it and realized he could only offer a time frame. "You can't peg me to something that's unacceptable to me, 'cause I don't know. I've told you enough times, I DO NOT KNOW. I'm not getting nailed for it to be definitive when I know it isn't."

In the fall of 2011, Robert McFadden arranged for Ainsworth to meet with the private investigator working for the defence, retired RCMP officer Jacques Ouellette. (Neither the defence nor Oland family lawyer William Teed would clarify who hired him.) Gold played a segment of Ainsworth's videotaped statement to Ouellette. On tape, the investigator mentioned their meeting was a follow-up to a July 27 telephone conversation and advised Ainsworth his statement could be used in court, even if he later changed or denied his version of events. He warned Ainsworth against making false statements, committing perjury, or obstructing justice, which can carry sentences of between five and fourteen years. Ainsworth agreed his participation was voluntary and swore an oath to tell the truth. Gold stopped the video. "That's what you were told, and those were your responses?" he asked.

"I'm not trying to mislead you," replied Ainsworth. "I'm trying to clarify circumstances. You make it sound like what I'm saying currently is misleading. It's not misleading. It's trying to clarify it... I've had lots of time to think about it, mind you."

Gold pushed to narrow the time frame of the noises. "It was approximately quarter to eight, seven thirty, quarter to eightish, is that correct, sir?"

"You're not going to give up on that, are you?"

"Sir, listen to the question, and answer the question," Morrison instructed.

"No, I don't agree with that," said Ainsworth, responding to Gold's question.

The video resumed. Ouellette asked Ainsworth what time he heard the noises. He replied clearly and without hesitation: "It was approximately quarter to eight, seven thirty, quarter to eightish."

The video stopped. "The time at which you heard these noises was approximately quarter to eight, seven thirty, quarter to eightish," Gold said. "Do you agree you said that at that time?"

"It's right there, sir," Ainsworth replied.

"Exactly. And do you agree, sir, that that is in fact the truth that you—"

"No, I don't," Ainsworth interrupted.

"— that you swore under oath?"

"In retrospect, I realize I didn't really know . . . I couldn't be that accurate. Throw me under the bus for it, but . . . I realize I do not really know. I DO NOT KNOW what time it was," he said, raising his voice. "I've been suffering with it for eight years! You think it doesn't bother me? Profoundly so, but I DON'T KNOW!"

The court took a short recess. When proceedings and the video resumed, Ouellette asked Ainsworth how he knew what time it was. He said he checked the clock when he left for the night. It was around "nine, ten after," and he calculated back. Gold questioned if that was accurate. "Not really, no," said Ainsworth. He described the customer's fax, time-stamped 8:11, as a "closer benchmark." Ainsworth had told Ouellette it seemed like the noises were about a half hour before the customer came in, Gold noted.

"Seemed. S-E-E-M-E-D! *Seemed* like it. Big bold letters. *Seemed* like it. Sixty-two-point bold letters," the print shop owner stressed. Gold, he argued, was giving "no credence to how distracted" he was with the brochure he was working on. "It's so critical. I've reiterated for seven years."

Gold asked Ainsworth if he had formed the opinion that Dennis Oland was guilty. Ainsworth paused before asking Morrison if he could plead the fifth, prompting a few chuckles. "We don't have that here, sir," Morrison replied, straight-faced. "I concur with the determination of the original jury," Ainsworth finally said. "I respect what they determined."

"Am I correct your general attitude is you want to bring the killer of Richard Oland to justice?" Gold asked.

"Absolutely."

"And you certainly don't want to do anything to help the killer of Richard Oland escape justice. That's in your mind too, correct?"

"Absolutely."

"So if you think that Dennis Oland is the killer, you're not going to say or do anything that might possibly get him acquitted, isn't that the truth?"

"Absolutely, unequivocally wrong! No! I'm not that kind of person," Ainsworth retorted indignantly. "That has absolutely nothing to do with this."

"You want to do everything possible to get him convicted," pushed Gold.

"I don't agree with that."

Gold displayed a comment Ainsworth posted on a media website the day Oland was convicted: "The jury deserves the greatest respect for their time, effort and insight," Ainsworth wrote. He also posted on Facebook that day: "Toasting... justice being served equitably saving face for the judicial system by respecting the findings of a jury and providing some sense of justice for Richard." When Oland was released on bail after the appeal court overturned his conviction, Ainsworth posted a photo of a young woman wearing a pink off-the-shoulder dress and a costume crown, gripping a metal pipe in her white-gloved hands, and spattered with blood. "What so many people seem to think the perpetrator should of looked like," he wrote. "Imagine going out into the streets of saint john even for a minute looking like this when it is still light outside on an early summer evening... oh! what coveralls can cover up!" And in November 2018, Ainsworth allegedly had a conversation with a man named Butch about his upcoming testimony in the retrial and told him Oland was "guilty as sin," that he was "one hundred per cent sure of it." Ainsworth said he didn't recall that specific conversation, but he acknowledged he may have said something similar to one or two friends. "We're not allowed to surmise stuff relative to what has transpired in the news? Wow. OK. Big Brother on us now?"

Gold introduced some emails Ainsworth sent to the Crown in which he made "a number of helpful suggestions" right up to a month before he took the stand. In November 2018, for example, after the media reported on a defence-created video that demonstrated how the killer could have escaped out the back door, climbed on top of a small garage and over a low retaining wall, ducked down a narrow passageway, and gone through a gate onto Germain Street, he wanted to make sure prosecutors knew that Dennis Oland and his wife owned the Germain Street building the gate was attached to at the time the defence made the video. Ainsworth acknowledged he sent the email. The gate might not have been as accessible on the night of the killing, he argued. It could have been locked or broken in 2011. "Did anybody check?... It just made me wonder, as a conscientious person." He vehemently denied he was implying the Olands might fabricate evidence.

Gold noted that before Oland was charged in 2013, Ainsworth's time estimate was seven thirty to seven forty-five p.m. He alleged Ainsworth had altered his account to fit when Oland was at his father's office to "get him convicted." He asserted that Ainsworth's position was that he would not "commit in any way at all to anything that might be helpful to Dennis Oland's defence."

"How dare you?" Ainsworth fired back. "I want to see justice done, period. I have nothing against Dennis ... I don't know the man, and I'd hate to see him wrongfully go to jail."

Their heated exchange marked the close of the Crown's case.

Gold advised the court the defence wished to file a so-called KGB application, to have a previous inconsistent statement admitted into evidence for the truth of its contents. P.J. Veniot eventually agreed, noting it would be up to Morrison to determine the "ultimate reliability" of the statement, and the remainder of Ouellette's interview with Ainsworth was played. Ainsworth said he was "in shock" when he found out Oland had been murdered. If he had gone upstairs, he mused, he might have seen who did it. But then, he noted, he might have become a victim, too.

As Alan Gold's cross-examination of Ainsworth indicated, the defence's strategy was to prove that Richard Oland was murdered *after* his son left at around 6:36 p.m. The first witness the defence called was also a new witness: Saint John Liberal MLA Gerry Lowe. The former city councillor had not testified at the first trial, but he had become almost a regular fixture at the courthouse as he fought — and won — a legal challenge of his ten-seat win in the 2018 provincial election.

Police canvassed the neighbourhood in the days following the murder, looking for witnesses. They spoke to one woman who said she heard "loud yelling" while walking along Princess Street in the block between Canterbury and Germain at around seven thirty p.m. on July 6. Police didn't follow up with her for more than six years, and never conducted a formal interview with her, instead taking a statement from her via email in October 2017. An officer also spoke to Gerry Lowe, who said he was at Thandi, the restaurant across the street, sometime after seven thirty p.m. He saw a man exit the street-level door that led to Richard Oland's office. But in court, Lowe, a frequent patron who estimated he'd eaten at Thandi "four hundred or five hundred times since" the murder, wasn't certain if he saw the man on July 5 or July 6. "I've racked my brains the last couple of months," he testified. "It's just been so long. Eight years is a long time."

Keith Copeland, a member of the major crime unit, had been one of the officers who interviewed Lowe. Copeland did not attempt to clarify which night Lowe saw someone exiting 52 Canterbury. He did not ask if Lowe had been at Thandi on other nights that week. Nor did he ask if anybody was with him, if he knew which waiters or bartenders had served him, or if he had paid by credit card — all questions, Copeland acknowledged under cross-examination, that might have helped pinpoint the date. He was more interested in the description of the man, Copeland explained, and Lowe couldn't remember.

"Sir, isn't it obvious that if it turned out someone had witnessed someone leaving 52 Canterbury Street after seven thirty p.m. on July 6, 2011, that means Dennis Oland wasn't the last person to leave that address before Richard Oland was discovered dead?" Michael Lacy had asked. Copeland agreed. That's why he'd contacted Lowe to try to get more information about what the man looked like. He assumed other officers would follow up on Lowe's information "if they believed there was reason to," he said.

"Of course, as of July 8, 2011, you were aware that investigators already had decided that Dennis Oland was the suspect in the murder, correct?"

"Yes, sir," Copeland, the officer whom Morrison described as taking over Oland's interview and turning it into an interrogation, replied.

"And the investigative mindset was: 'Now we have to find evidence to help support our suspicions,' right?"

"Yes, sir." Copeland could not remember where he interviewed Lowe or whether it was in person, but he said it was brief. He did not record the interview, didn't ask Lowe to write a statement, and he didn't take any notes himself, he said. He said he did enter it in the computer system the next day.

The defence submitted security video of Gerry Lowe entering Thandi with a woman on July 6 at 7:40 p.m. and leaving at 8:35 p.m. Police did not obtain any video from July 5. Lowe testified he didn't remember being interviewed by police on July 7 or 8, but he did remember his interview with Stephen Davidson on May 29, 2015, before Oland's first trial. He'd told the constable that he'd thought he'd seen a man come out a door and turn toward King Street East. He pointed to the Far End Corporation door in a photograph, noting that the photo was taken from the same perspective he had from his seat at the bar. He remembered "they were doing advertisement, or they were doing something out front" (a photographer from Nova Scotia hired to do a marketing shoot for the city took photos at Thandi on July 6, arriving at 7:46 p.m.). Davidson returned to the stand and confirmed that Lowe had told him about seeing the photographer. But under cross-examination, Jill Knee questioned Lowe's memory. She pointed out that he never mentioned any photography to the first two officers he spoke to in the days immediately following the murder and noted he used words to the effect of, "I believe I seen."

"I know what I seen," Lowe insisted. "I seen a male come out of that door where that plaque is [the Far End Corporation sign] and make the turn towards King Street East."

"But you have no recollection of what date it was?"

"Not for sure, no."

"You have no recollection of what time it was?"

"Only what I told the police officer." Whatever he told police at the time was the truth, Lowe said. "I'd have no reason to lie, ma'am."

Lowe did recall that he was with a woman on the night in question. Knee suggested his focus would have been on conversation with her and the bartender and on what was going on inside the restaurant, not outside. Lowe, who drove a cab for years, said he has a "tendency to look around. I've always done that." But Lowe couldn't tell police whether he was at the bar or going out the front door when he saw the man, argued Knee, and the only description he gave was that the man "wasn't black." That, she said, was "an interesting turn of phrase." She posited that the man was of "another ethnic background," probably an allusion to Anthony Shaw and John Ainsworth's testimony about the man who sent a fax that evening. Lowe couldn't be sure, but he was certain that the man he saw was standing in the Far End Corporation doorway. Knee asked if the man could have been smoking. Lowe acknowledged the possibility. Shaw went outside four or five times to smoke cigarettes that evening, and he said he may have walked back and forth between Printing Plus's entrance and the double doors to its loading dock. Ainsworth, absorbed in his work, said he "never moved" out of his seat until he left at around nine.

To bolster their argument that the mystery man Lowe said he saw was "the real killer," the defence focused on a partial footwear impression found near the main blood pool, just northeast of the victim's head. Forensic officer Mark Smith testified that he noticed the "brownish, reddish" markings on the hardwood floor at some point on July 7, but he believed he and Duane Squires created them when they removed the body. Only three years later, while preparing for the preliminary inquiry and comparing photos he took that morning with photos he took five days later after spraying Leucomalachite Green (LMG) to detect latent blood did he realize the markings had been on the floor before the body was removed, he said. Smith agreed with Lacy's assertion that he had missed "a very important thing." (Lacy also showed the court a photograph Smith took of the desk and zoomed in on a red smear on a piece of paper, asking Smith to agree that it could be a fingerprint or palm print "or something that has to do with someone's unique characteristics from their hands" in blood. Smith said it could be, but he couldn't answer with certainty because police had not seized or tested the blood-spattered papers.)

The RCMP conducted an independent comparative analysis to determine if the markings on the floor were indeed created on July 7. Smith put together a package of crime scene photos, photos of footwear seized from Dennis Oland's home, and sole impressions of the footwear, security-video screenshots of Oland before he visited his father and during his police interview on July 7, as well as more than twenty close-ups of the shoes he wore in both videos, which Oland identified as the shoes he wore when he visited his father. Smith also sent photographs and impressions of Squires's footwear, even though he was wearing protective booties when they removed the body. Corporal Brian Babin conducted the analysis, but the Crown never called him to testify. Instead, the defence put the now-retired officer on the stand at the retrial. Babin said only one of the crime scene photos in Smith's package was suitable for comparison purposes, the others "lacked clarity." In the zoomed-in photo of the faint green marks on the floor, Babin identified what he believed to be "lug patterns" consistent with footwear. He compared those eight "lugs" with the photos and impressions of Oland's six pairs of footwear, including the brown square-toed shoes Oland said he wore on July 6. None were a match, he testified. He also eliminated Squires's footwear as a possible source. In fact, "no footwear impressions could be identified," his written report concluded.

The court had already heard that Oland's shoes were forensically examined and no blood was detected. No blood was found on the victim's shoes, either, suggesting the impressions could not have been made by him during a struggle with his attacker. P.J. Veniot argued that didn't mean the impressions were made by an unidentified suspect or that they were even a bloody footprint. They "appear to be footwear," Babin testified, but he couldn't say with certainty, noting missing pattern and lack of clarity. The quality of the photos, Babin acknowledged, put him at a "disadvantage" in conducting his analysis. Another complication was the crime scene itself. He could recall only a couple of occasions where the body had already been removed. If officers stepped around in the crime scene, that made his work more difficult. About twenty-four people, including numerous police officers and the former prosecutor in the Oland case, Patrick Wilbur, were in and out of the office before the bloodstain pattern analyst examined it, and few wore protective booties, the court had heard. Of those, at least fifteen had entered before Smith took the photo that showed the possible footwear impression was present before the body was removed. Only one of the paramedics testified to being close enough to touch the body, but he said he "wouldn't have walked through the blood." Police never asked to see his footwear, he said.

Babin could not say if the impression was made by someone who stepped in blood. Although it reacted to the LMG, LMG is not a confirmatory test and can produce false positives, the Crown's bloodstain pattern analyst, Brian Wentzell, had testified. No confirmatory test was done. Wentzell also noted the absence of bloody footwear impressions leaving the scene. "If the spatter had been deposited on the floor, had not dried, and someone had walked through the spatter, there should be evidence of that, and that's not present," he testified. He did not see any evidence of transfer stains outside the office, either. The Crown proposed the impression pre-dated the killing, and Babin agreed that he couldn't tell when it was made.

Despite their focus on the front door of the building and Lowe's account of seeing an unknown man leaving the building, Oland's lawyers did not abandon their contention that the "killer or killers" could have escaped out the back. The door, which locks from the inside with a deadbolt and from the outside with a key, was never tested for evidence. The defence introduced the enactment video they produced to demonstrate the possible escape route. The video wasn't shown to the jury in 2015, and Jill Knee objected to its inclusion at the retrial, arguing that Maureen Adamson had testified she'd locked the back door when she left the office on July 6, and "Anything beyond that is purely speculation and would be highly prejudicial." (According to McFadden, Adamson "was a bit fastidious" about ensuring the door was locked.) Besides, the video was filmed nearly three years after the killing and may not accurately depict the area as it was in 2011, Knee said. Gold countered that the defence was entitled to present the video in response to Duane Squires's testimony about the difficulty of leaving the property from the back. Gold wanted to show the judge that Squires had made it sound harder than it was. The defence was not introducing the video as evidence that the back door was used as an escape route, Gold said. "It's being introduced as something else the police did not investigate."

The video showed a bird's-eye view of a young man, a law student at the time, exit the back door, walk to his right, scrabble over some debris, use both hands to pull himself up on top of a small garage, vault over a low retaining wall to a grassy backyard, turn left down a narrow passageway between two buildings, fiddle with the latch of a tall wooden gate at the end (the gate Ainsworth referred to in his email to the Crown) and exit onto Germain Street—all within one minute.

Former lead investigator Rick Russell had offered what appeared to be important new evidence for the Crown about the back door. He told the court that in the spring of 2018 he remembered a conversation he'd had with Stephen Davidson at the crime scene on July 6. "I asked if he checked it [the back door], and he replied that he did and it was locked," said Russell. "Davidson was either by the back door or in the vestibule area, and I would have had a conversation with him about the back door then." They'd had the conversation within five minutes of his arrival at the scene, he told the court. Three months later Russell retired and wanted to "put everything behind him, including this case," he said, and must have forgotten when he testified at the preliminary inquiry and the first trial. But the "heightened awareness" of the first trial "caused me to really go through my mind all the steps that I did on that day to further my recall." Once he remembered the conversation, he said, he had, "in good conscience, to speak the truth." It quickly proved to be a false memory, however, or what Gold suggested was "wishful thinking." Records showed that Russell and Davidson were never together at the scene that day—Davidson left "a considerable period of time" before Russell arrived. "It's agreed between the defence and the Crown that you could not have had physically that conversation that you say you had," Gold told Russell. Russell apologized for his mistake. "Sir, you're only human. The other members of the Saint John Police Force are only human. Our problem is that this is a murder case," Gold observed, "and when people make honest mistakes it can be just as fatal to the truth as intentional mistakes."

twenty-one

DENNIS OLAND SPEAKS – AGAIN

Dennis Oland strode calmly and confidently past the prosecutors' two tables and settled into the witness box beside the judge. He wore a burlap-coloured suit, a light blue collared shirt, and a dark purple and orange-striped tie. About half a dozen of his relatives and friends looked on, but his wife was noticeably absent, as she had been for several weeks. Oland, now 51, faced Michael Lacy directly and did not look around the courtroom. He appeared at ease, his arms casually crossed and his hands resting in his lap. He told the crowded room that it was his decision to testify. "I want to clear my name," he said. "I think it's important that people hear from my own voice that I did not kill my father."

With that, Lacy plunged in. He asked Oland about the Crown's assertion that he flew into a rage on July 6, 2011, and brutally bludgeoned his father.

"Did you do that?"

"No," Oland replied, an insistent note underscoring the word.

Lacy raised the Crown's motive that Oland was "desperate financially" and went to visit his father that night looking for money. Again, Oland denied it. Then Lacy cited Richard Oland's extramarital affair. He asked Oland if he'd raised the issue with his father that day, resulting in a rage-inducing argument.

"Did any of that happen?"

"No," said Oland, shaking his head, his brow furrowed.

Next Lacy turned his attention to Oland's statement to Saint John police. At Oland's first trial, the defence and Crown agreed to submit only the first half of the approximately five-hour-long interview. The Crown wanted to submit the first half again for the retrial, but the defence tried to have the entire statement thrown out, arguing that it wasn't "the product of a meaningful, informed choice" because Oland believed he was simply a witness. He didn't realize he was "already the subject of a focused investigation and suspicion" even before the interview started. Police didn't caution him or advise him of his Charter rights until nearly halfway through the interview, and then officers interfered with his ability to retain and instruct a lawyer, the defence alleged, and "thus detained him without legal authority." Morrison agreed Oland was "subjected to a relentless and aggressive interrogation" that amounted to psychological detention but did not find his Charter rights were violated. Information from the statement formed the basis of search warrants and production orders, and exclusion of the statement would jeopardize the admissibility of evidence obtained through those search warrants and production orders. It was "critically important to the Crown's case." He ruled the "probative value" of the statement "outweigh[ed] any prejudicial effect it might have," and denied the defence's application.

Lacy asked Oland about his description of his father as not "the easiest guy in the world to get along with" and someone who "would say and do things that could be hurtful." Oland acknowledged that his relationship with his father was not a perfect one; at times, they had "issues." He said he had tried to accurately portray what Lacy termed "the peaks and valleys" in his police interview. Oland appeared emotional at times as he talked about his father. He spoke fondly of how "Dad" offered to buy him a Honda Civic if he maintained a B average in university, motivating him to improve his marks. His father also paid so he could join the family on skiing trips in Maine and Vermont. And when he was thinking about becoming a financial adviser, his father encouraged him to "go for it" and offered to be his first client. Oland said he often sought his father's counsel when making life decisions. "The person who seemed to be in the know was Dad."

His father had negotiated a deal so he could afford to buy his late grandfather's Rothesay home. Richard Oland convinced the executors, his siblings Derek and Jane, to parcel the property and purchased for himself the adjacent horse pasture that had to remain with the house. As a child, Dennis made regular Sunday visits to the estate, when his father would take him and his two sisters to visit their grandparents. After Oland moved into the house with his own family in 1998, the Sunday visits continued. If his father was in town, he would drop by unannounced "most Sundays" to see him. They'd chat about politics and community activities over a beer, he said.

In 2000, Oland purchased the adjacent farmhouse property. His father financed the purchase, and Dennis's payment was about $10,000 a year. He wasn't always able to make the payment, but it was never a problem. He would just tell McFadden, who would add a year to the payment schedule and recalculate the interest accordingly. His father never threatened to take possession of the property because Oland couldn't make the payment, he said. (McFadden had testified that Dennis fell behind in repaying loans from his father several times over the years, but Richard was never overly concerned.) Later, to keep the family home during his costly divorce, Oland said his father told him he would give him an advance on his inheritance in the form of an interest-only loan. (McFadden said the senior Oland considered the $500,000 a loan, but "wasn't worried about collecting it," because the sum could be deducted from Dennis's share of the estate.)

"My father was concerned that I was receiving a benefit that my two sisters were not receiving," Oland testified, "so he thought that I should pay for that benefit to ensure that things appeared to be equal, fair."

He confirmed his father wanted him to sign a domestic contract with his then common-law wife Lisa as part of the arrangement. His father also wanted a mortgage on the property and a right of first refusal to buy the house, but the paperwork was never signed, and Richard Oland advanced the money without it. (McFadden's testimony confirmed that Richard Oland hadn't "expressed any dissatisfaction" about the paperwork not being finalized. He hadn't even inquired about the status of the loan for at least "six months to a year.")

Lacy noted that Oland told police that his father didn't give him things. "Were you trying to suggest your dad never did anything at all for you?"

"[He] didn't spoil us," Oland explained. "We didn't have trust funds."

Lacy turned to Oland's finances in the months before his father's death, asking about three major trips he and his wife took: Hungary and Italy in the fall of 2010, Florida for March break with their children in 2011, and then England in the spring. They racked up more than $20,000 on his Visa. Oland said he wasn't concerned about the debt. "It was just sort of stuff that we always did," he said. His $163,000 line of credit was maxed out, his $27,000 Visa was "getting up there," and on June 1 he asked CIBC Wood Gundy to advance him $16,000 on his pay. But, as the defence had argued earlier, this was nothing new, and Oland could have borrowed more. He planned to build his book of business to increase his income. In the email he sent his supervisor to request the advance, Oland wrote: "I had a good chat with Dick [his father] yesterday and the timeline to see some funds flowing this way looks to have firmed up to the August/September time period." He told the court this referred to $1 million his father had in his "play-money category." This was money his father liked to actively manage, making decisions about what to buy and sell. Oland already handled about $2.5 million of his father's money and was encouraging his father to bring the $1 million to him to manage. Oland's email also referred to another client who would be consolidating his assets in September: "We are looking at total new assets in the $10-$20m range. So things are progressing very well." He expected August and onward to be "a new growth period," he told the court, plus the market "always picks up that time of year." He also anticipated his wife would go back to work that fall, earning between $75,000 and $100,000, after being off for about a year with back and shoulder problems that required surgery, he said.

Lacy asked him what he would have done if he found himself in a "desperate financial situation with nowhere to turn." Oland said he would have switched firms and received a signing bonus equivalent to the value of his book of business (which his supervisor had testified was worth approximately $200,000 to $300,000). He told the court he didn't know his latest post-dated payment to his father had bounced just the day before he visited his office. If he had known there wouldn't be enough money in his account to cover the cheque, he would have asked Maureen Adamson to avoid cashing it for "a day or two." Based on his past record, that would not have been a problem, he said, something Adamson corroborated in her own testimony. The cheque cleared on July 19, Lacey noted, and by the end of the month Oland had $572.68 in his chequing account.

It wasn't unusual for him to stop by his father's office, Oland said: if his father wasn't travelling, he visited about once a month. (Adamson and McFadden testified to seeing him visit a few times a year but agreed he may have visited when they weren't there.) His July 6 visit wasn't planned, but he'd done a stock trade for his father that day, so he knew he was around, and he wanted to show him a historical will he'd discovered while he was in England. He also wanted to pick up his uncle Jack Connell's logbook. His father had borrowed the logbook to scan it, but he'd had it for about a year, and Connell had expressed "frustration" it was taking so long to get the book back. Connell was returning to Toronto soon so, Oland said, "I took it upon myself to make a point of getting the logbook." (Although Connell had emailed Oland on July 7 saying, "I'm around all summer," Connell testified he meant he'd be in Toronto, not travelling abroad. He planned to leave Rothesay on July 13 and wanted the book back beforehand to show it to Marg Bourne.)

Oland said he drove to his father's office after work and parked in the same lot his father used for his BMW, at the corner of Princess Street. He headed up to the second floor and got to "sort of the foyer area" when he realized he had forgotten some genealogy "stuff": a green book containing "important" and "extremely rare" documents as well as some notes he'd prepared. Figuring he'd left them in his office, he returned to his car and drove back toward nearby Brunswick House, at the corner of Chipman Hill and King Street. He realized he didn't have the pass card he needed to operate the elevator after hours, though, so he "didn't bother." He turned back up King Street, right onto Canterbury Street, and parked at the curb, in front of the Thandi parking lot, across from his father's office. He noticed Maureen Adamson's husband parked out front, waiting to pick her up, but he didn't speak to him because, he explained, he didn't know him well at that time. Oland headed upstairs with the genealogy documents he did have in a red reusable grocery bag and entered the Far End Corporation. He greeted Adamson and chatted with her briefly. They did not discuss his bounced cheque, he said. He then went over to his father at his desk, and they had a conversation about his trip to England and the will he'd found. It was a significant find, Oland said, "the key" that allowed them to "explore back in time" and debunk a number of family myths. As they talked, Adamson brought over the logbook and "either placed it on the desk or gave it to Dad" before she left for the day.

He was with his father for about forty-five minutes, he said. They did not discuss anything other than genealogy: not Dennis's finances, and not Richard's extramarital affair. Oland had "broached" the issue with McFadden a year or two before his father "died," he said, avoiding unpleasant words like *killed* or *murdered*. He didn't expect McFadden to confirm the rumours of the affair, but he did propose McFadden suggest that Richard Oland could be more discreet or consider ending the relationship. (McFadden confirmed that Dennis raised the issue with him once, at least eighteen months before the homicide. McFadden had a more recent and lengthier conversation with Matthew Bustin, Richard Oland's son-in-law, about the affair in March 2010. Bustin wanted to know what was going on, McFadden said. Bustin did most of the talking, he said, and "alcohol was involved.")

When Oland left the office, he left behind the will and "some bad poetry" written by an Oland. His Blackberry records showed he sent a text at 6:12 p.m. "I am at my dads office doing history stuff. I shud not be too long." Oland said he sent it between his father's office and the car and intended to send it to his wife but sent it to his sister Lisa Bustin by "sheer accident." He started to drive away when he realized he'd forgotten the logbook, so he "wheeled around." He couldn't find a parking spot on Canterbury, so he drove the wrong way up Princess Street for a short distance and pulled into a gravel lot across from the lot where his father parked. (Constable Stephen Davidson had found this illegal turn significant and demanded to know why Oland failed to mention it when he first described his movements that evening. But the Crown and defence entered an agreed statement of facts from a long-term resident with a clear view of the gravel lot from his back deck who said he has "frequently" noticed motorists make illegal turns up Princess

Street to turn into the gravel lot at various times of day and night. John Ainsworth, on the other hand, testified he "probably saw a couple" of motorists make the illegal turn over thirty-some years.)

Oland said he went back up to his father's office and stayed for about ten minutes. "He wanted to show me that his maternal grandfather and my mother's maternal grandfather had built this camp together or worked on it together and were friends," he explained. A call from his wife at 6:24 went to his voicemail, his Blackberry records showed. (Oland testified that he thought the Blackberry was in his car.) She called again at 6:36, at which time he said he was back in his car in the gravel lot. The call lasted forty-one seconds. She wanted to know where he was and asked him to come home so they could go to the drug store for cold medicine, he testified. After the call, he headed toward home.

"The Crown is going to say that you had bludgeoned your father to death in his office by then," said Lacy.

"Absolutely not."

"Did you tell police about going back to get the logbook?"

"Unfortunately no, I did not."

"Were you trying to lie to police by omitting that?"

"Not at all, no."

Lacy played a time-stamped security video of Oland walking north on the sidewalk in front of Thandi at 6:12, carrying the red grocery bag. Oland explained that when he left his father's office after their forty-five minute visit, he initially turned left toward his father's parking lot, where he had parked the first time, before remembering his car was in the opposite direction, on the street by the Thandi lot.

Oland confirmed the bag he was carrying in the video was the one he had with him in his father's office. Lacy asked him if he'd carried "anything like a tool with a crosshatch hammer and a sharp edge on another side, weapon, anything like that" to his father's office and used such an object to strike his father "some forty-five times." Oland denied it. "It's absolutely ridiculous," he said. "I'm not that kind of monster. I'd never do that to my dad, or any person."

He told the court he stopped at the Renforth wharf on his way home in the hopes of seeing one or two of his kids; he explained it was something he did when he didn't have them for the week. He did not throw anything away at the wharf, he said. He did notice some beer bottles, and he picked those up. He walked to the end of the wharf where some kids were in the water. Not seeing his kids, he believed he sat down for a minute, and then he got up and left. When he arrived home, he changed and looked around the house and yard for his wife. His phone records showed three calls between them from 7:24 to 7:28. That, he explained, was "Lisa and I trying to find each other while I'm home." They ran some errands, and at 9:40 he took a call from Mary Beth Watt about a problem with the sailboat she co-owned with Lisa. He and Watt had talked about the problem earlier that day, and he'd left her a voicemail at 9:19 to see how she'd made out; she called back at 9:40. According to Watt, Oland told her he would go to the boat and try a new idea.

He didn't deliver his uncle's logbook that night. At around seven the next morning he dropped it off at his parents' home, leaving it on a wood shelf on top of a radiator inside the side door. Back then, he said, the door was left unlocked. (Jack Connell testified that Oland had called around seven thirty or seven forty-five p.m. on July 6 to tell him he had the logbook and would drop it off in the morning. Connell confirmed he found it on the radiator. The logbook tested negative for blood.) Oland then described the rest of his morning, corroborated by security video, store receipts, and phone records, as he purchased parts to fix the sailboat problem, picked up a new sail cover, stopped at a Canadian Tire, and went to his uptown office to do some work before emailing his assistant to explain that he had left to work on the boat. He was wearing a navy blazer and collared shirt. He also wore the same pants and shoes he'd worn the night before when he'd visited his father, he said.

His cellphone records showed he called his "Mum and Dad" at 10:24 a.m. The call lasted 26 seconds. Oland said he couldn't recall what it was about. Then, starting at 12:20 p.m., his cellphone logged a flurry of calls, each less than a minute: from his parents' home, to his parents' and back again, from Oland to his own house, and from his mother's cell. Oland said he believed the first call or two was his mother or uncle asking for Robert McFadden's number. (McFadden testified that Connie Oland called him from her home at around twelve thirty that day.) "The subsequent calls were my uncle Jack calling me, telling me that I needed to come home right away, that something bad has happened." He didn't know how his father had died, he said; he "just knew that he was gone."

Lacy displayed video security images taken of Oland on the morning of July 6, wearing a brown sports jacket. Oland confirmed it was the jacket he wore when he visited his father that night. Police had seized it and the blue-and-white check J. Crew dress shirt he wore with it. (Grant Fredericks, the Crown's forensic video analyst, could not verify the jacket or the shirt as the ones Oland wore in the video, only that they were "of the same class.") Oland denied changing his clothes in between any of the visits to his father's office, nor did he put on a jumpsuit or coveralls. Lacy did not ask him if he took off any clothing during his visits. He also didn't ask about the four small bloodstains and DNA matching Richard Oland's profile found on the jacket. Oland was not asked to recount the alleged incident in his father's workshop, when he described his father handling the jacket, but he did explain that in 2010 he and his family moved into his parents' home while theirs underwent renovations. His parents were "down south somewhere," so he and Lisa slept in his father's bedroom, and he put his clothes and shoes in his father's closet. His parents returned before the work was complete, so Oland and his family moved into the apartment above his parents' garage, but he and Lisa left their clothes in the house.

Oland told the court he had nothing to do with the brown sports jacket being dry cleaned the morning after police questioned him. He did not drop it off, arrange for it to be dropped off, or ask anyone to do so, he said. Nor could he recall when he learned the jacket had been dry cleaned, he said, only that his seventeen-year-old stepson tried on his dry-cleaned jackets on July 10. "They wouldn't fit, so we had an emergency." He emailed friends, asking if anyone had a navy blazer size 38 or 40 that Andru could wear for a visitation that afternoon. His friends came through.

"You told the police on July 7, 2011, that you were wearing the blue jacket on July 6. You were in fact wearing the brown jacket. What can you tell us about that?" asked Lacy.

"What I can say is that on the morning of July 7, I was wearing the blue blazer, and I think that just because it was briefly enough that I was wearing it, that I had it in my head that I must have been wearing it the day before," Oland replied. "That was a mistake; wrong. The information that I gave to Constable Davidson, wrong." He denied trying to deliberately mislead the police or to hide the fact that he'd been wearing the brown jacket.

P.J. Veniot had handled Oland's cross-examination at the first trial, and many expected that, as the senior member of the team, he would again. But Jill Knee went to the podium. Her cross-examination would be more aggressive than Veniot's had been, her questions more pointed and accusatory. She wasted no time in challenging Oland's warm depiction of his relationship with his father, leading him through a transcript of his police statement, virtually line by line, to force Oland to acknowledge that his father was difficult to get along with and that he sometimes stayed away from him to avoid conflict. He acknowledged his father's high and demanding standards, his expectation that things would be done the way he liked. They would get into arguments and "conversations where inappropriate things were said," he testified.

"You didn't have a close relationship with him," Knee posited.

"There were times when I did," Oland responded, "and there were times when I definitely did not.... I wish I had a better relationship with my father, and there were times when it was troubled."

Knee pointed out that Oland made numerous negative comments about his father within the first hour of his police interview. Although in court he portrayed their relationship as having "peaks and valleys," he never told police about any peaks, she argued. On the same day his father's body was found, Oland had told the police "how awful" his father was to him. Oland said he wanted to provide an "honest representation" of the "completeness" of their relationship. "He was a good dad. He was not the best dad. He was a good dad." Nowhere in his police statement did he mention the regular Sunday visits. She noted that Oland raised with Robert McFadden the issue of his father's extramarital affair and discussed it with his sister Lisa Bustin. Oland denied that he agreed with his sister when she called their father "a dirty pig."

"You were mad for your mother who was being deceived by your father in an affair," Knee proposed.

"I had no moral issues with my father having an affair," Oland replied.

Knee began to compare Oland's three accounts of what happened — one to police on July 7, the second during his testimony at his first trial, and the third during his direct examination by Michael Lacy — against each other and against known evidence, looking to expose any inconsistencies. The real reason Oland went to his father's office was to ask him for money, she suggested; genealogy was a ploy to get his father in a good mood before raising the financial issue. His credit was maxed out, he had cashed out his RRSPs, and his income for the first six months of 2011 — $34,124.02 — was the worst it had been in four years, despite improving markets. About $8,000 was an advance, and most of the rest would have gone to his ex-wife in his monthly spousal and child support payment of $4,322. Knee argued Oland misled his employer to secure advances in June and July, giving the impression he had between $10 million and $20 million in new business lined up for August or September, money that would come from his father and another client. Oland countered that his supervisor would have thought he was "a fool" if he suggested that. He expected about $2 million to come in, he told the court, and he planned to grow the rest. That wasn't how the email was worded, Knee fired back. Robert McFadden, she pointed out, had testified he had no knowledge of any plans to send Dennis new money to invest. Oland said McFadden wouldn't necessarily have known.

Oland was overspending by about $14,000 a month in the time leading up to his father's death. He was supposed to pay almost $4,000 on his over-limit Visa by July 5, money he didn't have. He was two months behind in his monthly interest-only payment to his father, and his latest cheque had just bounced. He maintained he was unaware the cheque would bounce, but Knee pointed out that he'd asked Maureen Adamson to hold off on cashing it until July 4 because his account was overdrawn. On July 4 he'd deposited a cheque from his wife's tenant and on July 6 a rent cheque from the tenant in the apartment above their garage, so he would have known his balance, Knee suggested. He was at risk of losing the family home again, just two years after his father loaned him more than $500,000 to ensure he kept it during his divorce, Knee argued, because he'd missed the June payment on the line of credit, which he had secured against the home without his father's knowledge. (Two CIBC employees testified they were unaware Oland had received $538,000 from his father, but one agreed under cross-examination that he wouldn't expect to be told that. The defence maintained that "there was nothing improper" about Oland encumbering the home, because the money from his father was an advance on his inheritance.)

"That was the financial distress you were in when you visited your father, correct?" "It was not financial distress," insisted Oland. "I agree it was tight, but..." He trailed off without completing the thought.

"You had no resources left except taking money on your credit card that morning, but, sir, you're going to suggest today you were not financially distressed?" Knee argued that Oland had spent himself into a corner, with his mounting debt, maxed-out credit, and shrinking income. "I'm going to suggest to you, you knew this conversation was going to come up because Richard Oland kept track of every penny."

"It did not," Oland replied. They talked about genealogy, he maintained. He could have borrowed more money from the bank if he needed it, he said. Knee pointed out he did not qualify for a credit limit increase on his Visa in May or June.

Knee turned to his movements that night. She argued he would have realized before he got up to the second floor that the green book, which was neither small nor light, wasn't in the bag he was carrying. If he was right outside his father's office, she questioned, why wouldn't he pop in to say hello and tell him he'd forgotten something and would be right back? He didn't know if his father would be there later, she noted. The "real reason" he climbed the stairs but turned around and left, she posited, was because he was nervous. There was already friction between the two men that day over a stock trade, she argued. Oland denied he was hesitant and, although the stock sale he handled for his father became complicated, it was not a problem, he said.

When Oland returned to the office a second time, Knee noted, he parked and sat in the car for roughly ten minutes. His Blackberry records showed no incoming or outgoing calls or texts during that period. Knee suggested he was "working up" the courage to talk to his father. "Absolutely not, said Oland. When Oland left the office after the visit, he turned left, crossed the street, turned right, crossed back, and then away again. Knee suggested he was distraught and "didn't know what to do next." He texted his sister instead of his wife because he was "flustered," she said. Oland insisted these were simple mix-ups.

Knee posited that after the genealogy talk, money came up, and they had a "big disagreement." She contrasted Oland's dire financial situation with his father's fortune. She noted that he would have to keep making the monthly interest-only payment for as long as his father was alive. "No, as long as Richard Oland and my mother were alive," Oland corrected. But, as Knee pointed out, he stopped making the payments in November 2011. She was alleging that Oland had, in fact, personally benefitted from his father's slaying, but he remained unflappable.

Knee revisited Oland's statement to police, noting that officers had only informed the family that Richard Oland had died; they did not provide any information about what had happened to him. Yet Oland, at the start of his interview, offered his own unsolicited theory that his father had been the victim of violence. Oland responded that he and his family had been waiting for hours prior to his interview. "We were aware that the death was suspicious, and so we were speculating a lot." Later on in the interview, Oland had suggested the perpetrator could have been someone his father had said something to who had had enough. Knee pointed out that Oland had told police and the court that his father had said many awful things to him over the years.

When he stopped at the Renforth wharf, she argued, he knew Emily was at her mother's, Henry wasn't home from New River, and that Hannah had finished kayaking. He knew his wife was sick and wanted him to come home. And yet he stopped at the wharf, took out the bag that contained his genealogical materials, and put dirty, broken beer bottles into it. He would have passed a garbage can twice when he walked to the end of the wharf and back. Why didn't he put the broken glass in that can? Oland said he didn't notice the can until he walked back. He said he may have disposed of the broken glass there or in the garbage at his home. If the broken glass was dirty, he said, he probably would have carried it and not put it in the bag.

Knee proposed that Oland had suggested robbery as a motive to police to explain why his father's iPhone was missing. She disputed his assertion that his first recollection of knowing his brown sports jacket had been cleaned was on July 10, when his stepson tried it on. She displayed a photograph of his full closet, tightly packed with jackets, shirts, and pants, arguing he would have noticed the gap left by the nineteen items taken to be cleaned. Oland agreed, acknowledging that, "at minimum" he knew before July 10. Knee showed a photo of the dry-cleaning receipt on top of Oland's dresser, suggesting that meant he had dropped off the cleaning. Oland said the receipt and other papers on top of the dresser had been moved from drawers or elsewhere by someone else. He and his wife shared a receipt drawer in his dresser, and she may have put it there. (The court heard it was possible the police moved the receipts while executing the search warrant.) He denied either taking the jacket to the cleaners or telling his wife to do so. Knee pointed out that the dry cleaner's records, dating back to November 2010, showed that no men's sports jackets had previously been taken for cleaning. The only reason Oland had it dry cleaned the morning after police accused him of involvement in his father's death, she argued, was to remove bloodstains. She further suggested that after his father was killed and before the jacket was cleaned, Oland washed it himself, creating the diluted stains—something he flatly denied.

Knee doubted his claim that he'd simply been mistaken when he told police he'd worn a navy blazer rather than the brown sports jacket. She argued he was able to remember other "minute" details about that night, such as which genealogy documents he and his father had looked at.

"You can't imagine how difficult a day that was," Oland replied. "You can't imagine the sadness and shock. I tried very, very hard to remember that day, to remember everything. It was a very, very difficult time."

"Sir, I'm going to suggest to you that you weren't mistaken when you didn't tell police the colour of your jacket that you were wearing. You were lying."

"I absolutely disagree with you."

Knee alleged that he tried to mislead police by telling them he'd visited the office twice rather than three times.

"Absolutely not. As I said before, it was the most difficult day in the world. And you don't know what's significant; you don't know what isn't. You're totally a mess. You do the best you can. I did the best I could." He remembered more details later, he said, once he was removed from the "stressful situation."

"Mr. Oland, you didn't tell them about the third visit because that's when you went back to kill your father."

"That is wrong. I did not kill my father."

The retrial lasted forty-four days spanning four months. It heard from sixty-one witnesses and featured 309 exhibits. Although the circumstantial facts of the case remained largely unchanged from the first trial, the evidence was extensive and complex. The defence requested until April 30 to file its post-trial brief. Morrison remarked that seemed "quite a ways out," but Veniot said, "these are monumental tasks." They settled on April 23 for the defence and April 30 for the Crown. Morrison cautioned both parties that "throwing everything at the wall and hoping it sticks is not generally a good approach." As for the oral arguments, both sides agreed on a time limit of thirty minutes each, just enough to cover anything not in the written submissions. Morrison set aside two days for the oral arguments, noting he would undoubtedly have questions for both sides, citing in particular the circumstances around the possible bloody footprint that was disregarded for three years. Morrison would hear the oral arguments on May 9 and 10, giving the lawyers fifty-six days to prepare. In the first trial, the jury could not be kept waiting, and the lawyers had just eleven days to prepare their final arguments. Morrison anticipated it would take him into June before he'd have his decision ready. "Unlike a jury that doesn't have to give reasons, I have to give detailed reasons," he observed. "It does take a fair amount of effort to make sure those reasons are cogent and can withstand judicial scrutiny."

The court had one unusual piece of business before it could adjourn. The accused, two of his lawyers, two prosecutors, two sheriff's deputies, a court stenographer, and the judge visited the scene of the crime. The defence asked for the visit, arguing that photographs didn't convey the office's compact size, "and that a view of the scene would help Morrison "fully assess" the cramped conditions, the steep stairs, the viability of the back door as an escape route, and the "probability that the assailant(s) would have significant spatter on his or her person." It would also assist Morrison in gauging the location of the thumping noises Shaw and Ainsworth had heard, the view Gerry Lowe had from across the street, and the different locations where Dennis Oland had parked that night. The court doesn't keep statistics on site visits, but staff say they are rare. Morrison approved the request, noting that the visit would be only an aid and not in itself evidence. No one else was allowed in (Robert McFadden watched from down the block), and talking was not permitted. Reporters, a documentary film crew, and a few curious onlookers lined both sides of the narrow one-way street. The two sheriff's deputies stood guard outside the door. The visit lasted less than ten minutes. Oland was the last to leave the building. He stared directly into the camera lenses as he left.

The Crown's written submission was 244 pages long; the defence's 224. Morrison praised them as well done and helpful, but he had "pages" of questions for both parties, he said. Morrison also accepted as an "aid" the defence's 54-page "corrections" report on alleged discrepancies in the Crown's brief; the Crown declined the opportunity to submit a response.

The proceedings began in earnest with a surprising admission on a crucial point. Morrison wondered if there was consensus on any facts. For example, did both sides agree that the noises Anthony Shaw and John Ainsworth had heard were connected to Oland's murder. "That is our position," P.J. Veniot replied. In the Crown's opening statement, Jill Knee had told Morrison that he would have to decide if the noises the two men heard were "caused by the perpetrator committing the unlawful act upon Richard Oland," but now the Crown's post-trial brief conceded: "It is likely the noises they heard related to the murder of Richard Oland." Morrison also wondered whether a 1991 Supreme Court of Canada instruction on assessing the credibility of an accused person—the so-called W.D. analysis—should apply to Shaw and Ainsworth's evidence, which was potentially exculpatory. Both defence and prosecution agreed: if Morrison accepted Shaw's evidence about the timing of the noises and believed Oland was killed at a time when his son was somewhere else, he could not convict.

Morrison also raised the thorny issue of Dennis Oland's post-offence conduct, specifically his incorrect statement to police about which jacket he wore when he visited his father. It was Justice John Walsh's instructions on the issue to the jury at the first trial that led the appeal court to overturn his conviction and order a new trial. Morrison said he must determine whether the untrue statement was a lie, as argued by the Crown, or an honest mistake, as argued by the defence. If he concluded it was a lie, he could use the lie to support an inference of guilt only if it was deliberately concocted to conceal involvement in the offence, and a finding of concoction could only be made on the basis of separate, independent evidence. He asked the lawyers if the finding of concoction should be on the balance of probabilities or beyond a reasonable doubt. Gold argued the burden was beyond a reasonable doubt. Veniot disagreed, noting the Crown had researched the issue while preparing its post-trial brief and could not find any case law indicating what the burden should be.

After a short recess, Gold began the defence's closing arguments. Saint John police wrongly fixated on Dennis Oland early on and viewed everything through that prism without considering possibilities that didn't fit that theory, he contended. The Crown fell victim to the same error of reasoning, filling in blanks to bridge gaps in the evidence, he alleged. Gold said the Crown urged the court to "cast aside" evidence about the time the thumping noises were heard because prosecutors were "trying to knock out something that affirmatively disproves guilt." Prosecutors argued Anthony Shaw's "guesstimate" about the time was not reliable when weighed against the digital and cellphone evidence but, Gold argued, "The evidence of the time of the noises can only be weighed against the digital and cellphone evidence if you assume that Richard Oland was already dead at the times reflected in the digital cellphone evidence." The Crown focused on the "lack" of computer activity after Oland arrived at his father's office and a "lack" of any response from Richard Oland to calls or text messages — "negative evidence" rather than "affirmative evidence," said Gold. The Crown relied on the missing cellphone connecting with the cell tower in Rothesay as proof, but the significance of that connection was "very much up in the air," Gold said.

"You can't assume it proves guilt by assuming Dennis had [the phone]. You have to prove he had it."

"That's the four legs of their case," he derided. "And with the greatest of respect, if one is aware of the proclivity of the human mind to interpret evidence consistent with a pre-existing theory, [this] is a textbook example of that." The Crown's post-trial brief also contained examples of confirmation bias, according to Gold. The Crown considered the lack of activity on Richard Oland's office computer and cellphone after approximately 6:30 p.m. as evidence the elder Oland was dead by then, but there was no activity between 6:12 when Dennis left after his second visit and 6:21 when he said he returned to get the logbook, either. "So even with Dennis gone, there's a ten-minute period of no activity."

Gold argued that the "Fairvale ping" at 6:44 was evidence that Richard Oland had left the office. He pointed to the small amount of alcohol found in Oland's urine and the fact that no alcohol was kept in the office. And while the Crown made much of the iPhone going silent by 6:46, Gold contended it was unclear how that advanced the theory that the phone was in Dennis's possession and destroyed rather than in Richard's possession and turned off or in do-not-disturb mode. "It would be understandable," Gold suggested, if Richard ignored his phone to delay speaking "with the somewhat pestering Ms. Sedlacek."

As for the brown jacket, Gold noted that prosecutors had no evidence that Oland was responsible for getting the jacket dry cleaned and disputed the assertion that the dry cleaning of the jacket supported the inference that the stains inside the cuffs were blood. The fact of the dry cleaning did not make a stain on the garment more likely to be blood "unless, of course, you assume the dry cleaning was done for the purpose of removing blood." The Crown argued the lack of blood on the jacket "could very well have been caused by the dry cleaning," yet also acknowledged a lack of evidence of the effect dry cleaning would have on a bloodstained jacket, said Gold. Similarly, the Crown asserted that Oland went to the wharf to conceal evidence but later in its brief was "forced to admit" there was no proof that Oland actually destroyed any evidence at the wharf.

John Ainsworth's testimony that the thumping noises could have occurred as early as six o'clock should not be believed, argued Gold. For three months after the murder Ainsworth agreed with Shaw that they'd heard the noises sometime after seven thirty, but once he realized his estimate helped Oland's case, his story changed. Ainsworth's demeanour in the KGB statement was "plain, normal, helpful," Gold said. At the retrial, he was "combative, argumentative, unresponsive." Ainsworth claimed that learning on July 7 that Richard Oland was murdered had prompted him to think more carefully about when he'd heard the thumping, but he'd corroborated Shaw's statement on July 27, 2011, both over the phone to the private investigate and again in his statement on October 27, when he had no idea whether his time estimate was helpful or harmful to the prosecution. He had a motive to fabricate at the time of the trial, though, because "by that time he formed his opinion that Dennis Oland was guilty and wanted to do everything possible to convict the killer," Gold alleged. "His conduct in this case demonstrates that he is motivated by bias in his testimony."

Although the Crown attempted to diminish the reliability of Shaw and Ainsworth's evidence, describing it as "subject to the 'everyday hazards of imperfect recognition or imperfect memory,'" they both accessed their memories just twelve hours after hearing the noises, Gold pointed out. He also noted that the Crown was "highly critical" of Oland's imperfect memory of trivial events without making allowances for "everyday hazards," let alone the stress of having just lost a loved one. The errors that Oland made, such as misidentifying the jacket he wore and forgetting the third trip to the office to get the logbook, the defence argued, were "exactly the type of errors that could be expected from an innocent person, as opposed to a guilty one. For an innocent person, such inconsequential details would likely go unconsidered." The killer "would have had a rehearsed, easy flowing story prepared for the police." (In its written submission, the Crown argued that Oland "was capable of remembering several minute details... yet 'forgot' the two most inculpatory portions.")

The Crown faulted Gerry Lowe's evidence because he could not be certain which night he saw a man exit the victim's office building, but Gold said prosecutors also appeared to concede Lowe saw the man on either July 5 or 6. He argued other evidence made it clear Lowe saw the man on July 6, rebutting any suggestion that Lowe's evidence was "something new for the purpose of the trial."

The Crown's alleged money motive was next on Gold's list. Prosecutors' post-trial brief, he said, made it clear that this was "crucial, almost critical" to their case: approximately 13 per cent of the brief's 1,054 paragraphs focused on what prosecutors described as Oland's "dire financial situation" and "financial despair." But the Crown could not offer any evidence to prove that Oland discussed money with his father during the visit or even intended to do so, Gold stressed. The theory was unclear, speculative, and contradictory, Gold argued. The Crown's argument that Oland had no choice but to ask for money from his father, who denied him further assistance, leading to a "rage" killing, "raises the question of the mysterious weapon being at hand." The suggestion that Oland had to kill his father "to save himself from financial ruin" ignored the fact that Richard Oland's will stipulated that his money would go to Connie and only be divided among the children upon her death. And despite describing the killing as a "crime of passion" born "of an enraged mind," the Crown also contended that Oland felt "disappointed, distraught, and distressed" when he left his father's office. The "shifting and alternate suppositions," Gold argued, "cogently indicate" prosecutors' "gap-filling overreach" in its efforts to "establish motive and identify the killer."

Gold also attacked the Crown's "unconvincing" effort to "sweep away" the flaws in the investigation. Prosecutors acknowledged the "deviation from standard practices," "investigative shortcomings," and "inadequacies," he argued, "but then they say, 'Oh, well, but the defence can't show that any of this matters. In our respectful submission, that completely misses the point." As Gold put it, "Negligence on the part of state actors relating to the accumulation of potential evidence is directly related to the strength of the inferences that the Crown asked the court to draw about the available evidence." Perhaps the errors the police made in processing the scene destroyed evidence "implicating the actual third-party killer." The defence's written brief contended that the person who killed Richard Oland was the man Gerry Lowe saw leaving 52 Canterbury Street after 7:40 p.m., the man who, in the course of his murderous attack, made the noises that Anthony Shaw and John Ainsworth heard, who killed Oland with a hammer-like weapon he brought with him and took away, who wore the footwear visible in the bloody imprint, and who, for a reason known only to him, took the victim's iPhone with him when he left, "All for some reason or motive we will never know unless and until someday he is identified."

Gold noted that the Crown's brief quoted an Alberta Court of Appeal decision: "Any one piece of Crown circumstantial evidence may leave a huge doubt. But eight or ten may yield an ironclad case for the Crown." Gold proposed that Morrison look at it from the opposite perspective: "any one piece of defence circumstantial evidence may not leave a huge doubt, but eight or ten may yield an ironclad case for innocence." He identified ten circumstances consistent with Dennis Oland's innocence. The Crown could not explain why Oland would take his father's phone, could not identify the weapon used, and could not connect Oland to anything that could possibly have been the weapon. Gold also cited the alcohol in Richard Oland's urine, which he argued suggested that the victim left his office after his son's visit. He pointed to the location, pattern, and timing of the thumping noises that Shaw and Ainsworth heard, and Gerry Lowe's "significant observation" from across the street. The "complete absence" of any spatter and "only a few blood-DNA stains" on the brown sports jacket, stains the defence contended were the product of "innocent transfer." And, finally, "the amazing coincidence" of a footwear impression "in the right location, by the victim's head, where the killer would have been bloodied by the murder" but that did not match any of the accused's shoes.

Morrison leaned forward as he listened thoughtfully, his elbows on the bench and his hands clasped in front of his mouth. When Gold was finished (and, with the court's permission, he far exceeded the self-imposed thirty-minute limit), Morrison spent nearly an hour asking him questions, including about the Crown's statement that the only item missing from the crime scene was the victim's iPhone. Gold noted that one of Diana Sedlacek's texts had referred to a note. "What's the significance of that?" Morrison asked. "Because I'm having difficulty putting that into the puzzle."

"The court will bear in mind the defence position: if the pieces don't fit, you must acquit," Gold joked, echoing Johnnie Cochran's famous exhortation about the bloody glove in the O.J. Simpson case. "It's not a big deal," said Gold, "but the point is, it's just another little piece that doesn't fit into the puzzle that the Crown would have us see."

"Another mystery," Morrison remarked.

P.J. Veniot began by addressing the defence's allegations of errors in the Crown's written submission. He acknowledged six mistakes, including one reference to 6:36 that should have read 6:44, like the other thirty-four instances it was mentioned. A reference to the iPhone being "off or disabled" should have read simply "off," because the word *disabled* wasn't used in testimony. Other errors, however, were just arguments, according to Veniot. Contrary to what Gold had said, the case wasn't about confirmation bias on the part of the police or the prosecution, Veniot told the judge. "It's about a father and son, one being wealthy, the other not." He noted that the Crown presented evidence that didn't support its case, such as the forensic examination of Oland's car that found no blood and the testimony of Anthony Shaw. The totality of the evidence pointed to Dennis Oland, he said, and authorities simply followed it. Veniot noted that Shaw was preoccupied with helping Ainsworth and didn't make note of the time; he could only "guesstimate" when the thumping occurred. The Crown's position that Shaw and Ainsworth were wrong was "a reasonable inference" to draw, he said. The appeal court found the judge at the first trial "rightly concluded" there was some evidence from which the jury could infer that Richard Oland's lack of response to his phones was inconsistent with Shaw's estimate.

Veniot's argument focused on the known evidence: the lack of human interaction with the office computers after Dennis Oland arrived; the victim's failure to respond to calls or texts after 6:44 p.m.; the iPhone's inability to receive texts after that time and all calls going directly to voicemail, indicating the phone was turned off or destroyed; and the 6:44 text that communicated with the Fairvale tower, indicating the phone was no longer in uptown Saint John but in the same area where Dennis Oland stopped on his way home. The only reasonable inference, said Veniot, is that death occurred when Dennis Oland had "exclusive opportunity" before 6:44 p.m. He was "the only one who could have committed this offence."

With regard to the brown jacket, the Crown's position wasn't that "the accused is guilty solely because there is blood on the jacket, so therefore it must have been worn during the crime," as the defence had asserted. The "reasonable inference" was that Oland wore the jacket when he committed the crime: he wore it when he visited his father and "lied" to police about it to mislead the investigation. The jacket was dry cleaned less than ten hours after police told Oland that search warrants would be executed against him, and blood and DNA matching Richard Oland's profile were later found on the jacket. Veniot also pointed to the "strained" father-son relationship, to Dennis's alleged disapproval of his father's affair, and the fact that he visited on a day when his finances were "the worst they had ever been." In addition to his heavy debt-load, he had spent about $80,000 more than his income during the first half of 2011. "The financial walls, so to speak, were closing in," the Crown wrote in its brief.

Oland visited his father unannounced. First he went up to the second-floor foyer, but he didn't go in; he was "hesitant" to face his father and discuss money, Veniot alleged. Before his second visit, he sat in his car for roughly ten minutes; Robert McFadden and his son would otherwise have seen him. When he did go up to the office, the Crown submitted, he raised the issue of finances with a father whom the court had heard was "tight" with his money. And after the visit Oland, the last known person to see his father alive, behaved in a way that was "distracted and distraught," walking in the wrong direction, crisscrossing the street, mistakenly texting his sister instead of his wife, driving the wrong way up a one-way street. He did not mention the third visit in either his written statement or videotaped police interview. This third visit was when the Crown alleged the murder occurred. The forty-five blows were "way beyond what was required to kill him," Veniot argued. "This was a crime of passion. This was personal. It was not a random killing by a crack head."

No single piece of evidence in isolation proved guilt beyond a reasonable doubt, the Crown wrote in its brief. But when the evidence was assessed cumulatively, it revealed the "completed puzzle . . . Richard Oland's killer is Dennis Oland."

Morrison had several detailed questions for Veniot, starting with the Crown's contention that the killing was "a crime of passion." He noted that the murder weapon must have been brought to the scene and then removed, which suggested premeditation. Premeditation, of course, would bring a charge of first-degree murder, not second degree. Veniot said the decision to proceed with second-degree was made before he joined the prosecution team, but the Crown didn't believe there was the evidence to support first-degree. Morrison asked if Oland deliberately failed to disclose his third visit because that's when the murder occurred, and if he stopped at the wharf to destroy evidence, why didn't he conceal that visit, too? "He was seen," Veniot pointed out, referring to the couple in the parked car at the wharf. But despite the bloody crime scene and extensive testing, no blood was found on Oland's shoes, in his car, on his Blackberry, or on the grocery bag he carried, Morrison said, summarizing the defence's argument. "Because this is the evidence one ought to have seen, the fact that that evidence is not there not only goes to the weight of the Crown's case but is exculpatory," Morrison continued. "What can you say to that?"

Veniot countered that the Crown's bloodstain pattern analyst testified that there are too many unknowns about the bloodletting. The murder was a "dynamic event" with an unknown weapon used in an unknown manner. There may not have been a lot of blood, the analyst testified. The small amount, he argued, should not be viewed as exculpatory.

Morrison commended both teams for the work they'd put into the case and for their professionalism. "You're a credit to your profession," he said, "and I thank you." Although he had hoped to have a verdict by June 7, he realized that was "wildly optimistic." He acknowledged the "strain" that a long deliberation would impose, "but it's important that I get it right." He set his decision for July 19, eight years to the month after Richard Oland was killed.

twenty-two
JUDGMENT

Peple began lining up outside the courthouse an hour before the doors opened and two and a half hours before Morrison was scheduled to deliver his verdict. Many were Oland's supporters, including childhood friend Val Streeter. Others, though, were interested observers who had followed the case as it unfolded and wanted to witness the outcome. "It's been a huge event," explained Mary Stilwell. "I think many people in Saint John felt a personal connection, even though we don't have a personal connection to it." Saint John native Ray Arseneault made the trip from Ontario, scheduling a Saint John stop as part of a sixtieth wedding anniversary tour of New Brunswick he and his wife were making so he could hear the judge's decision in person.

Staff set up overflow seating in an adjacent courtroom equipped with closed-circuit video. Once everyone made it through the security check, they had to line up again in the fifth floor hallway outside courtroom 12 to wait for those doors to open and the rush for seating to begin. How close to the front could they get? Which spot offered the best view of the accused? Three rows were set aside for media, but reporters still had to squeeze over to accommodate their colleagues. It was standing room only by nine a.m., and spillover into the next courtroom began.

Oland arrived at the courthouse hand-in-hand with his wife, accompanied by his son, Henry, and his daughter Hannah, just ten and thirteen years old when the ordeal began, now grown. His mother, uncles Jack Connell and Derek Oland, and aunt Jacqueline found their usual spots, joined by his stepson Andru, his sister Jacqueline, and his cousins

Andrew and Patrick Oland of Moosehead Breweries. Oland's former defence lawyer Gary Miller was also present. The mood in the courtroom was electric, and voices reached a dull roar. When Oland entered, the noise level dropped and tension built.

Morrison cautioned the packed gallery that he would not tolerate any outbursts. "If you are not confident that you can control yourself, please leave the courtroom now," he said. "I think all of us want to avoid the unpleasantness of having the sheriffs intervene." No one stirred.

His written decision was 146 pages, much of it "technical" and "scientific," he said. His oral summary would be brief. Like anyone, Oland was presumed innocent unless and until the Crown proved its case beyond a reasonable doubt Morrison said. Reasonable doubt is not a far-fetched or frivolous doubt; it is not a doubt based on sympathy or prejudice, he explained. It is a doubt based on reason and common sense that logically arises from the evidence, contradictions in the evidence, or the lack of evidence. "It is not enough for me to believe Oland is probably or likely guilty," he said. "But I need not be satisfied with absolute certainty as to guilt. However, proof beyond a reasonable doubt falls much closer to absolute certainty than to proof on the balance of probabilities. In short, before I can find Dennis Oland guilty, I must be sure that it was he that struck the blows that killed Richard Oland."

Morrison outlined the "central two pillars" of the Crown's case: the blood and DNA found on the brown sports jacket, and the lack of activity on the victim's computer and cellphone after his son's visit, which prosecutors argued suggested he was dead by the time Oland left. He then reviewed the defence's position, including what they argued was a lack of evidence linking Oland to the crime and the two witnesses who heard thumping noises coming from the victim's office at a time when Oland was shopping with his wife in Rothesay.

"There is much to implicate Dennis Oland in this crime," said Morrison. "He was the last known person to have seen his father alive on July 6. The brown jacket he wore during that visit was found to have his father's blood and DNA on it. When interviewed by police, he told them he was wearing another jacket. The brown jacket was dry cleaned the morning after that untrue statement. Richard Oland's iPhone was the only item missing from the crime scene, and it happened to connect to a cell tower in the Rothesay area at approximately the same time that Dennis Oland was in the same general area, ten minutes after leaving his father's office. One might consider these circumstances to be more than mere coincidence. But more than suspicion is required to convict a person of murder said Morrison. Probable guilt is not enough. In a circumstantial case such as this, there must be a sufficient assembly of the pieces of the evidential puzzle to form a picture that is consistent with guilt—and only guilt."

The Crown, Morrison noted, had failed to establish motive. That utterance set off a wave of elated gasps and "Oh my Gods!" before hands shot up and clapped over mouths, recalling the judge's warning. Motive is not an essential element of the offence, Morrison continued, but it "provides context for the interpretation of the evidence. Without motive, the trier of facts is being asked to put the jigsaw puzzle together without the benefit of seeing the picture on the puzzle box."

"As expected, there are missing puzzle pieces," he said. "Despite extensive searches, no murder weapon was found or linked to the accused. Despite a bloody murder scene, careful forensic examinations of Dennis Oland's car, his Blackberry, the shoes he was wearing, and the grocery bag carried in and out of his father's office revealed no blood or other trace evidence linking the accused to the crime. While the presence of his father's blood on the brown jacket could be indicative of the accused's presence during the murder, the small number and size of the bloodstains on the jacket is inconsistent with the bloody crime scene and no plausible explanation for the lack of blood has been demonstrated."

A "central and critical piece" of the evidential puzzle, said Morrison, was the time of Richard Oland's death. He concluded the thumping noises heard by Anthony Shaw and John Ainsworth were the sounds of the brutal murder. The timing of the noises was therefore key. He accepted Shaw's testimony that the noises occurred at around seven thirty p.m. as "credible and reliable." He also relied on Ainsworth's sworn statement to the private investigator, when he put the time at seven thirty to seven forty-five. If Richard Oland was killed at this time, then Dennis Oland "could not have been the killer" because he was shopping in Rothesay, said Morrison. At the very least, as the defence had argued, it raised a reasonable doubt as to his guilt.

"Notwithstanding the credibility and reliability" of Shaw's evidence, Morrison could not "wholeheartedly accept it" because of the inconsistent digital evidence that suggested Richard Oland was dead by 6:44 p.m. That evidence, he said, was "persuasive" but inconclusive. "In short, I have a reasonable doubt as to whether Richard Oland was killed prior to 6:44 p.m., or when Mr. Shaw says he heard the murder at 7:30 p.m."

Morrison identified "some frailties" in Dennis Oland's testimony. "In light of those and the evidence as a whole, I cannot accept outright the accused's denial of guilt," he said. His words triggered another shockwave and put Oland's supporters on shaky ground. "However," he continued, I am not confident that I can accept the Crown's version of events."

Morrison asked Oland to stand. "There are too many missing puzzle pieces to form a cohesive portrait of guilt beyond a reasonable doubt," Morrison said. "In short, I am not satisfied that the Crown has proven beyond a reasonable doubt that it was Dennis Oland who killed Richard Oland.

"Dennis Oland, I find you not guilty of the murder of Richard Oland." Morrison rose and quietly left the courtroom.

Dennis Oland immediately turned to Alan Gold and gave him a bear hug and then hugged Michael Lacy and James McConnell. He wiped away tears and shared long embraces with his family members; his daughter sobbed openly. Slowly he made his way through the crowd of other relatives and supporters, sharing more hugs, handshakes, and pats on the back. It was a stark contrast to his reaction three and a half years earlier, when the jury found him guilty.

The prosecutors showed no reaction and offered no comment before leaving. Neither did the police officers who were sitting at the back of the courtroom. Oland beamed as he left the courthouse a free man. He declined to comment. Only Jack Connell offered a remark. "It's great," he said. The crowd of supporters outside erupted into applause as Oland and his family passed through the throng of reporters wielding microphones and cameras, piled into a waiting SUV, and sped away.

Within an hour, the defence held a news conference. Gold said it was an important day to "acknowledge the fact that Dennis did not kill his father." Justice Morrison, he noted, had "spent months considering whether the Crown could prove Dennis was the killer" before concluding that it could not. He said he hoped that the 27 per cent of Saint Johners who believed Oland was guilty (a reference to the pre-trial poll) would admit they were wrong. "I hope that everybody in Saint John now understands and appreciates that Dennis Oland did not kill his father and understands the misery that he and his family and his friends and supporters have gone through the last eight years."

Gold was dismissive of the judge's observation that there was "much to implicate" Oland. "If there wasn't much to implicate, we wouldn't have had a trial," he said. Gold was uncomfortable with well-wishers congratulating him and saying it was a day to celebrate. "Dennis lost his dad to a brutal murder," he stressed. The day when the "actual perpetrators" are finally caught and brought to justice would be the day to celebrate. Gold had strong words for the Saint John police. "Based on a flawed investigation, they never took their eyes off him," he declared. He called on police to "start doing the investigation that should have been done eight years ago." If the local force won't, he said, then "perhaps some outside force should come in."

Asked whether Oland planned to sue, Gold said he didn't know; he only practised criminal law. Oland's immediate plans were to spend quality time with his family and "mentally regroup." No one could truly understand what he'd endured, Gold noted. He urged the media and the public: "Leave him in peace, and let him come to the wonderful realization that it's finally over."

Saint John Police Chief Bruce Connell said only, "The Saint John Police Force respects the decision of Mr. Justice Morrison."

Morrison's verdict divided public opinion — again. "That's wrong," said Allen Horsman. "He got off." But another observer, Susan Ainsworth, wasn't surprised. "There was no evidence," she said. "If the man is not guilty, he's not guilty," said Jonnelle Lake. "He's been through hell and back, and he's probably destroyed. Whatever part of his life he's lost he's never going to get back. I can't imagine going through something like that, so I wish him the best." Some who were shocked by the verdict were quick to point to the family's wealth as the reason. "As someone said, money talks," said Melanie Clark. Law student Alex Hoyt noted that while people with money undoubtedly have an advantage when it comes to mounting a defence, "you can't fault someone for finding good representation."

Why did the judge reach the opposite conclusion of the jury in the first trial? His written decision was indeed detailed. Before considering the physical evidence, expert analyses, and witness testimony, he began with the three-pronged motive the Crown had put forward: the troubled father-son relationship, the extramarital affair, and the financial issue. Morrison noted more than once in his analysis a contradiction between the Crown's argument that Dennis Oland, driven into a rage, had committed an impulsive crime of passion and prosecutors' claims that Oland went to the office prepared to kill his father.

Morrison said he had no doubt the two men had a "difficult" relationship, noting the father's "demanding, controlling, and difficult personality." But he believed Dennis "learned to adapt" by keeping his distance and focusing on their shared passion for genealogy "as a touchstone for conflict-free communication." He wasn't convinced their relationship was "so dysfunctional" as to be abnormal. "Human experience, and an examination of our own extended families, teaches us that many filial relationships suffer from many of the same stresses that were the hallmarks of the Oland family dynamic." He disagreed that Oland's characterization of the relationship to the police was disproportionately negative, feeling that Oland mentioned both positive and negative aspects in his statement and in his testimony. That Oland was a co-executor of his father's will "strongly" suggested that his father had "trust and confidence" in him, said Morrison. In short, he did not believe that any resentments in the relationship could, on their own, account for the murder.

Nor did he believe the extramarital affair played any role in a possible motive. Oland, he noted, disclosed to police his knowledge of the "potential affair" and his conversation about it with McFadden. That conversation was a "rather tepid suggestion made in a one-off, unrelated conversation at least a year and a half before the murder," which "hardly belies a burning resentment, let alone red-eyed rage," said Morrison. The Crown offered no proof that Oland raised the subject again or that it was "a matter of pressing, or any, concern" when he visited his father on July 6.

Although Morrison didn't doubt that Oland's financial situation was "bleak," he accepted his testimony that he wasn't particularly concerned, although "perhaps [he] should have been." But, he wrote, Oland's testimony regarding his request for an advance on his salary was "simply not credible." The "clear and unequivocal meaning" of his email was that he expected his father and another client would invest $10 million to $20 million, not that his growth target was $10 million to $20 million. The judge dismissed as "unrealistic" Oland's testimony that simply increasing his book of business would allow him to "extricate himself from his financial morass," calling that "a long-term plan, not an immediate solution." Still, Morrison did not find a "tipping point" in Oland's finances "that drove [him] to desperation" on July 6. Neither Maureen Adamson nor Robert McFadden's evidence supported the Crown's suggestion that Richard Oland knew about the missed interest-only payments or that it concerned him, Morrison asserted. He also found no evidence of the Crown's suggestion that Oland was at risk of losing the ancestral home to foreclosure because he had missed one payment of $481.

Even if he did find Oland was in a financial crisis that required his father's assistance, he wrote, he saw no evidence to support the inference that he would have approached his father directly. McFadden had previously acted as intermediary, the court had heard, and "when Dennis Oland sought financial help in the past, his father did not refuse it. Morrison argued that while the Crown's theory that Oland and his father had a discussion about money that resulted in a confrontation "cannot be characterized as mere speculation, the evidence in support of that proposition is weak." He pointed out that Shaw and Ainsworth did not hear shouting or sounds of an argument coming from the office. No evidence suggested that Oland planned to "speak to or confront" his father about money that day, "Nor does the record disclose the level of upset, animosity or emotional break that would justify the Crown's murderous rage theory."

Morrison also rejected the argument that Oland killed his father to benefit financially from his death. The will provided a spousal trust for Connie, and only upon her death would the remainder be divided among Oland and his two sisters. (Of course, Connie could arguably give money to her son if she wished. Oland and McFadden are trustees of the spousal trust.) Besides, Morrison observed, financial gain as the motive implied premeditation, "which would fly in the face of the Crown's theory that this was a crime of passion born of an enraged mind and would be inconsistent with the charge of second-degree murder found in the indictment."

As for the bloodstained jacket, Morrison noted the evidence supported the inference that three of the stains were from Richard Oland's blood, given the single-source DNA profile. Although the fourth stain did not provide sufficient DNA to confirm a profile, Morrison found it too was most likely Richard Oland's blood. But in a strange twist, Morrison felt those stains supported the defence's case more than the Crown's. The small number and "very small" size of the stains were inconsistent with "a gruesome and bloody murder" with 360-degree blood spatter. He rejected the Crown's argument that three reddish stains inside the cuffs were also blood. "I believe it is very dangerous to accept as blood something that the hemochromogen test has not confirmed," he wrote. The Hemastix test, he noted, is not specific for blood, and the positive results could have been the result of other substances. The presence of DNA at a site, even in conjunction with blood, does not necessarily mean that blood is the source of the DNA, given the mixed profiles, he observed, citing Joy Kearsey's expert evidence.

The Crown had argued the lack of a blood trail leaving the office or evidence of cleanup at the scene suggested the killer walked away with little blood on him or her, but Morrison accepted the opinion of the defence's bloodstain pattern analyst, Patrick Laturnus, that if the brown jacket had been worn during the murder, it would have been significantly and visibly stained with blood. "In my view, the absence of a bloody footwear trail does not preclude me from drawing the inference that the attacker had significant blood spatter on them."

Although the Crown argued dry cleaning could have removed bloodstains from the jacket, the judge pointed to "a dearth" of evidence about the effect of dry cleaning on bloodstained clothing. The most compelling evidence, he wrote, was that of the dry cleaners, who said they carefully examine clothing for stains before and after cleaning and noted no bloodstains. "While I appreciate that the brown colouring of the jacket may obscure the visibility of the bloodstains, Ms. Choi's evidence is that if the jacket had been covered in blood, she would have remembered it." Prosecutors' suggestion that the jacket was washed before it was taken to the dry cleaner "falls into the realm of impermissible speculation." Nor was there evidence that the killer donned coveralls. "Indeed, the taking of such precautions would necessarily imply planning and premeditation which is antithetical to the Crown's theory of the case: a crime of passion born of an enraged mind."

The absence of blood spatter on Oland's other clothing, shoes, reusable grocery bag, Blackberry, and car "calls into question the inference that the blood on the jacket is blood spatter," Morrison concluded.

Moving on to the time of death issue, Morrison analyzed the Crown's position that the victim was killed sometime between 5:45 and 6:36 p.m., when his son was alone with him. Prosecutors presented evidence that the last human interaction with Richard Oland's main computer was at 5:39 p.m., and Morrison found that credible. There was no reliable evidence of Richard Oland's normal computer usage patterns or whether it was unusual for him to stop his computer activity at that time. Morrison concluded the reason for the lack of computer interaction was "probably because something was amiss," but he could not give it undue weight, he explained, because the evidence showed Richard Oland ignored his computers between 6:12 and 6:21 p.m. — from the end of his son's second visit until his third return — "when he was still very much alive."

The Crown further argued the lack of cellphone communication from Richard Oland after 6:44 p.m. supported the inference that he was dead by that time. The Crown had also claimed that since the iPhone connected with the cell tower in Rothesay at 6:44, and since the phone was the only known item missing from the crime scene, the only reasonable inference was that the killer took the phone and either turned it off or destroyed it, and that Richard Oland was therefore already dead. Given his attachment to his iPhone, Morrison deemed it unlikely that he would have turned it off or switched it to do-not-disturb mode. Nor was it likely the battery was dead, since it had been connected to Oland's computer that afternoon while it was backed up. Since Oland "was indeed dead" at some point on July 6, and the other possible explanations for the lack of response were unlikely, Morrison concluded that the victim had likely stopped responding "because he was unable."

That a cell tower near the wharf where Dennis Oland stopped on his way home sent the iPhone's final communication was, Morrison wrote, "potentially potent evidence against the accused." But, he noted, "it is also evidence which must be approached with caution." A general rule, he pointed out, is just that: general. Joseph Sadoun's opinion regarding the likely location of a cellphone based on his propagation maps proved wrong several times, Morrison observed. Moreover, Sadoun's opinion that it was unlikely a cellphone located uptown would connect to the Fairvale tower, about fourteen kilometres northeast, failed to account for the fact that the Fairvale tower was likely on the "neighbour list" for the uptown Saint John tower and could take over during peak periods or technical problems. In Morrison's view, Sadoun's opinion that it was "very unlikely" a cellphone uptown would connect to the Fairvale tower was "significantly undermined" by the neighbour-list evidence. Although determining the probability was impossible, Morrison concluded it was greater than Sadoun's "pessimistic probability assessment." The evidence, however, was simply not conclusive, he noted.

On the other hand, the only reasonable inference about the thumping noises was that they were the sounds of the killing, Morrison asserted; "Indeed, the Crown concedes the point." Despite the Crown's argument that Shaw's "guesstimate" of the timing was unreliable, Morrison reviewed Shaw's testimony and found he used the term *I guess* as a substitute for *I think* (something the defence had observed in its closing argument). Asked what tenants were above Printing Plus, he said Oland's office and one other tenant, "I guess." Morrison disagreed that Shaw simply picked the halfway mark between his arrival at six and departure at nine, noting that Shaw also used the "Middle Eastern" customer who sent a fax at around eight as a reference point. "Temporally, this is much closer in time to Mr. Shaw's time estimate than either when he arrived at six p.m. or when he left at nine p.m." The fax was sent about thirty minutes after Shaw said he heard the noises. Ainsworth testified he could only estimate the noises occurred sometime between 6:00 and 8:11 p.m., but Morrison accepted Ainsworth's sworn statement to the private investigator, when he put the timing between 7:30 and 7:45.

Ainsworth was "calm, direct, and cooperative" when he made the sworn statement, Morrison observed. "His demeanour at trial was quite the contrary. Mr. Ainsworth was angry, combative, and argumentative. In many instances he refused to answer the questions posed, and he often editorialized." Although Ainsworth "bristled" at the defence's suggestion that he wouldn't do or say anything that might help Oland's case, "one would be forgiven for believing otherwise," Morrison said. When Ainsworth spoke to the private investigator, Oland had not yet been charged, so "there was no motive for Mr. Ainsworth to colour his evidence in a light unfavourable to the accused. The same cannot be said by the time Mr. Ainsworth testified at this trial," he said. In addition, Morrison found Ainsworth's explanation that he didn't realize the "criticalness" of what time he gave the police because he believed Oland had died of natural causes "simply implausible." He knew when he spoke to the private investigator that Richard Oland had been killed, and still he repeated his initial time estimate of seven thirty to seven forty-five. And once Ainsworth learned it was a homicide, he could have immediately contacted police if he believed he'd made an error. "Incredibly, he did not." Morrison acknowledged other evidence was inconsistent with Shaw's time estimate but concluded that Shaw's testimony and Ainsworth's statement raised "a serious question with respect to the time of death." Morrison also found some support for the seven thirty to eight p.m. time frame — "albeit tenuous" — in Gerry Lowe's testimony.

The defence had theorized that the cellphone may have connected with the Fairvale tower because Richard Oland left his office after his son, pointing to the small amount of alcohol in Richard Oland's urine and their toxicology expert's opinion that the level was consistent with Oland drinking a beer or glass of wine about an hour before his death. Morrison found the expert's evidence of little assistance because it was "based on assumptions that do not necessarily accord with the toxicology findings," he wrote, and Mayer was not asked to provide an opinion as to the time of alcohol consumption. Morrison found "not a scintilla of evidence" that Richard Oland left his office at any time before his death. "When and in what quantity alcohol was consumed to leave the small quantity of alcohol in the bladder remains a mystery."

Another unexplained "puzzle piece" was the possible footwear impression near the victim's head. The impression was probative evidence only if it could be linked to the murder, Morrison wrote. Although the Crown claimed the impression could have pre-dated the homicide, the fact that it turned green when sprayed with LMG was "at least presumptive evidence of the presence of blood." Morrison wasn't convinced that not one of the fifteen people who entered the office before Sergeant Smith took crime scene photographs could have made the impression. At least three of them were "very close" to the body, he observed, and their recollections of where they stepped may be understandably imprecise. "If one could be confident that none of the fifteen people who entered the FEC offices before eleven thirty a.m. on July 7 could have made the impression, then this would be very cogent evidence that the impression was made by the killer and that the killer was not Dennis Oland," Morrison wrote. "However, I do not have that degree of confidence."

In the end, Morrison didn't consider the footwear impression "as compelling as the defence makes out," but he didn't accept the Crown's position that it should be "dismissed as meaningless," either. "The best I can make of the footwear impression is that it is a piece of circumstantial evidence that raises the possibility of an unknown assailant," he wrote. Although the defence argued the man seen by Lowe leaving Oland's office was the real killer and that the footwear impression supported that, Morrison said it was only speculation "without substantially more evidence linking this unknown person to the crime."

Morrison had unanswered questions about the murder weapon too. "Where did the murder weapon come from?" he wondered. "Was it just coincidentally available?" The evidence was "clear" that the killer had to have brought the weapon and removed it from the scene. "This bespeaks premeditation and does not fit with the Crown's theory of the case: a crime of passion born of an enraged mind." If Oland was the killer, Morrison observed, the red reusable grocery bag he had with him that night would seem the logical receptacle for a murder weapon and would "likely" have trace evidence either in or on it, yet none was found. The Crown argued that, other than Oland's testimony, there was no way to know if the bag seized and tested by the police was the same bag. Morrison concluded it was. It appeared similar to the one seen in the security video, the Crown offered no evidence to suggest it wasn't, and he noted Sergeant Smith expected to recover trace evidence from the bag. The Crown theorized Oland took the bag with him after his second visit and didn't bring it back on his third trip, but that still left the lingering question of a weapon.

Similarly, if the logbook remained on the table where Maureen Adamson recalled last seeing it or was "anywhere in the vicinity of Richard Oland's desk," it "certainly" would have received blood spatter, Morrison noted. The Crown contended the logbook left with Oland after his second visit and was not present during the murder. Other than his testimony, there was no evidence as to when he took the logbook from the office.

Morrison found some inconsistencies between Oland's statement to police and his testimony regarding his stop at Renforth wharf on his way home that tended to "undermine his credibility." Nevertheless, Morrison noted, Oland had volunteered to police the fact he stopped at the wharf. The Crown alleged Oland stopped to conceal or destroy evidence, but Morrison wrote that was not supported by the evidence. Neither of the witnesses who saw Oland at the wharf saw him throw anything away, and an extensive search didn't find a murder weapon, Richard Oland's missing cellphone, or any other item of interest. (Divers did find a cellphone and a welding hammer during the search, but neither was connected to the Oland case; the defence elicited this evidence to suggest that the failure to locate either the missing iPhone or the weapon in the water wasn't necessarily because small objects would be difficult to find.) While the Crown challenged as implausible Oland's testimony about noticing a beer bottle at the wharf and placing it in his reusable grocery bag that contained valuable genealogical documents, Morrison noted, "I reject this attack completely." Oland's testimony, he wrote, was consistent with the agreed statement of facts of the two witnesses who observed him at the wharf.

"At first blush," Morrison agreed that Oland's wandering around Canterbury Street, wrongly sent text, and illegal left turn could be considered the behaviour of a "distraught and distressed individual." Similarly, the change in his demeanour during his police interview from talkative and laughing to quiet and guarded, along with his confusion in answering certain questions, could be evidence of "panic or an attempt to obfuscate." On the other hand, Morrison wrote, his actions could be consistent with his explanations: his change in demeanour could be a response to more aggressive questions and his confusion could be attributed to the shock of losing his father that day. The evidence of Oland shopping with his wife, chatting with his aunt, and making a couple of phone calls "certainly seems to be more in keeping with 'normal' behaviour and thus inconsistent with someone who had committed a brutal murder less than an hour earlier," Morrison observed. But "it could be that Dennis Oland is particularly adept at concealing or controlling his emotions or that he lacks empathy." A person's outward appearance does not necessarily reflect their state of mind, he noted. The problem with demeanour evidence is it assumes a "normal" range of reaction to highly stressful situations applicable to everyone, and case law advises caution in drawing any conclusions from such evidence. Consequently, Morrison wrote, he gave the demeanour evidence from either side "very little weight."

The Crown presented two pieces of Oland's "after-the-fact" conduct as circumstantial evidence of his guilt: his "lie" about the navy blazer and the dry cleaning of the brown jacket the morning after his police interview, purportedly to destroy evidence. Only a person involved in the murder would attempt to mislead police, prosecutors argued. The defence responded that Oland simply made a mistake about which jacket he'd worn and that the jacket was cleaned in preparation for visitations and the funeral. Analyzing post-offence conduct is "susceptible to and carries an elevated risk of speculative reasoning," Morrison wrote, and the evidence "may appear more probative than it really is." It was Justice John Walsh's instructions to the jury on this thorny issue that led to the new trial. Morrison said he had to consider the post-offence conduct in light of all the evidence, weigh the competing inferences, consider reasonable alternative explanations for the conduct, and then determine what inferences to draw and what weight to give them, if any. He found evidence to support the Crown's inference, including the blood and DNA on the jacket and the fact it had been dry cleaned. Other evidence pointing to Dennis Oland's involvement included the likely time of death and the iPhone's connection to the Rothesay cell tower.

On the other hand, Oland knew Maureen Adamson had seen him, and police told him they would be checking surveillance video. "One could very well ask the question, 'Why would Dennis Oland deliberately lie knowing that he was likely to be caught?'" Morrison said. "Although it is not clear cut, I believe the inference that the false statement is a lie is the more cogent of the inferences." Morrison divided the Crown's list of nineteen circumstances it said constituted independent evidence of fabrication into five general categories. First, circumstances surrounding the interview; second, the level of detail of the statement; third, other instances of obfuscation; fourth, demeanour; and fifth, subsequent discovery of blood and DNA and dry cleaning.

Prosecutors said Oland was not a suspect at the time of his interview and suggested he gave his statement in circumstances where one would expect him to tell the truth. Morrison agreed. They also argued he gave police a detailed description of the jacket, identifying the colour as navy without prompting, and made the false statement twice during the interview. But Morrison found no "embellishment," unlike other cases where an accused provides precise details of time, place, circumstances or "elaborately implausible explanations." He said it was a "simple response" to a simple question posed by police: "What were you wearing?" Oland identified other clothing he wore during his visit, including the pants and shoes he was wearing at the time of his interview. "If his intent was to divert the police attention from key pieces of evidence," Morrison argued, "then it seems that he would have lied about these as well."

As for the Crown's assertion of Oland's "premature knowledge" of the manner of his father's death, Morrison wasn't convinced. The family didn't know any details about the cause of death, but they could reasonably suspect foul play, based on the police response. "In my view, the accused's statements do not betray any detailed knowledge of the cause of Richard Oland's death and certainly not knowledge that would be known only to the killer."

Morrison did find "some merit" to the Crown's contention that Oland "deliberately obfuscated" certain facts during his police interview, given the fact he "entirely omitted" the third trip to his father's office even though he recalled having parked three times. This, combined with the blood and DNA on the brown jacket and its dry cleaning, provided evidence "in favour of concoction," evidence "that an accused deliberately lied because he was conscious of having committed the crime." But given the other elements of Oland's statement, which Morrison deemed inconsistent with such a finding, he was not satisfied there was sufficient evidence to conclude Oland's untrue statement about the jacket was a lie fabricated to deceive police, and therefore he could not "consider the untrue statement to infer consciousness of guilt." The receipt found on Oland's dresser did not prove he knew about or participated in the dry cleaning, said Morrison. Oland was under surveillance from the moment he left his police interview on July 7, and there was no evidence he attended the dry cleaner on July 8.

As for the flawed police investigation, Morrison found "numerous shortcoming, failings, and inadequacies" in the way police handled the crime scene. The crime scene should have included the doors of the inner office, the foyer, stairways, and both exits. And the back door, "a natural escape route for an assailant to consider," ought to have been forensically examined, even if police possibly contaminated it. Morrison called the "uncontrolled access" to the office both before and during its processing "another failing." Even the forensic officer, he noted, failed to follow "basic crime scene hygiene" regarding shoe coverings to avoid contamination of evidence. But "this trial is not a judicial inquiry into police conduct," he wrote. As the Alberta Court of Appeal stated in another case, a trier of fact should "focus on the quality of the evidence, not the quality of the investigation." The police failings were just "part of the mix" to consider in deciding whether or not the Crown had met the onus of proof beyond a reasonable doubt and did not "weigh heavily in the final determination of this case."

POSTSCRIPT

The province of New Brunswick spent more than $1.5 million prosecuting Dennis Oland: $637,000 for his first trial and subsequent appeal, and at least $930,000 on the retrial; this figure doesn't include the cost of the preliminary inquiry, which spanned thirty-seven days over six months in 2014. Of the retrial expenses, approximately $490,000 went to P.J. Veniot, pulled out of retirement for the first trial and kept on to lead the prosecution team (this includes Veniot's travel-related expenses from his home in Bathurst). Another $120,000 was spent on the jury selection process for the jury trial that never transpired. The federal government paid Justice Morrison's expenses and does not release those figures. The investigation and two trials cost Saint John police an additional $150,581 in overtime, DNA testing, and forensic accounting services.

The public cost pales in comparison to how much was spent on Oland's years of legal wrangling. Lawyer David Lutz estimates that the defence cost $10 million. At least $15,000 per day was spent just on the three lawyers, he figures.

On August 13, 2019, Public Prosecution Services announced it had reviewed "the policy and legal considerations" and concluded that the Crown had no legal basis for appealing the acquittal of Dennis Oland. Legal experts were not surprised. Crown appeals are limited to points of law, and the threshold with judge-alone trials is high, observed Toronto lawyer Christopher Hicks. An error of law alone on the part of the judge was insufficient grounds, prosecutor Kathryn Gregory said. The Crown would have to satisfy the appellate court that "there is a reasonable degree of certainty" that the judge had made an error of law likely to have affected the outcome of the case.

The Oland family was, of course, very happy. "In our opinion, the Crown could not have come to any other conclusion," family lawyer William Teed wrote. "Perhaps now the police investigation to actually solve the case, if that is possible, will move forward," Alan Gold commented. Chief Bruce Connell told CBC News that the force does not intend to resume the investigation, although police will consider any additional information or evidence that "comes to our attention." The Oland family has renewed its 2011 offer of a reward (amount unspecified) for information that might help find the real killer. "Notwithstanding this offer, we would have thought that the complete re-examination of the evidence by fresh eyes — a common step used by many police forces in reviewing old cases — would have been the obvious next step," the family's statement read. "Sitting and waiting for clues to be delivered... is a very disappointing response. As a family, we believe our husband and father deserve better."

The retrial brought to light more problems with the police investigation: a possible bloody fingerprint on a piece of paper on Richard Oland's desk that was overlooked; the forensic officer wearing dirty shoe coverings in the foyer, down the stairs, and out onto the street; and an officer who didn't file any reports on his involvement in the case until seven years after the fact, to name a few. "The Crown does not dispute that the Saint John Police Force's handling of the crime scene was not without deviation from what should have been standard practice," prosecutors acknowledged in their post-trial brief. "Several officers, in their testimony, admitted that the crime scene was mishandled and that in the future they would handle such a scene in a different manner." Justice Morrison may not have given the faults in the investigation much weight, but the defence set out to "impugn the conduct and credibility" of various officers, alleged that some of the force's applications for search warrants contained misleading or outdated information, and accused police of treating the crime scene like a "tourist attraction."

The New Brunswick Police Commission is currently weighing whether to proceed with its review of how police handled the homicide investigation, a review the commission committed to in 2015 and put on hold once Oland filed his appeal. "The incident occurred eight years ago," Jennifer Smith, the current executive director of the commission, explained. "There have been two trials, a number of related public documents, and a change in senior leadership at both the Saint John Police Force and the New Brunswick Police Commission, all of which adds to an already complex investigation and court proceedings." The force has addressed its involvement in the jury selection, she said, and the commission "is satisfied with the action taken." Smith declined to elaborate, and neither the police chief nor the police board responded to requests for comment. Less than two months after the mistrial, Sean Rocca was promoted to staff sergeant, skipping the rank of sergeant entirely.

The New Brunswick Police Commission is itself the subject of an independent review. Retired RCMP Assistant Commissioner Alphonse MacNeil, who previously reviewed the 2014 fatal shootings of three Mounties in Moncton, is examining the commission's policies, practices, and procedures. The commission's board of directors requested the review after the New Brunswick Police Association condemned the commission for the way it handled the conduct investigation of Mike King's allegations against Glen McCloskey and called for the removal of then executive director Steve Roberge. The provincial integrity commissioner concluded that the New Brunswick Police Commission twice breached McCloskey's privacy by disclosing his personal information to the Crown and the defence in the Oland case. Shortly after the integrity commissioner's findings were made public, Roberge was "no longer employed by the province." McCloskey, the former deputy chief, is now suing the police commission and Roberge for allegedly failing to conduct the Police Act investigation of him without bias, deliberately engaging in unlawful conduct in exercising their public function, and violating the public trust. McCloskey, who is seeking damages and costs, contends that the commission anticipated a settlement conference before the investigation of him was complete, demonstrating that the investigator's findings were "foregone conclusions." None of McCloskey's allegations have been proven in court. In their statement of defence, the commission and Roberge deny any wrongdoing. They call the lawsuit "frivolous and vexatious" and argue it should be dismissed with costs.

Justice Terrence Morrison noted a dominant theme in the roughly six hundred social media comments he reviewed before the retrial: "Sentiment that there is a law for the rich and one for the poor, and that the accused is a spoiled rich kid who killed his father for money." Associate law professor Nicole O'Byrne doesn't believe Oland received special favours because of his wealth — certainly the Saint John Police Force had no hesitation in investigating him. Oland did, however, have the means to hire top lawyers and pursue every possible avenue, all the way to the country's highest court. Exhaustive legal battles are expensive, O'Byrne observes. "The fact is the average person doesn't have the resources to hire the defence team that was put together for this case." This highlights a problem with access to justice, she says. "Any of us could wake up tomorrow facing very serious charges, and we shouldn't have to face financial ruin to be able to defend ourselves properly." The legal aid system, O'Byrne contends, is "profoundly underfunded."

Oland's case starkly contrasts another Maritime murder case, one that made headlines at the same time Oland was acquitted. In 1999, Glen Assoun of Halifax was wrongfully convicted of second-degree murder in the 1995 stabbing death of Brenda Way and spent nearly seventeen years in prison. Assoun, who had a Grade 6 education, was forced to represent himself after he fired his legal aid–appointed lawyer and could not obtain another. According to Innocence Canada, a non-profit organization dedicated to advocating for the wrongfully convicted, Assoun always maintained his innocence but "lacked the education and skill" to mount a successful defence against two experienced prosecutors. A federal review of Assoun's case showed that investigators focused on him at the expense of other suspects, that prosecutors failed to disclose information, and that the RCMP deleted files that pointed to other possible suspects, including a serial killer.

Many people wondered how Oland paid for his high-priced defence, given the evidence presented about his financial situation. In 2011, his net income was $250,068.02, according to tax-related documents his wife filed in a child support dispute. In 2012, the documents show, it jumped to $674,928.49. No information about the source of that income is provided. CIBC Wood Gundy paid him a forced retirement settlement sometime after police searched his home, but the amount of the buyout was unclear. As a co-executor of Richard Oland's will, co-trustee of the spousal trust for Connie Oland, and co-director of his father's main holding company and two subsidiaries (responsibilities he shared with Robert McFadden), Dennis received roughly $200,000. By 2015, his net income had dropped to $26,062.85, where it has continued to hover; he was, of course, in prison for approximately ten months in 2016. He is still listed as co-director of his father's companies. Exchange on Germain, the designer consignment shop Lisa Andrik-Oland had opened in 2012, closed at the beginning of 2018. The sale of Handworks Gallery was also announced by Lisa Andrik-Oland in August 2018.

To date, William Teed has declined to comment on the possibility that Oland will sue the police and the Crown. When the family issued a statement urging the New Brunswick Police Commission to resume its probe of the force's investigation, it stated: "We are confident that findings from such an inquiry will support the conclusions that the investigation was filled with missteps and Dennis should never have been charged."

Dennis Oland is a free man. But will he ever be free of the shadow of doubt that has hung over him since July 2011? Justice Morrison's detailed verdict is, by all accounts, above reproach legally, but it hasn't provided the finality some had hoped. "The last thing any of us wants is to have a verdict... with an asterisk," Morrison had said when he declared a mistrial. But not guilty is not the same as innocent, and Morrison made it clear that he found "much to implicate" Oland in the crime. Oland's guilt or innocence continues to be a subject of gossip, speculation, and heated debate. It seems everyone in Saint John has an opinion, and they aren't afraid to share it, whether in hushed conversations in coffee shops, boisterous debates in bars, or on social media with hundreds of their closest "friends." And more than eight years after Maureen Adamson arrived at work and discovered her boss's bludgeoned body, the murder of a Saint John icon remains unsolved. Who killed Richard Oland?

Readers interested in the complete text of
Justice Terrence J. Morrison's Decision can
receive an eBook version free of charge
from Goose Lane Editions.

Download your free copy of
R v Oland 2019 NBQB 151
at http://bit.ly/RvOland
using the promotional code
QX3ZJKSKW5

gooselane.com

ACKNOWLEDGEMENTS

I would like to thank the talented team at Goose Lane Editions, notably Susanne Alexander and Karen Pinchin, who took a leap of faith on me for the first edition in 2016.

Thanks to production editor Alan Sheppard, who steered this edition through to production with patience and professionalism, creative director Julie Scriver for the book design, Nathaniel Moore for his publicity efforts, and proofreader Paula Sarson for her meticulous work.

I am especially indebted to my exceptional editor Jill Ainsley for her vision, collaborative approach, and skill.

This book would not have been possible without the support of CBC News. To the national, regional, and local managers who allowed me to take on this project and to use material I gathered reporting on the case, thank you.

Special thanks to my supervisors Darrow MacIntyre and Mary-Pat Schutta, who accommodated my time off to write, as well as time away from my web editor duties to cover the lengthy trial. Many thanks are also due to my CBC colleagues for their contributions to our coverage, particularly the ever-insightful Robert Jones.

I am also grateful to CBC lawyers Sean Moreman and Judith Harvie, media lawyer David Coles, and University of New Brunswick associate law professor Nicole O'Byrne, who provided invaluable assistance navigating this complex case. Thanks as well to lawyer David Hutt and the Court of Queen's Bench of New Brunswick staff.

To colleague, fellow author, and friend Jacques Poitras for his guidance and encouragement, I am deeply grateful. I would also like to acknowledge agent Hilary McMahon for her early counsel.

Finally, heartfelt thanks to my family and friends for their unfailing understanding and enthusiasm during this challenging undertaking.

Bobbi-Jean MacKinnon is a reporter and web editor for CBC New Brunswick. She previously worked at the *Toronto Star*, the *Ottawa Citizen*, and the *Telegraph-Journal*. She is the winner of a Saint John Arts Award and an Atlantic Journalism Award, and a finalist for two National Newspaper Awards and three Atlantic Journalism Awards. The first edition of *Shadow of Doubt* was a national bestseller and a finalist for an Arthur Ellis Award from the Crime Writers of Canada. It won the New Brunswick Book Award for Non-Fiction.